# The Economics of Non-Market Goods and Resources

Volume 17

**Series Editor**

Ian Bateman, Land, Environment, Economics and Policy Institute (LEEP), Department of Economics, University of Exeter Business School, Exeter, UK

More information about this series at http://www.springer.com/series/5919

Petr Mariel · Danny Campbell ·
Erlend Dancke Sandorf · Jürgen Meyerhoff ·
Ainhoa Vega-Bayo · Rebecca Blevins

# Environmental Valuation with Discrete Choice Experiments in R

## A Guide on Design, Implementation, and Data Analysis

Springer

Petr Mariel
School of Economics and Business
University of the Basque
Country (UPV/EHU)
Bilbao, Spain

Danny Campbell
Stirling Business School
University of Stirling
Stirling, UK

Erlend Dancke Sandorf
School of Economics and Business
Norwegian University of Life Sciences
Ås, Norway

Jürgen Meyerhoff
Department of Business and Economics
Berlin School of Economics and Law
(HWR)
Berlin, Germany

Ainhoa Vega-Bayo
School of Economics and Business
University of the Basque
Country (UPV/EHU)
Bilbao, Spain

Rebecca Blevins
Basque Centre for Climate Change (BC3)
Leioa, Spain

ISSN 1571-487X
The Economics of Non-Market Goods and Resources
ISBN 978-3-031-89337-7 ISBN 978-3-031-89338-4 (eBook)
https://doi.org/10.1007/978-3-031-89338-4

This work was supported by University of the Basque Country.



This Springer imprint is published by the registered company Springer Nature Switzerland AG
The registered company address is: Gewerbestrasse 11, 6330 Cham, Switzerland

# Preface

This book, *Environmental valuation with discrete choice experiments in R*, builds on the foundation set by Mariel et al. (2021) with a new perspective, delving deeper into the intricacies of discrete choice experiments (DCEs), and emphasising their practical applications. In writing this book, we aim to provide more than just a technical description of the DCE methodology—our goal is to share a resource that offers actionable advice and suggestions in a non-prescriptive manner, serving as a flexible guide for researchers and practitioners at various stages of the DCE process.

We share insights from our experience of over two decades conducting DCEs, particularly in environmental economics, to equip readers with hands-on tools and practical strategies to tailor to their own research needs, recognising that there is no "one-size-fits-all" approach in DCE research.

Our insights have been further enriched by a decade of collaboration within the ENVECHO network—a community dedicated to advancing discrete choice modelling in environmental valuation (www.envecho.com). This collaborative effort has shaped the way we think about DCEs, and we hope that this book reflects the flexibility, creativity, and rigour needed to successfully apply this method.

While this book provides guidance on conducting DCEs, it is important to note that it does not prescribe or assume responsibility for the specific choices readers make during the design or execution of their studies. Our intention is to offer a thoughtful exploration of the potential implications of many choices researchers and practitioners face, providing a comprehensive overview of the methodological considerations that underpin DCEs. We encourage readers to critically engage with the material, adapting the methods and suggestions to best suit their own research questions and unique contexts.

In this book, we cover a comprehensive range of topics related to DCEs, from the initial stages of experimental design and data collection to the preliminary analysis, estimation, and post-estimation analysis. To support both learning and practical applications, each of these steps is accompanied by detailed R scripts, offering readers a clear and actionable framework for implementing the methods in their own research. All scripts and datasets used in this book are freely accessible through our GitHub repository (https://github.com/edsandorf/evdce), so that readers have the necessary resources to apply and practise the methods discussed.

This book is designed to be a resource for researchers and practitioners looking to design, conduct, and analyse DCEs with a greater understanding of the underlying methodology. By offering detailed explanations paired with easy-to-replicate R scripts, we aim to bridge the gap between theoretical knowledge and practical implementation. A key motivation behind writing this book is to enhance the validity and reliability of stated preference studies, particularly in environmental economics, while also inspiring further research into the methodologies and applications of DCEs.

Achieving this requires both new and experienced researchers to understand the methods comprehensively. We hope that the experience and knowledge shared throughout this book will prove valuable to all researchers and contribute positively to the field of environmental valuation. Through this work, our goal is not only to inform but also to encourage critical thinking and innovation in the use of DCEs, fostering a deeper understanding and more effective applications of this method in real-world decision-making contexts. If this book contributes even in a small way to advancing these goals, we will consider it a success.

Bilbao, Spain — Petr Mariel
Stirling, UK — Danny Campbell
Ås, Norway — Erlend Dancke Sandorf
Berlin, Germany — Jürgen Meyerhoff
Bilbao, Spain — Ainhoa Vega-Bayo
Leioa, Spain — Rebecca Blevins

## Bibliography

Mariel P, Hoyos D, Meyerhoff J et al (2021) Environmental Valuation with Discrete Choice Experiments: Guidance on Design, Implementation and Data Analysis. Springer Nature. https://doi.org/10.1007/978-3-030-62669-3

**Acknowledgements** Petr Mariel acknowledges financial support of MCIN/AEI/10.13039/501100011033 through grant PID2020-113650RB-I00, the Basque Government through grant IT1508-22 (UPV/EHU Econometrics Research Group) and FEDER "Una manera de hacer Europa"/Unión Europea "NextGenerationEU"/PRTR. Danny Campbell acknowledges the research funding that supported part of his work while writing this book, specifically the ReSOW UK project (NE/V016024/1), jointly funded by the UK Natural Environment Research Council and the Economic and Social Research Council, and the CAVEAT project (AH/Y000528/1), jointly funded by the UK Arts and Humanities Research Council and the Department for Digital, Culture, Media and Sport. Jürgen Meyerhoff would like to acknowledge partial funding by the University of Catania, Italy (contract for external collaboration to the research project "Advancing environmental valuation methods" directed by Prof. Giovanni Signorello).

We extend our sincere thanks to Peio Alcorta, Tobias Börger, Klaus Glenk and Ulf Liebe for their thorough review of this book. Their comments and suggestions have provided valuable input, helping improve the clarity and quality of the text. Any remaining shortcomings are the responsibility of the authors of this book.

**Competing Interests** The authors have no competing interests to declare that are relevant to the content of this manuscript.

# R Packages

The scripts presented in this book were executed using the following R packages.

- Apollo: version 0.3.4
- googledrive: version 2.1.1
- googlesheets4: version 1.1.1
- gt: version 0.10.1
- janitor: version 2.2.0
- kableExtra: version 1.4.0
- patchwork: version 1.2.0
- purrr: version 1.0.2
- shiny: version 1.8.1.1
- shinyjs: version 2.1.0
- shinythemes 1.2.0
- shinyWidgets: version 0.8.7
- spdesign: version 0.0.5
- tidyverse: version 2.0.0

# Contents

# Abbreviations

| | |
|---|---|
| AIC | Akaike Information Criterion |
| BIC | Bayesian (Schwarz) Information Criterion |
| BWS | Best-Worst Scaling |
| CAPI | Computer Assisted Personal Interviews |
| CVM | Contingent Valuation Method |
| DCE | Discrete Choice Experiment |
| DM-MXL | Discrete Mixture Model |
| G-MXL | Generalised Mixed Logit |
| LC-MXL | Latent Class Mixed Logit |
| MNL | Multinomial Logit |
| mWTP | Marginal Willingness to Pay |
| MXL | Mixed Logit Model |
| ROOR | Repeated Opt-Out Reminder |
| RP | Revealed Preference |
| RP-MXL | Random Parameters Mixed Logit |
| RRM | Random Regret Minimisation |
| RUM | Random Utility Model |
| SP | Stated Preference |
| WTA | Willingness to Accept |
| WTP | Willingness to Pay |

# Chapter 1
# Introduction

**Abstract** This chapter introduces this book, *Environmental valuation with discrete choice experiments in R.* We describe our motivation for writing a book on discrete choice experiments (DCEs), with a focus on the methodological details and practical applications of DCEs. We briefly introduce the DCE approach and its importance in the field of environmental valuation, where it allows us to capture the value of goods and services when preferences are not sufficiently represented in the market. Finally, we emphasise the importance of a thorough review of the literature before beginning to conduct your own DCE, and offer a short guide on how to read this book based on the focus of your research and your experience implementing DCEs.

## 1.1 Motivation

Discrete choice experiments (DCEs) are frequently used in the nonmarket valuation of environmental goods and services. Compared with contingent valuation, which focuses on eliciting preferences for the overall value of a good or service, DCEs provide deeper insights into individual preferences by capturing the trade-offs people are willing to make across different attributes. This added richness supports more informed decision-making (Bateman et al. 2002). However, DCEs require the specification of additional aspects, such as detailed definitions of the environmental good or service to be valued, the selection of attributes (characteristics) and their levels, the generation of the underlying experimental design, the employment of appropriate econometric models, and a thorough post-estimation analysis, to name a few.

Against this backdrop, our goal is to share our knowledge and experience from decades of combined experience carrying out DCEs in the field of environmental valuation and beyond. A key motivation for writing this book is to encourage the exploration and enhancement of DCE research in the future, with our main target audience being the new generation of PhD students, whose research we aim to support as they dive deeper into the world of DCEs. This book is written for new and experienced practitioners alike, and no matter if you are planning to implement a DCE

 
P. Mariel et al., *Environmental Valuation with Discrete Choice Experiments in R*,
The Economics of Non-Market Goods and Resources 17,
https://doi.org/10.1007/978-3-031-89338-4_1

in the future, or you find yourself in the midst of the project already, this book will help guide you through the questions that arise along the way.

While there are already several publications, including journal articles and books, that support the design and analysis of DCEs, we believe that a new book on this topic is needed for two main reasons. First, certain aspects of the methodology we consider essential have not been adequately considered in publications so far. These include exploring the raw data before jumping to modelling, understanding the basics of the maximum likelihood approach and the risk of landing at local maxima, and a comprehensive post-estimation analysis that considers the variance caused by sample and preference heterogeneity.

Second, in our reading of the literature, a comprehensive documentation of the steps of a DCE project from start to finish is missing in the current literature. Conducting a DCE survey means (much) more than choice modelling in a narrow sense, i.e. running econometric models, as the quality of the results depends heavily on the correct implementation of the prior steps (and subsequent post-estimation analysis), all of which are necessary to carry out a high-quality DCE study.

These prior steps not only include the selection of attributes and the design of the experiment, but also a thoughtful consideration of the hypothetical market that is constructed in a stated preference study, writing a good questionnaire, and collecting a representative sample. Things that go wrong when designing the DCE survey or collecting the data cannot be corrected later with fancy models—thus, the first steps of a DCE are crucial in ensuring reliable results. This book aims to provide a comprehensive guide to conducting DCEs, emphasising the importance of these prior steps as well as a comprehensive raw-data analysis, sound modelling and the subsequent post-estimation analysis in providing robust results, helping you avoid potential pitfalls along the way.

**ⓘ There is no "one-size-fits-all" approach in DCE research**

This book does not claim to serve as a definitive guide for all DCEs, and we do not prescribe standards that, if met, will ensure a high-quality study. All decisions related to the implementation of the DCE remain in your hands, and it is up to you to make the best choices for your specific research context. This book aims to help guide you through the important methodological decisions and considerations along the way, and provide you with the necessary tools to carry out a DCE project, covering a wide range of possible experimental designs, model specifications, and methods for data analysis. In addition, a large number of references are given, and we would highly encourage the reader to consult them as there is often not enough space in this book to explore certain topics more depth.

Throughout the book, we use as a case study a DCE on the landscape externalities of onshore wind power. It is based on a project that was conducted in Germany

(Meyerhoff et al. 2010), as a case study. The design of this DCE has been slightly adjusted for the purposes of this book, and instead of using the original data, synthetic data are generated. A detailed description of this case study is given in Chap. 4 but the externalities of wind farms are already addressed when going through the steps of a DCE in Chap. 2.

## 1.2 The DCE Approach

When we make a choice between two or more competing options, we make a trade-off. Imagine you are at the grocery store, and after buying all your ingredients for dinner (pasta, tomatoes, cheese, etc.), you find yourself in the ice cream aisle. You look past the glass pane and see a selection of different flavours—chocolate, vanilla, and strawberry. You may stand in the freezer section for a while, weighing the different options—you prefer chocolate, but the strawberry flavour is on sale, while the vanilla flavour is from a local brand you like. After thoughtful consideration, you make your choice and leave with your ice cream in hand—or, you leave without buying any (maybe your favourite flavour is missing, or you are trying to eat healthier, or it is just too hot to get home without the ice cream melting). This choice of selecting one ice cream option among many is a simple example of the choices made in DCEs. These involve trade-offs between different aspects of each choice (cost, flavour, and brand in this case). With the methodology used in DCEs, these trade-offs can reveal how much you value different aspects of different choices (ice cream options) in monetary terms, which then can be used to estimate the demand for a good or service.

Markets, however, do not always provide complete information about the values individuals hold, as many environmental goods and services are public goods or have characteristics of public goods. To gain information about the non-market values of environmental goods and services, a set of methods has been developed. These methods can broadly be assigned to two groups (Freeman et al. 2014): revealed preference (RP) methods, which aim to infer individuals' values from their observed choices in related markets, and stated preference (SP) methods, which become essential when information about individuals' preferences cannot be derived from market transactions.

Contexts in which preferences are not reflected in market transactions are common in environmental valuation research. These include the following contexts: (1) when individuals are thought to place value on environmental goods or services they do not use at all (so-called non-use or passive-use values), (2) when individual values of future goods or services are of interest (e.g. for new technologies to generate renewable energy), and (3) when there is insufficient variation with respect to certain characteristics of goods or services (Freeman et al. 2014). When individuals do not use goods or services, their preferences are not captured in the market; when technologies are not present yet, no existing market can indicate how people will value them; and, if all choices of a good have the same characteristics, no inferences about preferences can be made (for example, if all lakes in a certain region have the same poor water quality, observable transactions in the related markets will not reveal whether individuals prefer improved water quality and to what extent).

Generally, SP methods are survey-based and employ a hypothetical market, with respondents asked to make transactions in this market by selecting preferred alternatives or stating their willingness to pay for a certain good or service directly. Among the methods that analyse choices made in a hypothetical market, DCEs have become a widely applied method to record preferences in environmental valuation. Originating from marketing research, DCEs are now used in a range of other fields such as health economics, tourism, transportation, and environmental valuation.

DCEs are grounded in the microeconomic theory of consumer behaviour, where individuals who choose among bundles of goods reach their decision based on utility maximisation (i.e. choosing the option that gives them the highest utility) given their preferences and budget constraint. In the DCE context, utility maximisation leads to the choice of a single alternative from a finite, mutually exclusive and exhaustive set of alternatives that gives the individual the highest utility. In contrast to classic consumer theory, discrete alternatives are selected in a DCE setting. DCEs also assume that the *attributes* (i.e. cost, flavour, and brand of ice cream) describing the *alternatives* (ice cream choices) determine the utility individuals derive from the alternatives, instead of assuming homogeneous goods as in classic consumer theory. This assumption draws from the theory presented by Lancaster (1966), in which the latent (i.e. unobservable) utility of an alternative that an individual experiences can be subject to changes in these attributes, leading to discrete switches (changing of choices) among alternatives if attributes change. For more information on microeconomic consumer theory and the underlying assumptions of welfare theory, see Freeman et al. (2014) and Phaneuf and Requate (2017).

DCEs also differ from classic consumer theory by assuming that behaviour is not deterministic but intrinsically probabilistic. Building on seminal work in psychology by Thurstone (1927), and later extended by Marschak (1960), the *random utility theory*, presented by McFadden (1974), serves as the basis for discrete choice modelling (see Chap. 3 of this book for a detailed discussion of the *random utility maximisation* (RUM) model based on this theory). In DCE research, we assume that the individual knows exactly the amount of utility derived from an alternative; however, this does not apply to the researcher who investigates individual choice behaviour. The researcher only observes attributes related to alternatives and certain characteristics of the individual but not the individual's utility. Therefore, from the analyst's perspective, utility is assumed to consist of two parts: a deterministic part (which is explainable) and a random part (which is unexplainable). The former is influenced by the observed attributes that describe the alternatives and is modelled by estimating the parameters of the utility function, while the latter can be influenced by several factors, including unobserved attributes and measurement errors and is captured by the error term.

There are a number of model specifications used to capture the deterministic and random components of stated preference data, ranging from simple multinomial logit

(MNL) models to more complex mixed logit (MXL) models, such as random parameters (RP-MXL) and latent class (LC-MXL) models. We cover these models and their specifications, which can easily be tailored to different research contexts, in detail in this book and walk you through the theoretical basis and practical applications of each one.

## 1.3 Read, Read, Read!

Getting a good feel for the state of the literature is critical for any research project, and is especially important for DCE research. We recommend reading as much relevant DCE literature related to your research topic as possible, as it will help you situate your project within the greater context of DCE literature and contrast your research and methodologies with those of other authors.

In your review of the literature, you will see how other authors defined important aspects of DCEs, such as the environmental good or service in question, the survey mode, the payment vehicle, or the sampling strategy for the corresponding target population. We urge you to look beyond subject areas or journals that you are familiar with, and explore new research topics and methodologies. DCEs are employed in many different areas of research, and the problems you encounter in the field of environmental valuation may have already been solved (or at least addressed) in other fields such as transportation research, health economics, or marketing.

In addition to the literature discussed above, we offer a few specific recommendations for highly informative recent publications on DCEs. These aim to document the state of the art of DCE research and give guidance on how to implement, conduct, and analyse stated preference surveys, i.e. both contingent valuation and choice experiments. A good starting point is the following paper: Johnston et al. (2017) *Contemporary Guidance for Stated Preference Studies* in the Journal of the Association of Environmental and Resource Economists. The article comprehensively discusses the state of the literature at the time and derives best-practice recommendations for the design and conducting of SP studies with a focus on applications to public goods in environmental and human health contexts. The book by Mariel et al. (2021), *Environmental Valuation with Discrete Choice Experiments. Guidance on Design, Implementation and Data Analysis*, focuses on DCEs, with a deeper emphasis on the estimation of statistical models. Another recent book is Shang and Chandra's (2021) *Discrete Choice Experiments Using R. The How-To Guide for Social and Managerial Sciences*, which covers the entire process of carrying out a DCE study and introduces a suitable set of R-packages. However, several topics in the book deserve more detailed discussion, such as the experimental design, the analysis of recorded choices, and the models used for estimation, which we cover in this book.

Another useful source is the online tutorial *Non-market valuation in R* (NMVR Project Team 2021) and the book *Stated preference methods using R* by Aizaki et al. (2014). Both provide valuable resources for designing and analysing stated preference surveys in R, including DCEs, but are narrower in scope. While not intended to be a comprehensive guide, a valuable resource for an in-depth overview of the implementation of DCEs is the *Handbook of Choice Modelling* by Hess and Daly (2024). Finally, three older sources that continue to provide valuable insights for designing, conducting, and analysing stated preference studies including DCEs are the books by Bateman et al. (2002), Kanninen (2007) and Champ et al. (2017).

While working your way through these sources and reading this book, keep in mind that not all guidance on conducting DCEs will necessarily apply to your research context, and that the ultimate responsibility for making the best choices for the design, execution, and evaluation of your project lies on your shoulders. We do not recommend taking any single source (even this book) and basing all of your decisions on that reference. Also, remember that methods continue to evolve, so do your best to keep up to date with the literature as your development as a DCE researcher continues.

Above all, use your own judgement to determine if your design and analytical choices are defensible to your peers—whether they are conference delegates, thesis examiners or journal reviewers. You will see that a truly informed judgment can only be made after thoroughly engaging with as much relevant literature as possible, as a strong foundation in the literature will provide the context and support needed to justify your decisions.

## 1.4 How to Read This Book

The chapters of this book are designed such that they can be read independently, and where you pick up your reading will depend on your level of prior knowledge and experience implementing DCEs. If you are an experienced DCE researcher interested in how to generate an experimental design using the *spdesign* package (Sandorf and Campbell 2023) that is introduced in this book, then jumping directly to Chap. 5 will be the best path for you. However, if you are a beginner, we strongly recommend going through the book sequentially, as the chapters build on each other.

Working your way through the fundamentals may seem tiring at first, but this step is essential to gain a comprehensive understanding of DCEs and to correctly apply the methods in chapters later on. Thus, we do not recommend jumping straight to the estimation chapter and trying to use the scripts provided to estimate complex models without first understanding the basics. Our teaching experience and exchanges with many PhD students has shown us that this phenomenon is common, with inexperienced researchers estimating models without sufficient knowledge of the theoretical background and awareness of the potential pitfalls along the way.

The chapter following this introduction (Chap. 2) gives an overview of the steps of a DCE project focussing not only on DCE specific aspects but also addressing other topics, such as the development of the questionnaire or sampling strategies, among others. Chapter 3 presents the random utility maximisation (RUM) model, the basis for all choice models presented in this book. It explores the theoretical foundations of the models used in this book, including the multinomial logit model (MNL), variants of the random parameters mixed logit (RP-MXL), and the latent class mixed logit (LC-MXL) model. Chapter 4 presents the case study used throughout the rest of the book, and Chap. 5 details the process of generating an experimental design, introducing basic concepts and walking you through how to use the *spdesign* package in R.

Chapter 6 details how a DCE survey is implemented in R Shiny, providing a basis for readers to expand on, depending on their specific goals and research context. Before jumping to modelling the recorded choice data, we highlight the importance of getting to know the data first in Chap. 7. This step is (in our experience) too often skipped, even by experienced researchers, but is crucial in setting up the model estimation discussed in Chap. 9. In preparation for the model estimation, Chap. 8 provides insights into the maximum likelihood approach. It reviews essential information about the methodology behind the model estimation and covers the problem of local maxima and the importance of using various sets of starting values, an issue often ignored even by experienced researchers.

Chapter 9 walks the reader through the models described in Chap. 3 (MNL, RP-MXL, LC-MXL) using the *Apollo* package (Hess and Palma 2019) and provides detailed scripts that can be replicated and adjusted to your data and research needs. In most cases, the final model will not be the main output of a DCE study, but the prerequisite for calculating welfare measures such as the willingness to pay and changes in consumer surplus, which are covered in Chap. 10. Finally, the book concludes with some final thoughts (Chap. 11), giving a brief overview of models not treated in this book, and highlighting potential future developments in DCE research, as seen from today's point of view.

> ⓘ **R scripts and data**
>
> All scripts and datasets used in the book are freely accessible through our GitHub repository (https://github.com/edsandorf/evdce), so that readers have the necessary resources to apply and experiment with the methods discussed

## Bibliography


Aizaki H, Nakatani T, Sato K (2014) Stated preference methods using R. CRC Press, Florida, USA. https://doi.org/10.1201/b17292

Bateman IJ, Carson RT, Day B et al (2002) Economic valuation with stated preference techniques: a manual. Edward Elgar, Cheltenham. https://doi.org/10.4337/9781781009727

Champ PA, Boyle KJ, Brown TC (eds) (2017) A Primer on Nonmarket Valuation, vol 13. The Economics of Non-Market Goods and Resources. Springer Netherlands, Dordrecht. https://doi.org/10.1007/978-94-007-7104-8

Freeman AM III, Herriges JA, Kling CL (2014) The measurement of environmental and resource values: theory and methods. Routledge. https://doi.org/10.4324/9781315780917

Hess S, Daily A (eds) 2024. Handbook of choice modelling, 2nd edn. Edward Elgar, Cheltenham https://doi.org/10.4337/9781800375635

Hess S, Palma D (2019) Apollo: a flexible, powerful and customisable freeware package for choice model estimation and application. J Choice Model 32:100170. https://doi.org/10.1016/j.jocm.2019.100170

Johnston RJ, Boyle KJ, Adamowicz W et al (2017) Contemporary guidance for stated preference studies. J Assoc Environ Resour Econ 4(2):319–405. https://doi.org/10.1086/691697

Kanninen BJ (ed) (2007) Valuing environmental amenities using stated choice studies: a common sense approach to theory and practice, vol 8. The economics of non-market goods and resources. Dordrecht, Springer Netherlands. https://doi.org/10.1007/1-4020-5313-4

Lancaster KJ (1966) A new approach to consumer theory. J Polit Econ 74:132–157

Marschak J (1960) Binary choice constraints on random utility indications. In: Arrow K (ed) Stanford symposium on mathematical methods in the social sciences. Stanford University Press, Stanford, pp 312–329

Mariel P, Hoyos D, Meyerhoff J et al (2021) Environmental valuation with discrete choice experiments: guidance on design, implementation and data analysis. Springer Nature. https://doi.org/10.1007/978-3-030-62669-3

McFadden D (1974) Conditional logit analysis of qualitative choice behaviour. In: Zarembka P (ed) Frontiers in econometrics. Academic Press, New York, pp 105–142

Meyerhoff J, Ohl C, Hartje V (2010) Landscape externalities from onshore wind power. Energy Policy 38:82–92. https://doi.org/10.1016/j.enpol.2009.08.055

NMVR Project Team (2021) Non-market valuation with R. Retrieved January 24, 2025, from http://lab.agr.hokudai.ac.jp/nmvr/index.html

Phaneuf DJ, Requate T (2017) A course in environmental economics. theory, policy, and practice. Cambridge University Press, Cambridge. https://doi.org/10.1017/9780511843839

Sandorf ED, Campbell D (2023) spdesign: designing stated preference experiments. R package version 0.0.5. https://CRAN.R-project.org/package=spdesign

Shang L, Chandra Y (2021) Discrete choice experiments using R. Springer, The how-to guide for social and managerial sciences. https://doi.org/10.1007/978-981-99-4562-7

Thurstone LL (1927) A law of comparative judgment. Psychol Rev 34(4):273–286. https://doi.org/10.1037/h0070288

# Chapter 2
# Steps of a Discrete Choice Experiment

**Abstract** This chapter provides an overview of the key steps of conducting a discrete choice experiment (DCE). We begin with the research questions guiding the study design, move through several design issues related to the DCE and the questionnaire, and conclude with important considerations for the model estimation and post-estimation analysis. The main objective of this chapter is to highlight the decisions involved in conducting a DCE and the potential consequences of these choices for the realisation of the final study and subsequent results. Instead of offering step-by-step guide for the implementation of DCEs, we draw on our research experience in this field to offer insights and practical knowledge for you to consider in a DCE project.

## 2.1 Step 1: Research Questions and Hypotheses

### *2.1.1 Key Considerations*

The starting point for any discrete choice experiment (DCE) design process should be a clear research question and hypothesis. Research in this field is often motivated by either: 1) an interest in understanding people's preferences and their willingness to pay for non-marketed goods or services, or 2) a focus on methodological aspects that contribute to the development of DCEs and enhance the understanding of stated preferences. These objectives may overlap, depending on the research funding and the broader objectives of your overall research.

If your research is primarily motivated by the estimation of welfare measures for decision-making, it is important to develop a design with attributes, levels, and a sampling strategy that aligns with this objective. Using established precedents in the literature and considering previous applications based on similar methodologies will help you choose the right approach and justify your methodological choices. While it may be appropriate to replicate the design and analysis of a well-regarded

 
P. Mariel et al., *Environmental Valuation with Discrete Choice Experiments in R*,
The Economics of Non-Market Goods and Resources 17,
https://doi.org/10.1007/978-3-031-89338-4_2

DCE study in certain cases, you must always ensure that your methods have sufficient justification for your research context—citing others who have used the same methods is not considered sufficient justification.

In this context, hypotheses help you assess the validity of the survey responses. For example, testing for a plausible and assumed distance-decay-effect guides the data analysis and supports the evaluation of the validity of the recorded choice data. The association between an increasing distance toward the good or service of interest and a decreasing willingness to pay (WTP) have been found in many studies (Glenk et al. 2020). Thus, showing that this association is also present in your data helps to demonstrate their validity.

Similarly, if your research is focused on contributing to methodological advancements, you must be able to defend your design and analysis decisions to ensure that the study incorporates the newest advancements in the field. However, in this context, it may be reasonable to place less emphasis on the representativeness of the sampling strategy, as the primary goal is to identify gaps in the literature where deeper insights into individuals' choice behaviours can enhance understanding and make a meaningful contribution to the field.

While some fortuitous results—unexpected, accidental, and beneficial findings that were not anticipated initially—may occur by chance, it is important to have your research questions and hypotheses clearly defined before beginning the data collection. Formulating testable hypotheses in advance is essential in determining the specific experimental setup and information needed to effectively meet the goals of your research. This setup may involve designing the choice task instructions, structuring the presentation of the choice tasks, or implementing controlled experimental variations in the survey. Formulating testable hypotheses also involves considering how alternative variables, either directly or indirectly linked to the choice tasks, may influence choice behaviour and outcomes. Try to imagine which other variables could explain the recorded choices in case you cannot reject your hypothesis.

**ⓘ Preregistration of hypotheses**

The importance of having set informative hypotheses is evidenced by the recent uptick in the preregistration of hypotheses, which some journals promote or require. Preregistration guarantees that the analysis is guided by predetermined hypotheses rather than hypotheses generated after an exploratory data analysis. Preregistration also requires the specification of the statistical tests and models to be used, as well as the sampling procedure and data cleaning methods.

While preregistration is not mandatory, it is becoming increasingly important, particularly to publish in certain high-ranking journals. Therefore, you should consider early on whether you need to preregister your hypothesis and methods, and what implications this will have for your work plan. Once the data is collected, it may become apparent that there are better model choices based on the nature of the observed data, but an implication of preregistering your hypothesis is that you are bound by the models specified in the pre-registration. One available platform that offers preregistration is OSF (Open Science Framework) Registries (https://osf.io/registries), where you can find examples of preregistered hypotheses for stated preference research. An example of a DCE study based on a preregistered hypothesis is Perino and Schwickert (2023), which applied a DCE to food choices.

Regardless of your research questions and hypotheses, it is important to justify their exploration. Justifications include testing the validity of existing or new theoretical expectations or corroborating or challenging previous empirical findings. However, avoid using this stage as an opportunity for a "fishing expedition" where multiple hypotheses are tested with the hope that something significant will emerge. Instead, be selective and intentional in your approach. The key is to think in advance about the specific mechanisms or relationships you expect to observe, how they connect to your theoretical framework, and the type of data you need to collect to support or refute your hypotheses. This planning ensures that your study is focused, methodologically sound, and capable of yielding meaningful and interpretable results.

For example, if you want to investigate choice uncertainty and would like to use the response time per choice task as an independent variable (Uggeldahl et al. 2016), you must ensure that this information can be recorded before collecting the data. Response time, a type of *paradata* (Kreuter 2013), is not directly available in all survey modes, and while online survey platforms record timestamps and other forms of paradata routinely, this is often limited to specific milestones (e.g. when the survey page opens and when the final page is submitted). Therefore, to test this hypothesis, you must ensure that timestamps are recorded for each individual choice task.

### 2.1.2 Further Important Aspects

- **Is there a better way?** A key aim of a DCE is to get respondents to make trade-offs not only between the provision of the good or service in question and their willingness to give up money, but also between all the attributes used to define the good or service. Although the DCE and the Contingent Valuation Method (CVM), the other main stated preference method that has a history of more than 50 years of application (Smith 2006), are increasingly seen as merging methods (Haab et al. 2020), significant differences remain. A DCE, as used in this book, considers all trade-offs between all attributes. A CVM, on the other hand, typically considers only one trade-off between the provision of a good or service and the willingness to give up or receive money. Thus, while both DCE and CVM as stated preference methods share many advantages and, above all, problems, the evaluation exercise in a CVM might be less demanding for respondents because the trade-offs are not as comprehensive. At the beginning of a study using stated preference methods, it is therefore always important to ask whether the information gained by increasing the number of trade-offs that respondents have to make is justified by the greater burden that the required trade-offs place on them.

- **Relevance is of utmost importance.** If we expect respondents to make well-considered choices based on the trade-offs among the alternatives presented in a choice task, relevance is a prerequisite. However, some studies in the literature indicate that researchers' interests in certain goods or services seem to drive DCE studies more than the relevance of the good or service to the target population. Using a less relevant good or service might still yield interesting insights, but if we expect respondents to behave in our survey-based hypothetical markets as they would in real markets, relevance is crucial. Without genuine engagement and understanding, the reliability of the conclusions drawn from responses may be compromised, and the validity of the study could be called into question. Thus, it is essential to consider the relevance of the good or service for the potential target population early on in the design process. First test interviews, ideally face to face, or focus group meetings could help you get an idea of how relevant the selected good or service is for people from the target population.
- **Conducting an in-depth literature review.** Select a large number of papers from your area of interest, and document how the authors addressed the issues and decisions you face in your research. What experimental designs did they use? How was pretesting organised? How did they justify the number of choice tasks each respondent faced? How was the target population defined? This analysis and documentation will give you an overview of how important considerations related to the design were addressed in other studies and help you make more informed choices. This analysis is at the same time likely to show that important details are frequently missing from published papers, even though they are crucial for assessing study quality. An inspiring reference in this context is Lew et al. (2022), who investigated the adherence to best practices for stated preference studies in the U.S. Marine Ecosystem Services literature.
- **Consider whether a willingness-to-pay (WTP) question is the appropriate format**. Generally, in stated preference studies respondents are asked whether they are willing to give up money to keep or achieve a certain quality of a good or service. In contrast, respondents might be asked whether they are willing to accept payments to forgo a certain environmental quality, for example. This choice depends on whether individuals have ownership or entitlement rights over a certain good or service: the willingness-to-accept (WTA) approach is suitable when they have these rights, while the WTP approach is appropriate when they do not. However, the empirical literature has largely moved away from the WTA approach, favouring the WTP approach. Thus, this book will focus solely on the WTP approach, but the reader should be aware that in some cases, the WTA approach may be more suitable. A useful starting point for considering whether the WTA format is appropriate for your survey is the review by Whittington et al. (2017), which synthesises the current literature and offers guidance on when and how to use WTA elicitation formats.
- **Define your treatment groups and plan how you will test your hypothesis**. Depending on your hypotheses, you may need to implement several treatments

(split samples), providing different groups of respondents with different sets of information. Determine how many treatment groups you can afford to include given your resources, and make sure that you have enough observations in each treatment to effectively test your hypothesis. With this number of treatments in mind, develop a plan early on for how to test your hypothesis: will you run separate models for each treatment group and compare marginal WTP estimates across treatments, or will you merge all treatments and use interactions to test for differences across treatments? Even if you have not decided on all aspects of testing and modelling at this early stage, you should consider these questions before you begin with the data collection.
- **Consider the significance of non-use values.** In the environmental valuation literature, there continues to be a debate over whether *non-use values* (also referred to as passive-use values) can be measured in a valid manner and thus be incorporated in subsequent analyses such as cost–benefit analyses. Generally, non-use values refer to the willingness to pay to maintain some good in existence even though there is no actual, planned or possible use of this good (Bateman et al. 2002). The elicitation of non-use values and related aspects of the design of a hypothetical market is beyond the scope of this book. However, if you think that non-use values may constitute an important share of the total value of your good or service, or if you wish to explicitly measure non-use values, it is important to familiarise yourself with the relevant literature. This will help you determine whether additional design measures are required to ensure the validity of your estimates (Johnston et al. 2003, 2017; Bateman et al. 2023).

## 2.2 Step 2: Defining the Good or Service

### *2.2.1 Essentials*

At the core of any DCE is the good or service for which preferences are elicited. The DCE framework generally requires a detailed definition of the good or service (e.g. the impacts of wind farm developments in a region) and the set of characteristics, referred to as *attributes*, that define this good (e.g. impacts on electricity prices or an endangered bird species). These *attributes* collectively represent the good or service of interest, and the objective is to capture the trade-offs individuals are willing to make between different attributes and their levels.

From an economic perspective, a key consideration is whether the good or service in question is a *private good* or a *public good*. By definition, public goods are non-rival and non-excludable (i.e. the fact that property rights are neither defined nor allocated), meaning that multiple individuals can simultaneously enjoy the good or service and that people cannot be prevented from accessing it (Phaneuf and Requate 2017). The characteristics defining public goods can result in markets with incomplete information about the value of the good or service, since when individuals have an incentive to free ride (benefit from resources without paying for them), their true preferences are not revealed. This prevents the market from supplying the good at the level that matches actual demand. In some cases, the characteristics defining public goods can even lead to markets not emerging at all. Therefore, non-market valuation methods, such as DCEs, can be employed to assess the value of environmental public goods.

Designing a DCE for a public good requires additional considerations to address the challenges associated with this type of good. In this book, we assume that the goods or services of interest are public goods, as is usually the case in environmental economics. However, many of the considerations discussed here are also applicable to private goods.

The *attributes* (characteristics) and their levels define the differences between *alternatives* (choice options) and convey the characteristics of the good to respondents. Conclusions about trade-offs can only be drawn based on the attributes and their levels as defined in the design, so it is critical to choose them carefully. For example, if you aim to explore NIMBY (Not in My Backyard)-ism in the analysis of a planned wind farm project, an obvious attribute to include is the distance between the wind farm location and the respondent's residence. Sometimes, the most important and relevant attributes are less obvious, and conducting literature reviews, consulting with experts, and interviewing representatives of the target population are essential steps in identifying meaningful attributes for your research context.

Although the selection of the attributes and their levels is an essential step when carrying out a DCE, the literature offers limited guidance on this, likely because the selection of attributes is highly dependent on the specific research topic and context of each study. The most comprehensive instructions on how to select attributes and their levels are provided by Shang and Chandra (2021). We recommend starting by consulting their chapters on attributes and attribute levels, where they propose five criteria for the selection of attributes:

- *Relevance*: The attributes must be pertinent to the good or service of interest and appropriate in the context of the study.
- *Significance*: The attributes should be important and meaningful to the individuals expected to make choices between the alternatives.
- *Clarity*: The attributes must be defined clearly to avoid ambiguity.
- *Completeness*: The attributes should be comprehensive and cover all aspects of the good or service in question.
- *Measurability*: The attributes and their levels should be measurable, either qualitatively or quantitatively.

When selecting the attribute levels it is important to keep in mind that their range and their number depend on the assumed functional form of the relationship. For example, if only two levels (1000 m or 2000 m distance) are chosen for the attribute *distance of wind turbines from residential areas*, you can calculate welfare measures for any distance between 1000 and 2000 m if you assume that respondents value each unit (in this case, each metre) the same, i.e. assume a linear relationship.

Assuming a linear relationship means that each additional metre of distance is expected to have the same value for respondents, whether the turbine is placed at 1100 m or 1500 m distance from their residence. However, if the value of each metre changes at a certain threshold (e.g. it matters more when the distance is under 1000 m), more level values will be needed to capture how respondents value the distance attribute. Therefore, deciding on the number and range of attribute levels requires an understanding of whether changes are valued linearly or if they vary based on specific thresholds.

Another issue to keep in mind when selecting attributes is that it should in principle be possible for attributes to vary independently from each other. For example, the *size of a wind farm* (number of turbines) is independent of the *height of the turbines*. Thus, one of these attributes can vary independently from the other. In contrast, if one attribute is embedded in another attribute, this independence is not given, and the question of what is measured when attribute levels change arises. In the context of wind farms, this would apply if the attributes *amount of electricity* and *turbine height* were chosen, as higher turbines in general provide greater amounts of electricity. If attributes cannot be considered independent, this may raise the question of whether discrete choice experiments are the right method for evaluating the good or service (Holmes et al. 2017).

**Cost as a key attribute**. For economic valuation, including a cost attribute in the discrete choice experiment is essential. An important output of DCEs are welfare measures, particularly the WTP estimates, as they offer useful insights for policy recommendations. To generate this estimation, a cost attribute (an attribute that captures the marginal utility of money) must be included in the DCE. This can take the form of an entrance fee, a surcharge on the electricity bill, an increase in income taxes, or taxes earmarked for a specific purpose, to name just a few examples. To specify the cost attribute, we must consider (1) the payment vehicle and the recipient of the payments (see Step 3 of this chapter), and (2) the range of the cost attribute, the number of levels, and their monetary values.

In theory, respondents are expected to know their maximum WTP for a certain good or service and pay any amount equal to or below this maximum, while rejecting any amount above it in choice tasks, independently of the design of the cost vector (Hanley et al. 2005; see also Glenk et al. 2019 for a brief review). However, the findings in the literature show that the cost vector design is not neutral with respect to the recorded WTP. Börger et al. (2024) tested four different cost vectors, each with eight cost levels but with markedly different ranges. All four vectors had the same four lowest cost levels (€10, €25, €50, €80), but the higher levels varied, with maximum values of €300, €500, €1,000 and €1,800. The welfare estimates for the otherwise identical DCEs showed that the marginal WTP (mWTP) estimates, which report the willingness to pay for a one-unit change of the non-monetary attribute, increased when the upper values of the cost vector were higher, with the cost vector playing an important role in shaping the resulting mWTPs. This example highlights the need to consider the lower and upper limits of WTP estimates when designing the cost vector, accounting for preference heterogeneity and the choke price (i.e. the price at which individuals are expected to stop demanding the good). Although it is impossible to know this before collecting data, extensive literature reviews, focus group discussions, and piloting can provide greater confidence that the cost vector used in the final design is as accurate as possible.

A faulty design of the cost vector can also contribute to what Glenk et al. (2024) refer to as "overshooting". It occurs when the overall WTP exceeds the highest cost level presented, meaning that respondents are willing to pay more than the highest value encountered in the choice tasks. For example, if study results indicate that respondents have on average a WTP of €280 for an environmental good, but the highest cost level respondents could have seen is €200, we must ask whether a mean WTP well above the highest cost level is a reliable result. Given that the highest cost level should represent the choke price (or at least be close to it), we would expect that this highest price is only accepted in a small number of choice situations, i.e. choice task in which at least one alternative includes this highest price level. Having WTP estimates for the investigated environmental change well above the highest cost level could thus indicate that this result is driven by design choices and does not reflect true WTP. Glenk et al. (2024) show that overshooting is at least partially influenced by the design of the cost vector, specifically the number of levels and the range, with a larger number of levels and a broader range between the highest and lowest levels reducing the likelihood of overshooting. Therefore, testing for overshooting early on using pilot data with a sufficient number of observations can help determine whether the cost vector is adequately defined. Glenk et al. (2024) provide two examples illustrating simple methods to test for overshooting.

Although there is limited guidance available on the design of the cost vector for a DCE in the current literature, we suggest taking the following aspects into consideration (Mariel et al. 2021, Section 2.10):

a) **The number of cost levels.** The cost parameter is essential for calculating the WTP estimates and should be estimated with high precision, even for small level changes. If cost enters linearly into the utility function (as is the predominant practice), technically, two levels suffice to generate WTP estimates, but having more levels is a more robust approach. With more levels, the marginal disutility becomes less sensitive to changes in the cost attribute, providing greater confidence in the validity of the retrieved estimate. While extrapolation always carries risks, having more intermediate cost levels offers a better basis for making informed estimates about the relationship beyond the observed range, which can be important when exploring overshooting. Moreover, while a linear relationship is often assumed, having a greater number of cost levels allows for the investigation of potential non-linear patterns that may not be detectable with fewer levels. In most studies, the number of cost levels ranges from 4 to 8, in addition to a zero level for the status quo alternative.
b) **The distribution of the cost levels.** Cost levels can be distributed evenly across the cost vector range (e.g. setting each level €10 apart) or with exponentially increased distances between levels. The exponential approach allows for finer granularity in the lower part of the vector, making it particularly useful when there are differences in the marginal disutility of cost across its range. The equal

spacing approach is effective when respondents perceive the cost levels linearly, and is simpler and easier for respondents to understand.

c) **The range of the cost levels.** Setting the range of the cost vector is a difficult issue, as respondents may consider the relative differences between the cost levels rather than the absolute cost amounts reflecting the money respondents would have to pay if they select an alternative (see Börger et al. 2024). In this context, the choke price, i.e. the price at which individuals are expected to stop demanding the good, becomes important (Mørkbak et al. 2009). If you set the highest cost level too low (i.e. below the choke price) respondents may not perceive the cost differences as meaningful, resulting in potentially biased estimates. Setting the highest cost level too high may result in respondents accepting cost values that are way above their true WTP, due to anchoring and the hypothetical nature of the choice situation.

d) **Distance from the status quo price.** If the choice tasks include a status quo alternative with zero cost, the gap from the status quo to the lowest cost level should be relatively small. This helps avoid the status quo constant capturing part of the cost sensitivity, which could bias the cost parameter. As Hess and Beharry-Borg (2011, Appendix) argue, this can result in a downward bias in the estimated cost coefficient and a consequent overestimation of WTP values.

### *2.2.2 Additional Points*

- **Only differences in utility matter**: Random utility maximisation (RUM) models, commonly used to analyse DCE data, focus on *utility differences*, meaning that only variations between different versions of the good or service are valued (Train 2009). Thus, DCEs do not reveal the absolute value of a good itself, but focus on differences between alternatives, representing variations in the provision of a good or service. For instance, DCEs can assess the benefits to individuals if wind farms are built in a particular region or the benefits of different configurations of wind farms (e.g. many small wind farms vs. fewer but larger wind farms). This aligns with the economic welfare perspective, which focuses on the change in societal welfare resulting from a policy shift.
- **Attributes and experimental design**. When defining the attributes, keep in mind that their specifications affect the experimental design. Some attribute levels cannot be combined due to factual incompatibilities or lack of plausibility and these constraints influence the efficiency of the experimental design. If you find that the defined attributes and their combinations have excessive constraints, you may have to revise the attributes and levels selected. See Chapter 5 for more details on attribute level combinations, constraints, and how they relate to the efficiency of the design.
- **Trade-offs in defining attributes**. On the one hand, attributes and their levels must be meaningful and understandable for respondents. On the other hand, they must be comprehensively and accurately describing the characteristics of the good to be

relevant for decision-making. It is often not possible to achieve both goals at the same time and therefore trade-offs are required. Interesting studies in this context are, for example, Strange et al. (2024) on measuring biodiversity in environmental valuation studies and Lupi et al. (2023) on disentangling water quality indices in the context of ecosystem service valuation for a discussion of the trade-offs arising from these conflicting objectives. See also Johnston et al. (2012).

- **Meaning of attribute levels.** Consider how you will interpret the results when selecting the attributes and their levels. Will using the levels *low*, *medium*, and *high*, for example, translate into meaningful results for relevant stakeholders? To assess this, check if "On average, respondents are willing to pay X amount to move from a *low* to a *high* level of biodiversity" will be informative in your research context. For a decision-maker implementing measures to protect biodiversity, these attribute levels may be too loosely defined to translate into actionable conservation measures. You should aim to describe attribute levels as clearly and precisely as possible to better inform stakeholders, without overwhelming respondents.
- **Prioritising attributes.** Resources permitting, a best–worst scaling (BWS) survey can help you understand how your target population ranks a longer list of attributes (Louviere et al. 2015) to guide your selection of attributes. To ensure robust results, you should run the BWS survey with a random and sufficiently large sample from your target population. Note that this ranking does not require running any models. Balancing the best and worst choices is sufficient for this task. See Webb et al. (2021) for an example of the application of BWS in health economics.

## 2.3 Step 3: Setting up the Hypothetical Market

### *2.3.1 Core Elements*

In environmental economics, stated preference methods are used when a market for an environmental good or service does not exist. These methods operate under the assumption that a market could exist in a hypothetical context, and present choices to respondents within this context. Setting up the hypothetical market, however, requires more than describing the goods or services being offered. Further information is needed to inform respondents about the functioning of the market. This includes details on how the exchange of money for the provision of a good or service would occur.

For responses to be considered valid, we must assume that respondents make choices in the hypothetical market as if it were real, i.e. consequential. If this is not true, hypothetical bias will be introduced, leading to inaccurate or unreliable results. Addressing and minimising this bias is therefore a key consideration when designing and conducting a DCE study. A gap between the two, however, will very likely always exist, as individuals in a hypothetical market only express a behavioural intention, such as agreeing or not agreeing to pay a certain amount for a good or service, but do not actually have to make the payment. The extent of the gap between the hypothetical and a real market will often remain unknown. For guidance on assessing the validity and reliability of the welfare estimates obtained from a DCE, start with Chapter 8 in Mariel et al. (2021) and Bishop and Boyle (2019). Given this context, we discuss some key considerations for designing a hypothetical market below.

**The institutional context.** For respondents to behave as if they are in a real market, they need to understand how the exchange—paying money for the provision of the good or service—will occur, specifically, (1) who is delivering it, and (2) how the respondent is expected to pay. The payment vehicle, discussed in Step 2 (Sect. 2.2), is of particular interest. An important question that arises is whether respondents will have to pay an (increased) entrance fee, a higher electricity bill, or higher taxes? Respondents must also know where the money they pay will go: will it go to the local community responsible for providing the good, or be collected by the national government and allocated to the national budget?

Both the *payment vehicle* and the *payment recipient* can influence respondents' choices. Respondents might prefer a tax as a payment vehicle because it would be applied universally within a community or a nation, but they may also distrust the local or national government's commitment to delivering the good as promised in the hypothetical market. Moreover, the plausibility of a tax being levied for a specific good depends on the fiscal system of a country. In some countries, the provision of public goods at the local level is funded through taxes, while in others, specially introduced fees may be charged for the good in question (e.g. a contribution to a fund for managing a local forest). However, newly introduced entrance fees, for example to a forest, can lead to protests by concerned individuals, as the fees affect their property rights. In other cases, as in our case study, surcharges or discounts to already existing payments such as the electricity bill are an option.

Another essential consideration is whether respondents trust the institutions responsible for providing the good or service. If they do not believe that the institution will deliver the promised good or service—or if they suspect the money might be used for other purposes—their stated WTP may decrease or be zero. For insights into the effects of distrust toward institutions providing environmental goods in the context of a developing country, see Manhique and Wätzold (2024).

**Incentive compatibility and consequentiality.** Incentive compatibility is important in the economic literature on stated preference (Carson and Groves 2007). Respondents should perceive revealing their true preferences as being in their own best interest in the DCE survey, as the contrary will increase the gap between stated and true preferences, potentially biasing the estimation results. For example, individuals may understate their preferences, expecting the good to be provided even if they state a lower WTP than their true preferences, or they may overstate their preferences to signal the importance of the good to decision-makers. While incentive compatibility is important in hypothetical markets in any field, it is particularly critical in environmental valuation (Carson and Groves 2007), which tends to deal with public goods. Whether a survey is incentive compatible or not depends on several conditions for truthful preference revelation (Vossler et al. 2012). Two conditions are particularly important (Carson and Groves 2007; Zawojska and Czajkowski 2017): first, that respondents perceive their responses as consequential, meaning that they care about the good or service they are evaluating and believe that their choices impact the provision decision; and second, that a single binary format is employed in the valuation question to discourage strategic misrepresentation.

Regarding consequentiality, two aspects should be distinguished (Herriges et al. 2010): *policy consequentiality* (i.e. respondents believe that the survey results will influence an outcome they care about) and *payment consequentiality* (i.e. respondents perceive that there is a positive probability they will have to pay). If both conditions are met, and the choice question is a single binary choice, this is called strong consequentiality (Herriges et al. 2010). Regarding the incentive compatibility properties of the binary question format, note that they are only preserved in a sequence of choices if respondents view each choice as independent from the other choices (Vossler et al. 2012). Presenting only one choice task in an interview, however, would result in a significant loss of information, as it would only provide one choice observation per respondent. Consequently, sample sizes would have to increase significantly.

Thus, in a recent study, Vossler et al. (2024) investigated whether an informational script could successfully encourage respondents to treat sequential choice tasks as independent. They reported that the scripts positively impacted validity. At present, the majority of DCE studies in environmental valuation use choice tasks with three or more alternatives, and it is common to present a sequence of choice tasks without explicitly instructing respondents to treat them as independent. Thus, a significant gap exists between survey designs that are considered incentive compatible and those implemented in the field.

**Devices to mitigate hypothetical bias.** To mitigate the effects of the hypothetical nature of stated responses, researchers have developed a set of tools that can be implemented in the hypothetical market, generally consisting of additional information scripts. For an overview related to DCEs, see Haghani et al. (2021a, 2021b), and for an overview in environmental valuation, see Penn and Hu (2019) and Penn et al. (2024). The rationale behind these tools is to encourage respondents to treat the money they are spending when choosing an alternative as "real money", similarly to how they spend money in real markets.

A widely known and often applied tool is the *cheap talk script* (Penn and Hu 2019), which explicitly discusses the hypothetical nature of the survey. The objective is to make respondents aware of its existence and consequences (Haghani et al. 2021b). However, the effect of a cheap talk script presented in the beginning of a sequence of choice tasks may fade as respondents make their way through the choice tasks, reducing its influence on stated choices over time. To combat this effect, researchers devised the repeated opt-out reminder (ROOR), providing a reminder before each choice task that prompts respondents to select the opt-out alternative if they genuinely are not willing to pay the amount associated with the hypothetical alternatives (Ladenburg and Olsen 2014).

In the context of novel food products, Alemu and Olsen (2018) found that the ROOR effectively mitigated the hypothetical bias for one attribute and reduced it for the remaining attributes when compared to a non-hypothetical setting. More recently,

Börger et al. (2024) found that the opt-out reminder combined with a cheap talk script mitigated the effects of cost vectors with varying ranges of cost amounts. Their study showed that using both tools together resulted in converging mWTP estimates across split samples that differed only by the values of the cost vectors. However, since the authors used the cheap talk script and the opt-out reminder jointly, and thus their effects might be confounded, it remained unclear whether one tool had a stronger effect or if the findings depend on both together. Studies investigating the effects of the opt-out reminder suggest that it may have a larger impact than the cheap talk script, but further evidence is needed before making a definitive recommendation.

Other tools in the literature include budget reminders, honesty priming, a "solemn oath", and more (see Haghani et al. 2021b). The jury is still out on whether the tools used to mitigate the hypothetical bias allow for the use of choice tasks with more than two alternatives while still revealing respondents' true preferences. The safest option is to employ binary choice tasks and ensure that respondents treat each task in a sequence as independent, but this may not always be feasible in real-world contexts. The lab experiment findings by Vossler and Zawojska (2020) indicate that when economic incentives are precisely controlled, mWTP distributions remain statistically indistinguishable, regardless of whether a single binary choice, double-bounded binary choice, payment card, or open-ended response format is used. If these results hold, a wider range of response format options would be feasible.

**Providing information.** An important objective when designing a DCE is ensuring that respondents make informed choices. Respondents will make trade-offs between attributes describing different alternatives in the DCE survey, and must have both a general understanding of the good or service and a more specific understanding of the meaning of each attribute and the corresponding levels. While some respondents may have extensive prior knowledge of the good in question, others may not be familiar with it at all (Sandorf et al. 2016), and thus a minimum level of information should be provided to all respondents. At the same time, it is also essential to avoid providing too much information, because (1) the respondents in the sample should represent the target population, which may not have access to the information survey participants receive, and (2) providing extensive information might result in an information overload which prevents the information provided from being taken in.

Generally, what is known from the literature is that the quantity and type of information, as well as how it is framed, can influence WTP estimates, so it is crucial to balance the goal of informing choices with avoiding unwanted influence on stated preferences (see Welling et al. 2022, 2023 or Needham et al. 2018 for a review of the effect of information on stated preferences). Given the limited survey time and attention span of respondents, it will often be impossible to provide detailed information on all aspects of the hypothetical market in a DCE survey. Therefore, researchers must decide which aspects to emphasise and which to provide less information on. Recall that the information given can influence responses, so testing is essential when preparing the survey information. This also applies to the format of information delivery: whether to use only text, a mix of text and images, or a video.

Mariel et al. (2021, Chapter 2.2) highlights the following considerations that should be taken into account when compiling information to present to respondents:

- Clearly define the attributes and their levels in a way that respondents will easily understand.
- Ensure that the proposed policy/scenario change leads to a specific outcome that is perceived as realistic by respondents, with at least some scientific evidence supporting this relationship.
- Make the scope and the timing of the valued policy/scenario change explicit.
- Distinguish between means, i.e. the measures with which a change in environmental quality can be achieved, and outcomes, with the latter representing the good or service in question.
- Confirm that the entities described as responsible for implementing the policy have the authority to do so and that respondents also find this plausible (suitability of the institutional setting).

### 2.3.2 Other Issues of Relevance

- **The *time frame* of the provision of the good in question.** Take the example of constructing wind farms: respondents might know that it could take months or even years before a new wind farm is built in their area. What does this imply for the provision of the good as described in the survey? For example, if the wind farm will be built in five years, do respondents start paying now or in five years? If the latter is true, you should be asking if they are willing to pay for a specific wind farm design in five years, not now.

  A longer time frame may heighten the hypothetical nature of the scenario and bias results, as people may report being willing to pay higher amounts knowing payments are far in the future. At the same time, asking respondents to start paying now for a good or service that will only be provided far into the future may not reflect real markets accurately.

  Additionally, preferences can change over time, as do environmental conditions and priorities, making the time scale a crucial aspect to consider when designing DCE surveys. A solution to this problem could be to limit the period during which individuals would have to pay. For example, Meyerhoff et al. (2021a) informed respondents that the payment "... was set up as a new coastal protection levy to be charged annually per household nationwide from 2021 on for the next 10 years. After this period, the measures would be reassessed, and a decision would be made on further financing." This procedure presents respondents with a time period that is clearly defined and foreseeable. Whether such a framing is possible in the end depends on the context of the study and the good at hand.
- **The format of the information presented.** Most often, information is presented as text in DCE surveys (often accompanied by images), however, information about the good or service in question and its attributes can be presented using various media (Vass et al. 2024). Depending on the survey mode, you may consider

presenting some or all of the information in audio or video format. As people are more and more accustomed to receiving information in such formats, using audio or video could capture their attention and better convey the information needed to make informed choices. Extensive pretesting, however, is essential in these cases, and will likely require more resources – time and financial resources - compared to text only information.

- **The *framing* of the changes in the good or service.** The framing of different attributes and alternatives can impact respondents' choices and welfare measures. Faccioli and Glenk (2021) investigated valence-based framing, where equivalent outcomes are presented by accentuating the same changes either as a) positive (e.g. more in good condition) or b) negative (e.g. less in bad condition). They obtained different WTP estimates for each framing approach, indicating that framing has important implications for the resulting estimates of welfare measures. To mitigate this effect, they recommend using neutral attribute descriptions and pre-testing for potential effects of different framings.
- **Considerations when using images.** When using images, make sure that they do not convey unintended information. In the wind power case study for example (see Chapter 4), the authors of the original study decided not to use images portraying the effects of wind turbines on landscapes, due to potentially misleading information. Specifically, depending on the camera angle, images could give the impression that turbines were much closer to houses than they really were, which could significantly influence respondents' choices, and thus images were not included. Parsons and Yan (2021) explored how visual cues can anchor respondents' perceptions and influence stated preferences, highlighting the importance of carefully selecting and using images to avoid bias. Also consider that when a survey is conducted over a large geographical area, landscapes are likely to vary and it becomes difficult to capture those differences in a few images. Moreover, the specific content of the image is also critical. If you are conducting a DCE to quantify the existence value of polar bears, a picture of a cute, cuddly polar bear cub will evoke positive emotions, leading to an inflated WTP. Conversely, an image of the same bear cub covered in seal blood after a meal will provoke a negative reaction, likely resulting in a much lower WTP.
- **Checking the effect of devices on the hypothetical bias.** When employing *tools to counteract hypothetical bias* (e.g. a cheap talk script or an opt-out reminder), including a split sample without the device can be useful to analyse whether the tool has an effect. If all respondents face the same device, you will have to trust that the effect goes in the expected direction based on previous studies, i.e. generally lower WTP estimates (Gschwandtner and Burton 2020). Note that employing such devices does not allow you to conclude that a hypothetical bias is not present in your data. Such a conclusion would require comparing hypothetical and real choices (Harrison 2024).
- **Individual vs. household WTP.** From a theoretical perspective, *individual* preferences are the focus in economic valuation, however, households' WTP are often elicited in DCE surveys. The few available studies on this topic indicate that differences exist between individually and jointly elicited household WTP estimates

(Bateman and Munro 2009; see Boto-García and Mariel 2024 for an overview). For example, a study by Alem et al. (2023) showed that women were willing to pay for improved cookstoves, but that men's preferences dominated the household's decision.

The implications for DCEs are as follows: First, the payment vehicle should be individual in nature, such as an income tax or an entrance fee. If it is at the household level, such as the electricity bill, this could affect the DCE's incentive compatibility as not only the interviewee has to bear the costs. Second, aggregating mWTP estimates across the target population may cause the estimations to significantly differ from true population values if the preferences of the interviewed person do not reflect the entire household's preferences.

Ultimately, the decision to use individual or household WTP depends on the context and the nature of the good or service being evaluated: individual WTPs tend to be better suited for goods or services that are personal, when the aim is to capture individual behaviour, or when analysing demographic differences, whereas household WTPs are generally better suited for goods or services that affect or are decided upon by the household as a whole.

## 2.4 Step 4: Designing the Discrete Choice Experiment

### *2.4.1 Fundamentals*

As the name of this method indicates, the experimental design lies at the core of any DCE. It involves the systematic variation of attribute levels, so that the influence of each attribute can be isolated and estimated in the subsequent analysis. The flexibility in designing the experiment gives us a clear advantage over other methods in certain situations, such as revealed preference methods used to determine preferences for non-market goods. For example, if all wind farms in a certain region are the same size, with a similar distance from residential areas, this lack of variation among existing wind farms makes it impossible draw conclusions about people's preferences using a revealed preference method. In contrast, when designing a DCE, we can generate sufficient variation in attribute levels to estimate these preferences, and even account for future developments, such as taller turbines due to technological advancements.

**Dimensions of the discrete choice experiment.** When deciding on the dimensions of a DCE, the following aspects must be considered: (1) the attributes, (2) their levels, (3) the range of these levels, (4) the number of alternatives per choice task, and 5) the number of choice tasks presented to each respondent (Hensher 2004; Caussade et al. 2005; Meyerhoff et al. 2015). Generally, the larger each of these five dimensions, the more information can be obtained from the DCE. While more attributes and a higher number of attribute levels provide more information about the characteristics of the good or service, including more alternatives per choice task yields more information about the trade-offs respondents make. The higher the number of choice tasks, the more data from each respondent is collected, which is important in supplying sufficient variation to provide reliable estimates, and is especially important when estimating more complex models. Varying the attribute level ranges affects the precision of the estimates (Bliemer and Rose 2024). Findings suggest that a wide attribute level range leads to smaller standard errors than a narrow range.

Given this information, it may seem that increasing the dimensions of a DCE will lead to better results. However, this positive effect is offset by respondents' ability to handle the complexity of the choice tasks, which increases when the dimensions increase. A concept used in this context is response efficiency, which refers to "measurement error resulting from respondents' inattention to the choice questions or other unobserved, contextual influences" (Johnson et al. 2013). Therefore, the dimensions of the DCE must balance the amount of information desired from your survey with the respondent's ability to manage its complexity. The lower the response efficiency, the less likely respondents are to identify the alternatives they most prefer, leading to lower choice consistency, i.e. making the same choices when faced with the same choice tasks (Rigby et al. 2015), and a greater variation in the error term, among other effects.

Your choice of the dimensions is likely to be revised several times during the design process. For example, focus groups or other early testing methods (see Step 7) might reveal that the response efficiency of a particular design is too low, requiring adjustments such as reducing one or more dimensions (e.g. dropping an attribute). Conversely, natural scientists on your interdisciplinary research team may need more information about the good or service and may advocate for adding attributes. Next, we cover several considerations that you may find helpful in informing this decision.

- **Number of attributes.** As mentioned in Step 2, the attributes lie at the core of any DCE. They describe the good or service in question and set the framework for the study results. The key question is how many attributes are needed to adequately describe the good or service, and at what point adding (or subtracting) an attribute would negatively impact individuals' choices.

  More attributes provide the opportunity to describe the good or service in greater detail and, of course, offer more information to decision-makers. It is common for DCE studies in environmental valuation to have between four and six attributes, but this does not mean that going beyond this range is inherently problematic. The appropriate number of attributes depends largely on the context of the study, including respondents' familiarity with and psychological distance from the good or service, as well as the complexity of the good or service itself and the number of attributes needed to reasonably describe it in order for respondents to make informed decisions.

  For example, presenting farmers with choice tasks about their specific farming practices, with which they are very familiar, may allow for the inclusion of more attributes compared to asking the public about biodiversity conservation, a concept that might be less familiar. A technique that allows you to use a larger number of attributes without significantly increasing the burden on respondents is *partial profile designs*. The basic idea is that the levels of some attributes are kept constant across alternatives, thereby reducing the complexity. If done systematically, coefficients for all attributes can still be estimated (Chrzan 2010; Meyerhoff and Oehlmann 2023; Jonker 2024).

- **Number and range of attribute levels.** From a statistical perspective, two attribute levels are sufficient if the marginal changes are linear, meaning that the slope for each additional level of the attribute is the same. Considering our case study, if each additional metre of distance between a turbine and residential areas is valued the same (i.e. the effect is linear), then two distance levels would suffice to capture how people value the distance to turbines. However, it may not always be reasonable to expect this to be the case, as people's valuation can change with increased distance. To test for potential non-linearity, more than two attribute levels are needed. Determining how many levels are sufficient to capture the non-linearity present is ultimately an empirical question, and pretesting in focus groups or other settings is thus needed.

  Studies investigating the impact of design dimensions on choices have found that a higher number of attribute levels can positively affect response efficiency and, consequently, choice consistency (Caussade et al. 2005; Meyerhoff et al. 2015), and the same was found for a narrower range of attribute level values. One explanation for this is that more attribute levels and a narrower range make it easier for respondents to identify the preferred alternative in a choice task. As discussed in Step 2 in relation to the cost attribute, recent findings indicate that using more levels may be beneficial in reducing the occurrence of overshooting (Glenk et al. 2024).
- **Number of alternatives.** When deciding on the number of alternatives, it is essential to remember that environmental valuation generally deals with public goods or services not traded in markets. Thus, the conditions for incentive-compatibility in stated preference surveys should be met (Vossler et al. 2012, 2024). From a theoretical standpoint, only binary choices are incentive compatible under conditions which are likely fulfilled in a survey concerned with environmental public goods. If the status quo is among the alternatives, only one hypothetical alternative should be included in the choice task (SQ + 1). In contrast, the choice task format most often used in environmental valuation includes the status quo and two hypothetical alternatives generated from the experimental design (SQ + 2).

  Weng et al. (2020) investigated both formats (SQ + 1 vs. SQ + 2), with their results supporting the use of the SQ + 1 format (see also Zhang and Adamowicz 2011) and advising caution when using choice tasks with more than one hypothetical alternative. The advantage of including more than one hypothetical alternative in a choice task is that it provides more information from a single choice observation. In private good settings, where incentive compatibility is not a major concern, such as those common in marketing, transportation or health, these advantages can be exploited. However, adding too many alternatives can increase the complexity to the point where respondents stop making trade-offs and instead rely on simplifying heuristics to make the decision-making process easier. Therefore, even in private good settings, the number of alternatives should be selected carefully to strike a balance between statistical efficiency and response efficiency, i.e. the cognitive capacity of respondents in a survey setting.

While it is true that in real market scenarios people often choose from a large number of alternatives (e.g. in a coffee shop with numerous combinations of coffee type, size, coffee bean characteristics, milk types, and flavourings—resulting in hundreds of possible combinations), the experience in a survey setting is different. It is not that people are incapable of handling many alternatives; rather, the context and format of a survey can alter how respondents process and engage with the options presented.

- **Number of choice tasks per respondent.** To decide how many choice tasks a respondent should face in a DCE survey, two important considerations must be taken into account. First, researchers often hesitate to present many choice tasks due to concerns about negative effects such as fatigue (Campbell et al. 2015); however, this concern is not consistently supported by the literature (Hess et al. 2012; Czajkowski et al. 2014; Meyerhoff et al. 2015). In fact, studies have shown that learning effects can occur with a large number of choice tasks.

  Two types of learning are identified in a valuation context: *institutional learning*, where respondents become familiar with the rules of the market (real or hypothetical), and *value learning*, where they refine their understanding of their own preferences for the good being evaluated (Campbell et al. 2015). To capitalise on these learning effects, it may be advantageous to include enough choice tasks to allow respondents to acquire the necessary knowledge to make more informed choices.

  However, it is crucial to balance the advantages of learning effects, while avoiding fatigue. Achieving this balance is not straightforward: Oehlmann et al. (2017) suggest that between 10 and 15 choice tasks can be used without negatively affecting study results, but this is not universally applicable and depends heavily on the specific empirical setting. While this range may be suitable in some contexts, it could be excessive in others, underscoring the importance of testing the number of choice tasks through focus group discussions and pilot studies.

  The second consideration relates to the conditions of incentive compatibility. Incentive compatibility can be expected only for the *first binary choice*; thus, presenting more than one choice task in a study evaluating a public good does not align with this condition. The current practice in DCE research, therefore, violates the prerequisites of incentive compatibility when presenting a series of choice tasks. The main justification for this approach is that sampling efficiency decreases significantly when only one choice observation is obtained per interview, requiring a corresponding increase in sample size. In a recent study, Vossler et al. (2024) reported promising results using information scripts to encourage respondents to treat the multiple valuation scenarios in a sequence of choice tasks as independent. They found that these scripts improved the construct validity (the validity of a study's estimation results, see Mariel et al. 2021, Chapter 8 for more information on the concepts of validity and reliability) of the study and increased the likelihood that stated beliefs aligned with theory-relevant assumptions. However, further research is needed in this area.

For now, we recommend using similar information scripts to Vossler et al. (2024), while continuing to present a sequence of choice tasks. If the sample is sufficiently large and the choice tasks are presented in a randomised order, it may be feasible to run choice models using only the first choice made by respondents and compare the results to a model that uses all choice observations. However, this comparison may be complicated by the potential learning effects, which could influence respondents' decisions as they progress through the choice tasks, making the results less straightforward to interpret.

**Opt-out option or forced choice.** An important issue to decide is whether respondents will be able to select an alternative that allows them to maintain the status quo, including not paying anything (i.e. the opt-out alternative, often called the status quo option), or whether they must select an alternative that involves a change to the current situation, including payments (non-SQ alternatives). To illustrate this, imagine you are going to a grocery store to buy ingredients for dinner. What happens if you cannot find anything you want to buy? Are you allowed to leave without purchasing anything, or are you forced to buy something before leaving? In the first scenario, you face an opt-out option; in the latter, you face a forced choice.

In most cases, including an opt-out option best reflects the choices people have in real-world contexts. This is important for welfare economic conditions, since including an opt-out option ensures that respondents reveal their true preferences, including the possibility that they do not find any of the offered alternatives preferable to their current situation. This is especially important when the objective of your study is to calculate overall (non-marginal) welfare measures, which involve comparing combinations of attribute level changes, with the status quo as a reference. If non-marginal welfare measures are a desired output, opt-out options must be included; with a forced choice, only marginal welfare measures (mWTP) can be calculated for the attributes incorporated.

However, in some situations, a forced choice might be appropriate. For example, if the government has committed to increasing electricity generation through wind power, and people can have a say in where this occurs, but not *if* it occurs (Ek and Persson 2014). Whether a forced choice format is suitable depends strongly on the context, and sufficient pretesting is necessary to determine whether respondents will accept this a forced format. If not, they might drop out of the survey or resort to random choice as a response strategy.

While including an opt-out alternative is common practice in DCEs, defining and presenting it to respondents can be challenging. You may define this alternative as "none of these", i.e. none of the other alternatives offered, or as an "actual" status quo that reflects the baseline or current attribute levels. In either case, the opt-out option should be credible and easily understood by respondents, allowing them to anticipate its impact on their welfare accurately. Note that an opt-out or status quo option can significantly influence the distribution of choices among other alternatives, affecting observed choice shares. Although selecting the opt-out option may genuinely reflect a respondent's preference, research indicates that this choice can be driven by factors beyond the attributes themselves (see Campbell and Erdem 2019 for a discussion on this and related topics).

**Generating an experimental design**. Once the key aspects of the DCE design have been defined, the next step is to generate the experimental design. The objective of the experimental design is to ensure that you can draw conclusions about the impact of each attribute and their levels on respondents' choices and infer economic welfare measures from the model results. To achieve this, the design must be structured in a way that ensures ceteris paribus conditions, allowing for clear and accurate inferences about how each attribute influences decision-making.

An experimental design is essentially a matrix, with the rows often representing the attributes and the columns representing the alternatives. The values in the matrix cells indicate the level of each attribute for each alternative. Depending on the survey mode selected and the software capabilities for online or CAPI (Computer Assisted Personal Interviews) surveys, this matrix can either be directly imported into the survey software (e.g. as an Excel file) or serve as a starting point for generating the choice tasks in a text or graphical editor. In the latter case, the choice tasks can be saved as image files and then uploaded to the survey software or copied to a paper questionnaire. If your survey is conducted by a company, be sure to confirm the capabilities of their platform and how you will need to provide the experimental design or choice tasks.

A comprehensive overview of different types of designs and their advantages and disadvantages is provided by Bliemer and Rose (2024). Details on how to generate an experimental design using the R-package *spdesign* (Sandorf and Campbell 2023) will be covered in Chapter 5. Here, we will focus on a few key considerations, especially at the planning stage.

A good starting point for developing an experimental design is the sample size you can afford. In recent years, efficient experimental designs have become standard in stated preference research, particularly in environmental valuation. The basic idea is that using prior knowledge about the preferences of your target population can make an experimental design more efficient, meaning that fewer observations are needed to achieve the same amount of precision. Prior knowledge can come from previously conducted studies available in the literature or from pilot studies.

Applied to our case study, results from other studies on wind farms indicate that distance matters, with people preferring wind turbines further away from their residence. Therefore, it is reasonable to assume that increasing the distance from residential areas will positively affect the probability of an alternative being chosen. The experimental design could incorporate this information by assigning a positive sign to the corresponding coefficient (a prior). Conversely, it is well known that higher costs decrease the probability of an alternative being chosen. In this case, a negative coefficient for the cost parameter could inform the experimental design. For more information on selecting priors, see Bliemer and Collins (2016).

However, an excessive focus on statistical efficiency can lead to unwanted side effects, as choices can become more difficult for respondents. Efficient designs enhance the ability to derive meaningful insights by promoting combinations of alternatives that are more *utility balanced*. When a design includes a clearly dominant alternative, it provides limited information, as the choice probabilities become highly skewed, making the "best choice" too obvious. In contrast, when alternatives are relatively similar in terms of overall utility (i.e. utility balanced), the choice probabilities are more balanced, and even a small change in one or more attributes can influence the most likely choice outcome. Researchers gain more information from balanced designs, as they provide a clearer view of how attribute changes affect choice behaviour.

A drawback is that more balanced designs place a higher cognitive burden on respondents. Such designs require respondents to consider trade-offs more carefully, as opposed to tasks with a dominant alternative, where the choice is straightforward and almost trivial. The more information the design provides, the fewer observations are needed overall to achieve statistical significance. Yet, as the difficulty of choices increases, respondents may resort to simplifying heuristics or even make random choices, which violates the underlying assumptions of the random utility model. Response efficiency, as discussed in Step 2, is also essential when generating an experimental design.

The need for efficiency largely depends on the obtainable sample size. The larger the sample size, the less critical it is to prioritise statistical efficiency in the design. Conversely, the smaller the sample size (or target group), the more important statistical efficiency becomes. Keep in mind that an efficient design is not a solution that compensates for very small samples—it has limits based on the quality of prior information (beyond just the sign, you might have additional information about the likely magnitude of the parameter) and the complexity (i.e. design dimensions) of the DCE. For example, as the number of attributes increases, a larger sample size is typically required to ensure sufficient degrees of freedom for accurate parameter estimation and to maintain the statistical robustness of the model.

**Labelled or unlabelled designs.** Another decision to make early on is whether your discrete choice experiment will be labelled, unlabelled or a combination of both. In our experience, most environmental valuation applications use unlabelled DCEs. Generally, a DCE is considered unlabelled if the alternatives are named without providing further details (e.g. Alternative A, Alternative B, Alternative C). In contrast, labelled DCEs, which are commonly used in transportation studies, work well when preferences for specific, named alternatives are meaningful (e.g. transport modes such as "car", "train", or "plane"). The attribute levels in labelled DCEs correspond directly to the characteristics of these specific alternatives.

An example from the environmental valuation field is Oehlmann and Meyerhoff (2016), who investigated preferences for renewable energy production sites and labelled the alternatives as "Electricity from solar", "Electricity from wind", and "Electricity from biomass". Labelled alternatives allow for experimental designs where certain attributes or attribute levels are assigned only to certain alternatives. For example, since solar panels require more space in a landscape than wind turbines to generate the same amount of electricity, a labelled design could assign different levels to the attribute "size of production site" for each alternative. However, the analysis of labelled experiments can become more complex, as estimating utilities often involves interactions between the attributes and the alternative specific constants (ASCs).

If the goods or services warrant the use of labelled alternatives, this approach can provide richer information from respondents and enhance clarity, as labels are often more meaningful than generic names like Alternative A and Alternative B. This can help respondents better understand the alternatives being presented. The extent to which labelled or unlabelled alternatives produce different findings has not been investigated, with the exception of Doherty et al. (2013), who compared both types of designs in the context of recreation and found that welfare measures differed significantly between labelled and unlabelled DCEs.

**Choice task design.** In addition to selecting the design dimensions of your DCE and generating an experimental design that allocates attribute levels to alternatives and choice tasks, you must decide how to present the choice tasks. Two considerations are key here: first, if a table format is used, and if so, whether the columns represent alternatives or attributes; and second, how the information conveyed by the attributes and their levels is presented to respondents.

The most common format in the literature is a choice task in the form of a table (also called the matrix format), where the rows represent the attributes, and the columns represent the alternatives. The attributes and their levels are typically described using text only. The choice tasks in our case study (see Chapter 4) are in this format. Recently, choice tasks increasingly include additional visual information, such as images or icons, to support the text describing attributes and/or their levels. Overall, there is limited evidence on whether additional visual information is beneficial.

DeLong et al. (2021) investigated this in the marketing field and compared a text-only representation to a visual version where pictures depicted the product alternatives using split samples. They found that participants paid more attention to the attributes in the text-only treatment. Another study on the effects of using text alone versus a combination of images and text, this time on green roofs, was conducted by Netusil et al. (2023) and found significantly higher mWTP estimates in the treatment that included images.

To date, few studies in environmental valuation have departed from the standard choice task format, i.e. the matrix format and text to describe the attributes and their levels. While a few authors like Rolfe and Windle (2012, 2015) have presented choice tasks with alternatives shown in the rows and attributes in the columns, Sandorf et al. (2018) are, to our knowledge, the first to investigate whether this change in format impacts the stated choices. They found that the orientation of alternatives and attributes matters and that the task format can influence respondents' choices and thus key outputs such as WTP estimates.

Among the studies that departed from the table or matrix format is Shr et al. (2019). To describe the neighbourhoods that were presented to respondents as choice options, the authors used a visual only treatment with three pictures, only text, or a combination of the three pictures and text, with three split samples to test differences among choice task designs. They concluded that including visual representations is preferable when DCEs are used to value goods and services connected to landscapes.

However, they also noted that adding information through images could increase decision complexity and result in less predictable responses.

The use of maps in choice tasks is particularly interesting when spatial dimensions are essential for the environmental changes being valued. For example, in a study on water quality in river sections, Meyerhoff et al. (2014) used simplified maps to represent the alternatives (different river sections with varying water qualities) in the choice task. Attribute levels were reflected by coloured levels on a water quality ladder. Another recent example is Johnston et al. (2023), who investigated the value of water quality in river networks using interactive maps generated through geographic information systems (GIS). Their maps displayed water quality measures at various zoom levels across the study area, providing spatially detailed information.

The matrix format was also abandoned in a study investigating the value of artificial lake ecosystems for anglers (Meyerhoff et al. 2019). The authors opted for a completely visual representation of the choice alternatives, using one image per alternative, in this case, gravel pits used for recreation. They assumed that respondents would better understand the changes across alternatives (different lakes) when each alternative was presented in a single image, rather than through text describing each attribute change separately. However, the subsequent analysis did not show clear benefits of the visual choice tasks (Meyerhoff et al. 2021b). Another example of a departure from the table format is Mokas et al. (2021), who recorded preferences for different types of urban green spaces, using split samples to investigate differences between text only, video and virtual reality presentations. They found that the presentation format could significantly impact mWTP estimates and that using virtual reality techniques could increase the choice certainty among respondents.

The evidence for using different choice alternative representations is still limited, as only a few studies have used split samples to explore differences between formats. However, going beyond the standard matrix format with text requires additional resources, especially if you aim to use attribute-accompanying icons or suitable images or maps, as the involvement of specialists may be required. This is especially true when creating videos or virtual reality content. Testing these formats is essential, preferably in individual interviews and group settings prior to implementing your DCE survey. Keep in mind that testing requires the creation of different versions of your choice tasks, which will be relevant for budget planning.

**Ordering effects.** Ordering effects can occur with several design elements in a DCE (Boxebeld 2024). First, the order of the attributes in the choice task could matter, as an attribute may receive more attention when presented first rather than last. In one of the few studies addressing this issue, Logar et al. (2020) found that the attribute order did not significantly affect welfare estimates under the standard assumption of full attribute attendance, i.e. respondents account for all attributes and their level changes when selecting the preferred alternative. However, when accounting for attribute non-attendance, i.e. respondents ignore one or more attributes, the welfare estimates for the attributes whose order was reversed and the share of respondents who ignored them differed significantly between treatments.

Ordering effects may also occur with the arrangement of alternatives (Campbell and Erdem 2015). If the status quo alternative is included, is it positioned first (leftmost) or last when reading from left to right? Various studies have shown that this ordering matters, as the opt-out alternative receives different levels of attention depending on whether it appears first or last in the choice task.

The order of alternatives may be even more influential when alternatives are labelled. For example, in a DCE evaluating preferences for different types of renewable energy sources (e.g. solar, wind, biomass), placing solar power as the first option could cause respondents who already favour solar energy to overlook the other alternatives. This ordering effect is particularly relevant if respondents are thought to use a satisficing strategy, where they choose the first acceptable option rather than evaluating all options comprehensively (see Sandorf et al. 2022; Sandorf and Campbell 2019). This behaviour can lead to biased results, as the position of the alternatives may disproportionately influence the choices made.

Therefore, careful consideration of the sequence and arrangement of alternatives is crucial to minimise such biases and obtain more accurate and reliable insights from DCEs. Randomising the order of alternatives or testing different arrangements during the pretesting phase can help mitigate these effects and improve the robustness of the study.

Another important ordering issue arises from the sequence of choice tasks. Respondents generally face a sequence of choice tasks, and if presented in a certain order, learning may occur, which affects choices. For instance, if the first choice task offers an alternative with a low cost and a highly valued combination of levels of the non-monetary attributes, respondents might use this as a reference point and reject subsequent alternatives that are seen as less favourable (Meyerhoff and Glenk 2015). While these effects cannot be systematically excluded at the individual level, randomising the order of choice tasks mitigates these effects at the sample level.

Randomisation is an important response to potential ordering effects, and a key question is the extent to which randomisation should be implemented. It is now common practice to randomise the sequence of choice tasks, but very few researchers (to our knowledge) randomise the order of attributes or alternatives. A look beyond the field of environmental valuation can be insightful: in political science, where conjoint analyses (a close relative of DCEs) are often used, fully randomised designs are common (Bansak et al. 2021). In this case, attribute levels are not allocated by an experimental design, but levels are all determined randomly. However, to avoid cognitive overload, we recommend only randomising the order of attributes or alternatives across respondents and not across choice tasks seen by the same respondent.

Ordering effects can also occur in other parts of the questionnaire, as the order of questions within a questionnaire can matter. For example, researchers often include sets of survey items to measure attitudes toward the good in question or other related aspects. Should these items be presented before or after the discrete choice experiment? Research has shown that order matters (Liebe et al. 2021). Answering attitudinal questions can activate beliefs that subsequently influence respondents' choices, so if we want to avoid this activation of attitudes or norms, the DCE should come first. This consideration also applies to other types of questions, such as knowledge questions presented in a quiz format, which may activate specific ways of thinking about the good or service.

However, these effects are not always undesirable. Presenting attitudinal and knowledge questions before the discrete choice experiment can serve as a "warm-up", helping respondents engage with the context and think critically about the topic, leading to more informed and consistent choices during the experiment. Activating existing views in this way can sometimes be beneficial, especially when it aligns with the study's objectives.

While it is impossible to eliminate ordering effects entirely, they can by mitigated through randomisation where appropriate. Most importantly, it is essential to consider these effects when designing the questionnaire and arrange the elements in a way that aligns with and supports the research objectives. As practical advice, we recommend deciding which elements you wish to randomise before asking a survey company for offers. While most companies can randomise the order of choice tasks, randomising the order of alternatives might pose an issue to some survey companies.

### *2.4.2 More Aspects to Consider*

- **Updating the experimental design.** If you are unsure whether your design will perform as expected, you can begin with only a portion of your planned interviews and estimate a choice model with this data. Results from this model can be used to inform and update the experimental design. Scarpa et al. (2007), who applied a sequential design approach, concluded that updating the experimental design delivers significant efficiency gains without losing respondent efficiency.
- **Attribute level balance.** When determining the number of attribute levels, the number of alternatives, and the number of choice tasks per respondent in a DCE, it is helpful to choose values that are common multiples (a multiple that is shared by two or more numbers, e.g. 12 is a common multiple of 2, 3, 4 and 6) as this approach facilitates balancing attribute levels across alternatives and blocks (a subset of choice tasks), if needed. For example, if your experimental design includes a single block, two alternatives, and five choice tasks per respondent, but your price attribute has seven unique levels, it will be impossible to achieve *attribute level balance*—where each attribute level appears an equal number of times—because $1 \cdot 2 \cdot 5 = 10$ is not divisible by 7 without a remainder. To achieve attribute level balance, at least one of these factors would need to be adjusted. Although it may not always be feasible, accounting for this can enhance the experimental design. As Bliemer and Rose (2024) state, while attribute level balance is not a strict requirement, maintaining some degree of it is generally considered beneficial to ensure a good coverage of all possible combinations of the selected attribute levels.
- **Interactions between attributes.** The valuations of the attributes used in the DCE might depend on each other, meaning that the levels of one attribute can influence how the levels of another attribute are valued. Consider the example of wind farms:

if respondents' valuation of turbine height depends on the distance between a wind farm and residential areas, there may be an interaction between these attributes. If the distance is short, respondents might reject high turbines, but if the distance is large, they may accept alternatives with taller turbines. If there are indications of interactions between attributes, they should be incorporated into the experimental design, so that their significance can be tested. Since incorporating interactions into the design increases its complexity, we recommend not accounting for all possible interactions, but selecting those that are meaningful in the context of your study.

- **Continuous vs. categorical variables.** It is important to determine which variables should be treated as continuous and which as categorical in the DCE and the experimental design. Categorical variables generally require more choice observations to achieve high-precision estimates. Therefore, an experimental design that accounts for categorical variables is usually larger, potentially resulting in more choice tasks to achieve the same level of statistical efficiency. If a variable coded as continuous in the experimental design is recoded as a categorical variable in the estimation, you might end up with an insufficient number of observations (choices) for your design, leading to insignificant coefficients or large confidence intervals.
- **Supplementing the status quo.** In many DCEs in environmental valuation, a status quo alternative is included, in which the attribute levels describe the current situation, and the cost attribute level is set to zero. If respondents select this alternative, they do not have to pay because the provision of the good or service remains unchanged. However, it is important to question whether this scenario is realistic. Often, even to maintain the status quo, resources are needed; otherwise, the current situation may deteriorate.

  If this is the case, one option is to include both a status quo alternative with a payment and a zero-price alternative that would lead to changes compared to the current situation. In Meyerhoff et al. (2021a), splitting the status quo alternative in this way resulted in a significant share of respondents who were unwilling to pay for further climate change adaptation measures but were willing to pay to maintain the current situation. If you anticipate that maintaining the current situation will require significant resources in your research context, employing these two options in a choice task can provide valuable insights for decision-making.
- **Smartphones as a frequent response device.** When designing an online survey, consider that a significant share of respondents may use devices with small screens, such as smartphones. This might limit the visibility of the choice tasks, as respondents cannot view them all at once. However, this is not necessarily a disadvantage; for example, Liebe et al. (2015) found that respondents took more time to complete choice tasks when using a smartphone, although this may be because exploring the choice tasks by scrolling takes more time. An unexpected side effect could be that this exploration increases respondents' familiarity with the choice tasks, potentially enhancing choice consistency. For a comparison across devices outside

of the environmental valuation literature see Décieux and Sischka (2024). Other references related to non-market valuation include Hartman and Craig (2019), Skeie et al. (2019), and Vass and Boeri (2021).

## 2.5 Step 5: Questionnaire and Survey Mode

### 2.5.1 *Central Topics*

The DCE questionnaire serves two primary purposes. The first is gathering the information necessary for the subsequent analysis, so a critical step at this stage is to ensure that the questionnaire collects all the information needed to answer your research questions and test your hypothesis—once the data collection begins, it is too late to add missing elements. Second, the questionnaire provides respondents with the context and information needed to make informed choices, including details about the environmental good or service, the study context, and the functioning of the hypothetical market.

Crafting an effective questionnaire involves principles that apply beyond DCEs, though some considerations are specific to this type of survey. General best practices in questionnaire design include structuring questions carefully; engaging or less sensitive questions often appear at the beginning to establish rapport, while the overall number of questions should strike a balance to sustain respondent engagement without causing fatigue. Only essential questions should be included, as irrelevant ones can reduce respondent motivation and thus data quality. A well-chosen mix of question types—such as open-ended, closed-ended, or ordinal—can yield insights into both factual knowledge and subjective opinions, though too many open-ended questions may burden respondents. Clarity, precise phrasing, and unbiased wording are also key to avoid confusion and unintended bias.

In DCE-specific questionnaires, thinking of the survey as a conversation can be especially useful. Start by welcoming participants and introducing the survey topic in an engaging and inclusive manner. While sparking interest in environmental issues or goods is ideal, the introduction should aim to appeal broadly, even to those less inclined toward these subjects. For instance, framing the topic in general terms (e.g. "quality of life in region [name of region], including environmental aspects") can broaden its appeal. Explicitly noting that all viewpoints are valuable can also help, as well as reassuring participants that no expert knowledge is required to answer the questions. Additionally, it is crucial to clarify the survey's objectives early on. If the survey results are intended to inform decision-makers about public preferences, conveying this from the start can increase a participant's sense of purpose and encourage genuine responses that reflect their true preferences.

It is important to note that there is no strict, universally applicable order for the sections of a DCE questionnaire—this should be adapted to your specific context and refined through focus group discussions and piloting. However, in our experience, there is often a logical flow to these sections (see Table 2.1). After the introduction, it is common practice to include general questions about respondent attitudes and behaviours related to the environmental good or service. These might cover how frequently respondents use or visit a specific landscape, their knowledge of the good or service in question, or their attitudes towards it. Such questions are typically closed-ended, often in the form of Likert-type scales, where responses are recorded on an ordinal scale (e.g. "completely disagree" to "completely agree"). Including these questions early on encourages respondents to reflect on the environmental good or service, priming them to consider specific aspects of the issue. This process can help respondents perceive and evaluate the choices presented in the DCE more clearly. These initial questions provide a natural transition to the main section containing the DCE, which typically includes essential information about the good or service, a description of the hypothetical market, and the sequence of choice tasks. The design and contents of these parts of the DCE survey were covered in detail in previous steps (see steps 2–4).

After respondents have answered all choice tasks, the next section typically includes a series of debriefing questions aimed at understanding the stated choices (Krupnick and Adamowicz 2006; Carson and Louviere 2011). While there are many potential lines of inquiry, the core objective of debriefing questions is to evaluate respondent understanding, assess task difficulty, identify behavioural strategies, and detect potential strategic responses or incentive compatibility issues. Equipped with this information, researchers can more accurately gauge the validity and reliability of respondents' choices. These questions often address the respondent's uncertainty in their choices (Lundhede et al. 2009; Dekker et al. 2016; Penn and Hu 2022), their attention to specific attributes (Scarpa et al. 2009; Koetse 2016; Lew and Whitehead 2020), and any heuristics or behavioural rules they may have used.

Debriefing questions can also go beyond stated choices to explore respondents' understanding of the survey, acceptance of the information and baseline scenarios provided, and perceptions of survey bias—whether they feel their answers were subtly directed toward certain responses (Krupnick and Adamowicz 2006). Additionally, follow-up questions can be used to evaluate the extent to which respondents perceived their answers as meaningful and whether their choices reflect how they would behave in a real market.

Motivations behind choice behaviours can also be explored, particularly to identify protest responses. For instance, respondents who consistently choose the status quo or zero-price alternative may be signalling discontent with the hypothetical market rather than a true unwillingness to pay for the good or service. In these cases, sets of statements can be presented, asking respondents to describe their motivations or to indicate their level of agreement with specific statements. See Mariel et al. (2021, Chapter 2) for potential approaches to identify and subsequently handle protesters.

Another set of questions often presented after the sequence of choice tasks addresses attitudes or norms that may influence respondents' choices. Sometimes, these questions are included in the opening section instead to prime respondents by encouraging them to think about the good or service before starting to respond to the choice tasks. This priming can be beneficial in some cases but can introduce

**Table 2.1** General structure and content of a DCE questionnaire

| Questionnaire section | Content and examples of related questions |
|---|---|
| Information given at the beginning | – What is the aim of the survey? |
| | – Who is eligible to take part? |
| | – Who is conducting the survey? |
| | – To what extent is anonymity or confidentiality of survey responses guaranteed? |
| | – How are the results going to be used / disseminated? |
| | – How long will it take to answer the survey? |
| | – Has ethical approval been obtained for the study? |
| | – How will the data be stored? |
| Behavioural questions | – How often have respondents visited the environmental good in question (e.g. a forest or beach)? |
| | – Which activities did respondents engage in at the location of the study? |
| Introduction to the valuation context | – What is the societal or environmental problem? |
| | – How is the environmental good at hand linked to it? |
| Information about the good or service at hand | – What are the expected changes in policy (meeting conservation objectives, etc.)? |
| | – What is the spatial scale (local, regional, national, global)? |
| Description of the hypothetical market | – Who is responsible for the provision of the good (public or private institution, etc.)? |
| | – How do respondents pay for the good (taxes, fees, contributions to a fund, etc.)? |
| | – Devices to mitigate hypothetical bias (budget reminder, cheap talk, opt-out reminder) |
| Choice tasks | – Presentation of the choice tasks in a random order |
| Follow-up questions | – How did the respondents make their choices? |
| | – How certain are respondents about their choices? |
| | – How difficult was it to answer the choice tasks? |
| | – What were the most important choice attributes?<br>– Have respondents paid attention to all attributes? |
| Questions on relevant attitudes, norms, etc | – To what extent are the respondents in favour or disfavour of the environmental good at hand (i.e. specific attitudes)?<br>– To what extent do the respondents endorse a pro-ecological world view (i.e. general attitude)? |
| | – To what extent does the social environment reward paying for an environmental good (i.e. social norm)? |

(continued)

**Table 2.1** (continued)

| Questionnaire section | Content and examples of related questions |
|---|---|
| | – To what extent does a respondent perceive a moral obligation to pay for the good at hand (i.e. personal norm)? |
| Questions on the socio-demographic background | – What is the respondent's gender, age, education, income, etc.? |

*Source* Based on Mariel et al. (2021, Chapter 2)

unintended bias in others. Therefore, the order of questions is a critical consideration and should balance the benefits of priming without introducing the risk of bias (see Step 4 for more details on ordering effects).

There is no strict rule to prescribe the order of questions in a DCE; instead, it should be chosen carefully to suit the survey's objectives. Whether included before or after the DCE section, employing attitudinal questions in the survey is important, as they can serve as explanatory variables for respondents' preferences. For example, responses may reveal whether respondents are generally concerned about the environment or have favourable views towards the good or service in question. Responses to norm-based questions (e.g. "It would be against my moral principles not to protect soils for the future in our state" with the response scale ranging from "1 = I do not agree at all" to "5 = I completely agree) may reveal whether respondents feel a sense of moral obligation or social expectation from others to engage in a particular behaviour. Validated scales are available in the literature to measure both attitudes and norms. For example, a widely used scale for attitudinal questions in environmental valuation is the New Environmental Paradigm scale, originally developed by Dunlap and Van Liere (1978) and later revised as the New Ecological Paradigm (NEP) scale (Dunlap et al. 2000). The NEP is a measure of endorsement of a "pro-ecological" world view, an example of its use in the context of a discrete choice experiment can be found in Faccioli et al. (2020). The norm activation model (Schwartz 1977) is another useful framework for incorporating social and personal norms into choice models (see Franceschinis et al. 2022).

To ensure the reliability and validity of your study as well as the comparability with other studies on attitudes and norms, we recommend using established and validated scales that align with your research objectives. For example, the NEP scale is appropriate for assessing general environmental concerns but may not accurately reflect attitudes towards specific local issues, such as wind turbine acceptance. If a more focused approach is needed, developing a custom scale can be advantageous, though this requires thorough validation to ensure its reliability and validity (Boateng et al. 2018; Hair et al. 2019).

The final section of the questionnaire is often dedicated to collecting socio-demographic information about the participant (e.g. gender, age, income, place of residence, membership in environmental organisations, etc.) and details about their household (e.g. household size, presence and number of children, income at both individual and household levels, etc.). If you are using quota sampling, i.e.

a non-probability sampling method that relies on the non-random selection of a predetermined number or proportion of respondents with certain characteristics, some of these questions may need to be asked at the beginning of the questionnaire to determine whether a participant qualifies to proceed with the survey. If your study requires aggregating data to represent the target population, consider designing socio-demographic questions that align with the variables and classifications used by national statistical agencies. For example, recording income in the same categories as official reports can facilitate comparisons and help you assess how well your sample reflects the target population's income distribution.

The ordering of questionnaire sections shown in Table 2.1 will likely be effective in most cases, however, their exact ordering will depend on your specific research context. For further aspects to take into consideration in the design of the survey and questionnaire, see the books by Dillman et al. (2014) and Stopher (2012), which both represent comprehensive and detailed introductions to the topic. We also highly recommend the work by Tourangeau et al. (2000), which explores the psychology of survey responses, and Bateman et al. (2002), which covers the implementation of stated preference surveys and data analysis in detail. While the field has advanced since these books were published, they continue to offer valuable insights, especially for beginners. We also recommend taking time to review questionnaires used in previous studies, particularly those published in high-ranking journals, which are often available as supplementary materials accompanying the journal article.

**Question order matters**

Question order can significantly influence responses. Not only do questions elicit answers, but they can also shape the way that respondents think about the good or service (see ordering effects in Step 4). This influence can sometimes be beneficial by priming or "warming up" respondents with questions related to the good but, at other times, may introduce undesirable bias.

For example, asking respondents at the start of the survey whether they are a member of an environmental organisation might heighten their environmental concerns, potentially affecting their subsequent answers, especially their stated choices. Anticipating whether and how these effects will arise is challenging, so we recommend examining their potential impact through a thorough, iterative process of focus group discussions and piloting. This approach helps ensure that the question order supports the study's objectives without introducing unintended biases.

Finally, when developing a questionnaire, we must balance the length of the interview with the desire to gather extensive information. While you may be tempted to ask a large number of questions, it is essential to prioritise questions that directly contribute to your research objectives. Each additional question beyond a certain point offers diminishing returns and increases the burden on respondents. As respondents' interest wanes, they may become fatigued, bored, or inclined to rush through the remaining questions. This is also an important ethical consideration: asking questions of limited relevance to the study wastes respondents' time and cognitive resources without a clear benefit to the research. Additionally, a shorter questionnaire allows for a larger sample size (given the same budget), potentially leading to more robust and generalisable findings. Therefore, a strategic approach to question selection and the balancing of depth and breadth can ultimately enhance the quality and efficiency of data collection.

**Survey mode.** The choice of survey mode significantly influences multiple aspects of data collection in a DCE. First, it determines the types of questions that can feasibly be asked. Different survey modes—such as face-to-face interviews, online surveys, telephone surveys, or mail surveys—each have their own strengths and limitations in terms of question complexity, length, and response accuracy. For example, face-to-face surveys allow for more complex questions and in-depth probing, whereas online surveys may require simpler, more straightforward questions to maintain engagement.

The survey mode affects how you can describe and present the hypothetical market and choice tasks to participants. In face-to-face or online formats, visual aids such as images, videos, and interactive elements can help clarify complex scenarios, making it easier for respondents to understand the context of the choices they are making. Telephone and mail surveys, however, lack these interactive options, which can limit the clarity of presentation, especially for complex or multi-attribute goods and services.

The survey mode also affects the quantity and quality of information gathered. Face-to-face interviews, for instance, allow for richer, more nuanced data collection through real-time clarifications and follow-up questions, which can reduce misunderstandings and improve data accuracy. In contrast, online surveys offer convenience and often attract a larger and more diverse sample but may suffer from a lack of engagement and lower response quality if participants speed through questions. Telephone surveys may provide a higher degree of interaction than online surveys but can be limited by time constraints and the inability to provide visual materials, which may hinder participants' understanding of the hypothetical scenarios.

Choosing the right survey mode is essential, as it impacts the depth of possible insights, the reliability of responses, and ultimately, the validity of the study. Each mode carries with it trade-offs between cost, convenience, sample reach, and data quality, requiring careful consideration based on the study's objectives and the size and characteristics of your target sample.

Online surveys are currently the dominant survey mode in many parts of the world. They are generally easy to implement, offer numerous opportunities for multimedia integration (such as images, audio, and video), can provide additional insights through response behaviour (paradata), and are often cost-effective. However, online survey may not always be suitable or feasible in all cases, depending on the characteristics of your target sample. To explore the advantages and disadvantages of the different survey modes, we recommend consulting Dillman et al. (2014) and Stopher (2012). In the rest of this section, we will highlight some considerations related to survey modes that are particularly relevant for DCE studies.

- **Mail surveys.** In the early days of non-market valuation, mail surveys were the dominant survey mode. Today, however, mail surveys are rarely used due to several disadvantages: the high logistical effort, limited control over how respondents complete the questionnaire, the need for manual data entry, lack of paradata (such as response times), and typically lower response and completion rates. Effective planning of reminders is important for mail surveys, including sending a second copy of the questionnaire if necessary (Dillman et al. 2014).

  Despite these drawbacks, mail surveys may still be the best option for certain target groups. For example, a low internet penetration rate among the target population or age-related resistance to online surveys may necessitate a mail survey. In a study on the value of gravel pits to anglers, Meyerhoff et al. (2019) conducted mail surveys with angling club members in parts of Germany. Since many members were over 70 years old, an online survey would likely have misrepresented the target population. By assessing membership lists, a random sample for each club was drawn, and survey invitations were mailed. This invitation also included a link to an online version of the survey, offering an option for those preferring digital participation and helping to save costs associated with digitising mail responses. If a mail survey is the best fit for your target population, we recommend the approach outlined by Dillman et al. (2014), particularly sending at least two reminders and including a second printed questionnaire in the final reminder for non-respondents.
- **Face-to-face surveys.** Compared to mail surveys, face-to-face interviews offer several advantages but are generally more expensive (Ozdemir et al. 2024). The primary distinction of this survey mode is that the interviewer is physically present with the respondent. Interviews can be conducted using paper forms, but CAPI, often using tablets, have become increasingly common. In this setting, the interviewer may administer the entire interview, assist respondents as needed, or allow them to complete the survey independently.

  One key advantage of face-to-face interviews over mail surveys is the control over the interview process, including the order of questions and choice tasks—in a mail survey, for example, a respondent might browse through all pages before beginning the survey. Having the interviewer present also allows for the clarification of complex survey designs, individual questions, or choice tasks, which can be particularly valuable for more complex surveys.

  However, this interaction with the interviewer also comes with potential drawbacks. Leggett et al. (2003), Bateman and Mawby (2004), and Loureiro and Lotade (2005) analyse interviewer effects in stated preference surveys, whereby interviewers unintentionally influence responses, either indirectly through their appearance or demeanour or directly by offering information beyond the researcher's intent or even suggesting certain responses. To mitigate this risk, extensive training for interviewers is essential, and increasing the number of interviewers can help to reduce the impact of any one interviewer on the study results. On the respondent side, a potential bias connected to interviewer effects is *socially desirable responding* in a stated preference survey (Börger 2013).

- **Online surveys.** Conducting stated preference surveys online has become the standard survey mode in industrialised countries, with most recent journal publications reporting an online survey implementation. Online surveys have gained dominance due to their cost-effectiveness, speed, and ability to reach a large and diverse audience quickly. They eliminate the need for physical materials and in-person interviewers, reducing logistical costs and enabling rapid data collection. Additionally, online surveys allow respondents to participate at their convenience, improving accessibility and potentially increasing response rates. Digital data collection also integrates seamlessly with statistical software, making online surveys a practical choice for many researchers.

  Like CAPI-scripted interviews, online platforms provide high control over the survey flow, allowing for the easy implementation of techniques to mitigate ordering effects, such as randomising choice tasks, questions, or response options. They also offer flexible design options, including multimedia elements like text, images, and videos to clarify complex questions. A key advantage of online surveys is the ability to collect paradata (Callegaro 2013), which provides valuable insights into respondent behaviour and survey design effectiveness. Paradata can include response times for each question, clickstream data showing the sequence and pattern of clicks, keystroke data indicating pauses or edits in open-text fields, mouse movements and hovering behaviour, and device information, such as whether a desktop, tablet, or smartphone is used. These insights can help improve the survey quality and design by deepening the understanding of respondent behaviour. Recent examples of the use of paradata in the context of DCEs are Vista et al. (2009), Liebe et al. (2015), Campbell et al. (2016), and Mattmann et al. (2018).

  While online surveys are generally more cost-effective and convenient than other survey modes, they come with notable drawbacks. Online surveys are susceptible to self-selection bias, as only motivated, tech-savvy individuals with internet access are likely to participate, which can skew the sample. Without an interviewer present, respondents may rush through questions, leading to lower-quality and more superficial responses. Additionally, the lack of control over the survey environment means that distractions may reduce respondents' focus, and technical issues across different devices or browsers can create inconsistent experiences, raising concerns about data quality.

  Survey fraud is also a risk, as anonymity increases the chances of fake or duplicate entries, particularly when incentives are offered. A frequent criticism of online surveys is the reliance on registered participants in online survey panels. These panellists' familiarity with survey structures can introduce response bias, as they may anticipate the expected answers or rely on past experiences, reducing the authenticity of their responses. Moreover, some panellists, motivated primarily by financial incentives, may have little genuine interest in the survey topic, leading to lower-quality data and the use of strategies to complete surveys quickly to maximise earnings. Over time, online survey panellists may also differ systematically from the general population regarding attitudes and experiences, potentially compromising the generalisability of findings. Thus, while online panels offer speed and convenience, frequent reliance on the same pool of respondents can impact both the data reliability and representativeness.

- **Phone surveys.** Conducting a DCE study by telephone is generally only feasible for very simple experiments, such as binary choices with few attributes, and even then, may not be advisable. While people can make meaningful choices over the phone, as seen with telephone ordering (especially for those less comfortable with digital options, such as older adults), phone surveys lack the visual aids that help respondents better understand choice tasks and options. Providing detailed attribute information over the phone is challenging, making this mode less suitable for complex DCEs. However, in specific cases—such as reaching hard-to-access populations like Sudanese migrants (see Tjaden et al. 2022)—phone surveys may be the most practical and cost-effective option, though rigorous testing and careful design of the survey are essential. In general, however, DCE studies by phone should be used sparingly and only when no other feasible option exists.
- **Mixed mode surveys.** Multi-mode surveys can enhance sample representativeness by reaching diverse demographics, including those without internet access or who prefer personal contact. This flexibility can mitigate biases, increase response rates and reduce nonresponse bias. By combining modes, researchers can overcome the limitations of each mode, such as providing clarifications by phone or using engaging online features. For example, if online panels lack rural representation, respondents can be recruited by phone via random digit dialling, with an option to send the survey link by email. The initial phone contact can also gather demographic data (for quota selection for example), or generate interest in the main interview. Likewise, if addresses are available, a survey link (e.g. a QR code) can be sent by standard mail to invite individuals to participate. However, mixed-mode recruitment can require significant resources, so adequate funding may be needed for this approach to be effective.

With the rise of online surveys in stated preference research, questions have emerged regarding how the survey mode might impact data quality and welfare estimates. Early studies comparing face-to-face with online surveys (Lindhjem and Navrud 2011; Nielsen 2011) and online with mail surveys (Windle and Rolfe 2011) found some socio-demographic differences, but generally no significant differences in welfare estimates. However, more recent DCE studies (Boyle et al. 2015; Watson et al. 2019; Cohen and Reichl 2022) suggest that the survey mode can influence DCE results, i.e. the recorded choices could differ, and thus subsequent welfare estimates might differ as well. If the results are confirmed by further studies, we may have to question whether the current dominance of online surveys can be justified.

### 2.5.2 Additional Factors

- **First impressions matter.** The landing page of the questionnaire can significantly impact participation rates—not only for online surveys but also for mail surveys. For instance, consider the case study presented in Chapter 4 on the externalities of wind power. City dwellers might assume the topic is irrelevant to them and choose not to start the survey at all. To address this, we recommend keeping the landing page as neutral as possible, revealing only general information such as "this survey is about the current energy policy in your country".

  Immediately following the landing page, participants are often presented with a participant information sheet to meet institutional ethical requirements. This sheet informs potential participants about the study's purpose, procedures, risks, and benefits, allowing them to make informed decisions regarding their participation. Efforts should be made to ensure that this information is presented clearly and accessibly, avoiding an overly legalistic tone, while still meeting ethical and institutional standards.
- **Questionnaires are a two-way street.** A questionnaire is ultimately a *dialogue* between the person asking the questions and the respondents answering them. While many researchers might view an interview as a one-way communication—where the researcher simply asks questions, and the respondent provides answers—this is a misconception that can affect survey outcomes (Tourangeau et al. 2000). Respondents are likely to pick up on subtleties in how questions are phrased, the wording used, or which aspects are emphasised, even unintentionally. Therefore, it is important to consider that a question can be more than just a request for a response; it may shape the way respondents think about issues in the survey or convey unintended information.
- **Open-ended text questions.** Open-ended text questions generally require more effort to analyse compared to closed-ended ones, as they involve reviewing and coding each response. While this can be challenging and time-consuming, including open-ended questions in your survey may be worthwhile depending on your research objectives. Open-ended questions allow respondents to answer freely, without being restricted to predefined options, which can yield valuable insights into their perspectives. For example, open-ended questions offer the opportunity to ask respondents to describe their decision-making process, i.e. how they proceeded, when choosing preferred alternatives in choice tasks. Similarly, another option is to provide an open-text field at the end of the survey to encourage participants to comment on the survey itself or share any additional thoughts on the topic. In online surveys, this is easily implemented with a prompt like, "We have now reached the end of the survey. If you would like to comment on the survey or share any additional perspectives, please use the text field below." Even if only a small number of respondents respond to this, the feedback can provide valuable insights into response patterns. To support various text analysis tasks, from simple word frequency analysis to complex machine learning models,

a number of software platforms and R packages are available. AI tools can also assist in analysing open-text responses (Morgan 2023).

Despite the advantages of open-ended questions, most questions in DCE questionnaires are typically closed-ended. Closed-ended questions are often preferred because they are quicker and easier for respondents to answer, reducing the survey time and cognitive load, which leads to higher response and completion rates. Additionally, closed-ended questions yield standardised, easily comparable, and quantifiable data, simplifying the statistical analysis and allowing researchers to control the range of responses, thus avoiding unexpected or irrelevant answers. Closed-ended responses can be analysed quickly using statistical software, saving time and resources.

Ultimately, you should aim for a balance between open-ended and closed-ended questions that aligns with your research objectives and yields rich, diverse, and reliable data. By carefully considering the strengths and weaknesses of each question type, you can design a questionnaire that provides meaningful and valuable insights.

- **Scale development.** Developing valid and reliable response scales to measure latent variables like environmental attitudes can be challenging (Boateng et al. 2018; Hair et al. 2019). This process often requires significant trial and error, multiple rounds of testing, and thorough validation, making it resource intensive. Validated item scales generally originate in psychology and sociology, where they are designed to measure personality traits, social attitudes, values, and beliefs. These scales are not typically developed within fields like environmental economics or other applied disciplines where DCEs are frequently used, so creating a validated scale may require expertise beyond your immediate skill set.

  For this reason, we recommend exploring resources such as the GESIS Leibnitz Institute for the Social Sciences (GESIS. n.d.), which offers an "Open Access Repository for Measurement Instruments" called *ZIS* (GESIS-ZIS. n.d.). The repository includes measurement instruments in areas such as "Environmental awareness", "Environmental knowledge and perception", and "Environmental responsibility", among others. This service is free, though scales may need to be translated into the language of your survey (GESIS-Items n.d.).
- **Survey navigation.** Survey software often allows respondents to return to the previous page of the survey and change their answers, but this functionality should not be included without a careful consideration of its implications. As respondents progress through the choice tasks, they may learn that better alternatives (e.g. with more positive qualities and lower costs) are also available, which could prompt them to review and alter their earlier choices. Although we theoretically assume that choices are independent across choice tasks to ensure incentive compatibility, this assumption would clearly be compromised if respondents revise previous choices based on insights gained later in the survey. Therefore, we recommend carefully evaluating the merits of allowing respondents to navigate backwards especially within the sequence of choice tasks.

- **Survey software capabilities.** Before signing a contract with a survey company, make sure that you have a clear idea of the survey software capabilities and information needed (in addition to the pure survey data) to reach your research objectives. Some examples include the following:
  - Check whether the software your survey company uses can provide all the capabilities needed for your survey implementation (e.g. specific randomisations, using a mouse-over to provide information, integrating maps in a survey to record geodata of locations, e.g. visited locations in a landscape, showing videos, etc.) and can provide the information needed for your analysis. In our experience, many software companies were not able to offer the specific options and tools needed at all or had to expand their software. The later might require additional resources.
  - If you use quotas for sampling (to have the same shares of females and males in your data, for example) or only want to interview a specific part of the population (e.g. people who have recently visited a specific natural area), we recommend also obtaining data from individuals who were screened out. Survey companies usually only provide the completed interviews, i.e. the interviews of those respondents who responded to the whole questionnaire and not only the quota questions.
  - Check whether all information on the survey company's sampling process and sample will be provided. Recently, we had an experience with a company that uses its own internet panel and was not able to provide the data needed to calculate the response rate. They did not know how many people were invited to complete the survey, as people in their panel who had finished one of the company's surveys were directly invited to another survey afterwards. Such issues can be avoided by checking these issues with the survey company beforehand.

## 2.6 Step 6: Market Size and Sampling

### *2.6.1 Primary Issues*

An essential but often challenging factor to define in a stated preference study is the size of the market in which the good or service in question is offered. The market size directly correlates with the definition of the population under study, and the key question here is: who will benefit from a change in the provision of the good or service, and who will be negatively affected? In many cases, these questions are far more complex than they initially appear.

Consider our case study on wind turbines as a source of renewable energy (for more details, see Chapter 4). While the electricity generated by a turbine is carbon-free, the turbine itself may have negative impacts on nearby residents, such as the visibility of turbines in the landscape and potential noise emissions. Determining the scope of welfare effects of building wind farms in a specific region raises important questions. Should we only consider people who live near the turbines, or should we also account for individuals who may pass by the turbines on their daily commute? Turbines may also affect local bird populations, and the question becomes whether only residents in the immediate area are affected, or whether individuals who live further away and only place a non-use value on the bird populations should also be included. Non-use values refer to a willingness to pay independent of any actual, planned or possible use (Bateman et al. 2002). If non-use values are considered, the relevant target population could be much larger than if only local residents are taken into account. For further insights on the distance-decay effect, see the review by Glenk et al. (2020) and recent contributions by Danley et al. (2021) and Bateman et al. (2023).

One technique to investigate the market size is to conduct preliminary interviews at varying distances from the good or service in question. If the stated preferences decrease or even disappear with distance—such as people being less concerned about the impact of turbines on bird populations—this could indicate that you are approaching the limits of the market. However, this technique can be costly and, in some cases, impractical, particularly for issues like biodiversity, where individuals even at great distances might feel affected by species under threat (i.e. if they hold values independent of any use). Aside from being resource-intensive, this approach also presents challenges for interpretation. For example, it may be difficult to determine whether people at greater distances truly have a preference about this issue—meaning that they would be willing to pay to protect a bird species from turbine impacts—or if their responses are primarily driven by a desire to signal the importance of biodiversity protection to decision-makers. In the latter case, these responses may not be informative enough to define the actual market size for your study.

A pragmatic approach often used to define the market size is to follow administrative boundaries, such as a county, state, country, or even larger entities like the European Union. One advantage of using administrative units, at least up to the national level, is that people within these areas typically share a common language, making it easier to conduct the survey, and often use the same currency. Defining the market size by administrative boundaries is convenient and resource efficient, however, administrative boundaries do not necessarily align with the true market size or area of environmental impact. Many environmental issues, such as water quality in rivers flowing through multiple countries or marine ecosystems spanning international waters, transcend these borders. Air quality and climate change, often classified as global public goods, theoretically require a market scope that includes the entire global population.

Selecting the appropriate market size is essential for both the plausibility and consequentiality of the DCE. If the market is defined too narrowly, respondents may find it too specific or unrealistic. At the same time, if it is too broad, they might view it as overly general and disconnected from their influence. In smaller, more localised markets, respondents may feel that their choices carry more weight, leading to higher incentive compatibility—a condition in which responses reflect true preferences as if real consequences were at stake. In larger markets (e.g. a nation of millions), this incentive could be diminished, impacting the study's reliability. Moreover, the choice of market size affects aggregation. Aggregating even modest mWTP estimates over a larger market can lead to substantially higher welfare measures. For example, aggregating mWTP estimates from a regional sample or a national sample, both for protecting the same threatened bird species living in the region from which the regional sample was drawn, could produce vastly different outcomes and significantly impact the results of subsequent cost–benefit analyses. Thus, it is always important to keep in mind that the market size can be a very influential factor, potentially having more influence on policy recommendations than the choice of the econometric model used for analysing the choice data.

The relevant market size for a DCE depends on the nature of the good or service being studied. For public goods like clean air or climate stability, which are non-excludable and non-rival, the total economic value (which combines use and non-use values) might span a jurisdiction or even the global population. For private goods that are excludable and rival, such as specific energy providers, the target market might be more narrowly defined to potential consumers. Goods with mixed characteristics (i.e. semi-public goods), like public parks or toll roads, might require a market size including both users and potential non-users. Understanding these characteristics is crucial in defining the target market size and ensuring valid DCE results.

**Sampling strategy.** Once you have defined your market size and identified your target population, the next step is to select the participants for your survey. Since surveying every individual within the target population is most often impractical or impossible, sampling offers several advantages, being both cost-effective and efficient: it reduces the time and resources needed while still yielding valuable insights. However, sampling also has limitations, especially regarding statistical inference. While there is limited guidance on selecting among alternative sampling strategies for DCE studies, choosing a suitable approach is essential. It is thus essential to establish a sampling strategy.

Attempting to infer the parameters of nonlinear choice models complicates the sample design, making the sampling process pivotal to the quality and reliability of the results. Therefore, developing a solid understanding of sampling and sample design theory is crucial. Various effective sampling strategies exist, with *simple random sampling*—where individuals are randomly selected from the population—being the most straightforward. Simple random sampling, though often not explicitly mentioned, is a foundational assumption for deriving maximum likelihood estimators for discrete choice models. Any departure from simple random sampling requires careful consideration of the potential effects on the estimation of DCE data and any adjustments necessary to estimate the model parameters accurately. This is usually not considered in the DCE literature, even when a different sampling strategy is known to have been employed.

The consistency of a given parameter estimation technique depends on the underlying sampling strategy. While this does not mean that parameter estimates based on DCE data collected through non-random sampling are inherently inconsistent or inefficient, ignoring or assuming this aspect can undermine the validity and reliability of the resulting estimates. The sampling strategy plays a crucial role in the estimation process, and adjustments (by weighting, for example) may be required in the estimation procedure to account for the chosen sampling approach. For a thorough exploration of sampling strategies in discrete choice analysis and parameter estimation across different sampling designs, Chapter 8 in Ben-Akiva and Lerman (1985) remains an indispensable reference.

Sampling strategies for DCEs can be divided into two main groups: *probability* and *non-probability sampling*. Probability sampling ensures that each member of the target population has a non-zero probability of selection for the survey. Common probability sampling methods include address-based sampling and random-digit dialling, both of which aim to achieve a representative sample. Probability sampling is preferred, as it minimises systematic bias in the representation of the population (Sandstrom-Mistry et al. 2023) and allows for known selection probabilities, which can be factored into the estimation if needed. Following Johnston et al. (2017), many studies opt for probability sampling (e.g. using addresses for mail or online surveys or lists of landline or mobile numbers for phone surveys). However, probability sampling has its drawbacks: it often incurs higher costs, requires longer time frames to reach the desired number of responses, and typically has higher non-response rates (Sandstrom-Mistry et al. 2023; Ozdemir et al. 2024).

A prominent probability sampling technique used in DCE studies is general stratified sampling, where the population is divided into mutually exclusive and collectively exhaustive strata (exhaustive because all possible members are included) and elements from each stratum are selected. One such strategy is to partition the population according to socio-demographic variables (e.g. based on age, gender, residential location, or income categories). This is commonly referred to as exogenous sampling, since choices made by potential respondents do not affect the stratum to which they belong, and is the most prevalent stratified sampling technique employed in environmental economics.

Stratified sampling can also be adapted to *choice-based sampling,* where respondents' choices determine their stratum. For instance, a DCE on transport mode choice might set quotas for each transport mode. Note that all on-site environmental economic studies, such as those conducted at recreational destinations, are inherently based on choice-based sampling. The classification of a stratified sample as choice-based or exogenous hinges on the good or service under study. For example, stratification by residential location would be exogenous when studying energy provider preferences but choice-based for windfarm location preferences.

It is also possible to combine exogenous and choice-based approaches into *enriched samples,* using multiple stratification criteria (e.g. both socio-demographic and choice-based dimensions). Stratified sampling allows for unequal inclusion probabilities across strata, which is useful for adequately representing subgroups with smaller population shares. For instance, if you are studying the preferences of specific minority groups relative to the broader population, even a large national sample might not provide enough participants from those groups to allow for a robust comparison. Note, however, that the estimation procedure for simple random samples is applicable to exogenous stratified samples, or to any general stratified sample where each stratum's sample fraction matches its population share.

- **Non-probability sampling.** An alternative that may involve some theoretical and practical compromise is *non-probability sampling*, where not all individuals in the target population have a possibility of being selected (Sandstrom-Mistry et al. 2023). In non-probability sampling, individuals are selected based on their availability or the researcher's judgement of their representativeness (Ozdemir et al. 2024). A common example of this approach is the use of opt-in panels. Respondents for many stated preference surveys today are drawn from such panels, where recruitment often involves online advertisements, allowing individuals to "opt-in" if they accept the incentives offered for participating.

  Other non-probability sampling approaches include convenience sampling—selecting participants who are easily accessible—and snowball sampling—where initial participants refer others who meet the study criteria. While both methods are typically quick and cost-effective, and snowball sampling is particularly useful for reaching hard-to-access populations, they often lack representativeness and can produce samples that are too similar, limiting diversity. This can lead to an underestimation of preference heterogeneity in the broader population.

  The main concern with non-probability sampling is that it may not accurately represent the target population, leading to biased welfare estimates. Our experience suggests that online panel samples often overrepresent highly educated individuals and those with higher incomes compared to the general population. If a cost-benefit analysis is a goal of the study, it is important to recognise that the sampling choice can significantly impact results.

  There are various methods to address potential bias from non-probability sampling. During the sample design stage, quota sampling among panel members can help create more balanced samples that align more closely with the target population, by setting quotas for characteristics such as age, gender, education, or income. As mentioned above, this type of sampling can have implications for the estimation, and it may be necessary to consider demographic weighting to adjust for any sample-target population discrepancies (Sandstrom-Mistry et al. 2023).
- **Comparing sampling strategies.** Overall, there is limited research on the differences between these sampling approaches, as few studies have applied different sampling strategies simultaneously with the same survey mode. However, existing results favour probability-based samples, especially when the goal is to make inferences about a broader population or when results are intended to inform policy decisions or other high-stakes decisions (Sandstrom-Mistry et al. 2023; Whitehead et al. 2023).

  As noted earlier in this chapter, the sampling strategies outlined have resource implications, and this should ideally be addressed during the funding application process at the study's inception. It is important to recognise that there is no universally optimal sample design for discrete choice data across all possible parameter values—the effectiveness of a sampling strategy depends on the unknown parameter values themselves. To address this, based either on initial data or the analyst's informed judgment, prior estimates can guide a more refined and potentially optimal sampling strategy, like how priors are used in the experimental design.

However, we rarely have complete foresight into the models that will emerge from a DCE dataset or the full array of environmental policies those models may eventually inform, which can limit the suitability of any single sampling strategy. Given the resources required for data collection, it is worth considering how the data supports the immediate analysis as well as a broader scope of future research, which may call for a more flexible sampling strategy. Ultimately, the choice of sampling strategy should balance theoretical and practical considerations. However, in reality practical constraints such as limited resources and access to respondent pools often dominate these considerations, leading to compromises in theoretical rigour.

- **Sampling alternatives.** It is essential to clarify that the sampling strategies discussed above pertain specifically to the sampling of individuals, not alternatives. In the DCE literature, recognising and distinguishing between the sampling of individuals and alternatives is crucial. Modelling choices can be challenging when dealing with many available alternatives, as the true number of alternatives may sometimes be indeterminate. For example, consider a scenario where an individual is selecting a recreational trip destination. Even if we narrow the options down to specific types of recreation (e.g. walking, cycling, or fishing) and restrict choices to a certain distance or travel time from the individual's residence, an almost infinite number of possible locations remain. This extensive range of alternatives can complicate the modelling process, making it advantageous, or even necessary, to sample from the set of alternatives during the estimation or use forecasting to manage the scope and complexity effectively.

  While this issue is traditionally more relevant in revealed preference data, the proliferation of online surveys and multimedia options has led to a virtually unlimited number of choices that can be presented. For a comprehensive discussion on alternative methods of sampling alternatives and corresponding estimators for the choice model parameters, refer to Chapter 9 in Ben-Akiva and Lerman (1985).
- **Sample size.** A frequently raised question is the necessary sample size for a DCE survey. First, you should ensure that the sample size is large enough to estimate all parameters of your model. A useful exercise to explore this is via simulation: first, generate synthetic data with varying sample sizes based on your experimental design and then test the models you plan to estimate on the final survey data. This allows you to easily explore how (for example) standard errors change with increasing sample sizes, providing valuable insights into the sample size required. For an example of this method, refer to Sect. 8.4 in this book (see also Sect. 3.3 in Mariel et al. 2021). This simulation approach does require assumptions about the values of unknown parameters and data can be simulated under a range of different parameter values. However, this method has limitations in determining the exact sample size requirement.

  Another option is to calculate the S-efficiency measure when generating your experimental design, which indicates the minimum sample size needed to estimate all parameters at a statistically significant level (Rose and Bliemer 2013). It is important to emphasise that this measure indicates a *minimum* number of observations and should not be interpreted as a sufficient sample size. Also, S-efficiency can only be calculated if all priors are non-zero, and the further they are from zero, the smaller the required sample size will be. Therefore, S-efficiency is useful mainly when testing whether a parameter differs from zero (though, of course, the S-efficiency measure could be adjusted to benchmark the parameters against any set of values of interest).

Comprehensive discussions on approaches and recommendations for determining the sample size can be found in de Bekker-Grob et al. (2015), Yang et al. (2015) and Assele et al. (2023), along with the literature cited within these studies. These discussions include various rule-of-thumb approaches for establishing sample sizes. While these guidelines can provide useful benchmarks, they remain general approximations. Rules of thumb may not fully capture the nuanced characteristics of a specific DCE design, so it is essential not to interpret them too literally, as they may lack precision and reliability in certain contexts.

The most important consideration in determining the sample size for a DCE is the complexity of your design, including the number of attributes, the levels within each attribute (and whether levels are represented qualitatively or quantitatively), and the number of choice tasks per respondent. Larger sample sizes are generally required as the number of attributes increases to ensure sufficient variation to estimate their effects. Similarly, designs with more levels per attribute introduce more complexity often necessitating larger sample sizes.

Qualitative attributes, which represent categorical choices without inherent numerical values, are usually coded with dummy or effects coding (Mariel et al. 2021, Section 5.2), and also increase the number of parameters to estimate, requiring a larger sample size for reliable and statistically significant results. While increasing the number of choice tasks per respondent can improve sampling efficiency—allowing for fewer respondents to achieve similar statistical precision—this must be balanced with the risk of respondent fatigue and potential biases that may arise, which can offset gains in sampling efficiency (see Step 2).

Sample size requirements also depend on whether you plan to analyse specific subgroups within the population. If so, each subgroup must have an adequate sample size to allow for a meaningful analysis. This is especially true for policy analysis, which may necessitate the comparison of results between different socio-demographic subgroups or across spatial jurisdictions. This also applies to designs involving experimentally controlled treatments (such as a control and one or more treatment groups), where each version of the DCE should have sufficient data to provide reliable parameter estimates.

In real-world applications, sample size is often constrained by available resources, especially the budget and time constraints. While it is essential to understand the statistical requirements, we understand that practical limitations often require a balanced approach. A key recommendation is to aim for the largest sample size feasible within your budget and time constraints and to adopt a sampling strategy that aligns with the sample size and the study's objectives.

- **Sample selection and non-response biases.** In some situations, despite all efforts to design a flexible and robust sampling strategy with a large sample size, it may not be feasible to sample from a specific subpopulation. In such cases, one option is to redefine the target population to exclude this difficult-to-reach group. Alternatively, it may be possible to assume that the preferences and corresponding parameters of this subpopulation align with those of a similar, more accessible group. Deciding between these options requires a case-by-case evaluation based on the study's context and objectives.

Another critical consideration is *sample selection bias*, which arises when the sample is not representative of the broader target population and can lead to biased results that misrepresent the preferences and behaviours of the population as a whole. For example, if respondents with specific socio-demographic characteristics or within certain choice-based stratum are more likely to participate, estimates of population parameters may disproportionately reflect these groups, resulting in skewed policy recommendations or welfare estimates. Sampling strategies must be designed to mitigate this risk, although it may not always be completely avoidable.

Additionally, it is essential to consider non-responses carefully, which occur when individuals do not respond to a survey. If non-response rates do not differ systematically across key socio-demographic variables and choice-based strata, the impact on estimates may be minimal, especially with a sufficiently large sample. However, if the non-response rate is higher within certain socio-demographic groups or choice-based strata, this could introduce significant bias. This is why examining the variation of non-responses across different characteristics is crucial (Johnston and Abdulrahman 2017; Bonnichsen and Olsen 2015).

While data collection typically does not capture information from non-respondents, panels that can provide basic demographics for all their members often make it possible to assess differences between respondents and non-respondents. In some cases, asking a few basic socio-demographic questions to those who decline participation can provide valuable insights. Although this opportunity will not always be available, gathering this information whenever possible is highly beneficial. In any case, assuming you know the population shares in each strata (which may be available from published sources or national statistical agencies), you always have the option of taking corrective measures when you compare the share of each stratum in the sample to the share in the population.

### 2.6.2 More on Size and Sampling

- **Selection of individuals within a household**. A less frequently discussed issue is how members within a household are sampled (Johnston et al. 2017). For example, imagine a target population represented by an address list that includes all households within the defined market. While it is straightforward to randomly select households from this list, the actual sampling units are individuals, not households. This raises the question of how to select individuals within each household. Gaziano (2005) and Smyth and Olson (2019) review and discuss potential solutions to this challenge.

- **Survey company panels**. When a survey company offers a random sample from their own or an external panel, the sample is not necessarily randomly selected from the target population—particularly when the panel consists of respondents who opt in. Therefore, it is essential to ask survey companies how they recruit their panel members. This is especially important if your focus is not on the overall national or regional population (for which survey companies may offer assurances) but on narrower subgroups. For instance, if your case study requires a sample of the rural population, it is essential to verify whether the panel adequately covers people living in rural areas.

  Other questions to consider include how frequently panel members are invited to survey over a specific time period (such as a week or a month). Frequent survey invitations may cause panellists to pay less attention to survey topics and questions, as their primary motivation may become compensation rather than engagement. Sandorf et al. (2020) provide insights into identifying professional respondents and potential consequences of this effect.

  Additionally, it is important to clarify how the survey company monitors response quality. Do they have minimum response time thresholds? What measures are in place to detect and prevent survey fraud? Understanding these practices will help ensure the reliability of your data.
- **Sampling strategy and survey mode.** Note that the sampling strategy and survey mode often go hand in hand, with the survey mode frequently dictating the sampling strategy. While closely connected, they are not the same. For instance, online surveys can employ probability sampling, though strictly speaking, this would require participants not to come from an opt-in panel. Often, the available resources—time and budget—will determine the sampling strategy and sample size, along with the study's objective, such as whether the welfare estimates will be applied in a cost–benefit-analysis or natural resource damage assessment. Using estimates from DCE surveys in such a policy context will require you to put more weight on a sound sampling approach, ensuring that the target population is well-represented and that the survey mode does not bias estimates.

  Note that all survey modes can use probability sampling if needed, though this often incurs higher costs. For example, conducting an online survey with a probability sample might involve randomly calling individuals and inviting them via phone to participate in an online survey. This approach is time-consuming and expensive, particularly if many people decline participation during the initial phone contact. In extreme cases, it may be necessary to abandon the goal of probability sampling altogether and instead rely on an opt-in panel.
- **Attention checks.** So-called attention checks may help identify respondents who pay less attention to your survey. While we are sceptical of their effectiveness in increasing the quality of the data, we make note of them here for the sake of completeness. A simple example for such a check is incorporating an attention

item in a set of items measuring environmental awareness, for example, by stating: "To respond to this item please tick the option 'I completely agree'". Respondents who do not pay attention to the content of the item statement have a high(er) probability of not selecting the required response level.

If you are considering applying attention checks, you should consider two key considerations: first, check whether your survey company is willing to accept such attention checks, i.e. whether it would be willing to replace the respondents who have not passed the check with other respondents. Second, have a plan for what you will do with the respondents who do not pass the test (even if they are replaced). Is it reasonable to drop them because they missed one or two attention items? Are attention items sufficient, or is a broader concept needed that incorporates response time and other characteristics of respondents? See Abbey and Meloy (2017), Gummer et al. (2018), and Berinsky et al. (2019) for more details on this topic.

- **Dominant choice task**. The incorporation of a dominant choice task in a DCE could serve as a valuable and straightforward method to assess internal validity. By introducing a clearly superior alternative among the choices, researchers can gauge the consistency of participants' responses with their underlying preferences. If respondents consistently favour the dominant alternative, it provides assurance that they are making logical and internally valid choices in the experiment.

  However, introducing a dominant alternative can run the risk of deviating from real-world scenarios. This may compromise the credibility of the study, as respondents' choices might not accurately mirror their decision-making in more complex, realistic situations. The goal is to strike a balance between the need for a controlled internal validity test and the experiment's external validity. Achieving this balance means that the findings remain robust and applicable while still providing valuable insights into respondents' decision processes. Any such test should be explored and tested in focus groups prior to data collection. Finally, it is important to have considered in advance how respondents who have failed the test should be treated. Are their answers sufficient to exclude them from further analysis?
- **Non-probability samples**. Non-probability samples are generally expected to differ significantly from those obtained through probability sampling. For example, using platforms like Facebook or Amazon Mechanical Turk for recruitment will likely produce a sample that does not fully represent the target population, especially when snowball sampling is applied. Nonetheless, researchers often opt for non-probability sampling because of its low cost and convenience. While this approach is less suitable for studies intended to inform policy decisions, it can be well-suited for testing survey instruments or exploring methodological features where representativeness is not a primary concern.

  If you plan to use a non-probability sample for a study aimed at informing policy recommendations, it is crucial to provide a clear rationale for why this sampling method is appropriate. Without such justification, the representativeness of your sample may become a significant issue when trying to convince policymakers of your findings or when seeking publication in reputable journals.

## 2.7 Step 7: Testing the Survey Instrument

### *2.7.1 Essentials When Testing*

Testing a survey instrument is essential to ensure its suitability for data collection. While researchers generally agree on the importance of this testing, there is less consensus on its specific methods, timing, and target audience. Ideally, testing should be conducted continuously throughout the design phase, from the initial concept to the final field deployment. Involving a diverse range of individuals from the target population and employing various testing methods will provide a more rigorous test of the survey instrument.

**Considerations for the testing sample.** Although it is convenient to recruit students, colleagues, friends, or family for this purpose, relying solely on these groups may not be sufficient to fully assess how the survey will be perceived and understood by the target population. While these individuals can offer valuable insights to refine the survey instrument, they may not adequately represent the target audience.

Extensive and ongoing testing with large, representative samples from the population will provide the most valuable feedback for improving a survey instrument, though it is not a guarantee of success. Such an approach may not always be practical or feasible due to time or budget constraints, however, even a limited testing effort can substantially enhance the quality of the survey instrument and improve the reliability of the data it generates. While no survey is perfect, a well-executed testing process significantly increases the confidence in the instrument's ability to produce valid and reliable results.

If you plan a survey at your university with students as the target population, conducting focus groups with students from your university is an effective and practical step to test the survey instrument. Engaging directly with individuals from your intended demographic ensures that the survey resonates with its audience, identifies potential issues, and generates feedback relevant to their specific experiences and perspectives. However, if your survey is intended for a national audience—for example, to measure preferences for different types of renewable energy in peoples' surroundings—relying solely on university students for feedback is unlikely to be sufficient.

University students typically share similar characteristics, such as age, income levels, and residential status. This homogeneity limits the insights gained, as it does not account for diverse characteristics of the broader target population. For a national survey, pretesting should ideally include individuals from a wide range of ages, educational backgrounds, household incomes, and geographic locations across the country. This diversity ensures that the survey instrument is comprehensible and relevant to all subgroups within the target population. It also helps identify biases or challenges that may arise when administering the survey at scale.

A common justification for relying on "convenient testing" with easily accessible groups is limited resources—such as time, funding or logistical support. To address this, it is important to plan for adequate provisions to allow for diverse pretesting as early as possible in the project timeline. Ideally, this planning should occur during the project's inception and, if applicable, be explicitly included in the funding application. This foresight can help secure the resources needed to recruit a representative pretest sample, ensuring that the survey instrument is robust, effective, and ready to deliver meaningful insights across the intended target population.

**Methods for pre-testing.** Various approaches are available to test the design of your hypothetical market and questionnaire, varying in the number of individuals involved—ranging from individual interviews to group meetings—and the timing of their application relative to the start of the final survey. Often, a combination of these methods is employed, as they complement each other and provide valuable information at different stages of the survey instrument's development process.

Pretesting should ideally incorporate both qualitative and quantitative approaches. Qualitative methods are essential for understanding how respondents perceive and engage with the design of the hypothetical market and the good in question. Quantitative pretesting, on the other hand, allows for statistical testing and the estimation of basic models, even if the results are preliminary. Together, these approaches provide a more comprehensive evaluation of the survey design.

Below, we outline some commonly used methods for pretesting DCEs and highlight important considerations based on our experiences. As always, additional references, such the section on survey development and implementation in Johnston et al. (2017), should be consulted for further guidance when planning and conducting survey testing.

- **Individual interviews.** A common step in testing is to conduct individual interviews using early drafts of the questionnaire or specific components, such as an initial version of the discrete choice experiment. The primary objective is to assess whether the attributes selected, the information provided to describe them, and the initial choice tasks are plausible and understandable to the respondents. These interviews are typically semi-structured, meaning that while you prepare specific questions targeting participants' understanding of the valuation exercise, there should also be enough flexibility to allow participants to share their thoughts and impressions.

  It is important to note that these interviews (and focus groups) are often the only stages in which you can obtain direct feedback from individuals who (ideally) belong to the target population. A particularly useful technique for these individual interviews is the *think-aloud-approach.* In this method, participants answer the survey while verbalising their thoughts, explaining how they interpret the questions, and detailing the reasoning behind their responses. This approach provides valuable insights into how participants understand the questions, information scripts, choice tasks, and other survey components. Examples of think-aloud-interviews applied in the context of DCE studies are Ryan et al. (2009) and Whitty et al. (2014).

  In addition to conducting individual interviews with the target audience, it is often highly beneficial to also interview stakeholders and individuals involved in policy design and implementation, particularly when the study aims to inform policy discussions. This approach ensures that the survey instrument collects information that is not only relevant to the target population but also valuable to policymakers and stakeholders. Relying solely on feedback from the target population risks prioritising their interests and perceptions in the survey instrument and not addressing the broader needs of decision-makers. This could limit the survey's utility in influencing policies and practical outcomes.

Expert interviews can play a critical role in selecting and refining the attributes for the DCE. Without their input, the final set of attributes may fail to meet criteria such as political acceptability, policy relevance, practicality, or feasibility. Accounting for these aspects ensures that your research can lead to actionable outcomes. For researchers, especially those in academia or working on publicly funded projects, demonstrating that their work has a tangible impact beyond academic circles is increasingly important. This includes showing that your findings contribute to societal, cultural, economic, or policy improvements or positively influence individual lives. Engaging policymakers and stakeholders early in the research process, particularly during the pretesting phase through individual interviews, not only strengthens the study's relevance but also enhances its potential to drive meaningful change in the real world.

- **Focus groups.** In contrast to individual interviews, focus groups (Stewart and Shamdasani 2015) bring together a small group of participants representing the target population. While having multiple participants in one session can save time and costs, the primary objective of a focus group is to encourage participants to discuss the survey instrument and the good in question amongst themselves. These interactions can provide invaluable insights into how people perceive the good and the hypothetical market setup. Based on our experiences, fostering exchanges among participants often yields rich and meaningful information, so we recommend exploring strategies to promote these discussions. During the focus group, various techniques can be employed, including open discussions or having participants complete the current version of the questionnaire or specific sections followed by a group discussion to gather their feedback. Resources permitting, employing a (professional) moderator can be particularly beneficial.

  For geographically dispersed populations, online focus groups provide a practical and flexible alternative. They are cost-effective, easier to organise, and allow for the inclusion of participants from diverse locations. However, they may lack the depth of engagement seen in in-person settings due to challenges such as technological issues, distractions, and the inability to fully observe non-verbal cues. In-person focus groups, by contrast, offer richer and more natural interactions. They allow facilitators to observe non-verbal communication like nodding or head shaking, and group dynamics, which can lead to deeper insights. While in person focus groups foster more engaging discussions, they require significant logistical planning, such as securing a venue and coordinating participant travel, which can make them costly and time-consuming.

  Preparing a detailed catalogue of questions helps ensure that all important topics are covered during the session, especially since participants typically cannot be re-contacted after the focus group concludes. However, it is important to maintain a relatively fluid agenda and use a semi-structured format. This approach allows the discussion to flow naturally, making the experience more engaging and less rigid, which can encourage participants to share their thoughts freely. Letting the conversation occasionally veer off topic can be valuable, as it may reveal unexpected but relevant insights and demonstrates to participants that their broader views are welcome. The moderator or facilitator plays a crucial role in striking a balance between allowing for an open discussion and steering the conversation back to the intended topics when necessary, ensuring that participant perspectives and the session's objectives are effectively addressed.

One key question to address is how many focus groups should be conducted. This depends on several factors, including the expected heterogeneity within the target population. For most applications, Johnston et al. (2017) recommend conducting a minimum of four to six focus groups, with more groups advisable if the good being studied is new, unfamiliar, or difficult to quantify. However, it is vital to prioritise quality over quantity. Unfortunately, many studies seem to conduct the "mandatory" four to six focus groups merely to satisfy reviewers or editors, reducing the process to a formality rather than a meaningful exercise. Conducting focus groups without genuine intent or purpose is counterproductive and diminishes their value.

Focus groups are an invaluable research tool and should not be treated as a box-checking exercise. In many cases, it is beneficial to conduct a larger number of well-designed and managed focus groups, even if this might require reducing the main survey sample size. This trade-off can yield deeper insights and significantly enhance the overall quality and relevance of the research.

- **Online communities.** The term *online community* is used in various contexts, such as marketing and social media. Here, we understand an online community as a group of people who are active on an online platform over several days, providing information and interacting with each other. Unlike focus groups, this format extends over multiple days, giving participants more time to consider the good or service in question, potentially providing researchers with richer insights.

  For example, for a project on private gardens and biodiversity, two chat-based online communities that each lasted for 10 days and involved 30 participants were conducted. The participants, recruited from an online panel and compensated for their time, engaged in a variety of daily activities, including short surveys about their gardens, group discussions, and testing early versions of the discrete choice experiment, and also had the opportunity to ask a wildlife gardening expert questions about gardening practices. While organising an online community requires more effort, it should generally offer deeper insights into people's thoughts about the good or service being evaluated compared to focus groups as participants stay much longer and are involved in more survey activities. This feedback is invaluable for developing a questionnaire that is both meaningful and accessible to respondents. Additionally, like online focus groups, an online community can cover large geographical areas; in the garden project participants from all over Germany were involved.

- **Pretesting and pilot study.** A pretest of the survey instrument is generally conducted once a reasonably complete initial version of the questionnaire is available. The primary objective of a pretest is to evaluate and refine specific elements of the survey or the entire instrument. Pretests focus on ensuring the clarity, relevance, and effectiveness of the survey (e.g. Are the survey questions easy to understand? Are the instructions clear?), rather than testing the survey with a representative sample. Pretests are generally smaller and more targeted than pilot studies, involving only a few participants. These participants are often recruited based on convenience and may not be part of the target population, as representation is not the primary concern. Instead, the aim is to identify and address design or content issues before the full implementation of the survey.

  To gather feedback, pretest surveys often include comment boxes on each page or in specific sections where input is particularly valuable. Participants are usually informed that the purpose of the pretest is to evaluate the survey instrument itself, rather than focusing on the accuracy of their responses. In some cases, participants may be encouraged to complete the questionnaire multiple times, providing different answers each time to test the logical flow, screening criteria, and redirection mechanisms within the survey, ensuring these work as intended.

  A pilot study is a broader trial run of the entire survey process, including recruitment, logistics, data collection, and analysis, and is often one of the final steps in testing a survey instrument. The primary aim is to evaluate the overall study design and methodology, identifying any remaining issues that may not have been detected in earlier testing phases such as the pretest. Unlike pretests, which focus on individual elements of the survey, pilot studies are more comprehensive and typically resemble a smaller-scale version of the full study. They provide critical information on feasibility, time requirements, resource allocation, and potential logistical challenges for the main study.

  While most fundamental issues are usually addressed during earlier stages of testing, pilot studies help identify minor but important adjustments. These tweaks, though small, can significantly enhance the efficiency and functionality of the survey. The pilot study is about testing the mechanics of the survey—such as recruitment strategies, question flow, data collection systems, and redirection logic—and about refining content to ensure that participants understand the information provided and can make meaningful choices.

  Since the pilot occurs shortly before the main survey begins, the data from the pilot can sometimes be incorporated into the final dataset, provided no major issues are detected. Another essential aspect of the pilot study is evaluating how data is stored and coded. This stage provides an opportunity to ensure that the data collection aligns with your expectations and the study requirements. Identifying and resolving issues—such as variables being incorrectly recorded or missing altogether—at this stage can prevent costly and embarrassing mistakes during the main study. Addressing these problems during the pilot can save significant time, resources, and effort later in the research process.

  In DCE studies, the pilot study serves an additional and critical purpose. One key objective is to gather priors for the experimental design. Priors are essential inputs for increasing the efficiency of the experimental design and the robustness of parameter estimates. As a result, a well-executed pilot study in DCE research not only ensures the survey mechanics function smoothly but also directly contributes to the quality and efficiency of the data and insights produced in the main study. The process of generating efficient experimental designs for DCEs is explored in detail in Chapter 5.

### 2.7.2 Further Points to Consider

- **Think early about resources for testing**. Remember that pretesting requires sufficient resources. For focus groups, you may need to recruit participants through a survey company, reserve rooms, hire an external moderator, and possibly travel to the locations where they are held. Online communities may require renting or purchasing suitable software. We highly recommend planning for testing expenses when applying for grants or other funding. Otherwise, you might have to rely on a convenience sample—an option that, while better than no pretesting, is far from ideal. As emphasised earlier, testing should be conducted with people from the target population.
- **Documenting makes life easier**. Keep in mind that reviewers and people evaluating your research often require details on how you tested your survey instrument. Be sure to document all tests thoroughly, including any conclusions drawn from each test. Did you make changes to the design of the hypothetical market or other parts of the questionnaire? What were the reasons for those changes?
- **Ensure that updating is possible**. Results from pretests and pilot studies can be used to generate priors for the experimental design (see Chapter 5 for more details). If you are working with a survey company, confirm that they are prepared to update the experimental design based on these priors while the survey is running, and interviews are conducted. Similarly, clarify in advance how many rounds of questionnaire revisions are included in their offer. Will you have only one opportunity to revise the survey, or are multiple rounds possible?
- **Testing the survey yourself.** Although it might seem obvious, it is worth emphasising the importance of thoroughly testing the survey yourself before it goes live. As the creator, you are the most familiar with its structure, objectives, and intended functionality. This makes you uniquely qualified to ensure that key elements such as question flow, data collection systems, and redirection logic work seamlessly and as planned.

  Testing the survey yourself allows you to identify issues that might not be apparent to others, such as unexpected question order, unclear instructions, or broken skip patterns. By walking through the survey as both a participant and a researcher, you can verify whether it meets the study's objectives and whether the user experience is smooth and intuitive. This step not only saves time but also helps prevent errors that could undermine the validity or reliability of your results. Taking this hands-on approach ensures that your survey is in the best possible shape before being tested by others or rolled out to participants.

- **Prepare code to analyse data.** Once you have decided on a version of the survey to use for a pilot study, ask the survey company to send you data from your previous tests. This would also be a good time to ask the survey company for a codebook describing the data format, variable names, etc. This will allow you to familiarise yourself with the data structure, i.e. how the survey software stores the data, and generate syntax for descriptive statistics and first simple models such as multinomial logit. You will then be prepared to quickly explore data from pilot projects or a soft launch survey.

## 2.8 Step 8: From Raw Data to Insights

While it may be tempting to jump straight to the estimation of complex choice models after obtaining your data, it is important to first explore the basic characteristics of your DCE dataset. This preliminary step helps you understand and describe the choices made and gain insights into the factors that may influence them. The goal at this stage is not to draw definitive conclusions but to identify promising trends or patterns to explore more deeply in subsequent stages of your research.

Unfortunately, this step is often overlooked. The increasing accessibility of complex choice models—enabled by tools such as Apollo (Hess and Palma 2019) and other specialist software—has led to a decreased focus on more straightforward exploratory methods. Before launching into sophisticated choice models, it is essential to assess whether your hypotheses are plausible and whether they can reasonably be tested with the available data. Insights obtained from this step often serve as a foundation for more advanced analyses, and results that cannot be supported by basic methods are unlikely to hold up under complex modelling. This exploratory phase is instrumental in guiding your choice of models and shaping the direction of your analysis.

The initial exploration of your data should be simple, clear, and focused. Start with summary tables and data visualisations to uncover basic patterns and trends. This could involve a table summarising the proportion of "yes" and "no" choices for a particular attribute level or a graph illustrating how choice shares change throughout the sequence of choice tasks. These initial results are not only easy to interpret but also highly valuable for communicating findings to stakeholders.

To avoid redundancy, we will not go into further details of this step here, as it will be covered in detail later in this book. For a comprehensive explanation and examples of data exploration techniques, please refer to Chapter 7.

## 2.9 Step 9: Model Estimation

While the preliminary analyses provide valuable insights and a strong sense of the expected results, the model estimation gives you a comprehensive picture of how behaviour and preferences influence choices. It transforms raw data into interpretable results by quantifying the influence of different attributes on choice probabilities. This way, it not only validates the prior analysis but also uncovers more nuanced insights, providing a robust framework for explaining and predicting behaviours. Ultimately, it is the model estimation phase that bridges the gap between the data collection and actionable, policy-relevant conclusions that are the hallmark of a successful DCE study.

Chapter 8 provides a basic example of estimating a discrete choice model (specifically, a MNL model with two alternatives and one attribute) using a self-coded log-likelihood function. Writing your own log-likelihood function gives you complete flexibility to estimate any model of your choice, which is a significant advantage. However, this approach has a steep learning curve and requires a substantial amount of time to set up and thoroughly test to ensure that it functions as expected. As a result, it is best suited for specialised modelling cases that cannot be implemented using standard software.

In most cases, it is more time-efficient to use software packages designed specifically for discrete choice modelling. There are several R packages available for estimating discrete choice models, including the *Apollo* package (Hess and Palma 2019) that we will use in this book. It enables the estimation of a wide variety of models, provides functions for post-estimation analysis, and offers full customisation to meet your specific research needs. The latest *Apollo* version, the manual, examples of a large set of choice models including data and a forum for *Apollo* users are available at Apollo Choice Modelling (n.d.).

Model estimation often begins with a standard MNL model that includes only the attributes and alternative-specific constants for all but one choice alternative. While simple, this model provides valuable insights into the drivers of choices at the sample level. Along with coefficient estimates, model diagnostics and fit measures are also retrieved, offering insight into the model's reliability. Socio-demographic and other interactions are then typically added to explore observed sources of preference heterogeneity.

Depending on the preliminary analysis, insights gained, and the research objectives, a wide range of modelling extensions and options are available. A commonly taken step is to account for unobserved sources of preference heterogeneity using a mixed logit (MXL) model specification. This could be a random parameters MXL (RP-MXL) or a latent class MXL (LC-MXL) model. The choice of the appropriate MXL specification depends on the objectives of the study, the data, the hypotheses to be tested, and the assumptions about the distribution of unobserved preference heterogeneity.

An RP-MXL model assumes continuous distributions of preferences across individuals, making it suitable when preferences are believed to vary smoothly and continuously. On the other hand, an LC-MXL model assumes discrete distributions, categorising individuals into distinct classes with homogeneous preferences within each class but heterogeneous preferences across classes, making it ideal when the population is believed to consist of identifiable segments with distinct preferences. Thus, MXL variants offer different perspectives on unobserved preference heterogeneity.

The model estimation, a critical step in the analytical process, involves the evaluation of different model variants and the testing of a broad range of specifications to identify the model that best fits the data and aligns with the research objectives. This ensures that the selected model provides the most accurate and meaningful representation of the preferences and behaviours reflected in the dataset. It is important, however, to acknowledge that no single model is likely to consistently outperform others across all datasets. In cases of empirical data with unknown generating parameters, the concept of a definitive "final" model is unrealistic.

For this reason, it is crucial to estimate a variety of models under different specification assumptions. Our recommendation is to begin with simpler models and progressively move to more complex model specifications. This approach not only provides a clear foundation for understanding the data but also facilitates the identification of potential issues, such as errors in the data, variable definitions, or model specifications, early in the modelling process. By systematically exploring different models, you can ensure the robustness and reliability of your findings while uncovering more profound insights into behaviours and preferences.

We intentionally kept the discussion of this step brief here, as it is explored in greater detail later in the book. Specifically, Chapter 9 provides step-by-step guidance on the modelling and estimation process, progressing from the foundational MNL model to various advanced MXL model variants.

## 2.10 Step 10: Postestimation Analysis

Constructing and estimating an econometric model is rarely the final goal of the analytical process. While these models can provide valuable insights, their true value lies in effectively interpreting and applying the results. The insights gained from the model estimation are meaningful only when understood within the context of the model's assumptions and structure. This is particularly true for discrete choice models, where each model requires a unique interpretation. Even the most sophisticated model is of little value without a clear understanding of how to interpret and use the results.

The post-estimation analysis in DCEs is essential for extracting meaningful information from model outputs. It ensures that the results are not only interpretable but also practically applicable. This phase involves several critical steps to derive insights and make informed decisions. First, we must evaluate the estimation performance and goodness-of-fit of the models. Then, we can examine the estimated coefficients to understand the impact of each attribute on choice probabilities, focusing on the significance and direction of these parameters. Robustness checks are a critical part of the post-estimation analysis, testing alternative model specifications to confirm the stability of results.

The validity of the results must also be assessed: external validity involves comparing findings with other studies or independent data sources to reinforce the credibility of your results, while internal validity requires checking the consistency within the dataset and model outputs. Finally, sensitivity analyses are necessary to explore how changes in assumptions or parameters influence results.

These steps ensure that the insights derived from your DCE are reliable and robust. In particular, the focus is generally on translating outputs from DCE models into practical and policy-relevant insights. In fields such as environmental economics, estimating mWTP or predicting changes in consumer surplus due to policy shifts represent key objectives. Taking full advantage of the post-estimation analysis ensures that models have real-world impacts and contribute meaningfully to decision-making processes. The post-estimation analysis is covered in detail in Chapter 10.

## 2.11 Key Takeaways

- Developing research questions and hypotheses is essential for any DCE study, as this guides the specifications of your DCE, including the information you need to collect, the population of interest, the survey method or sampling strategy needed, and further aspects of your design. Reviewing the DCE literature is crucial in informing your design.
- When starting your work, keep in mind that carrying out a stated preference survey employing discrete choice experiments requires more than choice modelling. To ensure a high data quality, knowledge of empirical social research is particularly important.
- It is essential to ensure that sufficient resources (i.e. time and money) are available for pre-testing and pilot surveys. Too often, the focus is on ensuring sufficient funding for the main survey, but testing is critical and requires adequate resources.
- The conditions for incentive compatibility are known but often not sufficiently accounted for in DCE designs. These include the number of alternatives in a choice task (a frequently ignored aspect), the independence of choices in a sequence of choice tasks, and other design aspects such as information scripts about the provision of the good or service at hand.
- Estimating willingness to pay measures requires a cost attribute to be included in the DCE. Its specification has important implications for the calculation of subsequent welfare measures and should be specified with careful consideration. In particular, the number of cost attribute levels and their range are important aspects to consider.
- Determining the market size can have tremendous effects on the study outcomes due to the association between market size and aggregated welfare measures.

- Developing a sampling strategy and careful selection of the survey mode are essential as going for an online survey inviting respondents from a survey panel is not automatically the best choice to represent your target population.

## Bibliography

Abbey JD, Meloy MG (2017) Attention by design: using attention checks to detect inattentive respondents and improve data quality. J Oper Manag 53–56(1):63–70. https://doi.org/10.1016/j.jom.2017.06.001

Alem Y, Hassen S, Köhlin G (2023) Decision-making within the household: the role of division of labor and differences in preferences. J Econ Behav Organ 207:511–528. https://doi.org/10.1016/j.jebo.2023.01.022

Alemu MH, Olsen SB (2018) Can a repeated opt-out reminder mitigate hypothetical bias in discrete choice experiments? an application to consumer valuation of novel food products. Eur Rev Agric Econ 45(5):749–782. https://doi.org/10.1093/erae/jby009

Apollo Choice Modelling (n. d.) Apollo: Choice modelling. Retrieved January 24, 2025, from https://www.apollochoicemodelling.com

Assele SY, Meulders M, Vandebroek M (2023) Sample size selection for discrete choice experiments using design features. J Choice Model 49:100436. https://doi.org/10.1016/j.jocm.2023.100436

Bansak K, Hainmueller J, Hopkins DJ, Yamamoto T (2021) Conjoint Survey Experiments. In: Druckman JN, Green DP (eds) Advances in Experimental Political Science. Cambridge University Press, Cambridge

Bateman IJ, Keeler B, Olmstead SM, Whitehead J (2023) Perspectives on valuing water quality improvements using stated preference methods. Proc Natl Acad Sci U S A 120(18):e2217456120. https://doi.org/10.1073/pnas.2217456120

Bateman IJ, Carson RT, Day B et al (2002) Economic valuation with stated preference techniques: a manual. Edward Elgar, Cheltenham

Bateman IJ, Munro A (2009) Household versus individual valuation: what's the difference? Environ Resour Econ 43(1):119–135. https://doi.org/10.1007/s10640-009-9268-6

Bateman IJ, Mawby J (2004) First impressions count: interviewer appearance and information effects in stated preference studies. Ecol Econ 49:47–55. https://doi.org/10.1016/j.ecolecon.2003.12.006

Ben-Akiva M, Lerman SR (1985) Discrete choice analysis. The MIT Press, Theory and application to travel demand

Berinsky AJ, Margolis MF, Sances MW, Warshaw C (2019) Using screeners to measure respondent attention on self-administered surveys: which items and how many? Political Sci Res Methods 9(2):430–437. https://doi.org/10.1017/psrm.2019.53

Bishop BC, Boyle KJ (2019) Reliability and validity in nonmarket valuation. Environ Resource Econ 72:559–582. https://doi.org/10.1007/s10640-017-0215-7

Bliemer MCJ, Collins AT (2016) On determining priors for the generation of efficient stated choice experimental designs. J Choice Model 21:10–14. https://doi.org/10.1016/j.jocm.2016.03.001

Bliemer MCJ, Rose JM (2024) Designing and conducting stated choice experiments. In: Hess S, Daily A (eds) Handbook of choice modelling. Edward Elgar Publishing

Boateng GO, Neilands TB, Frongillo EA et al (2018) Best practices for developing and validating scales for health, social, and behavioral research: a primer. Front Public Health 6:149. https://doi.org/10.3389/fpubh.2018.00149

Bonnichsen O, Olsen SB (2015) Correcting for non-response bias in contingent valuation surveys concerning environmental non-market goods: an empirical investigation using an online panel. J Environ Planning Manage 59:245–262. https://doi.org/10.1080/09640568.2015.1008626

Börger T (2013) Keeping up appearances: motivations for socially desirable responding in contingent valuation interviews. Ecol Econ 87:155–165. https://doi.org/10.1016/j.ecolecon.2012.12.019

Börger T, Glenk K, Meyerhoff J, Rehdanz K (2024) Mitigating cost vector effects in stated choice experiments using cheap talk and opt-out reminders. J Assoc Environ Resour Econ. https://doi.org/10.1086/731886

Boto-García D, Mariel P (2024) How well do couples know their partners' preferences? experimental evidence from joint recreation. Econ Politica 41(3):657–686. https://doi.org/10.1007/s40888-024-00346-x

Boxebeld S (2024) Ordering effects in discrete choice experiments: a systematic literature review across domains. J Choice Model 51:100489. https://doi.org/10.1016/j.jocm.2024.100489

Boyle KJ, Morrison M, MacDonald DH et al (2015) Investigating internet and mail implementation of stated-preference surveys while controlling for differences in sample frames. Environ Resour Econ 64(3):401–419. https://doi.org/10.1007/s10640-015-9876-2

Callegaro M (2013) Paradata in Websurveys. In: Kreuter F (ed) Improving Surveys with Paradata: Analytic Uses of Process Information, 1st edn. John Wiley & Sons

Campbell D, Boeri M, Doherty E, Hutchinson WG (2015) Learning, fatigue and preference formation in discrete choice experiments. J Econ Behav Organ 119:345–363. https://doi.org/10.1016/j.jebo.2015.08.018

Campbell D, Erdem S (2015) Position bias in best-worst scaling surveys: a case study on trust in institutions. Am J Agric Econ 97:526–545. https://doi.org/10.1093/ajae/aau112

Campbell D, Erdem S (2019) Including opt-out options in discrete choice experiments: Issues to consider. Patient 12:1–14. https://doi.org/10.1007/s40271-018-0324-6

Campbell D, Mørkbak MR, Olsen SB (2016) Response time in online stated choice experiments: the non-triviality of identifying fast and slow respondents. J Environ Econ Policy 6(1):17–35. https://doi.org/10.1080/21606544.2016.1167632

Carson RT, Groves T (2007) Incentive and informational properties of preference questions. Environ Resour Econ 37(1):181–210. https://doi.org/10.1007/s10640-007-9124-5

Carson RT, Louviere JJ (2011) A common nomenclature for stated preference elicitation approaches. Environ Resour Econ 49(4):539–559. https://doi.org/10.1007/s10640-010-9450-x

Caussade S, Ortúzar JD, Rizzi LI, Hensher DA (2005) Assessing the influence of design dimensions on stated choice experiment estimates. Transp Res B Methodol 39(7):621–640. https://doi.org/10.1016/j.trb.2004.07.006

Chrzan K (2010) Using partial profile choice experiments to handle large numbers of attributes. Int J Mark Res 52:827–840. https://doi.org/10.2501/s1470785310201673

Cohen JJ, Reichl J (2022) Comparing internet and phone survey mode effects across countries and research contexts. Aust J Agric Econ 66(1):44–71. https://doi.org/10.1111/1467-8489.12451

Czajkowski M, Giergiczny M, Greene WH (2014) Learning and fatigue effects revisited: investigating the effects of accounting for unobservable preference and scale heterogeneity. Land Econ 90(2):324–351. https://doi.org/10.3368/le.90.2.324

Danley B, Sandorf ED, Campbell D (2021) Putting your best fish forward: investigating distance decay and relative preferences for fish conservation. J Environ Econ Manag 108:102475. https://doi.org/10.1016/j.jeem.2021.102475

De Bekker-Grob EW, Donkers B, Jonker MF, Stolk EA (2015) Sample size requirements for discrete-choice experiments in healthcare: a practical guide. Patient 8(5):373–384. https://doi.org/10.1007/s40271-015-0118-z

Décieux JP, Sischka PE (2024) Comparing data quality and response behavior between smartphone, tablet, and computer devices in responsive design online surveys. Sage Open 14(2). https://doi.org/10.1177/21582440241252116

Dekker T, Hess S, Brouwer R, Hofkes M (2016) Decision uncertainty in multi-attribute stated preference studies. Resour Energy Econ 43:57–73. https://doi.org/10.1016/j.reseneeco.2015.11.002

DeLong KL, Syrengelas KG, Grebitus C, Nayga RM (2021) Visual versus text attribute representation in choice experiments. J Behav Exp Econ 94:101729. https://doi.org/10.1016/j.socec.2021.101729

Dillman DA, Smyth JD, Christian LM (2014) Internet, phone, mail, and mixed-mode surveys: the tailored design method, 4th edn. Wiley

Doherty E, Campbell D, Hynes S, van Rensburg TM (2013) Examining labelling effects within discrete choice experiments: an application to recreational site choice. J Environ Manag 125:94–104. https://doi.org/10.1016/j.jenvman.2013.03.056

Dunlap RE, Van Liere KD (1978) The 'new environmental paradigm.' J Environ Educ 9(4):10–19. https://doi.org/10.1080/00958964.1978.10801875

Dunlap RE, Van Liere KD, Mertig AG, Jones RE (2000) New trends in measuring environmental attitudes: measuring endorsement of the new ecological paradigm: a revised NEP scale. J Soc Issues 56(3):425–442. https://doi.org/10.1111/0022-4537.00176

Ek K, Persson L (2014) Wind farms—where and how to place them? a choice experiment approach to measure consumer preferences for characteristics of wind farm establishments in Sweden. Ecol Econ 105:193–203. https://doi.org/10.1016/j.ecolecon.2014.06.001

Faccioli M, Czajkowski M, Glenk K, Martin-Ortega J (2020) Environmental attitudes and place identity as determinants of preferences for ecosystem services. Ecol Econ 174:106600. https://doi.org/10.1016/j.ecolecon.2020.106600

Faccioli M, Glenk K (2021) More in good condition or less in bad condition? valence-based framing effects in environmental valuation. Land Econ. https://doi.org/10.3368/le.98.2.051920-0067R1

Franceschinis C, Liebe U, Thiene M et al (2022) The effect of social and personal norms on stated preferences for multiple soil functions: evidence from Australia and Italy. Australian Journal of Agricultural and Resource Economics 66:335–362. https://doi.org/10.1111/1467-8489.12466

Gaziano C (2005) Comparative analysis of within-household respondent selection techniques. Public Opin Q 69(1):124–157. https://doi.org/10.1093/poq/nfi006

GESIS (n.d.) Home. GESIS—Leibniz Institute for the Social Sciences. Retrieved January 24, 2025. https://www.gesis.org/en/home

GESIS-Items (n.d.) GESIS—Leibniz Institute for the Social Sciences. Retrieved January 24, 2025, from https://www.gesis.org/en/services/planning-studies-and-collecting-data/items-scales

GESIS-ZIS (n.d.) ZIS—Open access repository for measurement instruments. GESIS—Leibniz Institute for the Social Sciences. Retrieved January 24, 2025, from https://zis.gesis.org/en

Glenk K, Johnston RJ, Meyerhoff J, Sagebiel J (2020) Spatial dimensions of stated preference valuation in environmental and resource economics: methods. Trends and Challenges. Environ Resour Econ 75(2):215–242. https://doi.org/10.1007/s10640-018-00311-w

Glenk K, Meyerhoff J, Akaichi F, Martin-Ortega J (2019) Revisiting cost vector effects in discrete choice experiments. Resour Energy Econ 57:135–155. https://doi.org/10.1016/j.reseneeco.2019.05.001

Glenk K, Meyerhoff J, Colombo S, Faccioli M (2024) Enhancing the face validity of choice experiments: a simple diagnostic check. Ecol Econ 221:108160. https://doi.org/10.1016/j.ecolecon.2024.108160

Gschwandtner A, Burton M (2020) Comparing treatments to reduce hypothetical bias in choice experiments regarding organic food. Eur Rev Agric Econ. https://doi.org/10.1093/erae/jbz047

Gummer T, Roßmann J, Silber H (2018) Using instructed response items as attention checks in web surveys: properties and implementation. Sociological Methods & Research 50(1):238–264. https://doi.org/10.1177/0049124118769083

Haab T, Lewis LY, Whitehead J (2020) State of the Art of Contingent Valuation. In: HH Shugart (ed) Oxford Research Encyclopedia of Environmental Science. Oxford University Press, Oxford. https://doi.org/10.1093/acrefore/9780199389414.013.450

Haghani M, Bliemer MCJ, Rose JM et al (2021a) Hypothetical bias in stated choice experiments: part i. macro-scale analysis of literature and integrative Synthesis of empirical evidence from applied economics, experimental psychology and neuroimaging. J Choice Model 41:100309. https://doi.org/10.1016/j.jocm.2021.100309

Haghani M, Bliemer MCJ, Rose JM et al (2021b) Hypothetical Bias in stated choice experiments: Part II. conceptualisation of external validity, sources and explanations of bias and effectiveness of mitigation methods. J Choice Model 41:100322. https://doi.org/10.1016/j.jocm.2021.100322
Hair JF, Gabriel MLDS, Silva DD, Braga S (2019) Development and validation of attitudes measurement scales: fundamental and practical aspects. RAUSP Management Journal 54(4):490–507. https://doi.org/10.1108/rausp-05-2019-0098
Hanley N, Adamowicz W, Wright RE (2005) Price vector effects in choice experiments: an empirical test. Resource and Energy Economics 27(3):227–234. https://doi.org/10.1016/j.reseneeco.2004.11.001
Harrison GW (2024) Real choices and hypothetical choices. In: Hess S, Daly A (eds) Handbook of choice modelling. Edward Elgar, Cheltenham, pp 246–275
Hartman JD, Craig BM (2019) Does device or connection type affect health preferences in online surveys? The Patient - Patient-Centered Outcomes Research 12(6):639–650. https://doi.org/10.1007/s40271-019-00380-z
Hensher DA (2004) Identifying the influence of stated choice design dimensionality. J Transp Econ Polic 38(3):425–446. https://www.jstor.org/stable/20173065
Herriges J, Kling C, Liu CC, Tobias J (2010) What are the consequences of consequentiality? J Environ Econ Manag 59(1):67–81. https://doi.org/10.1016/j.jeem.2009.03.004
Hess S, Beharry-Borg N (2011) Accounting for latent attitudes in willingness-to-pay studies: the case of coastal water quality improvements in Tobago. Environ Resource Econ 52(1):109–131. https://doi.org/10.1007/s10640-011-9522-6
Hess S, Hensher DA, Daly A (2012) Not bored yet—Revisiting respondent fatigue in stated choice experiments. Transportation Research Part a: Policy and Practice 46(3):626–644. https://doi.org/10.1016/j.tra.2011.11.008
Hess S, Palma D (2019) Apollo: a flexible, powerful and customisable freeware package for choice model estimation and application. J Choice Model 32:100170. https://doi.org/10.1016/j.jocm.2019.100170
Holmes TP, Adamowicz WL, Carlsson F (2017) Choice experiments. In: Champ P, Boyle K, Brown T (eds) A primer on nonmarket valuation. The Economics of Non-Market Goods and Resources, vol 13. Springer, Dordrecht. https://doi.org/10.1007/978-94-007-7104-8_5
Johnson FR, Lancsar E, Marshall D et al (2013) Constructing experimental designs for discrete-choice experiments: report of the ISPOR conjoint analysis experimental design good research practices task force. Value in Health 16(1):3–13. https://doi.org/10.1016/j.jval.2012.08.2223
Johnston RJ, Schultz ET, Segerson K et al (2012) Enhancing the content validity of stated preference valuation: the structure and function of ecological indicators. Land Econ 88:102–120. https://doi.org/10.3368/le.88.1.102
Johnston RJ, Abdulrahman AS (2017) Systematic non-response in discrete choice experiments: implications for the valuation of climate risk reductions. J Environ Econ Policy 6:246–267. https://doi.org/10.1080/21606544.2017.1284695
Johnston RJ, Moeltner K, Peery S et al (2023) Spatial dimensions of water quality value in New England river networks. Proc Natl Acad Sci U S A 120(18):e2120255119. https://doi.org/10.1073/pnas.2120255119
Johnston RJ, Besedin EY, Wardwell RF (2003) Modeling relationships between use and nonuse values for surface water quality: a meta-analysis. Water Resour Res 39(12). https://doi.org/10.1029/2003wr002649
Johnston RJ, Boyle KJ, Adamowicz W et al (2017) Contemporary guidance for stated preference studies. J Assoc Environ Resour Econ 4(2):319–405. https://doi.org/10.1086/691697
Jonker MF (2024) Level overlap and level color coding revisited: Improved attribute attendance and higher choice consistency in discrete choice experiments. J Choice Model 52:100494. https://doi.org/10.1016/j.jocm.2024.100494
Koetse MJ (2016) Effects of payment vehicle non-attendance in choice experiments on value estimates and the WTA–WTP disparity. J Environ Econ Policy 6(3):225–245. https://doi.org/10.1080/21606544.2016.1268979

Kreuter F (ed) (2013) Improving surveys with paradata. Analytic Uses of Process Information. Wiley, Hoboken, New Jersey. https://doi.org/10.1002/9781118596869

Krupnick A, Adamowicz WL (2006) Supporting Questions in Stated Choice Studies. In: Kanninen B (ed) Valuing environmental amenities using stated choice studies. The Economics of Non-Market Goods and Resources, vol 8. Springer, Dordrecht, pp 43–65

Ladenburg J, Olsen SB (2014) Augmenting short cheap talk scripts with a repeated opt-out reminder in choice experiment surveys. Resource and Energy Economics 37:39–63. https://doi.org/10.1016/j.reseneeco.2014.05.002

Leggett CG, Kleckner NS, Boyle KJ et al (2003) Social desirability bias in contingent valuation surveys administered through in-person interviews. Land Econ 79(4):561–575. https://doi.org/10.2307/3147300

Lew DK, Anderson LE, Lipton DW et al (2022) Adherence to best practices for stated preference valuation within the u.s. marine ecosystem services literature. J Ocean Coast Econ 9(1). https://doi.org/10.15351/2373-8456.1159

Lew DK, Whitehead JC (2020) Attribute non-attendance as an information processing strategy in stated preference choice experiments: origins, current practices, and future directions. Mar Resour Econ 35(3):285–317. https://doi.org/10.1086/709440

Liebe U, Glenk K, Oehlmann M, Meyerhoff J (2015) Does the use of mobile devices (tablets and smartphones) affect survey quality and choice behaviour in web surveys? J Choice Model 14:17–31. https://doi.org/10.1016/j.jocm.2015.02.002

Liebe U, Mariel P, Beyer H, Meyerhoff J (2021) Uncovering the Nexus between attitudes, preferences, and behavior in sociological applications of stated choice experiments. Sociological Methods & Research 50(1):310–347. https://doi.org/10.1177/0049124118782536

Lindhjem H, Navrud S (2011) Are internet surveys an alternative to face-to-face interviews in contingent valuation? Ecol Econ 70(9):1628–1637. https://doi.org/10.1016/j.ecolecon.2011.04.002

Logar I, Brouwer R, Campbell D (2020) Does attribute order influence attribute-information processing in discrete choice experiments? Resource and Energy Economics 60:101164. https://doi.org/10.1016/j.reseneeco.2020.101164

Loureiro ML, Lotade J (2005) Interviewer effects on the valuation of goods with ethical and environmental attributes. Environ Resource Econ 30:49–72. https://doi.org/10.1007/s10640-004-1149-4

Louviere JJ, Flynn TN, Marley AAJ (2015) Best-worst scaling. Cambridge University Press, Theory, methods and applications

Lundhede TH, Olsen SB, Jacobsen JB, Thorsen BJ (2009) Handling respondent uncertainty in choice experiments: evaluating recoding approaches against explicit modelling of uncertainty. J Choice Model 2(2):118–147. https://doi.org/10.1016/s1755-5345(13)70007-1

Lupi F, Herriges JA, Kim H, Stevenson RJ (2023) Getting off the ladder: disentangling water quality indices to enhance the valuation of divergent ecosystem services. Proc Natl Acad Sci U S A 120(18):e2120261120. https://doi.org/10.1073/pnas.2120261120

Manhique H, Wätzold F (2024) Effects of institutional distrust on value estimates of stated preference surveys in developing countries: a choice experiment on conserving biodiversity within agricultural landscapes in a biodiversity hotspot. Q Open 4(1). https://doi.org/10.1093/qopen/qoae014

Mariel P, Hoyos D, Meyerhoff J et al (2021) Environmental valuation with discrete choice experiments: guidance on design, implementation and data analysis. Springer Nature. https://doi.org/10.1007/978-3-030-62669-3

Mattmann M, Logar I, Brouwer R (2018) Choice certainty, consistency, and monotonicity in discrete choice experiments. J Environ Econ Policy 8(2):109–127. https://doi.org/10.1080/21606544.2018.1515118

Meyerhoff J, Glenk K (2015) Learning how to choose—effects of instructional choice sets in discrete choice experiments. Resource and Energy Economics 41:122–142. https://doi.org/10.1016/j.reseneeco.2015.04.006

Meyerhoff J, Oehlmann M, Weller P (2015) The Influence of design dimensions on stated choices in an environmental context. Environ Resource Econ 61(3):385–407. https://doi.org/10.1007/s10640-014-9797-5
Meyerhoff J, Klefoth T, Arlinghaus R (2019) The value artificial lake ecosystems provide to recreational anglers: implications for management of biodiversity and outdoor recreation. J Environ Manag 252:109580. https://doi.org/10.1016/j.jenvman.2019.109580
Meyerhoff J, Boeri M, Hartje V (2014) The value of water quality improvements in the region Berlin-brandenburg as a function of distance and state residency. Water Resources and Economics 5:49–66. https://doi.org/10.1016/j.wre.2014.02.001
Meyerhoff J, Rehdanz K, Wunsch A (2021a) Preferences for coastal adaptation to climate change: evidence from a choice experiment. J Environ Econ Policy 10(4):374–390. https://doi.org/10.1080/21606544.2021.1894990
Meyerhoff J, Klefoth T, Arlinghaus R (2021b) Visual versus text-based choice sets: investigating differences in validity and value estimates. Conference Paper. Paper presented at the International Choice Modelling Conference, Kobe, Japan, 19–21 August 2019. https://doi.org/10.6084/m9.figshare.14013983.v1
Meyerhoff J, Oehlmann M (2023) The performance of full versus partial profile choice set designs in environmental valuation. Ecol Econ 204:107665. https://doi.org/10.1016/j.ecolecon.2022.107665
Mokas I, Lizin S, Brijs T et al (2021) Can immersive virtual reality increase respondents' certainty in discrete choice experiments? a comparison with traditional presentation formats. J Environ Econ Manag 109:102509. https://doi.org/10.1016/j.jeem.2021.102509
Mørkbak MR, Christensen T, Gyrd-Hansen D (2009) Choke price bias in choice experiments. Environ Resource Econ 45:537–551. https://doi.org/10.1007/s10640-009-9327-z
Morgan DL (2023) Exploring the use of artificial intelligence for qualitative data analysis: the case of ChatGPT. Int J Qual Methods 22. https://doi.org/10.1177/16094069231211248
Needham K, Czajkowski M, Hanley N, LaRiviere J (2018) What is the causal impact of information and knowledge in stated preference studies? Resource and Energy Economics 54:69–89. https://doi.org/10.1016/j.reseneeco.2018.09.001
Netusil NR, Dissanayake STM, Lavelle L et al (2023) Does presentation matter? an analysis of images and text in a choice experiment of green roofs. Q Open 3(1). https://doi.org/10.1093/qopen/qoad010
Nielsen JS (2011) Use of the internet for willingness-to-pay surveys. Resource and Energy Economics 33(1):119–129. https://doi.org/10.1016/j.reseneeco.2010.01.006
Oehlmann M, Meyerhoff J (2016) Stated preferences towards renewable energy alternatives in Germany—Do the consequentiality of the survey and trust in institutions matter? J Environ Econ Policy 6(1):1–16. https://doi.org/10.1080/21606544.2016.1139468
Oehlmann M, Meyerhoff J, Mariel P, Weller P (2017) Uncovering context-induced status Quo effects in choice experiments. J Environ Econ Manag 81:59–73. https://doi.org/10.1016/j.jeem.2016.09.002
Ozdemir S, Quaife M, Mohamed AF, Norman R (2024) An overview of data collection in health preference research. Patient:1–13. https://doi.org/10.1007/s40271-024-00695-6
Parsons G, Yan L (2021) Anchoring on visual cues in a stated preference survey: the case of siting offshore wind power projects. J Choice Model 38. https://doi.org/10.1016/j.jocm.2020.100264
Penn J, Hu W (2019) Cheap talk efficacy under potential and actual hypothetical bias: a meta-analysis. J Environ Econ Manag 96:22–35. https://doi.org/10.1016/j.jeem.2019.02.005
Penn J, Hu W (2022) Adjusting and calibrating elicited values based on follow-up certainty questions: a meta-analysis. Environ Resource Econ 84(4):919–946. https://doi.org/10.1007/s10640-022-00742-6
Penn J, Hu W, Ye T (2024) Efficacy of hypothetical bias mitigation techniques: a cross-country comparison. J Environ Econ Manag 125:102989. https://doi.org/10.1016/j.jeem.2024.102989

Perino G, Schwickert H (2023) Animal welfare is a stronger determinant of public support for meat taxation than climate change mitigation in Germany. Nat Food 4:160–169. https://doi.org/10.1038/s43016-023-00696-y

Phaneuf DJ, Requate T (2017) A course in environmental economics. Theory, Policy, and Practice. Cambridge University Press, Cambridge

Rigby D, Burton DM, Pluske J (2015) Preference stability and choice consistency in discrete choice experiments. Environ Resource Econ 65:441–461. https://doi.org/10.1007/s10640-015-9913-1

Rolfe J, Windle J (2012) Distance decay functions for iconic assets: assessing national values to protect the health of the great barrier reef in Australia. Environ Resource Econ 53(3):347–365. https://doi.org/10.1007/s10640-012-9565-3

Rolfe J, Windle J (2015) Testing attribute selection and variation in a choice experiment to assess the tradeoffs associated with increased mining development. Land Use Policy 42:673–682. https://doi.org/10.1016/j.landusepol.2014.10.006

Rose JM, Bliemer MCJ (2013) Sample size requirements for stated choice experiments. Transportation 40(5):1021–1041. https://doi.org/10.1007/s11116-013-9451-z

Ryan M, Watson V, Entwistle V (2009) Rationalising the 'irrational': a think aloud study of discrete choice experiment responses. Health Econ 18(3):321–336. https://doi.org/10.1002/hec.1369

Sandorf ED, Aanesen M, Navrud S (2016) Valuing unfamiliar and complex environmental goods: a comparison of valuation workshops and internet panel surveys with videos. Ecol Econ 129:50–61. https://doi.org/10.1016/j.ecolecon.2016.06.008

Sandorf ED, Campbell D (2019) Accommodating satisficing behaviour in stated choice experiments. Eur Rev Agric Econ 46:133–162. https://doi.org/10.1093/erae/jby021

Sandorf ED, Campbell D, Chorus C (2022) A simple satisficing model. PLoS ONE 17(10):e0275339. https://doi.org/10.1371/journal.pone.0275339

Sandorf ED, Campbell D (2023) spdesign: designing stated preference experiments. R package version 0.0.5. https://CRAN.R-project.org/package=spdesign

Sandorf ED, Crastes dit Sourd R, Mahieu PA, (2018) The effect of attribute-alternative matrix displays on preferences and processing strategies. J Choice Model 29:113–132. https://doi.org/10.1016/j.jocm.2018.01.001

Sandorf ED, Persson L, Broberg T (2020) Using an integrated choice and latent variable model to understand the impact of 'professional' respondents in a stated preference survey. Resource and Energy Economics 61:101178. https://doi.org/10.1016/j.reseneeco.2020.101178

Sandstrom-Mistry K, Lupi F, Kim H, Herriges JA (2023) Comparing water quality valuation across probability and non-probability samples. Appl Econ Perspect Policy 45(2):744–761. https://doi.org/10.1002/aepp.13375

Scarpa R, Gilbride TJ, Campbell D, Hensher DA (2009) Modelling attribute non-attendance in choice experiments for rural landscape valuation. Eur Rev Agric Econ 36(2):151–174. https://doi.org/10.1093/erae/jbp012

Scarpa R, Campbell D, Hutchinson WG (2007) Benefit estimates for landscape improvements: sequential Bayesian design and respondents' rationality in a choice experiment. Land Econ 83(4):617–634. https://doi.org/10.3368/le.83.4.617

Schwartz SH (1977) Normative influences on altruism. In: Leonard B (ed) Advances in experimental social psychology. Academic Press, New York, pp 221–279

Shang L, Chandra Y (2021) Discrete choice experiments using R. Springer, The how-to guide for social and managerial sciences

Shr YH, Ready R, Orland B, Echols S (2019) How do visual representations influence survey responses? evidence from a choice experiment on landscape attributes of green infrastructure. Ecol Econ 156:375–386. https://doi.org/10.1016/j.ecolecon.2018.10.015

Skeie MA, Lindhjem H, Skjeflo S, Navrud S (2019) Smartphone and tablet effects in contingent valuation web surveys—no reason to worry? Ecol Econ 165:106390. https://doi.org/10.1016/j.ecolecon.2019.106390

Smith VK (2006) Fifty years of contingent valuation. In: Alberini A, Kahn JR (eds) Handbook on Contingent Valuation. Edward Elgar, Cheltenham, pp 7–65

Smyth J, Olson KM (2019) Within-household selection methods: a critical review and experimental examination. In: Lavrakas PJ et al (eds) Experimental methods in survey research: techniques that combine random sampling with random assignment. John Wiley & Sons, Inc

Stewart DW, Shamdasani PN (2015) Focus groups: Theory and Practice, 3rd edn. SAGE Publications

Stopher P (2012) Collecting, managing, and assessing data. Cambridge University Press, Cambridge, Using Sample Surveys

Strange N, zu Ermgassen S, Marshall E et al (2024) Why it matters how biodiversity is measured in environmental valuation studies compared to conservation science. Biol Conserv 292:110546. https://doi.org/10.1016/j.biocon.2024.110546

Tjaden J, Liebe U, Bruscoli D (2022) Explaining re-migration preferences—evidence from a discrete choice experiment in Sudan. Paper presented at the 7th International Choice Modelling Conference, Reykjavík, Iceland, 23–25 May 2022

Tourangeau R, Rips LJ, Rasinski K (2000) The psychology of survey response. Cambridge University Press, New York

Train K (2009) Discrete choice methods with simulation, 2nd edn. Cambridge University Press, New York. https://doi.org/10.1017/CBO9780511805271

Uggeldahl K, Jacobsen C, Lundhede TH, Olsen SB (2016) Choice certainty in discrete choice experiments: will eye tracking provide useful measures? J Choice Model 20:35–48. https://doi.org/10.1016/j.jocm.2016.09.002

Vass CM, Boeri M (2021) Mobilising the next generation of stated-preference studies: the association of access device with choice behaviour and data quality. Patient 14(1):55–63. https://doi.org/10.1007/s40271-020-00484-x

Vass CM, Boeri M, Shields G, Seo J (2024) Making use of technology to improve stated preference studies. Patient 17(5):483–491. https://doi.org/10.1007/s40271-024-00693-8

Vista AB, Rosenberger RS, Collins AR (2009) If you provide it, will they read it? response time effects in a choice experiment. Canadian Journal of Agricultural Economics/revue Canadienne D'agroeconomie 57:365–377. https://doi.org/10.1111/j.1744-7976.2009.01156.x

Vossler CA, Doyon M, Rondeau D (2012) Truth in consequentiality: theory and field evidence on discrete choice experiments. American Economic Journal: Microeconomics 4(4):145–171. https://doi.org/10.1257/mic.4.4.145

Vossler CA, Keiser DA, Kling CL, Phaneuf DJ (2024) Information scripts and the incentive compatibility of discrete choice experiments. J Assoc Environ Resour Econ. https://doi.org/10.1086/731527

Vossler CA, Zawojska E (2020) Behavioral drivers or economic incentives? toward a better understanding of elicitation effects in stated preference studies. J Assoc Environ Resour Econ 7:279–303. https://doi.org/10.1086/706645

Watson V, Porteous T, Bolt T, Ryan M (2019) Mode and frame matter: assessing the impact of survey mode and sample frame in choice experiments. Med Decis Making 39(7):827–841. https://doi.org/10.1177/0272989X19871035

Webb EJD, Meads D, Lynch Y et al (2021) Attribute selection for a discrete choice experiment incorporating a best-worst scaling survey. Value Health 24(4):575–584. https://doi.org/10.1016/j.jval.2020.10.025

Welling M, Zawojska E, Sagebiel J (2022) Information, consequentiality and credibility in stated preference surveys: a choice experiment on climate adaptation. Environ Resource Econ 82(1):257–283. https://doi.org/10.1007/s10640-022-00675-0

Welling M, Sagebiel J, Rommel J (2023) Information processing in stated preference surveys: a case study on urban gardens. J Environ Econ Manag 119:102798. https://doi.org/10.1016/j.jeem.2023.102798

Weng W, Morrison MD, Boyle KJ et al (2020) Effects of the number of alternatives in public good discrete choice experiments. Ecol Econ 182:106904. https://doi.org/10.1016/j.ecolecon.2020.106904

Whitehead JC, Ropicki A, Loomis J et al (2023) Estimating the benefits to Florida households from avoiding another Gulf oil spill using the contingent valuation method: internal validity tests with

probability-based and opt-in samples. Appl Econ Perspect Policy 45(2):705–720. https://doi.org/10.1002/aepp.13352
Whittington D, Adamowicz W, Lloyd-Smith P (2017) Asking willingness-to-accept questions in stated preference surveys: a review and research agenda. Annual Reviews of Resource Economics 9:317–336. https://doi.org/10.1146/annurev-resource-121416-125602
Whitty JA, Walker R, Golenko X, Ratcliffe J (2014) A think aloud study comparing the validity and acceptability of discrete choice and best worst scaling methods. PLoS ONE 9(4):e90635. https://doi.org/10.1371/journal.pone.0090635
Windle J, Rolfe J (2011) Comparing responses from internet and paper-based collection methods in more complex stated preference environmental valuation surveys. Economic Analysis and Policy 41(1):83–97. https://doi.org/10.1016/s0313-5926(11)50006-2
Yang JC, Johnson FR, Kilambi V, Mohamed AF (2015) Sample size and utility-difference precision in discrete-choice experiments: a meta-simulation approach. J Choice Model 16:50–57. https://doi.org/10.1016/j.jocm.2015.09.001
Zawojska E, Czajkowski M (2017) Re-examining empirical evidence on stated preferences: importance of incentive compatibility. J Environ Econ Policy 6(4):374–403. https://doi.org/10.1080/21606544.2017.1322537
Zhang J, Adamowicz WL (2011) Unraveling the choice format effect: a context-dependent random utility model. Land Econ 87(4):730–743. https://doi.org/10.3368/le.87.4.730

# Chapter 3
# Random Utility Models: Theoretical Background

**Abstract** This chapter provides an overview of the random utility maximisation (RUM) model, reviewing its assumptions and delving into its theoretical foundations. We explore the multinomial logit (MNL) model, which is widely used in DCE literature due to its many advantages. These include its robustness, ease of estimation, and straightforward interpretation, with closed-form choice probabilities that simplify calculations. We also review advanced specifications of the mixed logit model, including the random parameters logit (RP-MXL) and latent class (LC-MXL) models, and walk you through the most common goodness of fit models used in DCE research.

## 3.1 Random Utility Maximisation Model

The origin of the Random Utility Maximisation (RUM) model approach lies in the concept of psychological stimuli developed by Thurstone (1927) and later extended by Marschak (1960), who interpreted the stimuli as utilities. Specifically, these models assume that among all available alternatives, the decision-maker selects the option that provides the highest utility. Models based on this assumption are called RUM models (see McFadden 1974 for the foundational paper on RUM models).

Utility is commonly defined as an indicator of the *perceived value of a good or service* by a decision-maker, and is generally derived from a set of attributes (characteristics) associated with different alternatives (choice options). For example, environmental policy alternatives for a protected natural area could be described by attributes such as the percentage of endangered species protected and the level of taxation required to ensure this protection, with different alternatives having different levels of protection and taxation.

The utility maximisation rule states that a decision-maker will select the alternative that provides the highest utility from the set of available alternatives. In other words, an alternative is chosen if its utility exceeds that of all other alternatives in the decision-maker's choice set. Next, we will walk you through how these assumptions allow us to derive the RUM model.



P. Mariel et al., *Environmental Valuation with Discrete Choice Experiments in R*,
The Economics of Non-Market Goods and Resources 17,
https://doi.org/10.1007/978-3-031-89338-4_3

Let us consider a decision-maker $n$ from a population or sample of $N$ individuals that faces a choice among $J$ alternatives over $T$ repeated choice occasions. It is assumed that the decision-maker $n$ derives a certain level of utility $U_{njt}$ from an alternative $j$ in a choice occasion $t$. The decision-maker selects the alternative that provides the highest utility. Therefore, alternative $i$ is chosen by decision-maker $n$ in choice occasion $t$ if and only if $U_{nit} > U_{njt}, \forall j \neq i$.

The researcher does not directly observe the decision-maker's utility; only the final choice, the attribute levels of each alternative, and some characteristics of the decision-maker (typically socio-demographic characteristics) are observed. Therefore, the utility $U_{njt}$ is decomposed in a deterministic and a random part as follows:

$$U_{njt} = V_{njt} + \varepsilon_{njt},$$

where $V_{njt}$ represents the observed part of the utility function, often referred as the representative utility, and $\varepsilon_{njt}$ is an unknown error term that captures factors affecting the utility $U_{njt}$ that are not included in $V_{njt}$. In RUM models, it is treated as a random term with a joint probability density function $f(\boldsymbol{\varepsilon}) = f(\varepsilon_{n11}, \ldots, \varepsilon_{nJT})$. The probability that decision-maker $n$, at choice occasion $t$, selects alternative $i$ is then defined as:

$$\begin{aligned} P_{nit} &= \Pr(U_{nit} > U_{njt}, \ \forall j \neq i) \\ &= \Pr(V_{nit} + \varepsilon_{nit} > V_{njt} + \varepsilon_{njt}, \ \forall j \neq i) \\ &= \Pr(\varepsilon_{njt} - \varepsilon_{nit} < V_{nit} - V_{njt}, \ \forall j \neq i) \end{aligned} \tag{3.1}$$

This defines a cumulative distribution function specifying the probability that the difference between the random terms, $\varepsilon_{njt} - \varepsilon_{nit}$, is less than the difference between the representative utilities, $V_{nit} - V_{njt}$.

Given the density $f(\boldsymbol{\varepsilon})$ of the error term, and defining an indicator function $I(\cdot)$, which equals one when the expression inside the parentheses is true and zero otherwise, the probability can be rewritten as:

$$\begin{aligned} P_{nit} &= \Pr\left(\varepsilon_{njt} - \varepsilon_{nit} < V_{nit} - V_{njt}, \ \forall j \neq i\right) \\ &= \int I\left(\varepsilon_{njt} - \varepsilon_{nit} < V_{nit} - V_{njt}, \ \forall j \neq i\right) f(\boldsymbol{\varepsilon})\, d\boldsymbol{\varepsilon}. \end{aligned} \tag{3.2}$$

This expression represents a multidimensional integral over the density of the random term, and its form varies depending on the specification of $f(\boldsymbol{\varepsilon})$, leading to models such as probit, multinomial logit (MNL) or mixed logit (MXL) models. For certain specifications like the MNL model, this integral has a closed form—meaning that a solution can be computed using a finite number of standard mathematical operations, without requiring approximation methods such as numerical simulations—significantly simplifying the estimation. However, for other models, such as probit or MXL models, the integral lacks a closed form and must be evaluated numerically through simulation.

Given the expression in Eq. (3.2), the identification of a RUM model is achieved through different approaches depending on the specifications of the model. However, the fundamental restrictions of a RUM model can be summarised by two key points: *the scale of utility is arbitrary* and *only differences in utility matter* (Train 2009, p. 19).

First, let us consider the restriction that *the scale of utility is arbitrary*. This means that multiplying the utility of each alternative by a constant does not change which alternative has the highest utility, and therefore does not affect the choice. As a result, the scale of utility must be normalised (more detail on this below). With this in mind, and assuming the representative utility $V_{njt}$ is linear in parameters, i.e. $V_{njt} = \mathbf{x}'_{njt}\boldsymbol{\beta}$, where $\mathbf{x}_{njt}$ is a $K \times 1$ vector of variables related to alternative $j$ and $\boldsymbol{\beta}$ is a $K \times 1$ vector of unknown coefficients, the model expression:

$$U_{njt} = V_{njt} + \varepsilon_{njt} = \mathbf{x}'_{njt}\boldsymbol{\beta} + \varepsilon_{njt} \tag{3.3}$$

is equivalent to:

$$U^*_{njt} = \lambda V_{njt} + \lambda\varepsilon_{njt} = \mathbf{x}'_{njt}(\lambda\boldsymbol{\beta}) + \lambda\varepsilon_{njt}.$$

Normalisation of the model is typically achieved by normalising the *variance of the error terms*. For instance, when the error terms are assumed to be independently and identically distributed (*i.i.d.*) with the same variance, normalisation is straightforward, and usually involves setting the error variance to a convenient value. In the case of *i.i.d.* standard extreme value type I distributed errors (also known as the Gumbel distribution) with a location parameter of zero and a scale of one, which define the widely used standard MNL model, $\lambda$ is set so that $\text{Var}(\lambda\varepsilon_{njt}) = \pi^2/6$.

Let us now focus on the second restriction: *only differences in utility matter*. According to Eq. (3.1), the absolute level of utility is irrelevant to the choice, since the selected alternative is determined by the differences in utility between them. In other words, if a constant is added to the utility of all alternatives, the choice remains unchanged, as the alternative with the highest utility will be the same. This implies that only the parameters capturing the differences between alternatives can be identified and estimated.

To illustrate this, we consider an example. Assuming linearity in the attributes as defined in Eq. (3.3), with three alternatives $j = 1, 2, 3$, and two attributes (*attr*1 and *attr*2), the utility functions of the RUM model are:

$$\begin{aligned} U_{n1t} &= ASC_1 + \beta_1 attr1_{n1t} + \beta_2 attr2_{n1t} + \varepsilon_{n1t} \\ U_{n2t} &= ASC_2 + \beta_1 attr1_{n2t} + \beta_2 attr2_{n2t} + \varepsilon_{n2t} \\ U_{n3t} &= \qquad\quad\; \beta_1 attr1_{n3t} + \beta_2 attr2_{n3t} + \varepsilon_{n3t} \end{aligned} \tag{3.4}$$

for $n = 1, 2, \ldots, N$, $t = 1, 2, \ldots, T$. The alternative-specific constants $ASC_1$ and $ASC_2$ account for the average impact on the utility of all factors not included in the set of attributes.

However, we cannot include alternative-specific constants for every alternative, due to issues with model identification. If $ASC_3$ were included in the $U_{n3t}$ equation above, the differences between $U_{n1t} - U_{n3t}$ and $U_{n2t} - U_{n3t}$ would be:

$$\begin{aligned} U_{n1t} - U_{n3t} = (ASC_1 - ASC_3) &+\beta_1(attr1_{n1t} - attr1_{n3t}) \\ &+\beta_2(attr2_{n1t} - attr2_{n3t}) \\ &+(\varepsilon_{n1t} - \varepsilon_{n3t}) \\ U_{n2t} - U_{n3t} = (ASC_2 - ASC_3) &+\beta_1(attr1_{n2t} - attr1_{n3t}) \\ &+\beta_2(attr2_{n2t} - attr2_{n3t}) \\ &+(\varepsilon_{n2t} - \varepsilon_{n3t}). \end{aligned} \tag{3.5}$$

In these equations, the new coefficients $(ASC_1 - ASC_3)$ and $(ASC_2 - ASC_3)$ are not identified unless one of the alternative specific constants is restricted to a specific value. This is analogous to the dummy variable trap, where including a constant for every alternative leads to perfect multicollinearity, making it impossible to estimate the model. Therefore, in the system of equations in Eq. (3.4), the alternative specific constant (in our case) $ASC_3$ is set to zero.

A similar problem arises with socio-demographic variables that are individual-specific but not alternative-specific. While attribute levels typically vary across alternatives, characteristics of the decision-maker, such as age or gender, remain constant. For example, if $\beta_3\, age_n$ is added to all three alternatives in Eq. (3.4), its effect, $\beta_3\,(age_n - age_n)$, would cancel out in the differences of the utilities defined in Eq. (3.5). To account for this, individual-specific variables (like age or gender) must be introduced in a way that creates variation in utility across alternatives.

A possible approach is to allow the parameters for variables like age and gender to vary across alternatives, meaning the effects differ for each alternative. A more complex approach involves interacting these variables with specific attributes so that the influence of factors like age on utility changes depending on the attributes of each alternative.

To illustrate this, the first approach would introduce age and gender as follows:

$$\begin{aligned} U_{n1t} &= \mathrm{ASC}_1 + \delta_{11} age_n + \delta_{21} gender_n + \beta_1 attr1_{n1t} + \beta_2 attr2_{n1t} + \varepsilon_{n1t} \\ U_{n2t} &= \mathrm{ASC}_2 + \delta_{12} age_n + \delta_{22} gender_n + \beta_1 attr1_{n2t} + \beta_2 attr2_{n2t} + \varepsilon_{n2t} \\ U_{n3t} &= \beta_1 attr1_{n3t} + \beta_2 attr2_{n3t} + \varepsilon_{n3t} \end{aligned} \tag{3.6}$$

Since only differences in utility matter, the utility differences corresponding to Eq. (3.6) are:

$$\begin{aligned}
U_{n1t} - U_{n3t} = ASC_1 &+\delta_{11} age_n \\
&+\delta_{21} gender_n \\
&+\beta_1 (attr1_{n1t} - attr1_{n3t}) \\
&+\beta_2 (attr2_{n1t} - attr2_{n3t}) \\
&+(\varepsilon_{n1t} - \varepsilon_{n3t}) \\
U_{n2t} - U_{n3t} = ASC_2 &+\delta_{12} age_n \\
&+\delta_{22} gender_n \\
&+\beta_1 (attr1_{n2t} - attr1_{n3t}) \\
&+\beta_2 (attr2_{n2t} - attr2_{n3t}) \\
&+(\varepsilon_{n2t} - \varepsilon_{n3t}).
\end{aligned} \tag{3.7}$$

This approach affects the interpretation of the parameters associated with the individual-specific variables. Here, the parameter $\delta_{11}$ represents the differential effect of age on the utility of the first alternative compared to the third, while $\delta_{12}$ reflects the equivalent effect of age on the second alternative relative to the third.

In the extreme case with no alternative-varying attributes ($attr1_{njt}$ and $attr2_{njt}$ in our case), the model in Eq. (3.6) would become:

$$\begin{aligned}
U_{n1t} &= \mathrm{ASC}_1 + \delta_{11} age_n + \delta_{21} gender_n + \varepsilon_{n1t} \\
U_{n2t} &= \mathrm{ASC}_2 + \delta_{12} age_n + \delta_{22} gender_n + \varepsilon_{n2t} \\
U_{n3t} &= \varepsilon_{n3t}
\end{aligned} \tag{3.8}$$

Strictly speaking, models that primarily use individual-specific variables (as defined in Eq. (3.8)) are referred to as *multinomial logit models*. These models are particularly well-suited when the focus is on the characteristics of the decision-makers and how these influence their choices across multiple alternatives. In contrast, models that primarily rely on alternative-specific variables (i.e. attributes that differ across alternatives but are constant for each decision-maker) are technically referred to as *conditional logit models*.

Despite this distinction, both models share the same underlying logit structure and principles (Long 1997, p. 180), and while it is not entirely accurate to use the terms interchangeably, doing so is common practice. Therefore, throughout this book, we will adopt the term *multinomial logit* to refer to these types of models, as this is the term widely accepted for models that include a mixture of individual-specific and alternative-specific variables.

This approach of directly incorporating of alternative-constant explanatory variables into the model can be combined with the interactions of these variables with attributes that vary across alternatives. To keep the model manageable and aligned with the pedagogical goals of this introductory chapter, we focus on a simplified case where only $attr1$ is interacted with the socio-demographic variables:

$$\begin{aligned}
U_{n1t} &= \mathrm{ASC}_1 + \delta_{11} age_n + \delta_{21} gender_n \\
&\quad + (\beta_1 + \delta_3\, age_n + \delta_4\, gender_n) attr1_{n1t} + \beta_2 attr2_{n1t} + \varepsilon_{n1t} \\
U_{n2t} &= \mathrm{ASC}_2 + \delta_{12} age_n + \delta_{22} gender_n \\
&\quad + (\beta_1 + \delta_3\, age_n + \delta_4\, gender_n) attr1_{n2t} + \beta_2 attr2_{n2t} + \varepsilon_{n2t} \\
U_{n3t} &= (\beta_1 + \delta_3\, age_n + \delta_4\, gender_n) attr1_{n3t} + \beta_2 attr2_{n3t} + \varepsilon_{n3t}
\end{aligned} \tag{3.9}$$

In this case, the new coefficient of $attr1$, defined as $(\beta_1 + \delta_3\, age_n + \delta_4\, gender_n)$, is not constant across individuals $n = 1, 2, ..., N$, but instead varies depending on the individual-specific values of the variable *age* and *gender*.

From an econometric perspective, when we introduce interactions between socio-demographic variables and explanatory variables, it is important to also include interactions between these socio-demographic variables and the alternative-specific constants (ASCs). This is because a change in the slope of a regression model is often accompanied by a corresponding shift in the intercept. To visualise this simply, consider a linear regression line: if its slope changes, the point where it intersects the vertical axis typically shifts as well. Therefore, the utilities in Eq. (3.9), in addition to the term $(\beta_1 + \delta_3\, age_n + \delta_4\, gender_n) attr1_{njt}$, also include interactions of the same socio-demographic variables with the intercepts $(\delta_{1m}\, age_n + \delta_{2m}\, gender_n)$.

The utility differences corresponding to Eq. (3.9), are given by:

$$\begin{aligned}
U_{n1t} - U_{n3t} &= ASC_1 + \delta_{11} age_n + \delta_{21} gender_n \\
&\quad + (\beta_1 + \delta_3\, age_n + \delta_4\, gender_n)(attr1_{n1t} - attr1_{n3t}) \\
&\quad + \beta_2\, (attr2_{n1t} - attr2_{n3t}) \\
&\quad + (\varepsilon_{n1t} - \varepsilon_{n3t}) \\
U_{n2t} - U_{n3t} &= ASC_2 + \delta_{12} age_n + \delta_{22} gender_n \\
&\quad + (\beta_1 + \delta_3\, age_n + \delta_4\, gender_n)(attr1_{n2t} - attr1_{n3t}) \\
&\quad + \beta_2\, (attr2_{n2t} - attr2_{n3t}) \\
&\quad + (\varepsilon_{n2t} - \varepsilon_{n3t})
\end{aligned} \tag{3.10}$$

This approach of incorporating socio-demographic variables into the model is commonly known as modelling *observed preference heterogeneity*. It is called this because the coefficient of $attr1$ in Eq. (3.9) varies for each individual, specifically based on their values of *age* and *gender*. This approach allows for individual-specific coefficients that are directly tied to socio-demographic or other individual-specific variables, making their interpretation straightforward.

Individual-specific variables can also interact with the scale parameter, offering another way to explore their impact on decision-making and choices (see Oehlmann et al. 2017). In this case, different values of the individual-specific variable correspond to distinct scale parameters. Therefore, interacting an individual-specific variable with the scale parameter results in a different error variance for different individuals, depending on the interaction coefficient and their specific variable values.

Keep in mind that the error term is included because we cannot observe all factors influencing a decision maker's choice. As a result, the perceived randomness in choices arises from the modeller's perspective and reflects our model's inability to fully account for all determinants, rather than suggesting that the decision maker is choosing at random.

It is important to note that it is not possible to separately identify both individual differences in scale parameters and preferences. Attempting to explain both scale differences and preference differences using the same individual-specific variables would result in confounded effects and obscure the true source of variation in the model (Hess and Rose 2012).

## 3.2 Multinomial Logit Model

The MNL model is the most widely used discrete choice model because of its robustness, ease of estimation, and straightforward interpretation. This popularity is primarily because the formula for calculating choice probabilities has a closed-form solution. In this section, we will walk you through the derivation of the MNL model and set up its estimation.

We assume that the utility derived by individual $n$ from alternative $j$ on choice occasion $t$ is given by:

$$U_{njt} = V_{njt} + \varepsilon_{njt}, \tag{3.11}$$

where $\varepsilon_{njt}$ follows an *i.i.d.* type I extreme value (i.e. Gumbel) distribution across choice occasions, individuals, and alternatives. Since the variance of this distribution is $\pi^2/6$, the assumption of the functional form of the errors implicitly normalises the scale of the utility.

The primary reason for choosing the extreme value distribution in Eq. (3.11) is that the difference between two extreme value variables follows a logistic distribution. Since only differences in utility matter, the differences in error terms (see Eq. (3.5), Eq. (3.7), Eq. (3.10)) will follow a logistic distribution. This distribution closely resembles the normal distribution but has a simpler functional form for both the probability density function and cumulative distribution function, making it more convenient for modelling.

The probability that decision-maker $n$ chooses alternative $i$ on choice occasion $t$ is given in Eq. (3.1). Since $\varepsilon_{njt}$, as a type I extreme value, is *i.i.d.* over choice occasions, individuals, and alternatives, the integral simplifies to a closed-form expression:

$$P_{nit} = \frac{\exp(V_{nit})}{\sum_{j=1}^{J} \exp\left(V_{njt}\right)}.$$

If the representative utility is specified to be linear in parameters, such that $V_{njt} = \mathbf{x}'_{njt}\boldsymbol{\beta}$, as in Eq. (3.3), then:

$$P_{nit} = \frac{\exp(\mathbf{x}'_{nit}\boldsymbol{\beta})}{\sum_{j=1}^{J} \exp\left(\mathbf{x}'_{njt}\boldsymbol{\beta}\right)}. \tag{3.12}$$

According to Eq. (3.12), the probability for each alternative is always between zero and one, making it a valid probability measure. Additionally, the sum of probabilities across all alternatives equals one, satisfying the requirement that the total probability distribution covers all potential outcomes. This property is essential for ensuring the model's consistency and making it suitable for representing choice behaviour in discrete choice analyses.

The MNL model is considered restrictive for several reasons. First, it can only account for observed sources of preference heterogeneity, meaning it can only handle preference variation linked to the observed characteristics of the decision-maker (as specified in Eq. (3.9)). Any unobserved, random preference variation that cannot be associated with these observed characteristics remains unaccounted for in MNL models.

Second, the MNL model assumes proportional substitution across alternatives, also known as the *independence from irrelevant alternatives* (IIA) property. While this assumption may be reasonable in some choice occasions, it is inappropriate in others. A well-known example illustrating this limitation is the red-bus-blue-bus problem (Train 2009, p. 46). In this example, initially, the car and red bus each have a 50% probability of being chosen. Introducing a blue bus, identical to the red bus in all aspects but colour, splits the probabilities into roughly 33% car, 33% red bus, and 33% blue bus—unrealistically increasing the total bus share to 66%. Due to the IIA property, adding a similar alternative (a blue bus to a red bus) artificially inflates the probability of selecting a bus, effectively doubling it over other options and forcing proportional substitution regardless of how alike they are.

Third, the MNL model is restrictive because the unobserved factors $\varepsilon_{njt}$ are assumed to be independent over choice occasions in repeated choice occasions. Consequently, the model cannot accommodate the dynamics associated with unobserved factors, similar to the issue of autoregression in classical linear regression models.

### *3.2.1 Maximum Likelihood Estimation of MNL*

Let us assume that the sample is drawn exogenously and that the explanatory variables $\mathbf{x}_{njt}$ are exogenous to the choice occasion, meaning that the variables entering the representative utility function are independent of the unobserved component of utility, $\varepsilon_{njt}$. Let $i_{nt}$ denote the alternative chosen by decision-maker $n$ in choice occasion $t$. the probability that decision-maker $n$ selects alternative $i_{nt}$ on choice occasion $t$ is given by:

$$P_{ni_{nt}t} = \frac{\exp\left(\mathbf{x}'_{ni_{nt}t}\boldsymbol{\beta}\right)}{\sum_{j=1}^{J}\exp\left(\mathbf{x}'_{njt}\boldsymbol{\beta}\right)}.$$

If $\varepsilon_{njt}$ are independent over choice occasions, the probability of decision-maker $n$'s sequence of choices $\mathbf{i}_n^{\star} = (i_{n1}, i_{n2}, \ldots, i_{nT})$ is:

$$P_n = \prod_{t=1}^{T} P_{ni_{nt}t} = \prod_{t=1}^{T} \frac{\exp\left(\mathbf{x}'_{ni_{nt}t}\boldsymbol{\beta}\right)}{\sum_{j=1}^{J}\exp\left(\mathbf{x}'_{njt}\boldsymbol{\beta}\right)}. \tag{3.13}$$

Assuming that each decision-maker's choices are independent of the choices made by others, using Eq. (3.13), the log-likelihood function can be expressed as:

$$\begin{aligned} \ln L(\beta) &= \ln\left(\prod_{n=1}^{N} P_n\right) \\ &= \ln\left(\prod_{n=1}^{N}\prod_{t=1}^{T} P_{ni_{nt}t}\right) \\ &= \sum_{n=1}^{N} \ln\left(\prod_{t=1}^{T} P_{ni_{nt}t}\right) \\ &= \sum_{n=1}^{N} \ln\left(\prod_{t=1}^{T} \frac{\exp\left(\mathbf{x}'_{ni_{nt}t}\boldsymbol{\beta}\right)}{\sum_{j=1}^{J}\exp\left(\mathbf{x}'_{njt}\boldsymbol{\beta}\right)}\right). \end{aligned} \tag{3.14}$$

The maximum likelihood (ML) estimator is the value of $\boldsymbol{\beta}$ that maximises the log-likelihood function, $\ln L(\boldsymbol{\beta})$. In the case of the MNL model, this maximisation is relatively straightforward because the log-likelihood function is globally concave when utilities are linear in parameters, ensuring a single (global) maximum. See Chap. 8 for more details on ML estimation.

To understand why we use the log-likelihood function, recall that the likelihood (probability) for each choice occasion is, by definition, always between 0 and 1. The natural logarithm of any value in this range is negative, which means that the log-likelihood function is always negative. Given that the natural logarithm is a monotonic transformation (in this case applied to the likelihood function), the maximisation of the log-likelihood function yields the same parameter estimates as the maximisation of the original likelihood function.

Maximising the log-likelihood function is equivalent to finding the value of $\boldsymbol{\beta}$ that produces the highest likelihood of observing the actual choices made by decision-makers. The higher the likelihood, the better the estimated parameters explain the observed choices. In other words, a higher log-likelihood indicates a model that fits the data more closely.

The reason we maximise the natural log of the likelihood rather than the likelihood itself is that it is computationally easier. The log-likelihood transforms the product of probabilities into a sum, simplifying the calculations. This transformation also helps avoid numerical issues, especially when dealing with very small probabilities.

However, the assumption of independent errors in the MNL model is often overly restrictive when there are multiple choice occasions ($T > 1$) and the data have a panel structure, as choices made by the same individual may not be independent. The MNL point estimate of the $\boldsymbol{\beta}$ parameter, as defined above, relies on the assumption of purely cross-sectional data ($T = 1$). When this assumption is used for panel data, the variance–covariance matrix estimation tends towards downward-biased standard errors (Hess and Palma 2019, p. 36).

The panel data structure can still be accounted for in the MNL model using the *sandwich* estimator (Huber 1967), which provides robust standard errors, as shown in Eq. (8.9) (Sect. 8.1). This adjustment corrects the bias introduced by not accounting for the correlation in repeated observations from the same decision-maker.

### 3.2.2 Welfare Measures in MNL

Despite its limitations, the MNL model has numerous advantages, particularly when measuring changes in *consumer surplus* associated with a specific policy or scenario. Under the MNL assumptions, the calculation of consumer surplus for a set of alternatives has a closed-form solution and is straightforward. Assuming one choice occasion ($T = 1$), the expected consumer surplus ($CS_n$) for individual $n$, represents the utility derived from the choice occasion, expressed in monetary units. It can be shown that in an MNL model with utility specified as linear over income:

$$E(CS_n) = \frac{1}{\alpha_n} \ln\left(\sum_{j=1}^{J} \exp(V_{nj})\right) + C$$

where $\alpha_n$ represents the marginal utility of income, and $C$ is an unknown constant reflecting the fact that the absolute level of utility is unobservable (Hanemann 1984). The expected change in consumer surplus resulting from a change in the alternatives and/or the choice set is calculated as

$$\Delta E(CS_n) = \frac{1}{\alpha_n}\left[\ln\left(\sum_{j=1}^{J^1} \exp\left(V_{nj}^1\right)\right) - \ln\left(\sum_{j=1}^{J^0} \exp\left(V_{nj}^0\right)\right)\right],$$

where $J$ represents the set of all available alternatives, $V_{nj}$ denotes the representative utility of alternative $j$, and the superscripts 0 and 1 correspond to conditions before and after the change, respectively. An example of computing this expected change in the context of environmental valuation can be found in Johnston et al. (2024) or Toledo-Gallegos et al. (2022). This expression can be simplified for the case of a marginal change in a non-monetary attribute to derive the widely used *marginal willingness-to-pay* (mWTP) values.

Alternatively, we can consider the *marginal rates of substitution* (MRS). Within the framework of a RUM as defined in Eq. (3.2) and Eq. (3.3), the MRS represents the rate at which individuals are willing to trade off one attribute for another within a given choice context. Specifically, it reflects the change in utility or preference associated with a small incremental change in one attribute relative to a small incremental change in another, while holding the overall utility constant. In this context, the model parameters estimated in an MNL model capture the marginal utility of each attribute, taking into account factors such as the scale of the error term.

To illustrate this, consider the model defined in Eq. (3.4), where $attr1$ represents the percentage of protected native forest in a specific area, and $attr2$ is an additional yearly tax paid to a local authority for forest protection. Suppose we want to determine the rate at which an individual is willing to exchange a one-unit increase in $attr1$ for a one-unit increase in $attr2$. The increase in utility corresponding to one-unit increase in $attr1_{njt}$ is $\Delta V_{njt} = \beta_1$. Since a tax increase is expected to reduce utility, the decrease in utility corresponding to one-unit increase in $attr2_{njt}$ is $\Delta V_{njt} = -\beta_2$. To maintain a constant utility level ($\Delta V_{njt} = 0$), exchanging one unit of attribute $attr1$ requires an adjustment in $attr2$ by the ratio $\beta_1/(-\beta_2)$. This adjustment represents the MRS, expressed as $\beta_1/(-\beta_2)$.

In other words, the MRS is the ratio of the partial derivatives of the utility function with respect to two attributes, which, in the case of Eq. (3.4), can be expressed as:

$$MRS = \frac{\partial U_{njt}/\partial attr1_{njt}}{\partial U_{njt}/\partial attr2_{njt}} = \frac{\beta_1}{\beta_2}.$$

This calculation of the MRS can be applied to any two attributes. However, if the attribute in the denominator is monetary, as it is in our case, the MRS can be converted into a monetary value, expressed in the same units as the monetary attribute. This measure is known as the mWTP, introduced earlier in this chapter. Given the marginal disutility associated with the monetary attribute, the MRS between the one-unit increase in $attr1$ (a 1% increase in protected native forest) and the monetary attribute $attr2$ (additional tax) represents the amount an individual is willing to pay for a 1% increase in protected native forest:

$$mWTP = \frac{\beta_1}{-\beta_2}. \tag{3.15}$$

Thus, mWTP values represent the marginal rates of substitution between a non-monetary and a monetary attribute. In the MNL model, when the monetary attribute is specified linearly, these values are calculated as straightforward negative ratios of the coefficients of the non-monetary and monetary attributes. The mWTP reflects the trade-off between the non-monetary benefit and the monetary cost, taking into account the negative impact of increased costs on utility.

## 3.3 Mixed Logit Models

Mixed logit models extend the traditional multinomial logit framework by introducing flexibility to account for unobserved preference heterogeneity and complex substitution patterns among alternatives. While the multinomial logit model assumes fixed coefficients and IIA, mixed logit models relax these assumptions by allowing for random variations in coefficients and incorporating more complex error structures.

Mixed logit models encompass a variety of modelling approaches, including random parameters models, error component models, or latent class models. Random parameter (RP-MXL) models focus on continuous unobserved heterogeneity by allowing coefficients to vary continuously across the population. Latent class (LC-MXL) models assume discrete unobserved heterogeneity by segmenting the population into distinct classes, each characterised by its own set of parameters and preference structures.

Estimating RP-MXL models involves simulation-based techniques due to the integrals over random parameters in the choice probabilities not having closed-form solutions. Despite their increased computational complexity, these models offer a more flexible tool for analysing choice behaviour.

Let us generalise Eq. (3.3) by assuming that the $\boldsymbol{\beta}$ coefficients are individual-specific, meaning that they differ across individuals. The utility derived from alternative $j$ on choice occasion $t$ by individual $n$ is then defined as:

$$U_{njt} = \mathbf{x}'_{njt}\boldsymbol{\beta}_n + \varepsilon_{njt}, \tag{3.16}$$

where $\varepsilon_{njt}$ remains an $i.i.d.$ type I extreme value distributed error term over choice occasions, individuals, and alternatives and the vector $\mathbf{x}_{njt}$ continues to represent the explanatory variables. If $\boldsymbol{\beta}_n$ were known in Eq. (3.16), the choice probability would follow the standard MNL model, since the errors are still $i.i.d.$ type I extreme value. Thus, given that $\boldsymbol{\beta}_n$ is unknown, the probability that decision maker $n$ selects alternative $i$ on choice occasion $t$, conditional on $\boldsymbol{\beta}_n$, is given by the standard MNL formula:

$$P_n(i|\boldsymbol{\beta}_n) = \frac{\exp(\mathbf{x}'_{nit}\boldsymbol{\beta}_n)}{\sum_{j=1}^{J}\exp\left(\mathbf{x}'_{njt}\boldsymbol{\beta}_n\right)}.$$

If the error terms are independent over choice occasions, the probability that the decision-maker $n$ chooses a sequence of alternatives $\mathbf{i}_n^\star = (i_{n1}, i_{n2}, \ldots, i_{nT})$, conditional on $\boldsymbol{\beta}_n$, is:

$$P_n(i_n^\star|\boldsymbol{\beta}_n) = \prod_{t=1}^{T}\left(\frac{\exp(\mathbf{x}'_{ni_{nt}t}\boldsymbol{\beta}_n)}{\sum_{j=1}^{J}\exp\left(\mathbf{x}'_{njt}\boldsymbol{\beta}_n\right)}\right). \tag{3.17}$$

The $\boldsymbol{\beta}_n$ coefficients are unknown and are assumed to follow a distribution described by a density function $f(\boldsymbol{\beta}|\boldsymbol{\Omega})$, which depends on parameters $\boldsymbol{\Omega}$. In mixed logit models, each element of $\boldsymbol{\beta}_n$ can follow either a continuous or discrete distribution (or a mixture of both), and different elements can follow different types of distributions. Additionally, the elements of $\boldsymbol{\beta}_n$ can be correlated, and some of them can be fixed.

The *unconditional probability* of the sequence of choices is obtained by integrating over all possible values of the unknown parameters. Consequently, the unconditional probability of the sequence of choices $\mathbf{i}_n^\star$ is given by the mixed logit probability formula:

$$P_n\left(\mathbf{i}_n^\star|\boldsymbol{\Omega}\right) = \int P_n\left(\mathbf{i}_n^\star|\boldsymbol{\beta}\right)f(\boldsymbol{\beta}|\boldsymbol{\Omega})d\boldsymbol{\beta}\ . \tag{3.18}$$

The density $f(\boldsymbol{\beta}|\boldsymbol{\Omega})$, which provides the weights, is known as the *mixing distribution*. The mixed logit probability is, therefore, a mixture of the logit formula $P_n\left(\mathbf{i}_n^\star|\boldsymbol{\Omega}\right)$, evaluated at different values of $\boldsymbol{\beta}$, with the weights determined by the density $f(\boldsymbol{\beta}|\boldsymbol{\Omega})$.

McFadden and Train (2000) demonstrated that a mixed logit model can approximate any discrete choice model derived from the RUM framework, regardless of the preference distribution, to any desired level of accuracy. The mixed logit model therefore imposes no inherent theoretical limitations on the choice model or the distribution of preferences. However, in practical applications, the researcher must specify the distribution $f(\boldsymbol{\beta}|\boldsymbol{\Omega})$, and this introduces constraints.

Below, we demonstrate how the specification of the mixing distribution $f(\boldsymbol{\beta}|\boldsymbol{\Omega})$ leads to the derivation of different models, here the MNL, LC-MXL, and RP-MXL models. We consider these examples using a single choice occasion ($T = 1$) for each individual for simplicity.

1. The MNL model is a special case in which the mixing distribution $f(\boldsymbol{\beta}|\boldsymbol{\Omega})$ is degenerate at fixed parameters $\boldsymbol{b}$, meaning that $\Pr(\boldsymbol{\beta} = \boldsymbol{b}) = 1$. In this case, the mixed logit probability simplifies to the standard MNL formula:

$$P_{ni} = \frac{\exp\left(\mathbf{x}_{ni}'\boldsymbol{b}\right)}{\sum_{j=1}^{J}\exp\left(\mathbf{x}_{nj}'\boldsymbol{b}\right)}\ .$$

2. If the mixing distribution $f(\boldsymbol{\beta}|\boldsymbol{\Omega})$ is degenerated at *multiple* discrete values, the mixed logit becomes a latent class (LC-MXL) model. Suppose that $\boldsymbol{\beta}$ can take on two possible values, denoted as $\boldsymbol{b}_1$ and $\boldsymbol{b}_2$, where $\Pr(\boldsymbol{\beta} = \boldsymbol{b}_1) = \pi_1$ and $\Pr(\boldsymbol{\beta} = \boldsymbol{b}_2) = \pi_2$, with the choice probabilities defined as follows:

$$P_{ni} = \pi_1\frac{\exp\left(\mathbf{x}_{ni}'\boldsymbol{b}_1\right)}{\sum_{j=1}^{J}\exp\left(\mathbf{x}_{nj}'\boldsymbol{b}_1\right)} + \pi_2\frac{\exp\left(\mathbf{x}_{ni}'\boldsymbol{b}_2\right)}{\sum_{j=1}^{J}\exp\left(\mathbf{x}_{nj}'\boldsymbol{b}_2\right)}\ .$$

3. If the mixing distribution $f(\boldsymbol{\beta}|\boldsymbol{\Omega})$ is specified as continuous, the mixed logit becomes a random parameters (RP-MXL) model. In most applications referred to as mixed logit, RP-MXL models are used. In these models, the density of the vector $\boldsymbol{\beta}$ can be specified, for example, as a multivariate normal distribution with mean $\boldsymbol{b}$ and variance–covariance matrix $\boldsymbol{\Sigma}$. In this case, the probability of individual $n$ choosing alternative $i$ is given by:

$$P_{ni} = \int \frac{\exp\left(\mathbf{x}'_{ni}\boldsymbol{\beta}\right)}{\sum_{j=1}^{J}\exp\left(\mathbf{x}'_{nj}\boldsymbol{\beta}\right)} f(\boldsymbol{\beta}\,|\,\boldsymbol{b},\boldsymbol{\Sigma})\,d\boldsymbol{\beta}\;.$$

With the three examples above, we have shown how the specification of the mixing distribution defines different mixed logit models. A key advantage of these models, which allow for heterogeneity in preferences, is the possibility of relaxing the IIA assumption and flexible substitution patterns. Next, we will go over the RP-MXL and LC-MXL models in more detail and walk you through their estimation.

### *3.3.1 Random Parameters Mixed Logit*

This subsection introduces the RP-MXL model as a flexible framework for analysing discrete choices that acknowledges and incorporates individual-level heterogeneity. In contrast to models with fixed parameters, the RP-MXL model specifies distributions of parameter values across individuals, providing not only mean effects but also measures of variability in preferences.

The utility in the random parameters mixed logit (RP-MXL) model is given by:

$$U_{njt} = \mathbf{x}'_{njt}\boldsymbol{\beta}_n + \varepsilon_{njt}, \tag{3.19}$$

where $\boldsymbol{\beta}_n$ are distributed according to the density function $f(\boldsymbol{\beta}|\boldsymbol{\Omega})$. To estimate this model, we need to specify $f(\cdot)$ and estimate the parameters $\boldsymbol{\Omega}$.

Defining an appropriate distribution for the coefficients is a nontrivial task that often requires careful consideration and theoretical justification. The complexity arises partly from the need to strike a balance between model flexibility and tractability, as overly complex distributions can render estimation computationally burdensome (Train 2009).

Moreover, selecting a particular distribution may impose certain restrictions on the shape or support of the parameter space, potentially affecting the ability to represent true underlying heterogeneity (Hess and Rose 2012). Empirical testing and model selection criteria can provide guidance, but these approaches still rely heavily on analyst judgment and experience in order to identify reasonable assumptions (Fiebig et al. 2010). Ultimately, defining distributions often involves iterative experimentation and sensitivity analyses, drawing upon both theoretical insights and practical considerations (Greene and Hensher 2010).

The distributions of monetary and non-monetary attributes are often assumed to be normal. The distribution of mWTP for an attribute is typically inferred from the distribution of the negative ratio of coefficients for the non-monetary and monetary attributes (see Eq. (3.15)). Since the monetary coefficient appears in the denominator of Eq. (3.15), its distribution plays a critical role in determining the distribution of mWTP.

Daly, Hess, and Train (2012) show that some commonly used distributions for the monetary attributes in RP-MXL models, such as the normal, truncated normal, uniform, and triangular distributions, can result in infinite moments for the distribution of mWTP. In practice, any distribution with support over zero is problematic to use in the denominator. They propose several solutions to this problem, including using the log-normal distribution for the coefficient of the monetary attribute, or re-parameterising the model in the WTP space (Train and Weeks 2005). Due to the random nature of the coefficients, mWTP values must be simulated. This topic is covered in detail in Chap. 10.

We will continue with the necessary steps of estimating an RP-MXL model, starting by defining 1) the unconditional probability of an observed choice sequence and 2) the log-likelihood function. As defined in Eq. (3.18), the unconditional probability of a given sequence of choices $\mathbf{i}_n^\star = (i_{n1}, i_{n2}, \ldots, i_{nT})$ for individual $n$ is defined as:

$$P_n\left(\mathbf{i}_n^\star|\boldsymbol{\Omega}\right) = \int \prod_{t=1}^{T} \left( \frac{\exp(\mathbf{x}'_{ni_{nt}t}\boldsymbol{\beta})}{\sum_{j=1}^{J} \exp\left(\mathbf{x}'_{njt}\boldsymbol{\beta}\right)} \right) f(\boldsymbol{\beta}|\boldsymbol{\Omega}) d\boldsymbol{\beta},$$

and the log-likelihood function of the RP-MXL model is defined as:

$$\begin{aligned} \ln L(\beta) &= \ln\left(\prod_{n=1}^{N} P_n\left(\mathbf{i}_n^\star|\boldsymbol{\Omega}\right)\right) \\ &= \sum_{n=1}^{N} \ln\left(\int \prod_{t=1}^{T} \left( \frac{\exp\left(\mathbf{x}'_{ni_{nt}t}\boldsymbol{\beta}\right)}{\sum_{j=1}^{J} \exp\left(\mathbf{x}'_{njt}\boldsymbol{\beta}\right)} \right) f(\boldsymbol{\beta}|\boldsymbol{\Omega}) d\boldsymbol{\beta}\right). \end{aligned} \tag{3.20}$$

Since there is no closed form solution to the likelihood function, the probability of a given sequence of choices is approximated as follows:

1. For each individual $n$, draw $R$ values of $\boldsymbol{\beta}_{nr} (r = 1, 2, ..., R)$ from the distribution $f(\boldsymbol{\beta}|\boldsymbol{\Omega})$, which represents the specified density of the random coefficients.
2. For each draw $\boldsymbol{\beta}_{nr}$, compute the probability of the observed choice sequence $P_n\left(\mathbf{i}_n^\star|\boldsymbol{\beta}_{nr}\right) = \prod_{t=1}^{T}\left[\exp(\mathbf{x}'_{ni_{nt}t}\boldsymbol{\beta}_{nr}) / \sum_{j=1}^{J} \exp\left(\mathbf{x}'_{njt}\boldsymbol{\beta}_{nr}\right)\right]$.
3. Finally, average these probabilities obtained in the previous step to approximate the overall probability of the sequence of choices:

$$\overline{P}_n\left(\mathbf{i}_n^\star\right) = \frac{1}{R} \sum_{r=1}^{R} P_n\left(\mathbf{i}_n^\star|\boldsymbol{\beta}_{nr}\right).$$

The average $\overline{P}_n(\mathbf{i}_n^\star)$ approximates the integral defined in Eq. (3.20). This averaged value serves as the simulated probability, providing an estimate of the unconditional probability of the observed choice sequence.

The log-likelihood function of an RP-MXL model defined in Eq. (3.20) is, therefore, approximated by its simulated counterpart:

$$\ln L_S(\boldsymbol{\Omega}) = \sum_{n=1}^{N} \ln\left(\frac{1}{R}\sum_{r=1}^{R}\left(\prod_{t=1}^{T}\left(\frac{\exp\left(\mathbf{x}'_{ni_{nt}}\boldsymbol{\beta}_{nr}\right)}{\sum_{j=1}^{J}\exp\left(\mathbf{x}'_{njt}\boldsymbol{\beta}_{nr}\right)}\right)\right)\right).$$

As mentioned above, an RP-MXL model allows each individual $n$ to have their own parameters $\boldsymbol{\beta}_n$ that come from a population (unconditional) distribution, typically assumed normal, lognormal, or another flexible distribution. The *unconditional distribution* is, therefore, the distribution of parameters before accounting for any specific individual's choice data. In a Bayesian interpretation, it can be viewed as the *prior* or, in frequentist terms, as the population-level distribution derived from all sampled individuals. By contrast, *conditional distributions* focus on individual-specific parameters refined by observed choices. In a Bayesian context, it corresponds to the *posterior* distribution.

Let the *conditional distribution* of the parameter $\boldsymbol{\beta}$, given the sequence of choices, be denoted as $h(\cdot)$. The *unconditional distribution* of the parameters $\boldsymbol{\beta}$, which is independent of any specific sequence of choices, is represented by $f(\cdot)$.

As defined in Eq. (3.17), the conditional probability (conditional on specific values of $\boldsymbol{\beta}$) that the decision maker $n$ will make a sequence of choices $\mathbf{i}_n^\star = (i_{n1}, i_{n2}, \ldots, i_{nT})$ is given by:

$$P_n(\mathbf{i}_n^\star|\boldsymbol{\beta}) = \prod_{t=1}^{T}\left(\frac{\exp(\mathbf{x}'_{ni_{nt}t}\boldsymbol{\beta})}{\sum_{j=1}^{J}\exp\left(\mathbf{x}'_{njt}\boldsymbol{\beta}\right)}\right).$$

The unconditional choice probability (unconditional on specific values of $\boldsymbol{\beta}$, but conditional on their distribution parameters $\boldsymbol{\Omega}$) of the sequence of choices is, therefore, obtained by integrating over all possible values of the unknown parameters, as shown in Eq. (3.18):

$$P_n(\mathbf{i}_n^\star|\boldsymbol{\Omega}) = \int P_n(\mathbf{i}_n^\star|\boldsymbol{\beta})f(\boldsymbol{\beta}|\boldsymbol{\Omega})d\boldsymbol{\beta}.$$

According to Bayes' rule:

$$P(A|B)\cdot P(B) = P(B|A)\cdot P(A),$$

So we get:

$$h(\boldsymbol{\beta}|\mathbf{i}_n^\star, \boldsymbol{\Omega})\cdot P_n(\mathbf{i}_n^\star|\boldsymbol{\Omega}) = P_n(\mathbf{i}_n^\star|\boldsymbol{\beta})\cdot f(\boldsymbol{\beta}|\boldsymbol{\Omega}).$$

Therefore, the conditional distribution of $\boldsymbol{\beta}$ is given by:

$$h(\boldsymbol{\beta}|\mathbf{i}_n^\star, \boldsymbol{\Omega}) = \frac{P_n(\mathbf{i}_n^\star|\boldsymbol{\beta}) \cdot f(\boldsymbol{\beta}|\boldsymbol{\Omega})}{P_n(\mathbf{i}_n^\star|\boldsymbol{\Omega})}.$$

An interesting value from an interpretative point of view is the mean of $\boldsymbol{\beta}$ in the subpopulation that selects the same sequence of choices when confronted with $\mathbf{x}_n$. The mean is defined as

$$\bar{\boldsymbol{\beta}}_n = \int \boldsymbol{\beta} \cdot h(\boldsymbol{\beta}|\mathbf{i}_n^\star, \boldsymbol{\Omega})\, d\boldsymbol{\beta}\ ,$$

that is,

$$\bar{\boldsymbol{\beta}}_n = \frac{\int \boldsymbol{\beta} \cdot P_n(\mathbf{i}_n^\star|\boldsymbol{\beta}) \cdot f(\boldsymbol{\beta}|\boldsymbol{\Omega})\, d\boldsymbol{\beta}}{\int P_n(\mathbf{i}_n^\star|\boldsymbol{\beta}) f(\boldsymbol{\beta}|\boldsymbol{\Omega}) d\boldsymbol{\beta}}.$$

The integral does not have a closed-form solution, so its value must be approximated through simulation as follows:

$$\bar{\boldsymbol{\beta}}_n \approx \sum_{r=1}^{R} \left( \frac{P_n(\mathbf{i}_n^\star|\boldsymbol{\beta}_{nr})}{\sum_{r=1}^{R} P_n(\mathbf{i}_n^\star|\boldsymbol{\beta}_{nr})} \right) \cdot \boldsymbol{\beta}_{nr}. \tag{3.21}$$

This distribution should not be interpreted as the conditional distribution of preferences across individuals. Instead, it represents the distribution of the means of the conditional distributions (or conditional means) across individuals (Hess 2010).

In summary, the RP-MXL model provides estimates of the distribution of taste parameters across individuals, capturing preference heterogeneity. On one hand it can deliver the unconditional (population-level) distribution capturing heterogeneity in preferences, and on the other hand the conditional (individual-specific) distribution can refine a particular individual's parameters by incorporating their observed choices.

The RP-MXL model is highly flexible, but poses several challenges in both specification and estimation. These challenges include the complexity of the model structure, the high dimensionality of the parameter space, the risk of encountering local maxima during estimation (see Chaps. 8 and 9), the need for high-quality data, and the computationally intensive nature of the estimation procedures.

### 3.3.2 *Latent Class Mixed Logit*

The LC-MXL model provides insights into different preference patterns within the population, allowing researchers to segment individuals into distinct, meaningful subgroups based on their choice behaviour. This segmentation can reveal variations in preferences that may not be apparent when analysing the population as a whole, offering a more nuanced understanding of decision-making processes.

The LC-MXL specification is particularly useful when the population is believed to be divided into $Q$ segments (classes), each exhibiting its own choice behaviour or preferences. For instance, in the case of two classes ($Q = 2$), two attributes, and three alternatives, the utilities can be defined as:

- Class 1

$$
\begin{aligned}
U_{c_1,n1t} &= ASC_{c_1,1} + \beta_{c_1,1}\, attr1_{n1t} + \beta_{c_1,2}\, attr2_{n1t} + \varepsilon_{n1t} \\
U_{c_1,n2t} &= ASC_{c_1,2} + \beta_{c_1,1}\, attr1_{n2t} + \beta_{c_1,2}\, attr2_{n2t} + \varepsilon_{n2t} \\
U_{c_1,n3t} &= \qquad\qquad\; \beta_{c_1,1}\, attr1_{n3t} + \beta_{c_1,2}\, attr2_{n3t} + \varepsilon_{n3t}
\end{aligned}
$$

- Class 2

$$
\begin{aligned}
U_{c_2,n1t} &= ASC_{c_2,1} + \beta_{c_2,1}\, attr1_{n1t} + \beta_{c_2,2}\, attr2_{n1t} + \varepsilon_{n1t} \\
U_{c_2,n2t} &= ASC_{c_2,2} + \beta_{c_2,1}\, attr1_{n2t} + \beta_{c_2,2}\, attr2_{n2t} + \varepsilon_{n2t} \\
U_{c_2,n3t} &= \qquad\qquad\; \beta_{c_2,1}\, attr1_{n3t} + \beta_{c_2,2}\, attr2_{n3t} + \varepsilon_{n3t}
\end{aligned}
$$

These two models could be seen as two separate MNL models, but they are related through the expression below. We assume that individuals can be classified into a set of $Q$ classes, with each class characterised by its own class-specific utility parameters $\boldsymbol{\beta}_c$. Given membership in class $c_q$, the probability of individual $n$'s sequence of choices is given by:

$$
P_{n|c_q} = P_n\left(\mathbf{i}_n^\star | c_q\right) = \prod_{t=1}^{T} \frac{\exp\left(\mathbf{x}'_{ni_{nt}t}\boldsymbol{\beta}_{c_q}\right)}{\sum_{j=1}^{J} \exp\left(\mathbf{x}'_{njt}\boldsymbol{\beta}_{c_q}\right)},
$$

where $\mathbf{i}_n^\star = (i_{n1}, i_{n2}, \ldots, i_{nT})$ is the sequence of choices over $T$ choice occasions for individual $n$.

The LC-MXL framework assumes that class membership is not directly observed but is instead latent. If the probability that individual $n$ belongs to a latent class $c_q$ is denoted as $\pi_{c_q,n}$, then the unconditional probability of a sequence of choices can be obtained by taking the expectation over all $Q$ classes, i.e.

$$
P_n\left(\mathbf{i}_n^\star\right) = \sum_{q=1}^{Q} \pi_{c_q,n} \prod_{t=1}^{T} \frac{\exp\left(\mathbf{x}'_{ni_{nt}t}\boldsymbol{\beta}_{c_q}\right)}{\sum_{j=1}^{J} \exp\left(\mathbf{x}'_{njt}\boldsymbol{\beta}_{c_q}\right)}.
$$

The unconditional probability of a sequence of choices for our case with two classes ($Q = 2$) is:

$$P_n\left(\mathbf{i}_n^{\star}\right) = \pi_{c_1,n} \prod_{t=1}^{T} \frac{\exp\left(\mathbf{x}'_{ni_{nt}t}\boldsymbol{\beta}_{c_1}\right)}{\sum_{j=1}^{J} \exp\left(\mathbf{x}'_{njt}\boldsymbol{\beta}_{c_1}\right)} + \pi_{c_2,n} \prod_{t=1}^{T} \frac{\exp\left(\mathbf{x}'_{ni_{nt}t}\boldsymbol{\beta}_{c_2}\right)}{\sum_{j=1}^{J} \exp\left(\mathbf{x}'_{njt}\boldsymbol{\beta}_{c_2}\right)}.$$

The class assignment probabilities $\pi_{c_q,n}$ in LC-MXL models are typically modelled using a logit structure, where class membership is a function of socio-demographic variables and their corresponding parameters $\lambda_{c_q}$, along with class-specific constants $\mu_{c_q}$ for class $c_q$. In our case, the probability of belonging to a specific class is given by a multinomial logit probability.

The probabilities $\pi_{c_q,n}$, for $q = 1, 2$, which depend on socio-demographic factors like age, gender and education, can be expressed as:

$$\pi_{c_q,n} = \frac{\exp\left(\mu_{c_q} + \lambda_{c_q,1} age_n + \lambda_{c_q,2} gender_n + \lambda_{c_q,3} education_n\right)}{\sum_{s=1}^{2} \exp\left(\mu_{c_s} + \lambda_{c_s,1} age_n + \lambda_{c_s,2} gender_n + \lambda_{c_s,3} education_n\right)}.$$

This approach yields Q sets of parameters corresponding to each latent class. However, to ensure the identification of the model, one set of parameters must be fixed, and is usually set to zero (e.g. $\mu_{c_1} = 0, \lambda_{c_1,1} = 0, \lambda_{c_1,2} = 0, \lambda_{c_1,3} = 0$). The sign of the remaining parameters $\lambda_{c_2,1}$, $\lambda_{c_2,1}$, and $\lambda_{c_2,3}$ indicates whether an increase in the respective variable will raise or lower the probability of belonging to a particular class. For example, a positive value of $\lambda_{c_2,1}$ implies that the variable *age* has a positive impact on membership to class 2 relative to class 1, meaning that older individuals are more likely to be assigned to class 2 rather than class 1.

In general, the assignment of probabilities $\pi_{c_q,n}$ depends on exogenous individual characteristics $\mathbf{z}_n$ and are defined as follows:

$$\pi_{c_q,n} = \frac{\exp\left(\mu_{c_q} + \mathbf{z}'_n \boldsymbol{\lambda}_{c_q}\right)}{\sum_{s=1}^{Q} \exp\left(\mu_{c_s} + \mathbf{z}'_n \boldsymbol{\lambda}_{c_s}\right)}, \tag{3.22}$$

where $\mu_{c_s}$ and $\boldsymbol{\lambda}_{c_s}$, ($s = 1,2$) are parameters to be estimated. As noted before, to ensure the identification of the model, one set of parameters is normalised to zero.

It is also common to estimate the LC-MXL model using only the constants of the class membership probabilities, $\mu_{c_q}$. In this case, the explanatory variables $\mathbf{z}_n$ are excluded, and the unconditional class membership probabilities depend solely on these constants. As a result, the class membership probabilities are the same for all individuals regardless of their specific characteristics. This approach essentially treats the population as homogeneous in terms of the likelihood of class membership.

**ⓘ LC-MXL is not a classification method**

It is important to clarify that the LC-MXL model is not a traditional class segmentation model. Rather than assuming that individuals belong to clearly defined, observable classes, the model operates under the premise that the underlying parameters—representing preferences—jointly follow a discrete distribution. This implies that class membership is latent, or unobserved, and is inferred from the data

In this framework, the preferences and behaviours of individuals are assumed to cluster around a finite number of distinct sets of parameters (classes), with each set representing a unique pattern of preferences within the population. Instead of assigning individuals to a specific class, the model estimates the probability of membership in each class for every individual, with the overall probability being distributed across all classes

The likelihood of a given choice sequence for individual $n$ is calculated as the weighted average of the class-specific contributions, with the weights $\pi_{c_q,n}$ representing the probabilities of belonging to each class:

$$\begin{aligned} P_n\left(\mathbf{i}_n^\star\right) &= \sum_{q=1}^{Q} \pi_{c_q,n} P_n\left(\mathbf{i}_n^\star | c_q\right) \\ &= \sum_{q=1}^{Q} \pi_{c_q,n} \prod_{t=1}^{T} P_n\left(i_{nt} | c_q\right). \end{aligned}$$

The log-likelihood function for the sample is given by:

$$\begin{aligned} \ln L &= \sum_{i=1}^{N} \ln\left[\sum_{q=1}^{Q} \pi_{c_q,n} \prod_{t=1}^{T} P_n\left(i_{nt} | c_q\right)\right] \\ &= \sum_{i=1}^{N} \ln\left[\sum_{q=1}^{Q}\left(\frac{\exp\left(\mu_{c_q} + \mathbf{z}_n'\boldsymbol{\lambda}_{c_q}\right)}{\sum_{s=1}^{Q}\exp\left(\mu_{c_s} + \mathbf{z}_n'\boldsymbol{\lambda}_{c_s}\right)}\right)\left(\prod_{t=1}^{T}\frac{\exp\left(\mathbf{x}_{ni_{nt}t}'\boldsymbol{\beta}_{c_q}\right)}{\sum_{j=1}^{J}\exp\left(\mathbf{x}_{njt}'\boldsymbol{\beta}_{c_q}\right)}\right)\right]. \end{aligned} \quad (3.23)$$

Maximising the log-likelihood function defined in Eq. (3.23) with respect to the $Q$ structural parameter vectors, $\beta_{c_q}$, and the $Q-1$ latent class parameters $(\mu_{c_q}, \boldsymbol{\lambda}_{c_q})$ is a standard problem in maximum likelihood estimation. However, the number of classes, $Q$, is not a parameter of the model and therefore cannot be estimated directly. Hypotheses about $Q$ cannot be tested directly; instead, the number of classes must be specified a priori by the analyst. To determine the appropriate number of classes, information criteria defined in Eqs. (3.27), (3.28), (3.29) and (3.30) are commonly used.

The mWTP values, key outputs in the LC-MXL model, are defined as:

$$mWTP_n = \pi_{c_1,n} mWTP_{Class1} + \pi_{c_2,n} mWTP_{Class2} \ ,$$

where the class allocation probabilities are defined in Eq. (3.22). If we estimate $\mu_{c_q}$ and $\lambda_{c_q}$, the unconditional estimates of the class probabilities are given by:

$$\widehat{\pi}_{c_q,n} = \frac{\exp\left(\widehat{\mu}_{c_q} + \mathbf{z}_n'\widehat{\boldsymbol{\lambda}}_{c_q}\right)}{\sum_{s=1}^{Q}\exp\left(\widehat{\mu}_{c_s} + \mathbf{z}_n'\widehat{\boldsymbol{\lambda}}_{c_s}\right)}.$$

Similar to the case of the RP-MXL model, Bayes' theorem can be used to obtain an individual-specific posterior estimate of the latent class probabilities, which is conditioned on the sequence of choices:

$$\widehat{\pi}_{c_q,n|\mathbf{i}_n^\star} = \frac{\widehat{P}_{n|c_q}\widehat{\pi}_{c_q,n}}{\sum_{s=1}^{Q}\widehat{P}_{n|c_s}\widehat{\pi}_{c_s,n}}. \tag{3.24}$$

These conditional probabilities $\widehat{\pi}_{c_q,n|i_n^\star}$ differ from the unconditional class probabilities $\widehat{\pi}_{c_q,n}$. These posterior class probabilities incorporate individual-specific choice data, whereas the unconditional class probabilities only reflect prior knowledge about the distribution of classes in the population. By conditioning on each individual's observed sequence of choices, the posterior probabilities update and refine what is known about that individual's likely class membership. Consequently, these conditional estimates differ from the unconditional probabilities, because they are tailored to the information revealed by the individual's actual choices.

The main differences between the LC-MXL and RP-MXL models lie in how they represent preference heterogeneity, handle parameter variation, and interpret parameters, as well as the complexity involved in estimation. The choice between these models depends on the specific research objectives, characteristics of the data, and assumptions about the underlying preference heterogeneity.

Greene and Hensher (2003) compare the RP-MXL and LC-MXL models, and conclude that each model offers a distinct approach to capturing unobserved heterogeneity. They note that there is no clear "winner" between the two; instead, the choice should be guided by the specific context and research objectives. The LC-MXL model offers a specification that frees analysts from making strong or potentially unsupported distributional assumptions about individual heterogeneity. However, it requires the number of classes to be determined exogenously. This topic will be discussed further in Chap. 9. In contrast, the RP-MXL model offers significant flexibility in specifying individual unobserved heterogeneity, although this flexibility requires a careful selection of distributional assumptions, which can be a complex task.

## 3.4 Goodness of Fit Measures

In discrete choice models grounded in RUM, such as MNL, RP-MXL or LC-MXL models, there is no universally accepted goodness-of-fit measure analogous to the $R^2$ in ordinary least squares regression (Ben-Akiva and Lerman 1985; McFadden 1974; Train 2009). Instead, researchers typically evaluate model performance relative to a benchmark log-likelihood that embodies minimal explanatory structure, such as the null (or equal-share) model or a constants-only model reflecting observed choice shares.

The percentage improvement in the estimated model's log-likelihood over this baseline forms the basis of pseudo-$R^2$ statistics, providing a comparative index of how well the estimated model explains observed choices. While higher values indicate better fit relative to the baseline, there is no absolute threshold corresponding to the conventional $R^2$ in linear regression. Consequently, assessing goodness of fit in RUM-based models is typically guided by these relative measures, along with additional information criteria and out-of-sample predictive performance (Train 2009).

McFadden (1974) introduced the measures reviewed in this section, based on the log-likelihood function of the estimated model, which have become some of the most commonly-used measures for assessing the goodness of fit of discrete choice models (Veall and Zimmermann 1996). The first measure, $\rho^2(C)$ is defined as:

$$\rho^2(C) = 1 - \frac{\ln L\left(\widehat{\boldsymbol{\beta}}\right)}{\ln L_C}, \tag{3.25}$$

where $\ln L\left(\widehat{\boldsymbol{\beta}}\right)$ is the log-likelihood of the full model, and $\ln L_C$ is the log-likelihood of a model in which all coefficients, except the alternative specific constants, are set to zero. To account for the number of explanatory variables $K$, Ben-Akiva and Lerman (1985) proposed an adjusted version of this measure, similar to the adjusted $R^2$ used in linear regressions:

$$\rho_a^2(C) = 1 - \frac{\ln L\left(\widehat{\boldsymbol{\beta}}\right) - K}{\ln L_C}. \tag{3.26}$$

These indicators cannot be interpreted in the same way as the classical coefficient of determination, $R^2$, in linear regressions, as they are based on the value of the log-likelihood function rather than the proportion of explained variance of the dependent variable. Various modifications of these measures are discussed and applied in Sect. 9.2.1 of this book.

While these measures does not represent the proportion of variance explained, higher values indicate better model fit. We usually interpret their values as a relative measure of model performance, comparing models or evaluating whether adding variables meaningfully enhances explanatory power.

Another goodness of fit indicator, proposed by Akaike (1973), is the Akaike Information Criterion (AIC). This statistical measure is used to compare and select the best-fitting model from a set of candidate models. The AIC balances model fit and complexity by penalising models with more parameters, thus helping us avoid overfitting. Typically, the model with the lowest AIC value is preferred, as it indicates a better trade-off between simplicity and accuracy. The AIC is defined as:

$$AIC = -2\ln L\left(\widehat{\boldsymbol{\beta}}\right) + 2K. \tag{3.27}$$

The AIC3 is a variant of AIC that imposes a stricter balance between model fit and complexity, making it especially useful when preventing overfitting is a priority. It is defined as:

$$AIC3 = -2\ln L\left(\widehat{\boldsymbol{\beta}}\right) + 3K. \tag{3.28}$$

The main difference is that AIC3 applies a heavier penalty for models with more parameters compared to the standard AIC. The CAIC (Consistent Akaike Information Criterion), a generalisation proposed by Bozdogan (1987), further adjusts the original AIC to account for additional model complexity, aiming for better model selection consistency, especially with larger sample sizes or high-dimensional models. It is defined as:

$$CAIC = -2\ln L\left(\widehat{\boldsymbol{\beta}}\right) + K(1 + \ln(NT)), \tag{3.29}$$

where $N$ represents the number of individuals and $T$ is the number of choice occasions faced by each individual.

The Bayesian Information Criterion (BIC), proposed by Schwartz (1978), is another measure used for model selection, similar to the AIC. Like the AIC, the BIC evaluates model fit while penalising the number of parameters, but it imposes a stronger penalty, particularly with larger sample sizes. This makes the BIC more conservative, often favouring simpler models compared to the AIC. The key difference between the two is that while AIC is rooted in information theory, the BIC is based on Bayesian probability, taking into account both the likelihood of the model and the prior probability of the model structure. The BIC is defined as:

$$BIC = -2\ln L\left(\widehat{\boldsymbol{\beta}}\right) + K\ln(NT). \tag{3.30}$$

It is important to note that the goodness of fit measures presented here are not standardised, and can, therefore, only be used to compare different models evaluated on the same dataset. In this context, a smaller (more negative) value indicates a better balance between model fit and complexity, with a lower value suggesting a better-fitting model. However, because these criteria depend on the specific data and model structures, they should not be used to compare models across different datasets or studies.

## 3.5 Key Takeaways

- The RUM model defines the underlying utilities determining choice behaviour, and serves as the foundational basis for most choice modelling frameworks.
- Different assumptions about preferences influence the predicted likelihood of selecting an alternative, which is why we see different choice probabilities across different types of models.
- We are inherently limited in observing the complete internal decision-making process of individuals. From analyst's perspective, this is reflected by a stochastic component in the decision-making process, which must be accounted for in DCE models.
- Moving beyond the MNL model allows for more flexible approaches, such as the RP-MXL or LC-MXL models, which can better capture unobserved heterogeneity, complex substitution patterns, and repeated choice data.
- The RP-MXL and LC-MXL models take distinct approaches to capture unobserved heterogeneity, with the former offering flexibility through customisable distributional assumptions and the latter relying on latent classes to avoid strong assumptions. The choice between them depends on the research context and objectives, as each model has strengths suited to different analytical needs.
- Goodness of fit measures can help us choose the best model for our data and research context. We review the main measures used in the DCE literature, including the $\rho^2(C)$, AIC, BIC, and variants of these measures.

## Bibliography

Akaike H (1973) Information theory and extension of the maximum likelihood principle. In: Petrov BC (ed) Second international symposium on information theory. Akademiai Kiado, Budapest, pp 267–281

Ben-Akiva ME, Lerman SR (1985) Discrete Choice analysis: theory and application to travel demand, vol 9. MIT Press

Bozdogan H (1987) Model selection and Akaike's Information Criterion (AIC): the general theory and its analytical extensions. Psychometrika 52:345–370. https://doi.org/10.1007/BF02294361

Daly A, Hess S, Train K (2012) Assuring finite moments for willingness to pay in random coefficient models. Transportation 39(1):19–31. https://doi.org/10.1007/s11116-011-9331-3

Fiebig DG, Keane MP, Louviere J, Wasi N (2010) The generalized multinomial logit model: accounting for scale and coefficient heterogeneity. Mark Sci 29(3):393–421. https://doi.org/10.1287/mksc.1090.0508

Greene WH, Hensher DA (2003) A latent class model for discrete choice analysis: contrasts with mixed logit. Transp Res B Methodol 37(8):681–698. https://doi.org/10.1016/S0191-2615(02)00046-2

Greene WH, Hensher DA (2010) Modeling ordered choices: a primer. Cambridge University Press. https://doi.org/10.1017/CBO9780511845062

Hanemann WM (1984) Welfare evaluations in contingent valuation experiments with discrete responses. Am J Agr Econ 66(3):332–341. https://doi.org/10.2307/1240800

Hess S (2010) Conditional parameter estimates from Mixed Logit models: distributional assumptions and a free software tool. J Choice Model 3(2):134–152. https://doi.org/10.1016/S1755-5345(13)70039-3

Hess S, Palma D (2019) Apollo: a flexible, powerful and customisable freeware package for choice model estimation and application. J Choice Model 32:100170. https://doi.org/10.1016/j.jocm.2019.100170

Hess S, Rose JM (2012) Can scale and coefficient heterogeneity be separated in random coefficients models? Transportation 39(6):1225–1239. https://doi.org/10.1007/s11116-012-9394-9

Huber P (1967) The Behavior of Maximum Likelihood Estimation Under Nonstandard Conditions. In: LeCam L, Neyman J (eds) Proceedings of the Fifth Berkeley Symposium on Mathematical Statistics and Probability. University of California Press, pp 221–233

Johnston RJ, Börger T, Hanley N et al (2024) Consequences of omitting non-lethal wildlife impacts from stated preference scenarios. J Environ Econ Manag 126:103011. https://doi.org/10.1016/j.jeem.2024.103011

Long JS (1997) Regression models for categorical and limited dependent variables, 1st edn. SAGE Publications, Thousand Oaks

Marschak J (1960) Binary choice constraints on random utility indications. In: Arrow K (ed) Stanford symposium on mathematical methods in the social sciences. Stanford University Press, Stanford, pp 312–329

McFadden D (1974) Conditional logit analysis of qualitative choice behaviour. In: Zarembka P (ed) Frontiers in Econometrics. Academic Press, New York, pp 105–142

McFadden D, Train K (2000) Mixed MNL models for discrete response. J Appl Econom 15(5):447–470. https://doi.org/10.1002/1099-1255(200009/10)15:5%3c447::AID-JAE570%3e3.0.CO;2-1

Oehlmann M, Meyerhoff J, Mariel P, Weller P (2017) Uncovering context-induced status quo effects in choice experiments. J Environ Econ Manag 81:59–73. https://doi.org/10.1016/j.jeem.2016.09.002

Schwartz G (1978) Estimating the dimension of a model. Annals of Statistics 6:461–464. https://cir.nii.ac.jp/crid/1571980075553706752

Thurstone LL (1927) A law of comparative judgment. Psychol Rev 34(4):273–286. https://doi.org/10.1037/h0070288

Toledo-Gallegos VM, My NHD, Tuan TH, Börger T (2022) Valuing ecosystem services and disservices of blue/green infrastructure. Evidence from a choice experiment in Vietnam, Economic Analysis and Policy 75:114–128. https://doi.org/10.1016/j.eap.2022.04.015

Train K (2009) Discrete choice methods with simulation, 2nd edn. Cambridge University Press, New York. https://doi.org/10.1017/CBO9780511805271

Train K, Weeks M (2005) Discrete choice models in preference space and willingness-to-pay space. In: Scarpa R, Alberini A (eds) Applications of simulation methods in environmental and resource economics. Springer Netherlands, Dordrecht, pp 1–16. https://doi.org/10.1007/1-4020-3684-1_1

Veall MR, Zimmermann KF (1996) Pseudo-$R^2$ measures for some common limited dependent variable models. J Econ Surv 10(3):241–259

# Chapter 4
# Case Study

**Abstract** This chapter introduces the case study used throughout the book to guide the reader through the steps of conducting a discrete choice experiment in R. The case study is based on the paper published as Meyerhoff et al. (2010), studying the landscape externalities of wind power generation. The original study was a choice experiment surveying preferences on the design of onshore wind farms in two regions in Germany, and the details of the study, particularly the attributes and their levels, demonstrate the real-world applications of discrete choice experiments. In this chapter, we familiarise readers with the wind power case study to prepare them for the estimation, data collection and analysis phase in the following chapters of the book.

## 4.1 Introduction

The case study presented in this chapter focuses on landscape externalities from onshore wind power, and will be used throughout the book to illustrate how discrete choice experiments are conducted, from the experimental design to the analysis and estimation phase.

The design of the choice tasks as well as the definition of the attributes and their levels are inspired by the stated preference study published as Meyerhoff et al. (2010). This study was among the first to look into potential negative externalities from onshore wind farms. Now, externalities from renewable energy production and transmission have become a common subject for the application of discrete choice experiments (DCEs) (e.g. Zerrahn 2017). Thus, this case study represents a typical example of a DCE in the field of environmental valuation.

The specific application of the DCE in this book is meant to be demonstrative, walking the reader through the process of designing and conducting a DCE in R. Therefore, the process, not the empirical findings, is of interest in this book. Instead

 
P. Mariel et al., *Environmental Valuation with Discrete Choice Experiments in R*,
The Economics of Non-Market Goods and Resources 17,
https://doi.org/10.1007/978-3-031-89338-4_4

of using the data collected in the original study, we create an artificial dataset which gives us more flexibility to demonstrate the prevalence of and solutions to specific issues in DCEs. The script for generating the dataset utilised throughout the book can be found in the accompanying GitHub repository: https://github.com/edsandorf/evdce.

## 4.2 Design of the Case Study

The objective of the original study was to evaluate the externalities of onshore wind power generation on landscapes in the regions of Westsachsen and Nordhessen, Germany (Meyerhoff et al. 2010). From an economic standpoint, the externalities of wind turbines on the landscape are generally not reflected in markets. An exception are the effects of turbines on property values (Schütt 2024). To fully understand the monetary impacts of these externalities, an economic analysis of the benefits and drawbacks of wind power generation must incorporate non-market valuation methods (Hanley and Barbier 2009).

The rationale for using a DCE as a non-market valuation technique is that onshore wind turbines have multiple impacts on the landscape that those affected will value differently. Knowing how people value these trade-offs is essential for further analysis, such as a cost–benefit analysis (Hanley and Barbier 2009) or the spatial optimisation of turbines in a landscape (Drechsler et al. 2011) that support decision making.

### *4.2.1 Attributes and Their Levels*

After conducting a series of expert interviews and focus groups, five attributes were chosen for the survey. These included four non-monetary attributes describing the impacts of wind turbines on the landscape: (1) the size of the wind farm, (2) the maximum height of turbines on the wind farm, (3) the effect of turbines on the red kite population, and (4) the minimum distance of wind farms to residential areas. A fifth attribute (cost) was added to allow for the calculation of marginal and non-marginal *willingness to pay* (WTP) estimates, which are crucial for the monetary evaluation of externalities on the landscape.

Below, we briefly introduce the attributes and describe the externalities they represent. Then, we review the levels of the attributes (Table 4.1) as set in the artificial dataset used in this book.

- The *maximum number of turbines* per wind farm affects both electricity costs and the visibility of wind farms. Increasing the size of a wind farm tends to decrease the overall cost of electricity production, and fewer wind farms are required to generate the same amount of electricity when farms are larger. However, larger

**Table 4.1** Attributes and their levels in the data generated for this book

| Attributes | Levels |
|---|---|
| Size of wind farms | Small farms (4–6 mills), medium farms (10–12 mills), large farms (16–18 mills) |
| Maximum height of turbines | Low height (110 m), medium height (150 m), high height (200 m) |
| Reduction of red kite population | 5%, 7.5%, 10%, 12.5%, 15% |
| Minimum distance to residential areas | 750 m, 1000 m, 1250 m, 1500 m, 1750 m |
| Monthly surcharge to power bill | € 0, € 1, € 2, € 3, € 4, € 5, € 6, € 7, € 8, € 9, € 10 |

*Note* The value € 0 only occurs as the surcharge in Programme A, the future status quo

wind farms have a greater impact on the landscape due to their visibility. In this case study, we set three possible sizes for wind farms: small, medium, and large, with a corresponding number of turbines for each size (see Table 4.1). The maximum number of turbines for large wind farms was established as 16–18 turbines, based on an analysis of suitable spaces in the target regions at the time of the study.

- The *height of turbines* was an important issue in public debates on the expansion of wind power in Germany at the time of the study. An advantage of taller turbines is that they can generate more electricity due to stronger and more consistent winds at higher altitudes, meaning that fewer turbines are necessary to produce the same amount of electricity. However, an adverse effect of higher turbines is their increased visibility, even from a greater distance. The attribute levels represent three possible heights of wind turbines in metres that reflect the state of technology for turbines at the time.
- The *impact on the red kite population* was selected to reflect the potential negative effects of the wind turbines on nature. While turbines are not typically installed in conservation areas, conflicts with conservation objectives such as the protection of birds can still arise outside of these designated zones. The red kite, a predatory bird with a primary habitat in the target regions, may experience a decline in population if wind turbines are installed. The percentage levels of the red kite attribute represent the potential reduction of the red kite population due to the deadly collisions of red kites with turbines. The levels were taken from an ecological model developed as part of the project, described in Eichhorn et al. (2012).
- The *minimum distance from residential areas* was another strongly debated issue among the German public at the time of the study. The objective of a minimum distance is to prevent, or at least mitigate, negative effects of turbines in operation, such as noise or shading, for nearby residents. Increasing this minimum distance, however, reduces the available space for economically viable locations, as certain sites with good wind conditions are excluded. The levels of this attribute describe five different minimum distances, with the shortest distance ensuring protection against noise and shading, and additional decreased visibility for larger distances. The shortest distance level was selected in accordance with regulations at the

**Table 4.2** Coding of the attributes and their levels in this book

| Attributes | Labels | Levels |
|---|---|---|
| Size of wind farms | *SmallFarms* | 0 |
| (discrete) | | 1 |
| (reference level: *LargeFarms*) | *MediumFarms* | 0 |
| | | 1 |
| Maximum height of turbines | *LowHeight* | 0 |
| (discrete) | | 1 |
| (reference level: *HighHeight*) | *MediumHeight* | 0 |
| | | 1 |
| Reduction of red kite population | *RedKite* | 5 |
| (continuous) | | 7.5 |
| | | 10 |
| | | 12.5 |
| | | 15 |
| Minimum distance to residential areas | *MinDistance* | 750 |
| (continuous) | | 1000 |
| | | 1250 |
| | | 1500 |
| | | 1750 |
| Monthly surcharge to power bill | *Cost* | 0 |
| (continuous) | | 1 |
| | | 2 |
| | | 3 |
| | | 4 |
| | | 5 |
| | | 6 |
| | | 7 |
| | | 8 |
| | | 9 |
| | | 10 |

federal state level in Germany, while the other two levels captured distances present in the public debate at the time.

- The *cost attribute* was defined as a surcharge to the electricity bill respondents would have to pay if they preferred a different development of wind power in their region over the one defined in the (future) status quo. The future status quo (Programme A) was introduced to respondents as a situation that would take place if they did not opt for either of the other developments presented in Programme B and Programme C. The future status quo was defined by specific levels of the non-monetary attributes that would favour building new wind farms: large wind farms, high turbines, a 10% reduction of red kite population, and a low minimum distance to residential areas, while not requiring any payments, in contrast to the other two alternatives. The electricity bill was chosen as a payment vehicle because it was assumed to be familiar to respondents, and because these bills have a contextual link to the good in question. The suitability of electricity bills as a payment vehicle was supported by the results of a series of focus groups carried out prior to the survey.

> **ⓘ Defining the cost attribute**
>
> While it is possible to use regulations or public debates to define the levels of non-monetary attributes (e.g. the minimum distance to residential areas), the same is generally not true for the cost attribute (see Chapter 2). In both the original study and the simulated data used in this book, the levels of the cost attribute rely at least partially on ad hoc assessments, with consequences for the welfare measures (Glenk et al. 2019), which are central outputs of non-market valuation studies. Even today, guidance on how to select levels of the cost attribute is hard to come by, and setting the levels requires an awareness of the potential consequences on subsequent results.

### *4.2.2 Coding of the Attribute Levels*

The attributes and their levels can be specified in two ways: as continuous or categorical (see Mariel et al. 2021, Sect. 5.2 for more details). In our case study, the attributes *Reduction of red kite population*, *Minimum distance to residential areas*, and *Monthly surcharge to power bill* are treated as continuous, while the *Size of wind farm* and the *Maximum height of turbines* are treated as categorical. Both of the categorically coded attributes have three levels, so two levels will be dummy coded and the third will serve as the reference level (see Table 4.2). The estimated parameters of the dummy variables will then represent the estimated impact on the utilities compared to the reference level. The effects of the continuous variables are specified as linear.

When an attribute is included in the utility function as a continuous variable, its effect is assumed to be linear for any value of the attribute level. This implies that an increase from 3 to 4% in the reduction of the red kite population has the same effect on the utility as an increase from 13 to 14%. However, when an attribute is incorporated as a dummy variable, its effect can be non-linear. If the level *small farms* is the benchmark level, and *medium farms* and *large farms* are two dummy variables included in the utility function representing the corresponding differential effects, the effect of a change from *small farms* to *medium farms* does not need to be half the change from *small farms* to *large farms*. The effect of dummy coded attribute levels depends on the specific value of the levels and therefore can capture non-linear effects.

Using dummy coded variables offers greater flexibility from a modelling perspective, allowing for more diverse effects of the attributes compared to the linear effects assumed by attributes coded as continuous. However, this flexibility comes with a cost. Using dummy coded attributes requires more columns in the design and more parameters to be estimated, which typically requires larger designs and sample sizes.

The variability of an attribute is directly related to the precision of its estimated parameter in a regression model, given a fixed sample size. Specifically, attributes with a broader range or greater variability provide more information for estimation, leading to lower variance in the corresponding parameter estimates. For instance, an attribute with values ranging from one to ten typically results in an estimated coefficient with lower sample variation compared to a dummy-coded attribute restricted to values of zero and one.

This relationship is a well-established result in regression analysis, frequently discussed in the context of linear regression models (Wooldridge 2020, Chapter 3). It reflects the mathematical structure of the variance of estimated coefficients, which is inversely proportional to the variability of the explanatory variable, emphasising the importance of attribute scaling and variability in achieving precise parameter estimates.

> ⓘ **Attribute coding**
>
> The choice between specifying an attribute as continuous or categorical must be made before generating the experimental design, and the design must be generated with the corresponding coding of the attribute levels. Coding attributes differently when estimating the choice models than in the experimental design can potentially distort results. For instance, if an attribute is coded as continuous in the experimental design but dummy coded in the data analysis, this re-coding does not account for the larger sample size needed to estimate the parameters of the dummy coded levels.

### *4.2.3 Choice Tasks and the Utility Functions*

In the case study, respondents were asked to choose between three alternatives (Programme A, B, and C) in each choice task (see Fig. 4.1). A quick look at the empirical literature reveals that a choice task with three alternatives, including one status quo alternative, is the most frequently employed form of a choice task in environmental valuation studies. Note, however, that the empirical suitability of this format is debated, as mentioned in Chapter 2.

| | Status Quo Programme A | Programme B | Programme C |
|---|---|---|---|
| **Size of wind farms** | Medium farms | Large farms | Medium farms |
| **Maximum height of turbines** | Medium height | High height | High height |
| **Reduction of red kite population** | 10% | 15% | 7.5% |
| **Minimum distance to residential areas** | 1000m | 1000m | 1000m |
| **Monthly surcharge to power bill** | 0 euros | 6 euros | 1 euro |
| **I CHOOSE** | | | |

**Fig. 4.1** Example of a choice task

**Incentive compatibility and the use of binary choice tasks**

Incentive compatibility is only ensured when people are presented with a binary choice, i.e. a choice task with two alternatives (Carson and Groves 2007; Vossler and Zawojska 2020). Thus, the study published by Meyerhoff et al. (2010) may not have been incentive compatible. Note that our use of an example with three alternatives does not mean that we (always) recommend this choice task format.

In each choice task, Programme A described the projected development of wind power over the next 10 years if respondents did not select an alternative option. Respondents were informed that choosing this future status quo would not incur any additional charges on their electricity bill. Programme A can thus be considered the *status quo* alternative. The attribute levels for Programme A remained the same across all choice tasks (see Fig. 4.1).

Programmes B and C, on the other hand, placed restrictions on wind power generation with regard to at least one attribute in comparison to Programme A. For instance, the maximum turbine height or wind farm size could be limited to low/small or medium, or the minimum distance could be set to a higher level. Respondents were told that all three programmes in each choice task would generate the same amount of electricity and therefore result in the same reduction of carbon dioxide emissions. However, implementing Programme B or C would lead to increased costs of electricity production because of the restrictions imposed by these programmes. As a consequence, the electricity bill would increase by the amount stated in these two programmes.

Respondents were informed that building turbines farther from residential areas would result in higher infrastructure costs due to longer power cables, and that increased maximum distances from residential areas would result in higher costs due to excluding potentially suitable locations for wind farms with favourable wind conditions.

The allocation of the attribute levels across the alternatives and choice tasks was carried out by a statistical experimental design. How experimental designs can be generated using the *spdesign* package (Sandorf and Campbell 2023) in R is detailed in Chapter 5 of this book.

Based on the alternatives presented in the choice tasks and the possible values of the attribute levels, utility functions are formulated to set up a RUM model Eq. (3.3). These utility functions represent the link between the theoretical model (RUM) presented earlier (Chapter 3) and the data analysis of the empirical case study (Chapter 9).

While we will not use these utility functions until later on in this book, we highly recommend starting to formulate them as early as possible over the course of a DCE project because of their essential importance for the analysis of the empirical data and the outcome of the study. Statements about peoples' preferences for inducing or preventing environmental changes (here: the use of specific designs of wind warms) rely on these utility functions.

$$
\begin{aligned}
U_{n1t} = \quad & \beta_{mf} MediumFarms_{n1t} + \beta_{sf} SmallFarms_{n1t} \\
& +\beta_{mh} MediumHeight_{n1t} + \beta_{lh} LowHeight_{n1t} \\
& +\beta_{rk} RedKite_{n1t} + \beta_{md} MinDistance_{n1t} \\
& +\beta_{cost} Cost_{n1t} + \varepsilon_{n1t} \\
U_{n2t} = ASC_2 \; & +\beta_{mf} MediumFarms_{n2t} + \beta_{sf} SmallFarms_{n2t} \\
& +\beta_{mh} MediumHeight_{n2t} + \beta_{lh} LowHeight_{n2t} \\
& +\beta_{rk} RedKite_{n2t} + \beta_{md} MinDistance_{n2t} \\
& +\beta_{cost} Cost_{n2t} + \varepsilon_{n2t} \\
U_{n3t} = ASC_3 \; & +\beta_{mf} MediumFarms_{n3t} + \beta_{sf} SmallFarms_{n3t} \\
& +\beta_{mh} MediumHeight_{n3t} + \beta_{lh} LowHeight_{n3t} \\
& +\beta_{rk} RedKite_{n3t} + \beta_{md} MinDistance_{n3t} \\
& +\beta_{cost} Cost_{n3t} + \varepsilon_{n3t}
\end{aligned}
\tag{4.1}
$$

The goal of this chapter was to introduce the study published by Meyerhoff et al. (2010), which serves as the basis for the wind power case study used throughout this book. With a greater understanding of the context of the case study, the attributes and their levels, and the importance of the utility functions, readers are now ready to combine all aspects of the design into choice tasks, and move on to the experimental design phase of their DCE project.

## 4.3 Key Takeaways

- In the course of the study design, the decision to specify an attribute as continuous or categorical must be made before the experimental design is generated, and the design must be generated with the appropriate coding of the attribute levels.
- The selection of the cost attribute levels can significantly impact subsequent welfare measures, thus defining the levels requires an awareness of the potential consequences.
- The choice task employed in the case study may not have been incentive compatible as instead of presenting a binary choice three alternatives were available in each task.

## Bibliography

Carson RT, Groves T (2007) Incentive and informational properties of preference questions. Environ Resour Econ 37(1):181–210. https://doi.org/10.1007/s10640-007-9124-5

Drechsler M, Ohl C, Meyerhoff J et al (2011) Combining spatial modeling and choice experiments for the optimal spatial allocation of wind turbines. Energy Policy 39(6):3845–3854. https://doi.org/10.1016/j.enpol.2011.04.015

Eichhorn M, Johst K, Seppelt R, Drechsler M (2012) Model-based estimation of collision risks of predatory birds with wind turbines. Ecol Soc 17(2):1. https://doi.org/10.5751/es-04594-170201

Glenk K, Meyerhoff J, Akaichi F, Martin-Ortega J (2019) Revisiting cost vector effects in discrete choice experiments. Resour Energy Econ 57:135–155. https://doi.org/10.1016/j.reseneeco.2019.05.001

Hanley N, Barbier EB (2009) Pricing nature: cost-benefit analysis and environmental policy. Edward Elgar Publishing. https://www.scopus.com/inward/record.uri?eid=2-s2.0-70549113975&partnerID=40&md5=a210cf30453967e9906ad837775c3dcd

Mariel P, Hoyos D, Meyerhoff J et al (2021) Environmental valuation with discrete choice experiments: guidance on design, implementation and data analysis. Springer Nature. https://doi.org/10.1007/978-3-030-62669-3

Meyerhoff J, Ohl C, Harte V (2010) Landscape externalities from onshore wind power. Energy Policy 38:82–92. https://doi.org/10.1016/j.enpol.2009.08.055

Sandorf ED, Campbell D (2023) spdesign: designing stated preference experiments. R package version 0.0.5. https://CRAN.R-project.org/package=spdesign

Schütt M (2024) Wind turbines and property values: a meta-regression analysis. Environ Resource Econ 87:1–43. https://doi.org/10.1007/s10640-023-00809-y

Vossler CA, Zawojska E (2020) Behavioral drivers or economic incentives? toward a better understanding of elicitation effects in stated preference studies. J Assoc Environ Resour Econ 7(2):279–303. https://doi.org/10.1086/706645

Wooldridge JM (2020) Introductory econometrics: A modern approach, 7th edn. Cengage Learning

Zerrahn A (2017) Wind power and externalities. Ecol Econ 141:245–260. https://doi.org/10.1016/j.ecolecon.2017.02.016

# Chapter 5
# Experimental Design

**Abstract** This chapter walks the reader through the process of generating an experimental design in R. We generate an experimental design by combining attributes and levels into alternatives and choice tasks, which allow us to estimate model parameters and understand preferences through trade-offs. In this chapter, we cover three different types of designs: orthogonal, random, and efficient designs, highlighting their respective advantages. We delve deeper into efficient designs, covering important concepts such as attribute level balance, utility balance, and priors. Using the *spdesign* package in R, we demonstrate how to use different efficiency criteria and estimation algorithms to generate efficient designs, and review important checks and considerations for your design.

## 5.1 What Is an Experimental Design and Why Do We Need Them?

With contemporary software, experimental designs are easy to generate, but hard to get right. This chapter serves as a brief introduction to experimental designs, where we delve into what experimental designs are, why we need them, and how to generate them in R. The process of generating an experimental design is driven by the main research question or hypothesis of your study. Having a clearly identified research question helps identify what the relevant choices and trade-offs are, guiding us towards the most appropriate experimental design.

We will be using the empirical case study presented in Chap. 4 to generate an experimental design in R. Recall the setting for the case study:

> Imagine that in your region, the government is considering extending the use of wind power by building new wind farms. The planning authorities have suggested certain rules that would apply to this expansion of wind power. Now they want to solicit public input on their preferences for these rules.

The collection of proposals a policymaker or homeowner can choose between (here, the wind power development plans) is called a *choice task*. You can see an example of a choice task in Fig. 4.1 (Chap. 4). Within a choice task, each proposal is called

 
P. Mariel et al., *Environmental Valuation with Discrete Choice Experiments in R*,
The Economics of Non-Market Goods and Resources 17,
https://doi.org/10.1007/978-3-031-89338-4_5

an *alternative* (or in some instances, a *profile*), which corresponds to the columns in Fig. 4.1. In our example, each proposal is described by the exact area to be zoned, the number and height of windmills allowed, environmental impacts, and expected running costs. These *attributes* describe each alternative and correspond to the rows in Fig. 4.1. The *levels* that each attribute can take, such as the height of the windmills or the range of costs, determine the variation between alternatives and across choice tasks. Each cell in Fig. 4.1 represents a specific level of an attribute. The attributes and levels used in our case study can be found in Table 4.2 (Chap. 4).

So, what is an experimental design? In short, it is a way of combining all attributes and levels into alternatives and choice tasks that allows us to estimate the parameters of our model, and by extension, provide meaningful information about people's preferences. Specifically, we analyse the trade-offs individuals make in their choices in order to estimate the parameters of our model.

The first steps of generating an experimental design were covered in Chap. 4, where we identified the problem, the attributes, and their levels. In this chapter, we will discuss different ways of combining them into an experimental design. Generating any stated preference experimental design begins with a model, and the design is conditional on the model used when generating it. Here, we use a random utility model to analyse the trade-offs people make when choosing between different wind power development plans (alternatives). The purpose of the experimental design is to help us create these alternative plans. For simplicity, we rewrite the utility function of our model, Eq. (3.3), in a general form:

$$U_{js} = ASC_j + \sum_{k=1}^{K} \beta_k x_{kjs} + \varepsilon_{js}, \tag{5.1}$$

where $U_{js}$ is the utility of alternative $j \in \{1, ..., J\}$ in choice task $s \in \{1, ..., S\}$, and $k \in \{1, ..., K\}$ indexes the attributes. This makes $x_{kjs}$ the level of the $k$th attribute in the $j$th alternative in the $s$th choice task.[1] $\varepsilon_{js}$ is an *i.i.d.* Gumbel distributed error term. Note that we have suppressed the notation for the individual $n$ because the design is generated as if one individual answered all choice tasks, as is customary for such models.

The main goal of generating an experimental design is to find the best combination of attributes $x_{kjs}$ such that we can identify the $\beta$ parameters. First, we need to define one utility function for each alternative available in a choice task. Then, once we have decided on the number of levels, attributes, alternatives, and choice tasks, as well as which model to use in the utility function, we can begin combining them into a design.

The simplest type of design is called a full factorial design. This type of design includes every single combination of attributes and levels for all available alternatives. With a full factorial design, we can identify all main effects and all interaction effects as long as every choice task has been answered at least once (Street and Burgess 2007).

[1] We use $S$ to indicate the number of choice tasks or rows in the experimental design. This may be different from $T$, which is the number of choice tasks answered by an individual, $S \geq T$.

Main effects refer to the independent impact of an attribute on choice, averaged over the levels of the other attributes, while interactions refer to the interactions between attributes and describe how the effect of one attribute depends on the levels of the other attributes.

This should not be confused with the number of respondents needed to detect significant effects or to estimate complex models with high data requirements. In cases where we have few attributes taking on just a few levels, using a full factorial design can be a feasible option. However, as the number of attributes and levels increases, the number of possible alternatives and choice tasks quickly grows to a level where it is unfeasible to have a respondent answer all choice tasks.

To demonstrate the scale of this challenge, let us consider our case study. We have five attributes: two can take on 3 levels, two can take on 5 levels, and one can take on 10 levels. Even without creating the full factorial, we know that the size of the full factorial, i.e. the number of rows for a single alternative is: $3^2 \cdot 5^2 \cdot 10^1 = 2,250$. That is, given the attributes and levels, we can create 2,250 unique alternatives. If each choice task contains two alternatives and a status quo (SQ) alternative defined as a constant, then we can create $\left(3^2 \cdot 5^2 \cdot 10^1\right)^2 = 5,062,500$ (or just over 5 million) possible choice tasks.

To create the full factorial of our design in R, we use the `full_factorial()` function from the *spdesign* package (Sandorf and Campbell 2023). The function takes a named list of attributes and levels in the `wide` format. In the code chunk below, we demonstrate how to create the full factorial for the wind power case study. For each alternative, we specify each attribute and the levels it can take in a systematic fashion, i.e. there is no randomness in creating the full factorial.

We employ a consistent naming convention, with the name of the alternative separated from the attribute name using an underscore. This naming convention aligns with how the *spdesign* package generates names based on the specified utility functions.

Note that we have specified a level for all attributes of the SQ alternative: zero in this case, due to the normalisation of the SQ alternative. Normalising the SQ alternative means subtracting the SQ levels from all alternatives *including* the SQ, such that non-SQ alternatives now represent deviations from the SQ. Importantly, this transformation (normalisation) preserves the relative order of the alternatives, and is possible since only differences in utilities matter. This transformation simplifies both the design generation and the model estimation.

For instance, the levels for the *RedKite* attribute have been determined as follows: (5–10, 7.5–10, 10–10, 12.5–10, 15–10). A similar method was applied to *MinDistance*: (750–750, 1000–750, 1250–750, 1500–750, 1750–750). Additionally, these values were divided by 100 to approximate the same scale or order of magnitude for the attribute levels, as outlined in Sect. 5.3.1.3.

Additionally, the attributes *Size of wind farms* and *Maximum height of turbines* are retained in their original coding (1, 2, 3), as this simplifies the generation of the full factorial design. After the design is generated, this coding can be converted into dummy coding if needed. Retaining the original coding during design generation is particularly advantageous for ensuring proper generation and implementing restrictions more effectively.

```
# Create the full factorial using a named list of attributes and levels in the wide format
full_fact <- full_factorial(
  list(
    alt1_sq = 1,
    alt1_farm = 0,
    alt1_height = 0,
    alt1_redkite = 0,
    alt1_distance = 0,
    alt1_cost = 0,
    alt2_sq = 0,
    alt2_farm = c(1, 2, 3),
    alt2_height = c(1, 2, 3),
    alt2_redkite = c(-5, -2.5, 0, 2.5, 5),
    alt2_distance = c(0, 0.25, 0.5, 0.75, 1),
    alt2_cost = 1:10,
    alt3_sq = 0,
    alt3_farm = c(1, 2, 3),
    alt3_height = c(1, 2, 3),
    alt3_redkite = c(-5, -2.5, 0, 2.5, 5),
    alt3_distance = c(0, 0.25, 0.5, 0.75, 1),
    alt3_cost = 1:10
  )
)

# Show the first six rows and 8th to 12th columns of the design matrix
full_fact[1:6, c(1, 8:12)]
  alt1_sq alt2_farm alt2_height alt2_redkite alt2_distance alt2_cost
1       1         1           1           -5             0         1
2       1         2           1           -5             0         1
3       1         3           1           -5             0         1
4       1         1           2           -5             0         1
5       1         2           2           -5             0         1
6       1         3           2           -5             0         1
```

As the number of attributes, levels, and alternatives rises, the full factorial becomes problematic in practice for a few other reasons beyond its dimensions:

1. Choice tasks in the full factorial may contain the same alternatives one or more times due to the nature of the generation process. These tasks provide no additional information on trade-offs and preferences.
2. Choice tasks may contain dominated or dominating alternatives. A dominated alternative exists in a choice task when this alternative is objectively worse compared to one or more alternatives (for example, comparing two alternatives when all attribute levels are equal except for one alternative being more expensive). Conversely, an alternative is dominating when its attribute levels are more favourable for all attributes compared to the other alternatives in the choice task. Neither dominated nor dominating alternatives are desirable for experimental designs because they provide no information about trade-offs. However, determining dominance a priori can be difficult because in many instances it depends on preferences.
3. We may want to impose restrictions on which attribute levels can co-occur, which is not possible in the full factorial. For example, we may want to restrict the impact of wind farms on the red kite population such that the highest impact cannot co-occur with the smallest and lowest wind farms, in line with the evidence found

in the literature. Imposing these types of restrictions can increase the realism of the experiment.

Choice tasks that fall into one or more of the categories above are referred to as problematic choice tasks. It is common practice to exclude these problematic choice tasks from the full factorial. With efficient experimental designs, as we will see later in the chapter, choice tasks with dominated and dominating alternatives tend to "drop out" because they provide no information on trade-offs. What we are left with is called the *candidate set* and includes only feasible (non-problematic) choice tasks.

### ⓘ Creating the candidate set in R

We can place restrictions on the full factorial created above using logical operators. For example, assume that tall windmills cannot be placed too close to residential areas. We therefore would like to restrict the maximum height of wind turbines to the lowest level when the distance to residential areas is less than 750 m, excluding cases where the maximum height is higher than the lowest level.

The first step is to identify the exclusion criteria (here, where the maximum height is higher than the lowest level and the distance to residential areas is less than 750 m) and then keep all cases where this is not true. Notice in the code chunk below that we have to do this for Alternative 2 and Alternative 3 but not for Alternative 1 (SQ), because the attribute levels are normalised to zero.

```
candidate_set <- full_fact[!((full_fact$alt2_height == 1 & full_fact$alt2_distance < 0.75)
| (full_fact$alt3_height == 1 & full_fact$alt3_distance < 0.75)), ]

candidate_set[1:6, c(1, 8:12)]

   alt1_sq alt2_farm alt2_height alt2_redkite alt2_distance alt2_cost
1        1         1           2         -5.0             0         1
2        1         2           2         -5.0             0         1
3        1         3           2         -5.0             0         1
10       1         1           2         -5.0             0         1
11       1         2           2         -5.0             0         1
12       1         3           2         -5.0             0         1
```

This data.frame has 3,240,000 rows. We have excluded 1,822,500 choice tasks that do not meet the exclusion criteria.

Even after we exclude all problematic choice tasks, we can still be left with far more potential choice tasks than any single respondent is able to answer. What we need is a way to select a subset of these 3.24 million choice tasks that is both manageable for respondents *and* enables us to estimate and identify the $\beta$ parameters. Note that we have not excluded dominant or dominating alternatives from the candidate set generated, as described in the textbox above.

## 5.2 Types of Experimental Designs

### *5.2.1 Orthogonal Designs*

Many early applications of stated choice experiments relied on orthogonal designs. Orthogonal designs are based on orthogonal arrays, and originate from the literature on linear models where these designs are common. Orthogonal designs have a desirable property called attribute level balance, where all attribute levels occur an equal number of times for each alternative across all choice tasks. This property provides excellent coverage of the attribute space, which aids in the estimation of model parameters. Orthogonal designs are appealing because they ensure that all main effects of the model are identified, that is, all estimated parameters are identified and there are zero co-variances between them (Mariel et al. 2021, Chapter 3).

However, there are at least three problems with orthogonal designs as they relate to stated preference research:

1. There is a limit on the number of attributes and levels within a design because orthogonal arrays may not exist for the combination of attributes and levels you want to use. Note, it is possible to use a larger orthogonal array and drop unwanted columns because orthogonality will still be preserved. However, dropping rows will lead to a loss of orthogonality.
2. Orthogonal designs are developed for linear models, whereas choice models are typically non-linear. In practice, this means that some of the desirable properties, e.g. zero co-variances between the attributes, may be lost or partially lost.
3. Even if your design is orthogonal, your data is likely not. Any non-response in the data will lead to a loss of orthogonality. This is equivalent to dropping rows in the orthogonal array. Again, in practice, this means that some of the desirable properties of orthogonal designs may be lost.

### *5.2.2 Random Designs*

We will not cover random designs in detail, but reviewing the different types of random designs will help us understand how the algorithms that search for efficient designs work (see Sect. 5.3.2.3). Here, we will briefly discuss two types of random designs.

The first type of random design is what we call a row-based random design. This type of design requires a *candidate set* of possible choice tasks (see the approach outlined in Sect. 5.1 above). The simplest way to create a design of the desired size is to randomly draw the desired number of choice tasks (rows) from the *candidate set*. If the candidate set is properly defined, i.e. you have excluded all choice tasks with dominant alternatives, all implausible or impossible attribute combinations, etc., then this random design will be a valid design. However, because we are drawing randomly from the *candidate set*, it is hard to achieve attribute level balance. If attribute level balance is a goal, e.g. you want even coverage of the attribute space to ensure that all levels are trade-off against one another, then you may have to draw and inspect numerous designs before finding one that meets your criteria.

The second type of random design is what we call a column-based random design. For this type of design, we randomly combine the attribute levels into a design of the desired size. The expanded list of attributes and levels used to create the full factorial can be used here, combined such that we end up with a design of the desired size. For this type of random design, it is easy to achieve attribute level balance, but it is almost impossible to ensure that certain attribute levels cannot co-occur or that other restrictions hold. To impose any exclusion criteria, they would have to be tested for every new design generated, resulting in a laborious and time-consuming process. Thus, it may take a long time to find even a single design meeting all exclusion criteria.

Creating a single random design for all respondents is not something we would recommend; however, random designs can work well if certain conditions apply. If there are few restrictions on attribute combinations or attribute level balance is not needed, and you are conducting a survey online, with the ability to do both real-time sampling and randomisation, random designs may be a suitable option. In this case, you can give every respondent a different random design following one of the procedures above, and the design will ensure plenty of variation in $x_{kjs}$ in your sample. This will allow you to estimate many if not all parameters of interest, as well as being free of design specific artefacts that may be present in your data. Design-specific artefacts could be tied to specific attribute level combinations being allowed or not, or a particular ordering of the choice tasks or alternatives. A variant of this type of design was used by Sandorf et al. (2022).

Note that this approach requires a large sample to ensure sufficient coverage of the variation in attribute levels. What "large" means depends entirely on the empirical setting. A design with many attributes, each of which have many levels, will require a substantially larger sample compared to a design with a small number of attributes taking on few levels.

### 5.2.3 *Efficient Experimental Designs*

Efficient experimental designs gained popularity due to their ability to reliably estimate models and significant model parameters with equal or smaller sample sizes compared to other types of designs such as orthogonal or random designs (Rose and Bliemer 2009). This is because efficient experimental designs seek to maximise the statistical information in the design. To understand what this means, we will define statistical information and how this relates to the standard errors of the model. A more detailed and technical discussion can be found in Chap. 8.

Let us rewrite the log-likelihood function defined in Eq. (3.14) of your model as:

$$\ln L(\boldsymbol{\theta}|\mathbf{X},\boldsymbol{y}) = \sum_{n=1}^{N}\sum_{s=1}^{S}\sum_{j=1}^{J} y_{nsj} \ln P_{nsj}(\mathbf{X}, \boldsymbol{\theta})$$

where $y_{nsj}$ is the binary response variable (0 or 1) and $P_{nsj}$ is the probability that alternative $j$ is chosen[2] and vector $\boldsymbol{\theta}$ includes all parameters of the model defined in Eq. (5.1). This general form of the log-likelihood function holds for both MNL and MXL (and other) models. The amount of information in the design is described by the Fisher Information matrix (see Eq. [8.4]).

The Fisher information matrix is the negative of the Hessian matrix of the model, which contains the second order derivatives of the log-likelihood function with respect to the parameters, and is directly linked to the asymptotic variance-covariance matrix ($\boldsymbol{V}_A(\hat{\boldsymbol{\theta}})$) (see Eq. [8.5]). For a given finite sample size $N$, the maximum likelihood estimator of $\boldsymbol{V}_A(\hat{\boldsymbol{\theta}})$ (see Eq. [8.6]) is

$$\hat{\boldsymbol{V}}(\hat{\boldsymbol{\theta}}|\mathbf{X}, \mathbf{y}) = \left[\boldsymbol{I}_A(\boldsymbol{\theta}|\mathbf{X}, \mathbf{y})_{\theta=\hat{\theta}}\right]^{-1} = -E\left[\frac{\partial^2 \ln L(\boldsymbol{\theta}, \mathbf{X}, \mathbf{y})}{\partial \boldsymbol{\theta}, \partial \boldsymbol{\theta}'}\right]^{-1}_{\theta=\hat{\theta}}.$$

This means that there is a direct relationship between the information in the design and the size of the standard errors: more statistical information implies smaller standard errors, *ceteris paribus* (Rose et al. 2018). Thus, you can get significance with a smaller sample size if your design contains more information, i.e. more informative trade-offs.

When we search for a more efficient design, we are effectively trying out different combinations of attribute levels (designs) to see if new combinations provide more statistical information compared to combinations already tested. However, it is difficult to compare one Fisher information matrix directly with another. This is because we would try to compare the informational content of individual matrix elements, and some designs might contain more information on some parameters than others. Determining how to weight these elements in a comparison is difficult.

To solve this problem, we rely on a set of efficiency criteria. These try to quantify the total information contained into a single number that makes comparisons easier. There are a number of efficiency criteria, all based on the variance-covariance matrix or probabilities in the model. Here, we will discuss only the D-efficiency criterion because it is the most widely used (see Olsen and Meyerhoff 2017; Rose and Bliemer 2014; Yao et al. 2015; Mariel et al. 2021 for a discussion of other efficiency criteria such as A, B, C, and S).

[2] This probability can come from an MNL, NL, or MXL model. This does not affect the discussion, however, recall that a design is only efficient for the model used to generate the design.

The D-efficiency criterion, or D-error, uses the determinant of the variance-covariance matrix. The goal is to minimise this measure, which all else equal, leads to smaller standard errors. This is equivalent to maximising the amount of statistical information in the design. Unlike the A-error, the D-error considers the co-variances as well as the variances and is less affected by large variances for single parameters. We scale the determinant with the factor $1/K$ where $K$ is the total number of attributes in the design. D-error is defined as

$$\mathrm{D} = \det\left(\hat{\boldsymbol{V}}\left(\hat{\boldsymbol{\theta}}\,|\mathbf{X}, \boldsymbol{y}\right)\right)^{1/K}.$$

So, how do we find an efficient experimental design? We can think of it as the opposite of fitting a model: when you fit a model, you have the data and try to find the parameters that maximise the likelihood of the data; conversely, when you generate a design, you assume a value for the parameters (priors) and try to "find" the combination of attributes and levels (design) that provides the most statistical information (smallest standard errors), i.e. the smallest possible D-error.

It should be clear that to calculate the determinant of the variance-covariance matrix, we need data and a model. The data in this instance is your design candidate, which is derived based on your utility functions including attributes and levels, the relationship between them, and the assumed priors (this is explained in more detail below). The model can be any random utility model. An important implication is that a design is only truly efficient for the model and utility functions assumed when generating the design. A move away from this, e.g. by estimating a different model on the data that was used to generate the design, leads to a loss in efficiency, with the practical implication of needing more respondents *ceteris paribus* to identify the parameters of interest. In practice, this is extremely common. Most designs are generated assuming an MNL model but we routinely fit different types of mixed logit models to the data in the estimation phase (see Chap. 9).

Efficient experimental designs are widely used in the stated choice literature due to numerous advantages over orthogonal and random designs, such as their superior estimation of parameters with smaller sample sizes through the maximisation of statistical information. To create an experimental design based on the wind power case study, we will employ an efficient experimental design.

## 5.3 Creating an Efficient Experimental Design in R

In this section, we walk you through the steps of generating an efficient experimental design in R, using the wind power case study introduced in Chap. 4. To generate our design, we use the *spdesign* package, which allows you to interact with the design objects, create utility functions, and more using standard R syntax. The package is well-documented and in active development as of the writing of this book and comes pre-packaged with easy-to-run examples. In this section, we will outline the steps of generating an efficient design using the *spdesign* package, and highlight potential pitfalls along the way.

### *5.3.1 The Utility Function*

As discussed at the beginning of the chapter, the generation of the experimental design depends on your research question and the model you wish to estimate. For random utility maximisation (RUM) models, the first step is specifying the utility functions.

In the *spdesign* package, we specify the utility functions as part of a named list, with one utility function for each alternative. The utility functions are defined as character strings specifying the priors, attributes, levels, and functional form. In the code chunk below, we show the utility functions specified for the example used in this book (see Eq. [4.1], Chap. 4). All parameters begin with `b_` and precede the attributes. The prior value and attribute levels are specified within the brackets `[]`. Because of how *spdesign* parses the utility expression, standard operators can be used directly. You only need to specify the levels and priors the first time they are used. In the following sections, we will cover all elements of the design in detail.

```
# Define the utility functions
utility <- list(
  alt1 = "b_sq[0] * sq[1]",
  alt2 = "b_farm_dummy[c(0.25, 0.5)] * farm[c(1, 2, 3)] +
          b_height_dummy[c(0.25, 0.5)] * height[c(1, 2, 3)] +
          b_redkite[-0.05] * redkite[c(-5, -2.5, 0, 2.5, 5)] +
          b_distance[0.5] * distance[c(0, 0.25, 0.5, 0.75, 1)] +
          b_cost[-0.05] * cost[seq(1, 10)]",
  alt3 = "b_farm_dummy * farm +
          b_height_dummy * height +
          b_redkite * redkite +
          b_distance * distance +
          b_cost * cost"
)
```

#### 5.3.1.1 Specifying Alternatives and the Role of the Status Quo Alternative

In the code chunk above, we have specified three alternatives, including the status quo (SQ). It is important to specify all alternatives, even when the SQ alternative is a constant, or an "opt out" or "buy none" alternative exists. This is because all alternatives have an associated utility, and not buying anything or sticking with the SQ also provides a decision maker with utility. A general rule is that all alternatives available to respondents should be included as part of the design.

> ⓘ **On normalising the utility of the SQ alternative**
>
> Only differences in utility matter. This allows us to simplify the specification of the SQ alternative to a constant by subtracting the SQ alternative from all alternatives. The non-SQ attribute levels now represent deviations from the SQ instead of their original absolute value in the experimental design, but you can still display the absolute value to respondents in the choice task.

Designs come in two broad categories: labelled and unlabelled designs. In labelled designs, each alternative has a "label" that carries behavioural meaning. For example, in an environmental context, a respondent could be asked to choose between different conservation policies labelled as "protected area", "restricted access", and "open access", each with their own attributes and levels. In labelled designs, the label itself contains important information about the alternative, and the design will need to consider this if you wish to estimate the effect of the label separately from the $J - 1$ constants.

Unlabelled designs are common in environmental applications where alternatives are given generic names like Policy A and Policy B that carry no additional meaning. These do not require extra care when generating the experimental design.

In many applications in environmental economics, we see a combination of these two types of designs, in which the SQ alternative is the only labelled alternative in an otherwise unlabelled stated choice experiment. This is the case in our example: alternatives 2 and 3 are unlabelled, while the SQ alternative is the only labelled alternative, representing the current development plan. There is extensive literature on the role of the SQ alternative and the behavioural interpretation of constants in choice models (see Oehlmann et al. 2017; Olsen et al. 2017; Johnston et al. 2017; Campbell and Erdem 2019; Sandorf et al. 2022).

**ⓘ Number of alternatives**

A question to consider carefully is how many alternatives to include in each choice task. Increasing the number of alternatives will lead to more information in your design because respondents are making more trade-offs. This will improve your ability to estimate more parameters (see Sect. 5.5), but may also cause respondents to perceive the choices as more difficult. In the literature, you will find applications using any number of alternatives, but three seems to be most common (Mahieu et al. 2017).

As discussed in Chap. 2, it is common to see more than two alternatives in environmental economics applications. However, only binary choices, or a sequence of binary choices, have properties consistent with theoretical incentive compatibility (Vossler et al. 2012; Carson and Groves 2007). That said, creating a choice set with more than two alternatives may be necessary to reflect real-world settings where more than two alternatives exist (Johnston et al. 2017), such as multiple competing development plans, transport modes, or minced meat in supermarkets.

#### 5.3.1.2 Attributes, Levels, and Attribute Level Balance

Attributes are specified directly in the utility function and must include at least two levels. As discussed above, your design should include enough attributes to answer your research question and enough levels to create sufficient variation in $x_{kjs}$ to reliably estimate the parameters of the model.

There are two main types of attributes: qualitative and quantitative attributes. Qualitative attributes are typically attributes whose numeric value does not matter. Environmental quality measured on a five-point scale (e.g. from very poor to excellent) or the size of the wind farm on a three-point scale (small, medium, large) are examples of qualitative attributes. These attributes typically enter the utility function as dummy variables.

Quantitative attributes, on the other hand, have meaningful numeric values. The distance to a wind farm in metres or the cost of the policy are examples of quantitative attributes. These typically enter the utility function linearly, although other functional forms can be considered. In our example, we specified the `redkite` attribute as continuous with the following levels: `redkite[c(-5, -2.5, 0, 2.5, 5)]`.

Attribute level balance, introduced in Sect. 5.2 above, is defined by each level of the attributes occurring an equal number of times in the design. Achieving attribute level balance is only possible under certain conditions: the number of rows in the design (number of choice tasks, also referred to as the size of the design) must be a multiple of the number of levels for each attribute. In our design, we have two attributes taking on 3 levels, two attributes taking on 5 levels, and one attribute taking on 10 levels. For this design to be attribute level balanced, the number of rows needs to be a multiple of 3, 5, and 10. Given that both 3 and 5 are prime numbers, the least common multiple is 30. In other words, the smallest design that can achieve attribute level balance has 30 rows.

Attribute level balance is often considered a desirable property because it ensures equal coverage across the attribute space in the design. However, it also restricts the designs we can create: restricting ourselves to designs that are attribute level balanced will lead to more statistically inefficient designs compared to designs that are not attribute level balanced. The most efficient designs, i.e. where we have maximal statistical information in the trade-offs, are found when we trade off one extreme attribute level against another (e.g. comparing the highest price to the highest environmental impacts against the lowest price to the lowest environmental impact). This, however, might impact the realism of the discrete choice experiment by introducing unrealistic trade-offs.

We, and others, argue that having some level of attribute level balance and accepting a less efficient design is desirable because it can increase the realism of the choice tasks, which is crucial to accurately answer the research question (Hensher et al. 2005). Efficiency, as we have seen in Sect. 5.2, only affects the standard errors and thus a less efficient design can be compensated for with larger sample sizes. Maximising efficiency should only be a goal when your potential sample size is constrained, such as in research on small vulnerable patient groups. Most research in environmental economics uses sufficiently large sample sizes to compensate for less efficient designs, and increased realism and attribute level balance are generally seen as more important factors.

In the generation of the experimental design, alternative specific constants take the form of single-level attributes in *spdesign*. For the wind power case study, we specified the ASC of the SQ alternative to take the value of 1 with a zero prior. This was the direct result of the normalisation of the SQ alternative. The specification of alternative specific constants in a design has the same identifying restriction as constants estimated in a model, that is, you can include at most $J - 1$. Alternative specific constants are straightforward to specify using standard R syntax, however, remember to only include $J - 1$ constants.

A final aspect to consider when specifying the attributes and levels of the utility function is the possibility of interaction effects between your attributes. For example, if you believe that people who prefer small wind farms also prefer lower wind turbines, you may want to allow for an interaction between these two attributes to capture this impact on utility and choice. If you suspect interaction effects to be present, these should be specified at the design stage to ensure that they can be identified after the data has been collected. If not specified, an insignificant interaction effect does not necessarily mean that there is no effect—it could be missed because it was not identified by the design. To specify an interaction effect between `redkite` and `distance` for example, we specify the interaction as well as its associated prior using R's formula syntax `I()`: `b_redkite_distance[0] * I(redkite * distance)`.

#### 5.3.1.3 The Role and Importance of Priors

A prior is the assumed parameter value, and is critical for finding suitable and efficient designs. The prior reflects the information you have about the true parameter value or, stated differently, the sign and magnitude of preferences. In the code chunk above (and for all prior values specified in the *spdesign* package), the priors start with `b_`, followed by the name of the attribute and a set of square brackets `[]` containing the value of the prior. We have specified the prior for the cost of the programme `b_cost` to be −`0.05`, and for the two highest levels of farm size `b_farm_dummy` to be `0.25` and `0.5`. Finding good priors can be difficult, but we outline a few useful strategies below.

First, the absence of any information on the sign and impact of a particular attribute on utility means that we assume a prior equal to zero. Importantly, this is still an assumption, and in the *spdesign* package, you have to explicitly assume a zero prior where relevant. If we assume all priors to be zero and we have an attribute level balanced design, then the most efficient design will be a (near) orthogonal design (see Sect. 5.2.1) (Hensher et al. 2005, p. 268).

Specifying (good) non-zero priors can lead to more efficient designs because generated choice sets are more utility balanced, meaning that utilities are more similar between alternatives (Huber and Zwerina 1996). Utility balance, while not a goal in itself, can provide important information about your design. A perfectly utility balanced choice set will have equal choice probabilities for all alternatives, which is effectively a random choice as seen from the analyst's perspective (choices are unlikely to be random from the decision maker's perspective, but the unobservable part, i.e. error term, of utility dominates). A perfectly utility imbalanced choice set includes a single dominating alternative with a choice probability of one. Neither of these extremes provide much information about preferences and should be avoided, however, a higher degree of utility balance forces respondents to make more difficult trade-offs, which reveals more information about their preferences.

There are a few different ways we can approach finding appropriate priors:

1. Rely on previous literature studying the same choices and trade-offs in other countries or other sites.
2. Rely on economic theory to provide the sign for the prior. For example, economic theory states that everyone has a positive marginal utility for money, which means that we can set a very small negative prior on our cost parameter, such as −`0.001`, to "sign" our prior.
3. Create an initial design with zero or near-zero priors and use this design in a pilot study. When we have gathered the pilot data, we can run the model used to generate the design on this data and use the estimated parameters as priors for our study.
4. A relatively simple method for how to find good priors can be found in Bliemer and Collins (2016).

Even with good guidance from theory, the literature, and pilot studies, the value of a prior is rarely known with certainty. We can consider this uncertainty using what is called a Bayesian prior (Sándor and Wedel 2001; Scarpa and Rose 2008; Rose and Bliemer 2014). The idea behind the Bayesian prior is that we assume the prior itself to follow a pre-specified distribution. For example, in the *spdesign* package, we could extend our design to consider a Bayesian prior for `b_redkite`. To capture this using a uniform prior between `−0.06` and `−0.04` (symmetric around `−0.05`), we can specify it as follows: `b_redkite[uniform_p(−0.06, −0.04)]`, where the `_p` indicates that the distribution is on the prior. When specifying a Bayesian prior, we also need to determine the number and type of draws to use in the simulation of the prior distribution. See the documentation and examples of *spdesign* for more details.

All of this said, a misspecification of the prior is not the end of the world. An "incorrect" prior does not affect or change people's preferences, but the loss of efficiency from an incorrect prior may mean that you need a larger sample to compensate for this loss.

**ⓘ On the magnitude of priors and attribute levels**

When deciding on the priors and attributes, know that the magnitude of one depends on the other. Ideally, we want the overall observed utility of each alternative to be in the range of −2 to 4, which is approximately the range of the standard Gumbel distribution (the assumed distribution of errors in the MNL model). For example, a prior of 0.1 combined with the attribute level 1 results in a utility contribution of 0.1. Likewise, a prior of 0.0001 and an attribute level of 1000 results in a utility contribution of 0.1.

From a practical standpoint and for reporting purposes, in both design and estimation, rescaling the attributes is preferred. When generating a design, making sure that all attribute levels are of roughly the same magnitude ensures that no attribute has an undue influence on the choice probability, which can result in a situation where the presence of one or more positive attributes cannot compensate for the presence of a negative one. This is especially important for the estimation, because it is easier to find maximum likelihood solutions when all attributes (and by extension parameters) are of roughly the same scale or order of magnitude. We can always obtain the original value by re-scaling our parameters after the estimation. See Chaps. 3 and 9 for more details.

## 5.3.2 Generating and Checking the Design

By this stage, we have already defined our utility functions and set the number of alternatives, attributes and levels, as well as the number of rows, i.e. total number of choice tasks, to include in our design. To finish generating the design, we need to specify a few more aspects of the design: the model, the efficiency criterion, and the estimation algorithm.

### 5.3.2.1 Model

The *spdesign* package requires a specification of the model used to generate the design. As of the writing of this book, the only available model in the *spdesign* package is the MNL model, however, most designs used in practical applications in the stated choice literature are based on the MNL model.

Recall that efficient designs are only efficient for the model used to generate the design, in this case the MNL model, and that the use of other models in the analysis phase will lead to a reduced efficiency. Larger sample sizes will be required to compensate for the reduced efficiency, which, *ceteris paribus*, leads to higher standard errors. For example, if the model used in your design is an MNL model and you wish to estimate an MXL model, then you will need more respondents (compared to the minimum necessary for the MNL model) to detect significant effects, due to both the loss of efficiency and the increased complexity of the MXL model. As discussed in Sect. 5.3.1, a strong focus on efficiency (and model choice in design) may only really be warranted with small and highly specialised samples where the predicted number of respondents is low, as samples in other contexts are typically large enough to compensate for reduced efficiency or increased model complexity. Thus, generating a design for an MNL model and using a latent class or random parameters mixed logit model in the analysis stage is still a robust approach (Bliemer and Rose 2010, 2011).

### 5.3.2.2 Efficiency Criteria

Another aspect of the design that must be specified in the *spdesign* package is the efficiency criterion. For our example, we use the D-efficiency criterion, the most common criterion used in stated choice literature, to optimise the design. We specify it as follows: `efficiency_criteria = "d-error"`. You may come across different types of D-efficiency criteria in the literature, which differ in their priors: $D_0$ specifies zero as a prior value for all parameters, $D_p$ specifies non-zero fixed priors, and $D_b$ specifies Bayesian priors. It is important to note that because the D-efficiency criteria are derived based on the variance-covariance matrix of the model used to generate the design, they are sample (data) specific and cannot be compared across designs for different samples. In practice, it makes little sense to compare the D-error from your design with the D-error of your sample.

#### 5.3.2.3 Estimation Algorithms

Finally, we must choose an estimation algorithm to generate our design. The *spdesign* package includes three different estimation algorithms: random, Modified Federov, and RSC. Which estimation algorithm you choose will depend on what you want to achieve with your design, e.g. implement restrictions or ensure attribute level balance. If you want to include restrictions in your design, you are best served using the random or Modified Federov algorithms. However, it is difficult to achieve attribute level balance with these algorithms. If you do not need to implement restrictions and absolute attribute level balance is desired, then the RSC algorithm is a better choice because it handles this automatically. Below, we review the strengths and weaknesses of the three estimation algorithms and the context in which they are best applied.

Random

The random design algorithm requires a candidate set. You can supply a candidate set to `generate_design()` by specifying it in the `candidate_set` argument. If you do not supply a candidate set, then the full factorial will be generated and used (subject to potential excluded choice tasks specified in `exclusions`, see `?generate_design`). Normally, the full factorial is generated in a systematic fashion and once generated, the row order of the full factorial is randomised in the random design. The design process is as follows:

1. Draw a random set of rows equal to rows from the candidate set.
2. Calculate the efficiency of the design.
3. Keep the design if the efficiency criterion of the new design is better than the old design.
4. Repeat steps 1–3 until the efficiency threshold or maximum number of iterations is reached.

> **ⓘ Thresholds and iterations**
>
> In the random, Modified Federov, and RSC estimation algorithms, the default efficiency threshold is set to an arbitrary value of 0.01 and the maximum number of iterations to 10,000. These values should be changed to ensure that you search through enough designs to find one that meets the needs of your study.

The random design algorithm quickly tests a large number of designs in a non-systematic fashion. In the default setting, attribute level balance is not taken into account. If we try to ensure attribute level balance with respect to the `redkite` attribute we can specify: `redkite[c(−5, −2.5, 0, 2.5, 5)](20)`, where the number inside the parentheses sets the attribute level occurrence for each level. With 100 rows and 5 levels, each level will need to occur 20 times to achieve attribute level balance, and every design where this is *not* true will be rejected. Due to the random sampling from the candidate set used in the random design algorithm however, the chances of finding any valid (attribute level balanced) designs are slim.

To solve this issue, we can specify a range of attribute level occurrences: `redkite[c(−5, −2.5, 0, 2.5, 5)](15:30)`. Here, each level will occur a minimum of 15 times and a maximum of 30 times. Importantly, the sum of the minimum level occurrences should be less than the number of rows in your design and the sum of the maximum level occurrences should be greater than the number of rows in your design. Otherwise, you may end up in a situation where no design is found.

One advantage of the random design algorithm over the Modified Federov algorithm is that the resulting design is completely independent of the order of the candidate set, since the algorithm searches through the candidate set randomly. In the Modified Federov algorithm, the order of the candidate set influences the designs found by the algorithm because it searches through the candidate set systematically. This may mean that depending on how long you have searched for a design, some potential choice tasks may never be evaluated or considered.

### Modified Federov

Like the random algorithm detailed above, the Modified Federov algorithm requires either a supplied candidate set or one generated from the full factorial. The design process is as follows:

1. Randomly draw a set of rows equal to `rows` from the candidate set to create a random design candidate and evaluate the design candidate using the chosen efficiency criterion.
2. Swap the first row of the design candidate with the first row from the candidate set.
3. Evaluate the design candidate using the chosen efficiency criterion.
4. If a better design is found, move to the next row of the design candidate and start at the first row of the candidate set. Otherwise, try the next row in the candidate set.
5. Continue to repeat steps 3 and 4, always keeping track of the best design candidate.
6. When all rows of the design candidate have been swapped once, start at Step 2 again.

7. The algorithm terminates when the maximum number of iterations is reached or the efficiency threshold is met.

The systematic process outlined above means that you need to let the model search for a longer period of time to allow choice task candidates later in the candidate set to be included in potential design candidates. If you only search for a short period of time, you will only use choice tasks at the beginning of the candidate set in the iterations.

When using the Modified Federov algorithm, there will be long periods of no improvement, i.e. when no better design has been found, before a burst of new and better designs are found. This is an artefact of the systematic fashion in which the algorithm works through both the design candidate and the candidate set, making it especially important to allow sufficient time for the Modified Federov algorithm to search for designs.

The Modified Federov algorithm will not (by default) check for attribute level balance, but we can achieve near attribute level balance using the same syntax specifying a range of attribute level occurrences as with the random algorithm.

#### Relabelling, Swapping, and Cycling (RSC)

The RSC algorithm will generate the design candidate directly using the supplied attribute levels without the use of a candidate set. Using the number of `rows` specified in the rows argument, the initial design candidate is created from the expanded list of attributes and levels (in the "wide" format) to create an attribute level balanced design candidate set. This is carried out in precisely the same way as the in random column-based designs discussed in Sect. 5.2.2. If we cannot obtain attribute level balance because the number of levels is not a multiple of the `rows`, the candidate set will be near attribute level balanced. The design process is as follows:

1. Create an initial design candidate.
2. Starting with the first column, relabel each column independently. The relabelling part of the algorithm will relabel the attribute levels to create a new design candidate (Hensher et al. 2005). For example, if the column contains the levels (1, 2, 1, 3, 2, 3) and 1 and 3 are relabelled, then the column becomes (3, 2, 3, 1, 2, 1), i.e. 1 becomes 3 and 3 becomes 1. Only a single attribute level is relabelled per column and iteration.
3. Evaluate the design candidate using the chosen efficiency criterion and keep the new candidate if it is better. By default, the algorithm will go through 10,000 column relabels before switching to a swapping algorithm.
4. The swapping part of the algorithm will swap the order of the attributes to create a new design candidate (Hensher et al. 2005). For example, if the attributes in the first and fourth choice task (row) are swapped, then (1, 2, 1, 3, 2, 3) becomes (3, 2, 1, 1, 2, 3). After 10,000 swaps (by default), the algorithm moves back to Step 2. Only one swap is executed per column and iteration.

5. If more than 10,000 candidates have been evaluated without an improvement, start over at Step 1.
6. The algorithm terminates when the maximum number of iterations is reached or the efficiency threshold is met.

The cycling part is rarely used and only really feasible when all attributes have the same number of levels (Hensher et al. 2005) and is not implemented in the *spdesign* package. It is currently not possible to implement any form of restrictions with the RSC algorithm, although this may be added to the package at a later stage. This is because every time a relabel or swap is made, we have to check whether the restrictions hold, which can be time-consuming and hard to ensure in practice.

#### 5.3.2.4 Generating Our Design

Now that we have decided on the model, the efficiency criterion, and the estimation algorithm, we can generate our design using the function `generate_design`. We specify an MNL model, the D-efficiency criterion, and the RSC estimation algorithm to generate our design.

```
# Generate design ----
design <- generate_design(utility,
                          rows = 100,
                          model = "mnl",
                          efficiency_criteria = "d-error",
                          algorithm = "rsc")
```

Searching for a design can be a time-consuming process. We recommend letting your computer search for an extended period of time (e.g. overnight) to allow for the testing of a sufficient number of designs. To see if a design is close to optimal, keep track of the development of the error measures: if improvements are very small and the errors are close to zero, this indicates that the design is close to optimal.

## 5.4 Inspecting Our Design

Once we have generated our design, we need to manually inspect it to determine its suitability. How to check a design is discussed in detail in Mariel et al. (2021), Sect. 3. 3. Designs should be checked for implausible or impossible attribute combinations and cases of dominance in choice tasks, and designs with such issues should not be used. If you are using the random or Modified Federov algorithm, it is normal to exclude these from the *candidate set*. Failing to do so, or if using the RSC algorithm, if priors are properly specified, clearly dominating alternatives should not occur, although in our experience, this can still happen when there are three or more alternatives per choice task (including the status quo). Therefore, we recommend assessing each choice task individually.

## 5.5 Summary of the Design

We can access a summary of the design using the `summary()` function.

```
# Print a summary of the design
summary(design)

---------------------------------------------------------------------
An 'spdesign' object

Utility functions:
alt1 : b_sq * alt1_sq
alt2 : b_farm_dummy * alt2_farm + b_height_dummy * alt2_height + b_redkite * alt2_redkite + b_
distance * alt2_distance + b_cost * alt2_cost
alt3 : b_farm_dummy * alt3_farm + b_height_dummy * alt3_height + b_redkite * alt3_redkite + b_
distance * alt3_distance + b_cost * alt3_cost


   a-error     c-error     d-error     s-error
0.11939271         Inf 0.03885682         Inf

---------------------------------------------------------------------

Printing the first few rows of the design
# A tibble: 6 × 16
  alt1_sq alt2_farm2 alt2_farm3 alt2_height2 alt2_height3 alt2_redkite
    <dbl>      <dbl>      <dbl>        <dbl>        <dbl>        <dbl>
1       1          0          1            0            0          5
2       1          0          0            0            0          2.5
3       1          0          0            0            1          2.5
4       1          0          1            0            0         -2.5
5       1          0          0            0            1          5
6       1          0          1            1            0         -2.5
# ℹ 10 more variables: alt2_distance <dbl>, alt2_cost <dbl>, alt3_farm2 <dbl>,
#   alt3_farm3 <dbl>, alt3_height2 <dbl>, alt3_height3 <dbl>,
#   alt3_redkite <dbl>, alt3_distance <dbl>, alt3_cost <dbl>, block <int>

---------------------------------------------------------------------
Correlation between the blocking vector and attributes:

# A tibble: 1 × 15
  alt1_sq alt2_farm2 alt2_farm3 alt2_height2 alt2_height3 alt2_redkite
    <dbl>      <dbl>      <dbl>        <dbl>        <dbl>        <dbl>
1      NA    0.00370    -0.0185      -0.0185       0.0407      -0.0492
# ℹ 9 more variables: alt2_distance <dbl>, alt2_cost <dbl>, alt3_farm2 <dbl>,
#   alt3_farm3 <dbl>, alt3_height2 <dbl>, alt3_height3 <dbl>,
#   alt3_redkite <dbl>, alt3_distance <dbl>, alt3_cost <dbl>

---------------------------------------------------------------------
```

At the top of the design summary, we see the assumed utility functions used to generate the design followed by the different efficiency criteria of the design. If you have not specified the denominator for WTP, then the `c-error` will always be `NaN` (see the *spdesign* documentation for this functionality), and if you have assumed zero priors or Bayesian priors with support over zero, then the `s-error` will be very large or infinite.

Below the efficiency criteria, you will see the first few rows of the design and as many columns as will fit in the printed output. The first row corresponds to the first choice task, where each column contains the attribute level for each alternative. If you have blocked the design, the correlation with the blocking column will also be printed. For more details, see below.

The design object is a list with the following elements, which can all be accessed with the `$` operator. You can see all elements of the design object using `str(design)`:

1. `utility`—The assumed utility functions with priors and attribute level information
2. `time`—A list containing the `Sys.time()` for the start and stop of the process of finding a design
3. `model`—A character string containing the name of the model used
4. `prior_values`—A list with the named vector of priors (can also be accessed using the generic `coef(design)`)
5. `design`—A tibble (a `tidyverse data.frame`) with the entire design including the blocking vector if the design has been blocked
6. `efficiency_criteria`—A named vector with the efficiency criterion of the design
7. `vcov`—The variance-covariance matrix of the design (can also be accessed with `vcov(design)`)
8. `blocks_value`—The mean squared correlation of the blocking column
9. `blocks_correlation`—The correlation vector between the blocking column and all other columns in the design
10. `blocks_iter`—The number of blocking columns tried

### *5.5.1 Correlation Between Attributes*

The next step of checking your design is to take a closer look at the correlation between the attributes of your design. If you have highly correlated attributes, then you have multicollinearity in the design and consequently will be unable to identify the main effect of all attributes. The *spdesign* package comes with the generic wrapper function `cor()` to quickly display the correlation matrix.

```
# Correlation matrix
cor(design)
```

### *5.5.2 Attribute Level Balance Within the Design*

We can check the attribute level balance of the design using the function `level_balance()`. If you have a blocked design, set the argument `block = TRUE`. The function will print a table with level occurrences for each column in the design. Below, we show what this looks like for the first three columns of the design.

```
# Print only the first three list elements
level_balance(design)[1:3]

$alt1_sq

  1
100

$alt2_farm2

 0  1
67 33

$alt2_farm3

 0  1
67 33
```

First, we see that the constant for the status quo alternative is present in all 100 rows of the design. Next, we see that wind farm size medium and small each occur 33 times, which means that the large level occurs 34 times. This design is near attribute level balanced, as expected, since the design was generated using the RSC algorithm. We may have seen a more attribute imbalanced design had we used the random or Modified Federov algorithm instead.

### *5.5.3 Dominating and Dominated Alternatives*

Dominant and dominated alternatives should be avoided, as they provide no meaningful information about trade-offs and may lead to bias in the estimated parameters (Hensher et al. 2005). The checks in this section ensure that we do not have any dominant or dominated alternatives in our design.

To inspect the utility balance of our design, which will help us identify dominant or dominating alternatives, we can take a look at the probabilities for each alternative. An alternative with a probability close to one will be dominating and an alternative with a probability close to zero will be dominated. The *spdesign* package comes with the function `probabilities()`, which calculates and prints the choice probabilities given your design and priors. The output below shows the probabilities of each alternative in each choice task. All rows sum to one.

```
# Check the utility balance by inspecting the probabilities. We use head() to avoid printing
all 100 rows in the book.
probabilities(design) |>
  head()

          alt1      alt2      alt3
[1,] 0.2894363 0.2894363 0.4211274
[2,] 0.2863329 0.1919347 0.5217325
[3,] 0.2238886 0.3880557 0.3880557
[4,] 0.1929639 0.2416531 0.5653830
[5,] 0.2823977 0.3364052 0.3811971
[6,] 0.2532035 0.5496015 0.1971951
```

To make it easier to spot potentially problematic choice tasks, we make a simple plot (see Fig. 5.1). There do not appear to be any dominating or dominated choice

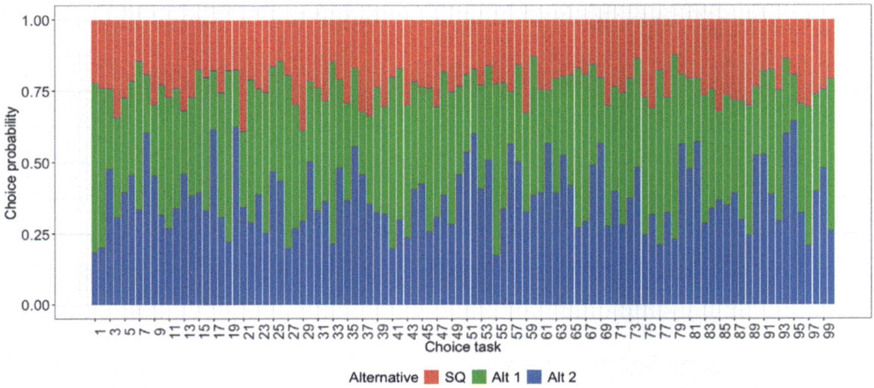


**Fig. 5.1** Choice probabilities

tasks in the design, which would be visible with very small or very large portions of the corresponding alternative colour. According to the plot, the probability of choosing the status quo (in red) is low, but not problematically so. How low is problematically low is hard to quantify and will depend on the context. For example, in labelled experiments, certain alternatives are expected to be chosen fewer times because they are less common. This is a consequence of the assumed prior of the status quo constant and of the other priors and attribute levels.

If the probability of choosing the status quo is too high or too low, based on your assumptions about the prevalence of status quo choices, the corresponding prior should be adjusted. A higher prior is warranted if you anticipate a greater share of status quo choices, while a lower prior is appropriate if you expect a lower share. This adjustment of priors based on the probabilities of different alternatives highlights the importance of inspecting the design and ensuring it aligns with expectations. It also emphasises the need for thoughtful consideration when selecting priors for the experimental design.

```r
# Create a plot to show the choice shares across the design
probabilities(design) |>
  as_tibble() |>
  rowid_to_column() |>
  pivot_longer(-rowid, names_to = "alt", values_to = "prob") |>
  ggplot(aes(x = rowid, y = prob, fill = alt)) +
  geom_bar(position = "fill", stat = "identity") +
  labs(x = "Choice task", y = "Choice probability", fill = "Alternative") +
  scale_x_continuous(breaks = seq(1, 100, by = 2)) +
  scale_fill_discrete(label = c("SQ", "Alt 1", "Alt 2")) +
  theme_bw() +
  theme(
    legend.position = "bottom",
    axis.text.x = element_text(angle = 315)
  )
```

To get a more exact measure of utility balance, we can calculate the utility balance of each choice task in our design using the following equation:

$$B_s = \prod_{i=1}^{J} \frac{P_{si}}{1/J}$$

where the balance in choice task $s$ is the product over the rescaled probabilities of choosing each alternative $i \in J$. Below, we show a simple general function that takes a matrix of probabilities x (with dimensions $S \times J$) and calculates the utility balance for each choice task. Matrix x may or may not include zero probabilities for unavailable alternatives, which could be the case in real data where only certain subsets of respondents see certain alternatives.

```
utility_balance <- function(x) {
  # Ensure that it is a matrix (and not a data.frame()/tibble())
  x <- as.matrix(x)

  # Find number of non-zero alternatives where 0 or NA can be non-available
  n_alts <- apply(x, 1, function(y) sum(y > 0, na.rm = TRUE))

  # Calculate for each alternative
  x <- x / (1 / n_alts)

  # Replace all zeroes with 1 to enable taking the product
  index_zero <- x == 0
  x[index_zero] <- 1

  # Take the product. This line requires the Rfast package.
  x <- Rfast::rowprods(x)

  return(x)
}

# Use the function for utility balance on the choice probabilities
utility_balance(probabilities(design)) |>
  head()
```

```
[1] 0.9525401 0.7741698 0.9102987 0.7118279 0.9777712 0.7409303
```

The function returns the utility balance of each choice task. The mean utility balance of the design is the mean of choice task-specific utility balance measures and is equal to 0.8478399. Typically, we will have a utility balance for efficient designs of around 70–90%, which means that designs are neither too balanced (e.g. utilities between alternatives are equal) nor too imbalanced (dominant alternatives exist) (Rose et al. 2018). In a perfectly balanced design, the choice probabilities are equal and indistinguishable from random.

If you find problems in your design, such as a choice task with a clearly dominated alternative, we recommend the following: check your priors and attributes to ensure that the utilities of each alternative are relatively balanced, correct the priors if needed, and dedicate more time to searching for a new design. With properly specified priors, dominated alternatives should not be part of the design.

The estimation of MNL, MX-RPL, and MX-LCM models (see Chap. 9) can also be used to validate the suitability of the generated design for these three models. This check is useful because it can reveal issues with parameter identification. Typically, issues of parameter identification in MNL, MX-RPL, and MX-LCM models present as follows: the problematic parameter will be an order of magnitude larger or smaller in scale compared to the other parameters of the model and the standard errors will be large.

## 5.6 Other Aspects to Consider

### *5.6.1 Size of the Design*

All designs are generated at the outset as if a single respondent answered all choice tasks. An obvious constraint then is how many choice tasks we can reasonably expect a single respondent to answer. The answer to this question is highly context dependent. Are the choice tasks complex with lots of detailed information, or are they simpler and more straightforward with easy-to-communicate attributes? Are the choices familiar to respondents, e.g. recreational trips, or are they unfamiliar, e.g. the impacts of conservation areas on biodiversity and economic opportunities for local communities?

In most applications in environmental economics, you will find that respondents typically answer somewhere between 6 and 12 choice tasks (see Chap. 2 and Mariel et al. 2021 for a detailed discussion). However, creating designs with such few choice tasks will impact your ability to estimate more complex models.

With only 10 choice tasks and 3 alternatives, for example, your ability to create variation in attribute levels across alternatives is limited, which impacts your ability to identify and estimate the parameters of your model. The total number of parameters that can be estimated with a given design is determined by (Rose et al. 2018):

$$K = (J - 1)\,S$$

In this example, we can estimate $(3 - 1)10 = 20$ parameters. This may be enough for simple multinomial logit models, but once you move to more complex models such as the mixed logit or latent class models, you will find that the number of required parameters increases rapidly.

The size of the design is defined by both the number of alternatives per choice task and, perhaps more importantly, the number of choice tasks (rows) in the design. A design that is too small can result in a log-likelihood function with flat regions, which makes convergence exceedingly difficult or even impossible (see Chap. 8). This then becomes a data problem that cannot be solved with more respondents.

With efficient designs, we can estimate the parameters and find significant effects with smaller sample sizes (Rose and Bliemer 2013). This is one of the reasons for their popularity and, we suspect, one of the reasons why we have seen a proliferation of small designs in the stated choice literature. Very efficient designs tend to be small designs, with a small number of choice tasks and few attributes varying over few levels.

By increasing the size of the design, i.e. including more levels for each attribute and additional rows, you can obtain more variation in $x_{kjs}$, which *ceteris paribus* will improve your ability to estimate the parameters of your model (Hensher et al. 2005) and potentially result in more realistic trade-offs. However, designs can quickly become too large for a single respondent to answer all choice tasks. A common solution to this problem is to divide the design into smaller blocks.

### 5.6.2 Blocking the Design

The design created in this chapter contains 100 rows, which is too many for a single respondent to meaningfully answer. In this section, we detail two ways to solve this issue. The first, and most common solution, is blocking.

Blocking the design entails creating smaller subsets of the design, called blocks, with each respondent facing only the choice tasks in a single block. Let us say that our pre-testing showed that respondents can reasonably answer 10 of our choice tasks. With 100 choice tasks, we would need 10 blocks of 10 choice tasks each for our design. Remember, we need each choice task to be responded to at least once. In practice, this means that we will need (at least) 10 respondents compared to a single respondent if each respondent answered 100 choice tasks. It is important to note that a larger design with blocking requires more respondents to get sufficient coverage of the choice tasks.

> ⓘ **Blocked designs**
>
> When implementing a blocked design, individuals responding to the survey will be randomly allocated to a block, with the order of choice tasks within a block randomised between respondents. Remember to always record the choice task so that you can recreate choices after you have gathered the data. See Chap. 6 for other tips and tricks on how and what to record when gathering data.

The blocking column of the design must be orthogonal, i.e. uncorrelated, to the rest of your design. The `block()` function from the *spdesign* package will find a blocking column such that the mean squared correlation is minimised, however, no attempt is made to keep attribute level balance within blocks. If your design overall is attribute level balanced, blocking does not affect this. However, in a blocked design, some respondents may never make trade-offs against all attribute levels potentially affecting the perceived realism of the choice tasks. Note that for some designs, finding the blocking column can take time.

```
# Add a blocking variable to the design with 10 blocks.
design <- block(design, 10)
```

To check the quality of the blocking column, the correlation between the blocking column and all attributes in the design is printed along with the `summary()` of the design, or can be accessed directly:

```
design$blocks_correlation

# A tibble: 1 × 15
  alt1_sq alt2_farm2 alt2_farm3 alt2_height2 alt2_height3 alt2_redkite
    <dbl>      <dbl>      <dbl>        <dbl>        <dbl>        <dbl>
1      NA    0.00370    -0.0185      -0.0185       0.0407      -0.0492
# ℹ 9 more variables: alt2_distance <dbl>, alt2_cost <dbl>, alt3_farm2 <dbl>,
#   alt3_farm3 <dbl>, alt3_height2 <dbl>, alt3_height3 <dbl>,
#   alt3_redkite <dbl>, alt3_distance <dbl>, alt3_cost <dbl>
```

Here, we see that the blocking column is practically uncorrelated with the rest of the design (mean squared correlation = 0.00069). The blocking column is stored as a `tibble`.

An alternative to blocking is to randomly draw the required number of choice tasks from the design for each respondent. For this approach, you will need to use survey software that can perform this randomisation. This approach has two main benefits over the blocking approach: it ensures that

(i) you will have no blocking effects in your data, e.g. choice patterns arising because some respondents saw choice tasks that were systematically different from those seen by other respondents,
(ii) the order of choice tasks between respondents will automatically be randomised

However, due to the nature of the random draws, it will likely require more respondents to achieve good coverage of all choice tasks (rows) in the design.

We have seen that larger designs provide more variation across choice tasks and that blocking allows us to give each respondent a manageable number of choice tasks. So, if budget is not an issue, why would we consider using small designs?

It depends on the context: researchers working with vulnerable populations or conducting research in developing countries may work under constraints related to both potential sample sizes and technical implementation. In these cases, small designs capable of detecting significant main effects may be much more important than the ability to estimate complex models. Additionally, without access to digital technology to handle randomisation, the implementation of large complex designs may be difficult.

At the end of the day, experimental designs are about ensuring that you are able to identify the effects of interest to answer your research question (Vega-Bayo et al. 2023). We have dedicated a large portion of this chapter to the discussion of efficient experimental designs, as they affect the standard errors and our ability to estimate significant parameters for each attribute in the design. That said, only in very specific cases, e.g. small potential samples, should efficiency be a goal in itself.

Other aspects of the design process, such as specifying appropriate priors or achieving (near) attribute level balance are just as important, as they help improve our design and the subsequent estimation. The goal is to use the concepts discussed in this chapter to generate the most suitable design for your specific research context, setting yourself up for data collection and analysis with confidence in your generated design.

## 5.7 Key Takeaways

- Experimental designs aim to identify the parameters and relationships necessary to address your research question effectively. In this chapter, we review orthogonal, random, and efficient designs.
- Efficient experimental designs minimise standard errors, enhancing the likelihood of obtaining significant parameter estimates for each attribute.
- Finding suitable priors can be challenging, but various strategies can help us identify them. Non-zero priors reduce dominating alternatives, making it important to assign the correct sign to all priors.
- Reviewing the generated design is essential to ensure that the choice tasks are realistic and free from dominating or dominated alternatives.
- The size of the design should reflect the complexity of the choice tasks and the number of parameters being estimated. The experimental design plays an even more critical role when working with smaller sample sizes.

## Bibliography

Bliemer MCJ, Collins AT (2016) On determining priors for the generation of efficient stated choice experimental designs. J Choice Model 21:10–14. https://doi.org/10.1016/j.jocm.2016.03.001

Bliemer MCJ, Rose JM (2010) Construction of experimental designs for mixed logit models allowing for correlation across choice observations. Transp Res b: Methodol 44:720–734. https://doi.org/10.1016/j.trb.2009.12.004

Bliemer MCJ, Rose JM (2011) Experimental design influences on stated choice outputs: an empirical study in air travel choice. Transp Res a: Policy Pract 45:63–79. https://doi.org/10.1016/j.tra.2010.09.003

Carson RT, Groves T (2007) Incentive and informational properties of preference questions. Environ Resour Econ 37:181–210. https://doi.org/10.1007/s10640-007-9124-5

Campbell D, Erdem S (2019) Including opt-out options in discrete choice experiments: issues to consider. Patient 12(1):1–14. https://doi.org/10.1007/s40271-018-0324-6

Hensher DA, Rose JM, Greene WH (2005) Applied choice analysis: a primer. Cambridge University Press

Huber J, Zwerina K (1996) The importance of utility balance in efficient choice designs. J Mark Res 33(3):307–317

Johnston RJ, Boyle KJ, Adamowicz W et al (2017) Contemporary guidance for stated preference studies. J Assoc Environ Resour Econ 4(2):319–405. https://doi.org/10.1086/691697

Mahieu PA, Andersson H, Beaumais O et al (2017) Stated preferences: a unique database composed of 1657 recent published articles in journals related to agriculture, environment, or health. Rev Agric Food Environ 98(3):201–220. https://doi.org/10.1007/s41130-017-0053-6

Mariel P, Hoyos D, Meyerhoff J et al (2021) Environmental valuation with discrete choice experiments: guidance on design, implementation and data analysis. Springer Nature. https://doi.org/10.1007/978-3-030-62669-3

Oehlmann M, Meyerhoff J, Mariel P, Weller P (2017) Uncovering context-induced status quo effects in choice experiments. J Environ Econ Manag 81:59–73. https://doi.org/10.1016/j.jeem.2016.09.002

Olsen SB, Meyerhoff J (2017) Will the alphabet soup of design criteria affect discrete choice experiment results? Eur Rev Agric Econ 44(2):309–336. https://doi.org/10.1093/erae/jbw014

Olsen SB, Meyerhoff J, Mørkbak MR, Bonnichsen O (2017) The influence of time of day on decision fatigue in online food choice experiments. Br Food J 119(3):497–510. https://doi.org/10.1108/BFJ-05-2016-0227

Rose JM, Bliemer MCJ (2009) Constructing efficient stated choice experimental designs. Transp Rev 29(5):587–617. https://doi.org/10.1080/01441640902827623

Rose JM, Bliemer MCJ (2013) Sample size requirements for stated choice experiments. Transportation 40:1021–1041. https://doi.org/10.1007/s11116-013-9451-z

Rose JM, Bliemer MCJ (2014) Stated choice experimental design theory: the who, the what and the why. In: Hess S, Daly A (eds) Handbook of choice modelling. Edward Elgar Publishing, pp 152–177

Rose JM, Collins AT, Bliemer M, Hensher DA (2018) Choice metrics. NGENE. http://choice-metrics.com/. Accessed 12 Dec 2024

Sándor Z, Wedel M (2001) Designing conjoint choice experiments using managers' prior beliefs. J Mark Res 38(4):430–444

Sandorf ED, Campbell D, Chorus C (2022) A Simple Satisficing Model. PLoS ONE 17(10):e0275339. https://doi.org/10.1371/journal.pone.0275339

Sandorf ED, Campbell D (2023) spdesign: designing stated preference experiments. R package version 0.0.5. https://CRAN.R-project.org/package=spdesign

Scarpa R, Rose JM (2008) Design efficiency for non-market valuation with choice modelling: how to measure it, what to report and why*. Aust J Agric Resour Econ 52(3):253–282

Street DJ, Burgess L (2007) The construction of optimal stated choice experiments: theory and methods. Wiley

Vega-Bayo A, Mariel P, Meyerhoff J et al (2023) Climate change adaptation preferences of winemakers from the Rioja wine appellation. J Choice Model 48:100534. https://doi.org/10.1016/j.jocm.2023.100434

Vossler CA, Doyon M, Rondeau D (2012) Truth in consequentiality: theory and field evidence on discrete choice experiments. Am Econ J Microecon 4(4):145–171. https://doi.org/10.1257/mic.4.4.145

Yao RT, Scarpa R, Rose JM, Turner JA (2015) Experimental design criteria and their behavioural efficiency: an evaluation in the field. Environ Resour Econ 62:433–455. https://doi.org/10.1007/s10640-014-9823-7

# Chapter 6
# Data Collection in Shiny

**Abstract** This chapter guides you through the process of using R Shiny to collect your own data for your DCE. We provide a sample code on how to implement a bare-bones DCE survey using Shiny, Google Sheets and Shinyapps.io, walking you through the following steps: (1) setting up the data storage location, (2) generating the choice tasks, and (3) creating the Shiny app. To create the Shiny app, we review the user interface, the server function, and the Shiny app function. Finally, we discuss the advantages and disadvantages of using R Shiny to implement DCE surveys.

## 6.1 Introduction

This chapter focuses on the process of data collection within the framework of the DCE methodology. After determining the attributes and levels, establishing the validity of our design through generation and testing, and finalising the remaining sections of the questionnaire (including socio-demographic and other pertinent inquiries for our research), this step involves the collection of data. Although there are several other options available for collecting data (see survey mode in Sect. 2.5), this chapter focuses on how to program a basic DCE using R Shiny. We guide you through the steps of collecting the data yourself, i.e. data collection without the use of a survey company, in R Shiny and discuss its advantages and disadvantages.

Note that the survey we implement in this chapter is relatively simple and bare-bones, but will still require significant effort on your part. In case you consider implementing your DCE survey using Shiny, make sure to account for this step both budget-wise and time-wise in your research.

> ⓘ **Ethics Committee**
>
> As mentioned in Chapter 2, you should be aware that in order to gather potentially sensitive data from individuals, your research organisation might require approval



P. Mariel et al., *Environmental Valuation with Discrete Choice Experiments in R*,
The Economics of Non-Market Goods and Resources 17,
https://doi.org/10.1007/978-3-031-89338-4_6

from an ethics committee before you can carry out the data collection. Therefore, you should make sure to look into the regulations your institution has in place, and factor sufficient time into your research plan to acquire the required permissions.

Failure to get approval from the ethics committee of your research institution can have significant repercussions, particularly concerning the publication of your findings. Ethics committees are responsible for ensuring that research complies with ethical standards, including the protection of participants' rights, privacy, and well-being. If your DCE has not undergone or failed to pass an ethical review, most reputable academic journals will refuse to publish the research due to concerns over ethical integrity and legal liability, thus rendering your research efforts null.

## 6.2 Why Shiny?

Using R Shiny for data collection in DCEs offers several advantages over other data collection methods: (1) R Shiny is an R package, whose syntax many of you will be familiar with from its use in the rest of this book or from previous programming experience, (2) we can keep everything in a single open-source platform, and (3) we have full control over our experiment.

Shiny allows us to create interactive and user-friendly web-based applications, making it an ideal tool for data collection, with a highly customisable and flexible interface for survey design. We can create visually appealing and intuitive surveys by leveraging the extensive set of built-in widgets, such as sliders, dropdown menus, checkboxes, and text inputs, among others. These widgets can be easily customised to match the specific requirements of our DCE, allowing for a seamless user experience and improved response rates.

R Shiny offers real-time data validation and error checking. This feature is particularly valuable for survey data collection, as it ensures the accuracy and integrity of the collected data. We can define rules and conditions to validate the input data in real time, providing immediate feedback to respondents if they make any mistakes or input invalid responses. This helps improve the data quality and reduces the need for manual data cleaning and validation after the survey is completed.

With dynamic survey question branching and skip patterns, we can create surveys that adapt to respondents' previous answers. Depending on the responses given, different follow-up questions can be displayed or skipped, providing a more personalised and efficient survey experience. This flexibility is particularly useful for DCEs, where there are typically requirements for multiple paths and conditional logic (e.g. only some respondents, such as "protesters", are asked to justify their choices based on previous responses; subsequent choice tasks can be tailored based on previous choices, etc.).

R Shiny provides seamless integration with R's powerful data analysis and visualisation capabilities. We can directly process and analyse the collected survey data using a wide range of statistical techniques and packages available in R. We can also generate interactive visualisations and dashboards to explore and present survey results, making it easier to derive meaningful insights from the collected data.

However, using R Shiny does have its downsides. Inexperienced R users might find it overly difficult or time-consuming to program their full survey in Shiny, especially if the DCE is complex. Therefore, we would only recommend this option for researchers or students with a limited budget, a simple DCE, and who are eager to add a new skill to their toolkit. The example we present in the following section will reflect this recommendation, and will not cover important issues such as secure data storage, respondent drop-outs, or complex adaptive designs. For advanced R users and programmers interested in incorporating these aspects into their R Shiny, we recommend reading through the INSPIRE Project (2020).

**General Data Protection Regulation**

When conducting online data collection, it is crucial to ensure compliance with the General Data Protection Regulation (GDPR), which mandates that researchers and data collectors avoid storing personal information that can directly or indirectly identify individuals without a proper legal basis and consent. Personal information includes, but is not limited to, IP addresses, email addresses, and detailed socio-demographic information. Under GDPR, such data is classified as personally identifiable information (PII), and its storage, processing, and use are subject to stringent requirements to protect the privacy rights of individuals.

Therefore, to comply with GDPR, researchers must implement data minimisation principles, i.e. collecting only the *essential* data necessary for the research purpose and ensuring that any personal information is anonymised or pseudonymised wherever possible. Moreover, they should avoid collecting data that could lead to the identification of individuals if it is not required for their research objectives.

As detailed in the INSPIRE Project (2020), persistent storage of any sensitive or identifiable information without a clear purpose, robust security measures, and informed consent could lead to severe legal consequences under GDPR regulations, including fines and penalties.

GDPR places an emphasis on transparency and accountability. In practice, this means that researchers must inform participants about the type of data being collected, the purpose of the collection, how it will be used, and the duration of its storage. Researchers should also periodically review the necessity of data storage and implement mechanisms for data deletion once the research purpose has been fulfilled, further minimising the risk of data breaches or misuse. Following these guidelines ensures not only legal compliance with GDPR regulations, but also fosters trust and ethical standards in research practices involving online data collection.

## 6.3 Programming the DCE in Shiny

If you have determined that Shiny is a suitable data collection method for your DCE, considering your programming capabilities, DCE requirements, time constraints, and funding availability, you can start the programming process. The implementation of the DCE in Shiny will consist of three main elements: (1) setting the data storage location, (2) generating the DCE choice tasks, and (3) creating the Shiny app. In this section, we review each of these elements and how to program them in R.

### *6.3.1 Data Storage Location*

First, we have to decide where to store the data to be collected. There are several options for persistent data storage using Shiny apps, depending on the type of data collected (Attali 2020):

- Arbitrary data, which can be stored as a file in a file system (e.g. a local file system, or cloud services such as Dropbox or Amazon S3)
- Structured rectangular data, which can be stored as a table in a relational database or table-storage service (e.g. Google Sheets, MySQL)
- Semi-structured data, which can be stored as a collection in a NoSQL database (e.g. MongoDB)

For both illustrative purposes and because of its ease of use, we will focus on remote data storage in Google Sheets, a type of structured rectangular data, in this chapter. This type of data storage requires an active Google account, which might have its implications in terms of data security. Note that this requires creating a Google account if you do not already have one.

The code chunks below represent an auxiliary script file that will code *where* in Google Sheets we wish to store the data that we collect, starting by creating a Google Sheet where we will store the results. We only need to run the following code chunks once to create the sheet. Once the sheet is created, every response to the survey will be added to this sheet.

Given the relative complexity of coding even a simple Shiny App, we strongly encourage you to read through the end of this chapter before you attempt to do so yourself, so that you understand how the different pieces of code relate to each other and what the file structure should look like.

```
# Load the necessary libraries

library(tidyverse)
library(shiny)
library(shinyjs)
library(shinyWidgets)
library(googledrive)
library(googlesheets4)
```

```
> gs4_auth()
The googlesheets4 package is requesting access to your Google account.
Select a pre-authorised account or enter '0' to obtain a new token.
Press Esc/Ctrl + C to cancel.

1: [redacted]@gmail.com

Selection: 0
```

**Fig. 6.1** Console prompt for selecting a Google account

In order to create the sheet, we need to (1) configure access to Google Sheets, and (2) set up the sheet with the column names of the data to be collected. We can configure access to Google Sheets by running the line of code below.

```
gs4_auth()
```

This should result in the console prompting you to select a pre-authorised account (if you have previously used the package) or obtain a new token, i.e. add a new account (Fig. 6.1).

If it is your first time setting up authorisation, enter "0" in the console. This will launch your computer's browser and prompt you to grant access to the Google account (Fig. 6.2) that you wish to link to RStudio. Once you hit continue, make sure you click "See, edit, create and delete all your Google Sheets spreadsheets".

You should then get confirmation that the authentication is complete in both the browser and your R console. Once the authentication is complete, you are ready re-run `gs4_auth()`, and select "1" (or the corresponding Google Account) to link RStudio and your Google account.

You are now ready to create the sheet where following information will be stored (with each respondent expected to answer two choice tasks):

- The choice *made* by the respondent, with one column per choice task (`cm1, cm2`)
- The choice task number *shown* to the respondent, with one column per choice task (`cs1, cs2`). The choice task actually shown to the respondent will be randomly drawn from all possible choice tasks each time someone accesses the survey. We therefore need to know what task each respondent is shown so that we can retrieve the corresponding attribute values prior to estimation.
- The socio-demographic variables to be collected as part of the survey, with one column per variable (`gender, age, edu`)
- If the respondent chooses the status quo option for all choices, a protest question asking why they are protesting (`protest`)
- A timestamp column `timestamp`

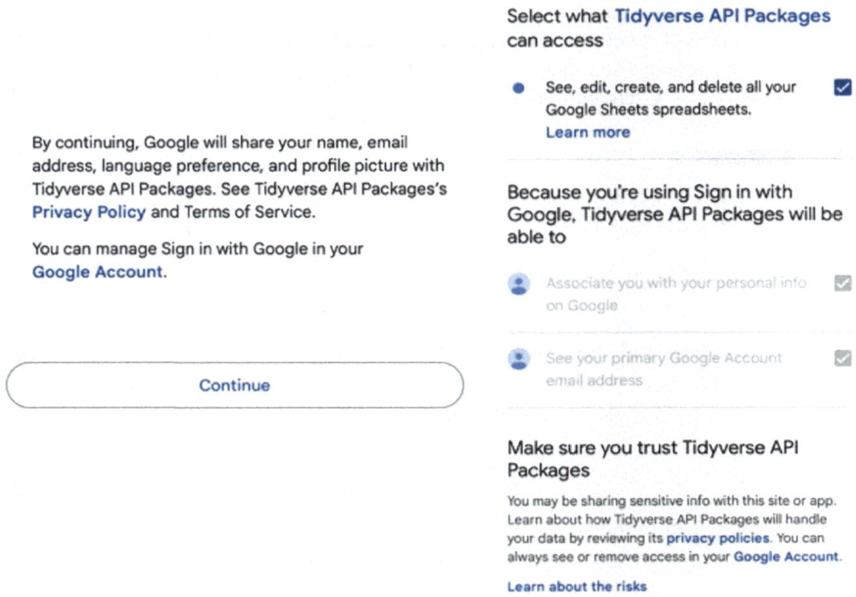


**Fig. 6.2** Browser-based Google sign-in and permission screen initiated by googlesheets4 for account authentication

Note that this data is in a wide format (one row per *respondent*, not per choice task). To initialise the sheet, we create an initial dataset with all variables set to zero, and define a global variable.

```
# Create an initial dataset to initialise the Google Sheet
initial_data <- tibble(
  cm1 = 0,
  cm2 = 0,
  cs1 = 0,
  cs2 = 0,
  gender = 0,
  age = 0,
  edu = 0,
  protest = 0,
  timestamp = 0
)

# Define global variable
gs_name <- "DCEBookTest"
```

Next, we create the Google Sheet file in the account previously linked, defining its name (here, `DCEBookTest`), and the sheet in which we wish to store the results (`DCEAnswers`). We pass that information, together with the `initial_data` column names on to the function `gs4_create()`.

```
# Create the Google Sheet file named DCEBookTest and initialise with the data above

gs_name <- "DCEBookTest"

gs <- gs4_create(
  gs_name,
  sheets = list(
    "DCEBookTest" = initial_data
  )
)
```

We then add a first (throwaway) row of data to make sure that everything is set up correctly and pass it on to the Google Sheet using `drive_get()` and `sheet_append()` from the `googledrive` and `googlesheets4` packages, respectively.

```
# We append some data to check if everything works as intended
appended_data <- tibble(
  cm1 = 1,
  cm2 = 1,
  cs1 = "Prog 1",
  cs2 = "Prog 2",
  gender = "Male",
  age = 25,
  edu = "Primary",
  protest = 0,
  timestamp = Sys.time()
)

sheet_append(
  ss = gs,
  data = appended_data,
  sheet = gs_name
)
```

We have now completed the setup of the Google Sheet. Figure 6.3 shows what the sheet looks like once it is up and running.

**Fig. 6.3** Screenshot of Google Sheets where the results will be stored

### *6.3.2 DCE Choice Task Generation*

In this step, we will generate the choice tasks of the DCE in an auxiliary script file that is not a part of the Shiny app. The goal of this script is to take the experimental design as an input and generate the choice tasks in the format required for the Shiny survey.

We start by reading the design generated using *spdesign* (Sandorf and Campbell 2023) in Chapter 5, saved elsewhere in our file system, and adding the design details to our R environment (see the end of this section for the recommended file organisation and relative file paths).

```
# Read the design
design <- readRDS(gzcon(url("https://raw.githubusercontent.com/edsandorf/evdce/refs/heads/main
/Data/design-windmills.rds")))
design <- design$design
```

In our example, based on the wind power case study (see Chapter 4), we have three alternatives, each described by five attributes. Below, we create a vector of attribute names that we will use throughout the Shiny App.

```
# Attributes
attrib <- c(
  "Size of wind farms",
  "Maximum height of turbines",
  "Reduction of red kite population",
  "Minimum distance to residential areas",
  "Monthly surcharge to power bill"
)
```

The number of alternatives, attributes, rows, blocks, and choice tasks can be inferred from the design. Due to space limitations, we will create a Shiny survey with just two choice tasks per respondent, although this number will typically be higher in DCE surveys.

The next step is to create a list of choice tasks, replacing the numeric levels from the experimental design (e.g. 0, 1 …) with the level names we want the respondents to see (e.g. small, medium, …). Note that we are showing respondents the actual levels of the attributes for each alternative, not the deviations from the SQ.

```r
# Apply user-defined function to each row of the experimental design

ct <- lapply(seq_len(nrow(design)), function(i) {
  return(
   # The function takes the design, creates the choice task, and modifies for correct display
    design[i, ] |>
      select(-block) |>
      pivot_longer(
        cols = everything(),
        names_to = c("alt", ".value"),
        values_to = "level",
        names_sep = "_"
      ) |>
      mutate(
        farm = farm2 * 2 + farm3 * 3,
        farm = ifelse(farm == 0 | is.na(farm), 1, farm),
        farm = case_when(
          farm == 1 ~ "Large",
          farm == 2 ~ "Medium",
          farm == 3 ~ "Small"
        ),
        height = height2 * 2 + height3 * 3,
        height = ifelse(height == 0 | is.na(height), 1, height),
        height = case_when(
          height == 1 ~ "High",
          height == 2 ~ "Medium",
          height == 3 ~ "Low"
        ),
        redkite = ifelse(is.na(redkite), 0, redkite + 10),
        redkite = paste0(redkite, "%"),
        distance = ifelse(is.na(distance), 750, distance * 1000 + 750),
        distance = paste0(distance, "m"),
        cost = ifelse(is.na(cost), 0, cost),
        cost = paste0("€", cost)
      ) |>
      select(farm, height,
             redkite, distance, cost, -farm2, -farm3, -height2, -height3, -sq, alt) |>
      pivot_longer(
        cols = -alt,
        names_to = "attribute",
        values_to = "level"
      ) |>
      pivot_wider(
        names_from = alt,
        values_from = level
      ) |>
      mutate(
        attribute = attribute_descriptions
      )
  )
})
```

This `ct` list has one item per design row, and will be the basis of our Shiny app, the third (and main) step of implementing a DCE in Shiny.

### 6.3.3 The Shiny App

For inexperienced Shiny users, we recommend following Posit (n.d.) as an introduction to Shiny apps. At a high-level, Shiny allows programmers to combine the computational strengths of R with the interactivity of web applications. Shiny provides a curated set of functions that generate the HTML, CSS, and JavaScripts necessary to create web applications (Wickham 2021). Shiny apps have three main components:

- A user interface object (`ui`), which controls the layout and appearance of the app
- A `server()` function, which contains the instructions to build the objects displayed in the user interface
- A call to the `shinyApp()` function that creates the app from the `ui/server pair`

You can choose to program the app fully in a single script, or divide it into chunks or scripts. For our purposes, we divide it into three different scripts: a `ui.R` script, a `server.R` script, and a `call-app.R` script. Depending on your R programming experience and the complexity of your experiment, you could also break down the `ui.R` and `server.R` scripts further, e.g. `ui-intro.R`, `ui-socdem.R`, `ui-choicetasks.R`, etc. Figures 6.4, 6.5, and 6.6 show what the app looks like once it is up and running.

Figure 6.4 shows the initial introduction text the respondent is shown when the survey is initially loaded. After they click next (note the greyed out vs. black 'NEXT' button in Fig. 6.4), the respondent will face the socio-demographic questions. They will not be able to click on next until they have answered the questions you have marked as required on the server.

Figure 6.5 shows how the 'NEXT' button on the socio-demographic questions becomes clickable once the respondent answers. Respondents are then shown standard pre-choice task information stating that answers are confidential and that there is no right or wrong.

Lastly, Fig. 6.6 shows a typical choice task as well as the screen only "protester" respondents (i.e. those who have selected Programme A as their answer in all of their choice tasks) are shown.

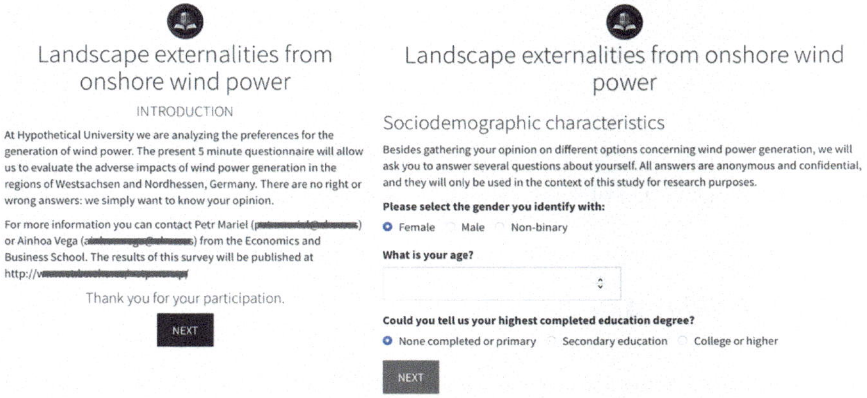


**Fig. 6.4** Screenshots of the introduction text and non-clickable 'NEXT' button due to incomplete socio-demographic questions

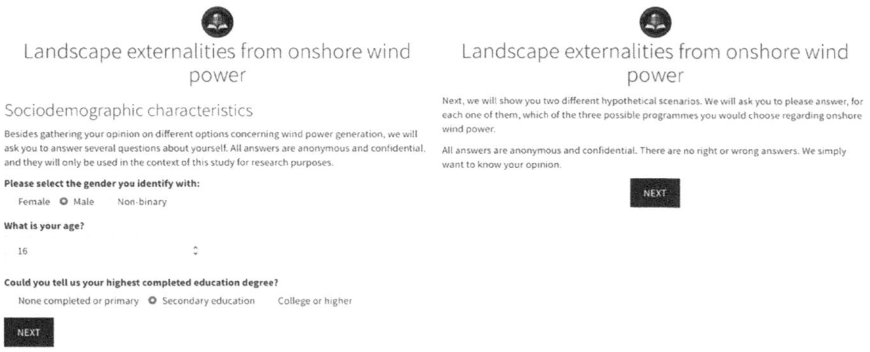


**Fig. 6.5** Screenshots of the clickable 'NEXT' button due to completed socio-demographic questions

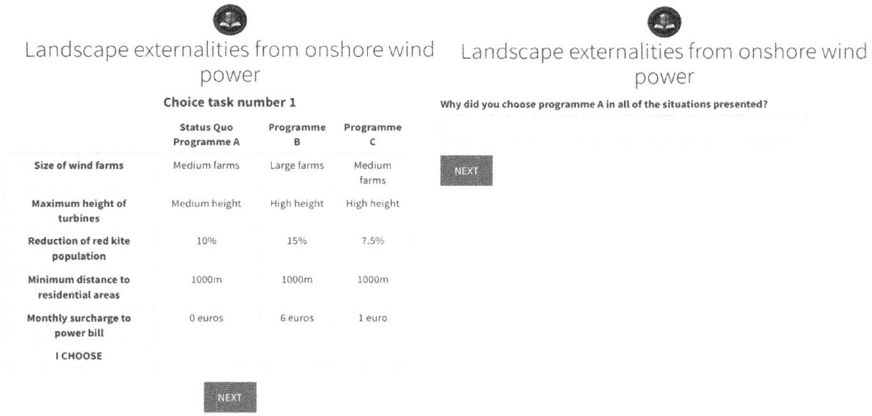


**Fig. 6.6** Screenshots of a typical choice task and follow-up question for protesters

#### 6.3.3.1 The User Interface (UI)

The next step is to write the code for the user interface (`ui.R` script). To simplify and shorten the code in this chapter, we only use two choice tasks per respondent. Although there are ways to "automate" the script for a higher number of choice tasks, we believe that copy-pasting the choice tasks as many times as you need is easiest, especially for novel programmers and for the purpose of improving the readability and flexibility of the script. You can find the code to this bare-bones Shiny survey, in full, in the book's GitHub repository.

The `ui` is wrapped inside a `fluidPage()` function, which we will fill with some basic settings in JavaScript, including theming, CSS, specifying a title, etc. Note that inside of the `fluidPage()` call, each "part" of the page has to be followed by a comma.

```
ui <- fluidPage(
  # State that we want to use JavaScript
  useShinyjs(),

  # Set the theme
  theme = shinytheme("cosmo"),

  # Define some CSS
  tags$style(
    type = "text/css",
    "tr:last-child {border-bottom:1px solid #D5D5D5;}
     td {border-left:1px solid #D5D5D5; border-right:1px solid #D5D5D5;}
     .choicebuttons .radio-inline {margin: 0 10% 0 3%;}",
    HTML("td:first-child { font-weight: bold }")
  ),

  # Set application title
  title = "Discrete Choice Experiment",
```

We continue filling our ui object with a `titlePanel`. In this case, aside from the title text itself, we are also including an institutional logo that we have saved in an "images" directory.

```
  # Set the title panel
  titlePanel(
    div(
      img(src = "images/your-logo.jpg", height = 50),
      p("Your title here"),
      align = "center"
    )
  ),
```

We can now start with the introduction to the survey inside a `div` with `id = "intro"`, which should include some basic information about the survey (see Fig. 6.4). Note that the introduction panel here includes an action button that takes the respondent to the next section of the survey when clicked, in this case the socio-demographic questions.

```
  # Survey introduction
  div(
    id = "intro",
    h4("Introduction"),
    p("Some basic information about your survey including how to contact the
      authors", style = "text-align: left;"),
    h4("Thank you for your participation"),
    actionButton(
      inputId = "click2socdem",
      label = "Next",
      style = "text-align: center;"
    )
  ),
```

The remainder of the survey is placed inside a `hidden()` panel that is not visible to the respondent until the first action button from the introduction is clicked. We will slowly fill in this panel with elements of the survey.

```
hidden(

)
```

In the code chunk below, we demonstrate how to collect information on three basic socio-demographic variables: sex, age, and educational level, using different Shiny widgets. As before, the div ends with an action button that takes the respondent to the following section—in this case, the explanation prior to the choice tasks.

```
# Socio-demographic questions
div(
  id = "socdem",
  h3("Socio-demographic characteristics"),

  # Gender
  radioButtons(
    inputId = "gender",
    label   = "Please select your gender",
    choices = c(
      "Female" = "female",
      "Male" = "male",
      "Other" = "other",
      "Prefer not to say" = "prefer_not_to_say"
    ),
    inline  = TRUE
  ),

  # Age
  numericInput(
    inputId = "age",
    label = "What is your age?",
    value = FALSE,
    min = 16,
    max = 100,
    step = 1
  ),

  # Education Level
  radioButtons(
    inputId = "edu",
    label   = "What is your highest completed education degree?",
    choices = c(
      "None completed or primary" = "primary",
      "Secondary education" = "secondary",
      "College or higher" = "tertiary"
    ),
    inline  = TRUE
  ),

  # Include the action button to send people to the next page of the survey
  actionButton(
    inputId = "click2explanation",
    label = "Next"
  ),
  style = "text-align: center;"
),
```

The following "explanation `div`" is quite basic and includes only text and an action button to the first choice task. However, it might be a good idea to describe the experiment attributes and levels in more detail in this step, and/or to include an example choice task for respondents to review.

```
# Explanation of the DCE
  div(
    id = "explanation",
    p(
      "Next, we will show you two different hypothetical scenarios.
      We ask you to please answer, for each one of them, which of the three
      possible programmes you would choose regarding onshore wind power.",
      style = "text-align: left;"
    ),
    p(
      "All answers are anonymous and confidential. There are no right or wrong
      answers. We simply want to know your opinion.",
      style = "text-align: left;"
    ),

    # Include the action button to send people on to the next page
    actionButton(
      inputId = "click2choice1",
      label = "Next"
    ),
    style = "text-align: center;"
  ),
```

The respondent is then shown each of the choice tasks, and has to select one of the alternatives to move on to the next one. In this example, we are only showing the respondents two choice tasks. Note that *which* choice task (of all of the possible ones based on the experimental design) is shown to each respondent is something that is determined on the *server* side of the app, which will be detailed later on.

```
# Choice task 1
  div(
    id = "choicetask1",
    h4(
      strong("Choice task number 1"),
      style = "text-align: center;"
    ),

    div(
      id = "ct1",
      class = "shiny-input-radiogroup",
      tableOutput("tct1")
    ),

    # Include the action button that sends people to the next choice task
    actionButton(
      inputId = "click2choice2",
      label = "Next"
    ),
    style = "text-align: center;"
  ),

  # Choice task 2
  div(
    id = "choicetask2",
    h4(
      strong("Choice task number 2"),
      style = "text-align: center;"
    ),

    div(
      id = "ct2",
      class = "shiny-input-radiogroup",
      tableOutput("tct2")
    ),

    # Include the action button that sends people to the next step
    actionButton(
      inputId = "click2protest",
      label = "Next"
    ),
    style = "text-align: center;"
  ),
```

If the respondent has selected the status quo alternative (here, Programme A) for all choices, they will be redirected to a "protest `div`" shown below. Ensuring that this panel is only shown to respondents who have exclusively chosen the status quo (or whatever pattern we define as protesting) is taken care of on the server side of the app, not the UI side.

```
  # Gathering data on potential protesters
  div(
    id = "protest",
    textInput(
      "protest",
      "Why did you choose Programme 1 in all of the situations presented?",
      width = 500
    ),
    actionButton(
      inputId = "click2thanksprotest",
      label = "Next"
    ),
    style = "text-align: center;"
  ),
```

Lastly, we include some panels (`divs`) to show a message while the answers are being saved, and a final thank you message to be shown once all answers have been saved correctly.

```
# Show a message while saving the results
    h3(
      id = "savingmessage",
      "We are saving your answers, this will take a moment ..."
    ),

    div(
      id = "submit",
      actionButton(
        inputId = "click2thanks",
        label = "Next"
      ),
      style = "text-align: center;"
    ),

    # Thank you slide
    div(
      id = "thankyou",
      h3("Thank you for participating in this survey."),
      p(
        "The results will be available on",
        a(href = "http://www.et.bs.ehu.es/~etpmaxxp/", "this website"),
        "shortly."
      ),
      div(
        tags$button(
          id = "close",
          type = "button",
          class = "btn action-button",
          onclick = "setTimeout(function(){window.close();},500);",
          "End survey"
        ),
        style = "text-align: center;")
    )
```

Note that you will have to enclose all the necessary panels (`divs`) in the `hidden()` and `ui <-fluidPage()` calls. This is hard to see with the code broken down into chunks as is the case here, but it means that after the end of the thank you panel above, if you have used the correct object structure, you will end with something like the chunk below. For the full code of the survey, not broken into chunks, we encourage you to check the book's GitHub repository.

```
  ) #end hidden

)#end UI fluidpage
```

#### 6.3.3.2 The Server Script

We can now start working on the corresponding `server.R` script that accompanies the previous `ui.R` script. The `server.R` script will have the following basic structure:

```
server <- function(input, output) {

}
```

First, we set up an `observeEvent()`, which hides the intro and shows the socio-demographic variables panel when a click on the `click2socdem` action button is detected (see the introduction `div` above). In the socio-demographic variables panel, we want to ensure that the action button that allows the respondent to continue to the explanation div is only clickable once the mandatory socio-demographic variables have been completed. We can define these questions as mandatory in the server script. This toggles the state of the `click2explanation` button shown at the button of the socio-demographic variables' panel (`div`), i.e. makes it clickable.

Note that names have to coincide with the inputIds specified above.

```
# Define a set of mandatory fields
  mandatory_fields <- c("gender", "age", "edu")

  # Observe and execute button click to advance to sociodem and reveal the
  # button to advance to the explanation of choice tasks if all mandatory fields are completed
  observeEvent(
    input$click2socdem, {
      hide("intro")
      show("socdem")

      # Only show next button when answers are completed
      observe({
        mandatory_filled <- vapply(
          mandatory_fields,
          function(x) {
            !is.null(input[[x]]) && input[[x]] != ""
          },
          logical(1)
        )

        # Check if all mandatory fields are completed
        mandatory_filled <- all(mandatory_filled)

        # Toggle the next button
        toggleState(
          id = "click2explanation",
          condition = mandatory_filled & input$age > 15
        )
      })
    }
  )
```

The `observeEvent` function below hides the socio-demographic panel and shows the next one (here, the explanation panel) once a click on the `click2explanation` button at the bottom of the socio-demographic div has been detected.

```
observeEvent(
    input$click2explanation, {
      hide("socdem")
      show("explanation")
    }
  )
```

We follow a similar approach in the code chunk below. The first `observeEvent()` registers a click on the `click2choice1` action button shown at the bottom of the explanation panel, hides the explanation panel, and shows Choice Task 1. It does not allow the user to click on the next button `click2choice2` until the respondent has chosen one of the alternatives presented in Choice Task 1. This is done via the `toggleState` and its corresponding `id` and `condition` arguments. We repeat the same step to move onto Choice Task 2. Note that we would need additional `observeEvents` if we were to add more choice tasks to our survey.

```
# Add observer for choice task 1
observeEvent(
  input$click2choice1, {
    hide("explanation")
    show("choicetask1")

    # Only show next button when a choice is selected:
    observe({
      toggleState(
        id = "click2choice2",
        condition = !is.null(input$ct1)
      )
    })
  }
)

# Add observer for choice task 2
observeEvent(
  input$click2choice2, {
    hide("choicetask1")
    show("choicetask2")
    show("submit")

    # Only show next button when a choice is selected:
    observe({
      toggleState(
        id = "click2thanks",
        condition = !is.null(input$ct2)
      )
    })
  }
)
```

Once the respondent has answered all choice tasks, we want to ensure that they are either (1) shown the "protest" question if they have chosen only status quo alternatives and then conclude the survey by saving the data and thanking them, or (2) skip the "protest" panel and go directly to saving their answers and thanking them. Inside the high-level `observeEvent` function, whenever we register a click on the button `click2thanks`, the following takes place:

```
If all answers are SQ/Prog1/whatever pattern we want:
  Hide last choice task
  Show protest to ask why
  Save answers and thank respondent

Else
  Hide last choice task
  Save answers and thank respondent
```

This can be coded as follows:

```
# Save the results to database when the submit button is clicked
observeEvent(
  input$click2thanks, {
    # Show protest question if all choices are SQ
    if (input$ct1 == "Prog 1" & input$ct2 == "Prog 1") {
      hide("choicetask2")
      hide("submit")
      show("protest")

      observe({
        toggleState(
          id = "click2thanksprotest",
          condition = nchar(input$protest) > 0)
      })

# Otherwise, hide the protest question and display saving and thank you message
      observeEvent(
        input$click2thanksprotest, {
          hide("protest")
          show("savingmessage")
          save_data("DCEBookTest", form_data())
          hide("savingmessage")
          show("thankyou")
        })

    } else{
      hide("choicetask2")
      hide("submit")
      show("savingmessage")
      save_data("DCEBookTest", form_data())
      hide("savingmessage")
      show("thankyou")
    }
  }
)
```

An important task of the server function is to randomly select choice tasks for different respondents, when necessary for the implementation of the experimental design. This can be done by applying `sample()` and drawing from the `ct` list object created in Sect. 6.3.2. above.

Note that what is, for example, Choice Task 7 on the server side from the `ct` object (i.e. design row 7) might appear as the first choice task (i.e. Choice Task 1) for the respondent due to the random drawing of choice tasks shown to each respondent. Therefore, we have to re-number choice tasks to ensure consistency with previous code chunks. We use this re-numbering as the input name below, such that the input names (i.e. `ct1` and `ct2` in the example below) match with the `input$ct1` and `input$ct2` used in previous code chunks. Otherwise, if a respondent is shown (what we call) Choice Task 7 and 13 out of all possible choice tasks, and we do not re-number them, the input will be registered and `ct7` and `ct13` (or whatever is drawn randomly).

```
# Set up the rendering of the choice tasks
nct_shown <- 2

# Randomly draw which choice tasks to show each respondent
rct <- sample(seq_len(nrow(design)), nct_shown)
ct_shown <- vector(mode = "list", length = nct_shown)

for(j in seq_along(ct_shown)){
  ct_shown[[j]] <- rbind(
    ct[[rct[j]]],
    c(
      "",
      paste('<input type="radio" name="ct', j, '" value="Prog 1"/>', sep = ""),
      paste('<input type="radio" name="ct', j, '" value="Prog 2"/>', sep = ""),
      paste('<input type="radio" name="ct', j, '" value="Prog 3"/>', sep = "")
    )
  )

  rownames(ct_shown[[j]])[nrow(ct_shown[[j]])] <- "?WHICH PROGRAMME DO YOU PREFER?"

}
```

We have now extracted the choice tasks to be shown to each respondent (randomised, as seen in the previous chunk, so that each respondent sees a different choice task), re-numbered them and saved them in the `ct_shown` list object. Next, we use the `renderTable()` function to create an output object for each choice task (two, in our case), named `output$tct1` and `output$tct2`. These have to match the id inside of the `tableOutput("tct1")` and `tableOutput("tct2")` calls in the UI chunks above.

```
# Render the choice task tables
  output$tct1 <- renderTable(
    ct_shown[[1]],
    sanitize.text.function = function(x) {
      x
    },
    align = c("lctc"),
    width = "90%",
    spacing = "s",
    striped = TRUE
  )

  output$tct2 <- renderTable(
    ct_shown[[2]],
    sanitize.text.function = function(x) {
      x
    },
    align = c("lctc"),
    width = "90%",
    spacing = "s",
    striped = TRUE
  )
```

Now, we need to ensure that respondents' answers are saved in the Google Sheet we created at the beginning of the chapter, using the necessary functions from the `googlesheets4` and `googledrive` packages. We also record a timestamp to see how long it takes each respondent to complete the survey. Note that the function named `saveDataFunction`, as well as the rest of the code chunk below, has been called inside the `observeEvent` function introduced above, and lies in between the thank you message and the previous panel.

```
# Define a timestamp as part of the collected data
end_time <- function() {
  format(Sys.time(), "%Y%m%d-%H%M%OS")
}

# Function to save the data
save_data <- function(sheetname, data) {
  # First get the ID for the sheet
  ss <- drive_get(sheetname)

  sheet_append(
    ss = gs,
    data = data,
    sheet = "DCEBookTest"
  )
}

# Reactive object to temporarily save the user's data
form_data <- reactive({
  tibble(
    cm1 = input$ct1,
    cm2 = input$ct2,
    cs1 = rct[1],
    cs2 = rct[2],
    gender = input$gender,
    age = input$age,
    edu = input$edu,
    protest = input$protest,
    timestamp = Sys.time()
  )
})
```

We can add the code below to make sure that the Shiny app stops running when the respondent has completed the survey. This is typically done when publishing Shiny apps to shinyapps.io to minimize runtime usage and avoid needlessly consuming subscription hours.

```
# Final observer to close the app when the user is done
observe({
  if (input$close > 0) stopApp()
})
```

#### 6.3.3.3 Final Steps and File Structure

Once we have set up our `ui.R` and `server.R` scripts, we need to call both the user interface and the server side of the app to create the Shiny app. This is typically done in a `call_app.R` or `app.R` script.

```
shinyApp(ui = ui, server = server)
```

Note that the final step, calling the user interface and the server side of the app, references the previous scripts using relative paths. Therefore, having a proper file structure before you start coding the Shiny app is crucial. We suggest the following structure (see Fig. 6.7), which is assumed in the code in this chapter. We begin with a directory containing all scripts and files for the implementation of your DCE in Shiny. Its contents are detailed below.

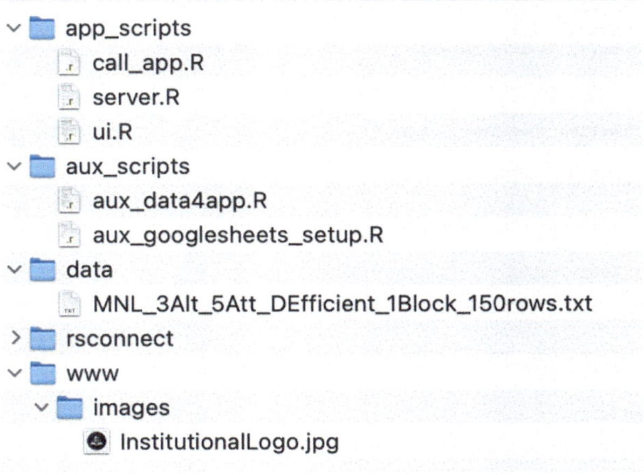


**Fig. 6.7** Recommended file structure for the Shiny app survey

**An "aux_scripts" directory,** which contains the auxiliary app files with the following two files:

a. The `"aux_data4app.R"` script that generates the choice task objects based on the design
b. The `"aux_googlesheets_setup.R"` script that sets up the data collection process …

**An "app_scripts" directory** that holds the actual app scripts (`"app_scripts"`)

a. `"ui.R"`
b. `"server.R"`
c. `"call_app.R"`

The "**data**" **folder** will contain the design previously generated (i.e. the output of Chapter 5), and the "**rsconnect**" and "**www**" **folders** are automatically created by RStudio when first saving the app. The "www" folder is used to upload and reference any images that we wish to include in our app.

### *6.3.4 Sharing Your Shiny Survey*

You have now learned how to implement a DCE survey using R Shiny—the next step is sharing it with respondents. Shiny apps are most easily shared as web pages, where users will be able to access your survey through the URL address you provide. Posit (formerly RStudio) offers three ways to host your Shiny app as a web page:

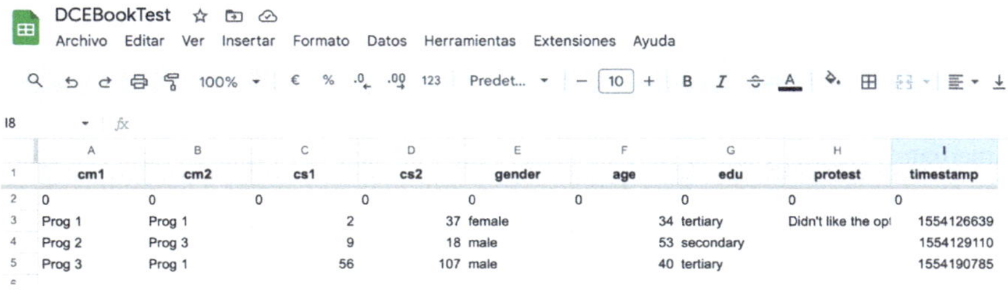


**Fig. 6.8** Screenshot of Google Sheets once several responses have been gathered

- ***shinyapps.io*** allows you to upload your survey app straight from your R session to a server hosted by Posit, where you have complete control over the app, including server administration tools. They offer several options, free and paid.
- ***Shiny Server*** is a free, open source, GitHub-available companion program to Shiny, which builds a web server designed to host Shiny apps. You will need a Linux server to run it.
- ***Posit Connect*** is a publishing platform which offers several server tools (password authentication, SSL support, etc.) and is free for non-profits.

Once you have uploaded your Shiny survey app to a web page, you can share the link and start collecting responses. You may want to use a professional survey company to send the link to respondents by email or send the link by email yourself. If you choose to use a professional survey company, they can send customised links for each respondent. This allows you to use URL Redirect to (anonymously) identify respondents and send them back to the survey company to be paid after completing the survey on shinyapps.io. You should take into account that capturing the personalised URL will require one of the more complete shinyapps.io paid packages as well as using JavaScript.

If you have decided to use the sample code outlined in this chapter to implement a basic survey, as soon as respondents finish the survey, your Google Sheet will be updated in real time, and will soon look something like Fig. 6.8.

Note that the first row is a throwaway, which we used to "initialise" the table in Google Sheets.

## 6.4 Pros and Cons of Using Shiny

Using a Shiny app to collect data for a DCE has advantages and disadvantages. One of the primary benefits is its high level of customisation and flexibility. Shiny allows you to design an interface that suits the specific needs of your DCE: you can control how questions are presented, modify the layout to be more user-friendly, and incorporate dynamic, interactive elements such as sliders or dropdown menus.

This ability to create a tailored experience is especially useful for experiments where subsequent questions depend on the participant's previous choices.

Another major advantage of using Shiny is its integration with R, which provides seamless data handling and analysis capabilities. Once the data is collected, it can immediately be analysed in R. This integration can save time and effort since there is no need to export and import data between different systems. Additionally, Shiny gives researchers complete control over the data collection process, with validation mechanisms that ensure data integrity, such as preventing incomplete or erroneous responses. It also allows for real-time monitoring, making it possible to track responses as they come in and respond to any issues immediately.

Cost-effectiveness is another positive aspect of a Shiny app. Being open-source, Shiny presents a free or low-cost solution, which may be particularly appealing to researchers or projects with limited budgets. It provides flexibility in deployment as well, as applications can be hosted on cloud services like ShinyApps.io or on local servers, depending on infrastructure requirements.

However, Shiny also presents some notable challenges. It requires significant programming skills, which can be a barrier for researchers without experience in R or Shiny. The process of building a DCE in Shiny can be complex and time-consuming, especially compared to other platforms like Qualtrics or Sawtooth that offer pre-built templates for DCEs. Shiny requires you to design the entire experimental structure from scratch, which can be daunting for more complex studies.

Another drawback relates to performance. Shiny applications can be resource-intensive, and as the number of respondents increases or the complexity of the experiment grows, the app might slow down. This makes scalability a concern, particularly if you do not have the resources to host the app on a robust server capable of handling high traffic. Moreover, ensuring optimal performance for a large-scale experiment could require significant technical expertise.

In terms of data security, Shiny places the responsibility for securing data on the developer. If sensitive information is being collected, it is essential to implement proper data security measures, such as ensuring secure data transmission with HTTPS and managing access controls. If you are hosting your app on ShinyApps.io, you will also need to be aware of their data privacy policies, which could introduce potential risks if not carefully considered.

The user experience of Shiny applications is another area that may fall short compared to dedicated survey platforms. While Shiny provides flexibility, its default interface can be less polished and less intuitive than professional survey software, which may result in lower engagement from participants. Designing a user-friendly and responsive interface across different devices, especially mobiles and tablets, may require additional optimisation efforts.

Finally, Shiny does not offer built-in tools for managing participant recruitment or distributing the experiment. You will need to handle invitations and sample management through external systems, which can add extra complexity. Unlike platforms that allow for easier integration with third-party panels, Shiny does not have native solutions for this, and collaboration with external data sources may require more manual intervention.

In summary, Shiny provides great flexibility, control over data collection, and cost-effectiveness for researchers who are proficient in R programming. However, it can be technically demanding, with potential challenges around performance, user experience, and data security. For researchers comfortable with programming and looking for a customisable solution, Shiny can be a powerful tool. For those seeking a more straightforward or user-friendly platform with built-in support, a specialised survey tool might be a better choice.

## 6.5 Key Takeaways

- Shiny is a great tool for creating interactive web apps using R, and can also be used to implement DCE surveys.
- Shiny is cost-effective, and offers great flexibility for researchers with R programming experience or those implementing simple surveys.
- Advantages include complete control over randomisation, a wide range of customisation options, and real-time data analysis.
- Downsides include the substantial R programming skills required, the difficulty of ensuring robust data security, and issues related to user experience and performance.

## Bibliography

Attali D (2020) Persistent data storage in Shiny apps. https://shiny.posit.co/r/articles/build/persistent-data-storage/#local. Accessed 7 Dec 2024

INSPIRE Project (2020) Persistent storage: Overview and recommendations. https://inspire-project.info/blog/2020/03/06/persistant-storage.html. Accessed 7 Dec 2024

Sandorf ED, Campbell D (2023) spdesign: designing stated preference experiments. R package version 0.0.5. https://CRAN.R-project.org/package=spdesign

Posit (n.d.) Shiny basics: Lesson 1. https://shiny.posit.co/r/getstarted/shiny-basics/lesson1/. Accessed 28 Nov 2024

Wickham H (2021) Mastering Shiny. O'Reilly Media, Inc.

# Chapter 7
# From Raw Data to Insights

**Abstract** This chapter highlights the importance of data exploration as a preliminary step in building choice models. By examining choice patterns and uncovering key influencing factors, you can establish a solid basis for the subsequent model development. This initial step involves a series of exploratory data analysis techniques that are simple yet informative. In this chapter, we demonstrate how to use R to effectively conduct this exploration, transforming raw data into meaningful insights. By creating summary tables and examining data visualisations, researchers can gain a deeper understanding of their data, paving the way for a more effective analysis and model building.

## 7.1 Introduction

While it may be tempting to jump straight into the estimation of complex choice models after obtaining your data, it is important to first explore the basic characteristics of your discrete choice experiment (DCE) dataset. At this stage, you should aim to understand and describe the choices made and get insights into what factors may affect them. Your goal is not to reach conclusions but to identify promising leads, which you will explore in greater depth in the next stages of your research.

In our experience, this step is generally not given sufficient attention. Complex choice models have become widespread in the choice modelling literature, and the increased ease of estimating these models (e.g. using the *Apollo* R package (Hess and Palma 2019) or other packages and specialist software) has led to a decreased emphasis on the use of comparatively simpler methods to explore choice data. We emphasise the importance of this step in determining the plausibility of your ideas and whether they can be reasonably tested using your data before launching into complex choice models.

Generally speaking, results that cannot be established using comparatively simple methods are unlikely to be supported by complex choice models. This preliminary step is instrumental in helping you choose which model to use in the following stages of the analysis.



P. Mariel et al., *Environmental Valuation with Discrete Choice Experiments in R*,
The Economics of Non-Market Goods and Resources 17,
https://doi.org/10.1007/978-3-031-89338-4_7

The initial exploration of your data should be simple and straightforward: summary tables and data visualisations are a great place to start. As we will see later in the chapter, this can involve graphs demonstrating how choice shares evolve throughout the choice sequence or a table illustrating the proportion of "yes" and "no" choices linked to specific levels for a particular attribute. Results from this stage are most accessible to non-expert audiences of your research and will be necessary for communications with relevant stakeholders.

Descriptive statistics and data exploration can be performed using standard R analytical procedures. In this chapter, we use these procedures to conduct a preliminary analysis and exploration of the data before the choice model development process that follows.

## *7.1.1 Prerequisites*

### 7.1.1.1 Packages

In this chapter, we make use of many of the `tidyverse` packages (Wickham et al. 2019), especially `ggplot2` (Wickham 2016) for creating graphics and visualisations, `dplyr` (Wickham et al. 2023) for data manipulation and `tibble` (Müller and Wickham 2023) to encapsulate best practices for data frames. Functions from other `tidyverse` packages are also called upon, so we recommend loading all `tidyverse` packages in your R session. We also use the `janitor` package (Firke 2023), which provides a collection of functions for cleaning and tidying data, making it easier for data analysts to work with messy datasets. To produce the tables of results presented in this chapter, we use the `gt` package (Iannone et al. 2023), and to combine multiple plots into a single, visually appealing graphic, we use the `patchwork` package (Pedersen 2024).

```
# Loading R packages
library(tidyverse)     # Version 2.0.0
library(janitor)       # Version 2.2.0
library(gt)            # Version 0.11.0
library(patchwork)     # Version 1.3.0
```

### 7.1.1.2 Data

As throughout the book, we will be working with a dataset called *Data_windmills.csv* in this chapter. This data is stored in a `tibble`, which is a type of `data.frame` (Müller and Wickham 2023), and is referred to throughout the chapter as `data_wind`. The data is based on the case study presented in Chap. 4. It contains 10,000 rows representing ten responses from 1,000 individuals, with some missing choice observations. The first six rows of the dataset are presented below.

```
# Importing data
data_wind <- read_csv(gzcon(url("https://raw.githubusercontent.com/edsandorf/evdce/refs/heads/
main/Data/data-windmills.csv"))) |>
  clean_names()

head(data_wind)

  id_individual choice_task alt1_sq alt1_farm2 alt1_farm3 alt1_height2
1             1           1       1          0          0            0
2             1           2       1          0          0            0
3             1           3       1          0          0            0
4             1           4       1          0          0            0
5             1           5       1          0          0            0
6             1           6       1          0          0            0
  alt1_height3 alt1_redkite alt1_distance alt1_cost alt2_farm2 alt2_farm3
1            0            0             0         0          0          0
2            0            0             0         0          0          1
3            0            0             0         0          0          1
4            0            0             0         0          0          1
5            0            0             0         0          1          0
6            0            0             0         0          0          0
  alt2_height2 alt2_height3 alt2_redkite alt2_distance alt2_cost alt3_farm2
1            0            1          2.5          0.00         4          1
2            1            0          0.0          1.00         5          1
3            1            0          0.0          0.75         2          0
4            0            0          0.0          0.25         7          1
5            0            1         -5.0          1.00         3          0
6            0            1          2.5          0.75         4          0
  alt3_farm3 alt3_height2 alt3_height3 alt3_redkite alt3_distance alt3_cost age
1          0            1            0         -2.5          1.00         9  66
2          0            0            0         -2.5          0.25         7  66
3          1            0            1         -5.0          1.00         3  66
4          0            1            0         -5.0          0.75         5  66
5          1            1            0          5.0          1.00         4  66
6          1            1            0          0.0          0.00         4  66
  female education choice
1      1         3      1
2      1         3      1
3      1         3      3
4      1         3      1
5      1         3      3
6      1         3      2
```

The choice data is in a wide format for consistency with subsequent chapters, where functions in the *Apollo* package are used to estimate the choice data. This means that each row corresponds to a single choice observation, observations from the same individual are (ideally) grouped together in adjacent rows, and identifier variables for individuals (`id_individual`) and choice tasks (`choice_task`) are included to denote each observation.

If your data is in a long format (i.e. with one row per alternative), we recommend reshaping it. To do so, you can use the function `pivot_wider()` from the `tidy` package (Wickham et al. 2024) or the `apollo_longToWide()` function in *Apollo*.

> ⓘ **Data format**
>
> The table below summarises the key distinctions between wide and long data formats when working with DCE data. Understanding these differences is crucial for efficient data manipulation and analysis. DCE data stored in a wide format simplifies

the computation of utilities for each alternative by eliminating the need for repeated reshaping or filtering of data. It also minimises redundant storage of identifiers and socio-demographic variables, such as participant IDs, age, and gender.

| Feature | Wide format | Long format |
|---|---|---|
| Initial structure | Simpler, reflects survey format | Less intuitive, requires familiarity with data manipulation |
| Viewing individual responses | Easier to see all choices for an individual | Less straightforward, requires filtering or aggregation |
| Scalability | Not scalable for many choice sets/attributes | Efficient for complex models |
| Analysis compatibility | Directly compatible with apollo | Requires data transformation for some software |

For convenience later on, we recommend creating several new variables, including the number of alternatives and the number of choice tasks presented to each individual in the DCE. In our example dataset, these are the same for every individual, though this need not be the case. With the same number of choice tasks for every individual, the number of respondents is the number of observations (given by `nrow()`) divided by the number of choice tasks per individual. However, to handle both balanced and unbalanced panels—where balanced panels mean all respondents complete the same number of choice tasks, and unbalanced panels mean they do not—it is better to utilise the `n_distinct` function from the `dplyr` package, which calculates the count of unique individual identifier variables. For the analysis, it is also helpful to specify which value of `choice` (i.e. alternative) denotes the status-quo alternative (SQ).

```
# Mutate some of the variables
data_wind <- data_wind |>
  mutate(
    choice = as_factor(choice),
    choice_task = as_factor(choice_task),
    female = as_factor(female),
    education = as_factor(education),
    age_group = cut(age, breaks = seq(15, 90, by = 15))
  )

# Create a set of global variables
n_alts <- 3
n_choices <- 10
n_rows_data <- nrow(data_wind)
n_individuals <- select(data_wind, id_individual) |>
  n_distinct()
sq_alt <- 1
```

## 7.2 Getting to Know Your Choice Data

First, we recommend using several functions to examine the dataset's contents and ensure the data looks as expected. In particular, we recommend the `glimpse` function, as it allows you to efficiently identify and address various data issues. It provides a quick overview of your data, allowing you to verify if variables align with your expectations.

For instance, you can easily see if variables intended to be integers (e.g. choice) are indeed integers or if they are miscoded as doubles, which could happen if a choice is recorded using a decimal number, if dates and times in the data are correctly interpreted, and if other issues, such as using commas as decimal separators, must be fixed.

```
View(data_wind)     # Invoke a spreadsheet-style view within RStudio
names(data_wind)    # List the variables in the dataset
str(data_wind)      # List the structure of the dataset
glimpse(data_wind) # Glimpse of the dataset
dim(data_wind)      # Dimensions of the dataset
```

### 7.2.1 *Missing Observations*

Any analysis you conduct with your choice data is only as good as the data itself, which is why missing data can be problematic. Missing data reduces the statistical power of the analysis and can distort the validity of the results. Therefore, the very first thing we recommend you assess in your choice data is, paradoxically, the choices you do not observe.

Here, we focus on missing choice observations. However, in the context of DCEs, missing observations relate not just to instances where the choice variable is unknown but also to cases where responses to the socio-demographic and attitudinal questions are missing. We emphasise the importance of exploring the occurrence of missing observations for all variables, not just the choice indicator variable. This is particularly pertinent for socio-demographic and attitudinal variables intended for inclusion in the analysis. As for variables that are not part of the analysis, their absence is of lesser concern.

The reasons behind missing choice observations can be varied, but it is important to understand *why* they might be missing wherever possible. In particular, try to establish whether the choice observations are missing at random or if there may be identifiable factors contributing to their absence. These could include measurement or recording errors due to ambiguities in the question, confusion, individuals' unwillingness to respond to the question, or other factors.

In general, the more the factors contributing to missing observations are correlated with individual characteristics or features of the DCE (e.g. number of attributes, alternatives, choice tasks, etc.), the greater the concern of generating biased results should be. It is also important to consider the impact of missing choice observations on the properties of the experimental design, as they can lead to a loss of efficiency in efficient designs and a loss of orthogonality in orthogonal designs. This occurs because missing data disrupts the intended balance and structure of the design, potentially reducing the statistical power to estimate parameters accurately. As a result, it is essential to investigate missing observations to ensure the experimental design's integrity is maintained.

While it may be tempting to drop rows from the dataset with missing choice observations, we do not recommend it. Retaining them is more transparent to other researchers with whom you share the data, facilitating open science, replicability, and reproducibility. We strongly advise against deleting respondents from the dataset who do not complete the entire sequence of choice tasks. If the pattern of missing data has any identifiable structure, removing these observations inevitably introduces bias into the results.

In R, missing values are represented by `NA`, a special value whose properties differ from those of other values. To identify missing values in the choice variable, we can use `is.na(data_wind$choice)`, which will return a logical vector with `TRUE` in the element locations that contain missing values represented by `NA`. Below, we summarise the missing choice observations in the data.

```
# Take the data, then identify choices with NA, count them, calculate the share
# and display the results in a table
data_wind |>
  mutate(
    missing = is.na(choice)
  ) |>
  count(missing, name = "frequency") |>
  mutate(
    share = round(100 * frequency / sum(frequency), 2)
  ) |>
  gt()
```

While there are 10,000 rows in the data, Table 7.1 reveals that only 8,633 are observed with a choice. A summary of the distribution of completed choice tasks per individual helps identify patterns in missing observations.

**Table 7.1** Share of missing values

| Missing | Frequency | Share |
|---|---|---|
| FALSE | 8633 | 86.33 |
| TRUE | 1367 | 13.67 |

**Table 7.2** Distribution of the number of completed tasks

| Completed_Tasks | Frequency | Share |
|---|---|---|
| 4 | 6 | 0.6 |
| 5 | 19 | 1.9 |
| 6 | 53 | 5.3 |
| 7 | 109 | 10.9 |
| 8 | 209 | 20.9 |
| 9 | 279 | 27.9 |
| 10 | 325 | 32.5 |

```
# Take the data, then exclude missing choices, count the number of choices per
# individual, count the number of individuals with a specific number of choices,
# calculate the share and display the results in a table
data_wind |>
  filter(!is.na(choice)) |>
  count(id_individual, name = "completed_tasks") |>
  count(completed_tasks, name = "frequency") |>
  mutate(
    share = round(100 * frequency / sum(frequency), 2)
  ) |>
  gt()
```

The results of the task completion analysis in Table 7.2 reveal that a little less than a third (32.5%) of individuals completed all ten choice tasks. While over 60% answered at least nine tasks, a small group of six individuals only completed four tasks—the lowest number of tasks completed by any individual. With nearly 40% of individuals completing eight or fewer choice tasks, this panel is an example of where missing observations may pose a risk of efficiency loss and compromise parameter accuracy.

If missing choice observations occur randomly and are not related to factors such as choice order, attribute levels, task complexity, or socio-demographic variables, their overall impact is likely limited. In such cases, the randomness of the missing data means that their effects may balance out across the dataset. However, if missing observations are linked to any of these factors, they become problematic, and further investigation into their occurrence is necessary.

To demonstrate how this can be explored, we provide an example in the code chunk below, where we examine missing observations across the sequence of choice tasks in conjunction with the variable `female` for illustrative purposes.

```
# Plot showing missing values by choice task
p1 <- data_wind |>
  group_by(choice_task) |>
  summarize(
    group_share = mean(is.na(choice)),
    .groups = "drop"
  ) |>
  ggplot(mapping = aes(x = choice_task, y = group_share, group = 1)) +
  geom_line() +
  geom_point() +
  scale_y_continuous(labels = scales::percent_format()) +
  labs(
    x = "Choice task",
    y = "Share of missing values"
  ) +
  theme_bw()

# Plot showing missing values by choice task and gender
p2 <- data_wind |>
  group_by(choice_task, female) |>
  summarize(
    group_share = mean(is.na(choice)),
    .groups = "drop"
  ) |>
  ggplot(mapping = aes(x = choice_task, y = group_share, group = female, col = female)) +
  geom_line() +
  geom_point() +
  scale_y_continuous(labels = scales::percent_format()) +
  labs(
    x = "Choice task",
    y = "Share of missing values",
    col = "Female"
  ) +
  theme_bw()

# Combine the plots
p1 + p2 + plot_layout(ncol = 2)
```

Figure 7.1 contains two panels showing the share of missing values across ten choice tasks. The left panel shows a steady increase in the share of missing values from around 4% in the first task to nearly 17% in the sixth task, after which the trend decreases. The right panel compares two groups, represented by color-coded lines for males and females. The blue line for females (coded as "1") rises more sharply than the red line for males (coded as "0"), indicating that females have a higher share of missing values, particularly in later tasks.

Interestingly, the plot suggests a potential ceiling effect around the sixth task, where missing observations appear to stabilise after a steep initial rise. This pattern indicates a link between the rate of missing observations and the order of the tasks in this dataset, which could be problematic. In a real case study, it would be important to investigate whether the trend continues or plateaus due to learning and fatigue. However, the implications of this upward trend in missing values depend on the task order. If choice tasks are consistently ordered, the ability to obtain accurate estimates is more uncertain, though randomising the task order can mitigate this concern.

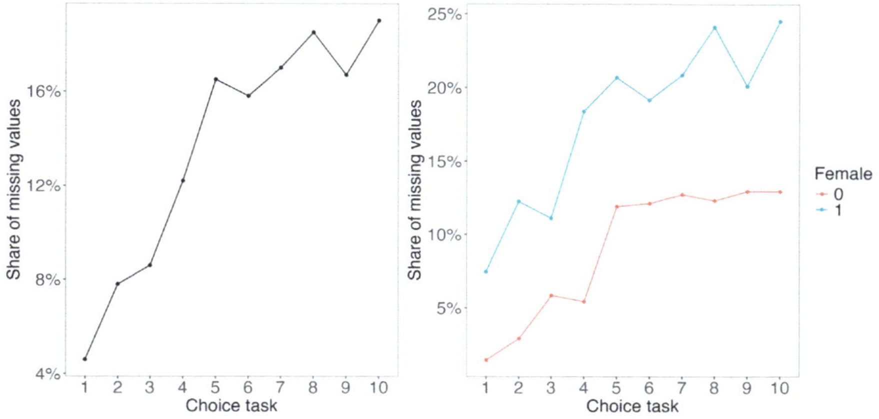


**Fig. 7.1** Share of missing values by choice task and gender

## 7.2.2 *Choice Shares*

After exploring missing choice observations, the next step is to explore choice shares to get an intuitive overview of the choice data (Table 7.3).

```
# Table showing choice shares
data_wind |>
  filter(!is.na(choice)) |>
  count(choice, name = "frequency") |>
  mutate(
    share = round(100 * frequency / sum(frequency), 2)
  ) |>
  gt()
```

Even from this simple summary table, we get first insights into the data: all else being equal, the future SQ alternative (i.e. Alternative 1: Programme A, see Fig. 4. 1) appears to be preferred, and among the non-SQ options, the first option (i.e. Alternative 2: Programme B) is slightly less preferred. Of course, confirming this requires a more robust analysis, but it illustrates a useful insight that can be obtained from this type of exploration.

Next, we can examine whether the choice shares differ by choice task.

**Table 7.3** Choice shares

| Choice | Frequency | Share |
|---|---|---|
| 1 | 4850 | 56.18 |
| 2 | 1885 | 21.83 |
| 3 | 1898 | 21.99 |

```r
# Plot showing choice shares by choice task
data_wind |>
  filter(!is.na(choice)) |>
  count(choice_task, choice) |>
  group_by(choice_task) |>
  mutate(
    share = n/sum(n)
  ) |>
  ggplot(mapping = aes(x = choice_task, y = share, group = choice, col = choice)) +
  geom_line() +
  geom_point() +
  scale_y_continuous(labels = scales::percent_format()) +
  labs(
    x = "Choice task",
    y = "Share of choices",
    col = "Choice"
  ) +
  theme_bw()
```

Figure 7.2 illustrates the share of choices (i.e. choice shares) across the ten choice tasks, with the three alternatives represented by different colours. The x-axis represents the choice task number from 1 to 10, while the y-axis represents the share of choices in percentages. The red line, representing the choice of Programme A, consistently shows the highest share of choices, fluctuating between 50 and 60% across all tasks, with a slight decline. Both Programme B and Programme C, represented by the green and blue lines, respectively, maintain relatively stable choice shares between 17 and 25% throughout the tasks.

The distribution pattern of choice shares across tasks suggests a preference shift as individuals progress through the tasks, possibly due to learning effects. Another possibility is that choice variability increases in later tasks, with the pattern of distribution of choice shares reflecting fatigue effects. Interestingly, while still far from equal, the observed shares for the three alternatives in the final choice task are closer to equal than at any other point in the sequence, indicating higher choice variability in the final choice task.

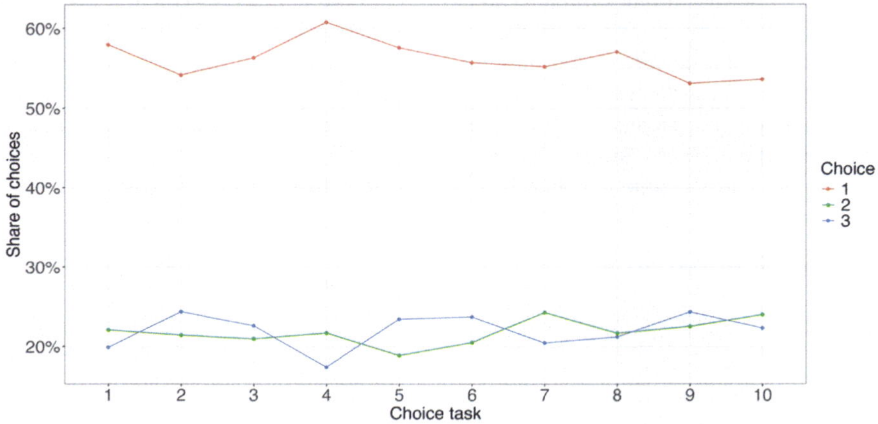


**Fig. 7.2** Choice shares by choice task

The observed choice shares offer clues about the scale parameter in the multinomial logit model: though slight, the pattern seen in Fig. 7.2 suggests a decrease in its relative magnitude across tasks, as discussed in Bradley and Daly (1994). The similarity in choice shares increases as the scale parameter decreases because a lower scale amplifies the influence of random errors, making choice probabilities more evenly distributed. However, our ability to definitively confirm this decrease is limited. As discussed in Chap. 3, it is not possible to separately identify marginal utilities (preferences) and the scale parameter, which makes it difficult to directly link the observed choice share pattern to a specific change in the scale parameter. Despite this limitation, this example shows that even basic summary statistics can provide valuable insights into potential choice behaviour. These observations can guide the iterative process of model refinement and selection, ultimately leading to a more efficient path towards the most suitable model specification.

Further investigation can explore whether any variable of interest explains choice behaviour. To illustrate this, we will now consider the `education` variable. By employing the faceting capabilities of `ggplot2`, we examine how choice shares vary across tasks for individuals with different educational backgrounds.

```
data_wind |>
  filter(!is.na(choice)) |>
  count(choice_task, choice, education) |>
  group_by(choice_task, education) |>
  mutate(
    share = n/sum(n)
  ) |>
  ggplot(mapping = aes(x = choice_task, y = share, group = choice, col = choice)) +
  geom_line() +
  geom_point() +
  scale_y_continuous(labels = scales::percent_format()) +
  labs(
    x = "Choice task",
    y = "Share of choices",
    col = "Choice"
  ) +
  facet_wrap(~education, labeller = label_both) +
  theme_bw()
```

Figure 7.3 displays the choice shares across the ten choice tasks, split into three panels based on different education levels (labelled as "education: 1," "education: 2," and "education: 3", and representing an ordered variable, with level 1 indicating the lowest education level and level 3 the highest). Each panel shows the distribution of the choices, colour-coded as red for Choice 1 (Programme A), green for Choice 2 (Programme B), and blue for Choice 3 (Programme C). Across all education levels, Choice 1 consistently dominates, with a share ranging between 50 and 65%, with some fluctuations. Choices 2 and 3 maintain lower shares, between 15 and 25%, with some variations throughout the tasks. The patterns of choices for each education level are pretty similar, with minor differences between groups in the fluctuation of choice shares across choice tasks.

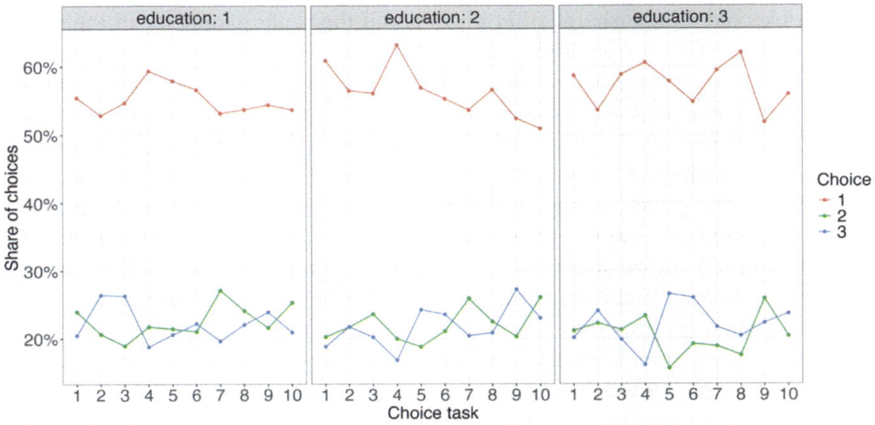


**Fig. 7.3** Choice shares by choice task and education

Although the differences are minimal, this example shows how distinct patterns in choice shares can be seen across different education levels. It also gives us an indication of how shifts in preferences and/or the scale parameter caused by learning or fatigue effects may be more pronounced in some education levels than in others. Notably, it may be useful to explore how education influences the alternative-specific constants and to examine whether adherence to the independence of irrelevant alternatives assumption varies between genders. Thus, the inspection of choice shares through simple summary statistics can provide useful insights and unveil potential research avenues for the next stage of analysis of your DCE data.

### *7.2.3 Status Quo Choices*

Numerous studies using DCEs have explored status quo (SQ) biases (e.g. Scarpa et al. 2005; Campbell and Erdem 2019), defined as the general tendency to stick with the status quo choice. One objective of the preliminary analysis should, therefore, be to explore the occurrence of SQ choices. The first step in identifying a potential SQ bias is to see if SQ choices are associated with their position within the choice task or with other factors, such as socio-demographic variables. This helps pinpoint whether the bias stems from task design (e.g. position effects) or respondent characteristics, allowing for targeted adjustments.

First, it is essential to obtain a broad understanding of the frequencies of SQ and non-SQ choices across the panel. This can be accomplished by generating a `tibble` containing the frequency of choices for each alternative for each individual. Note that we are excluding missing choices.

```
## Create a table with choices
choice_table <-  data_wind |>
  filter(!is.na(choice)) |>
  count(id_individual, choice, .drop = FALSE, name = "frequency")

# We can add socio-demographics to this table by joining it with our data
choice_table <- data_wind |>
  select(id_individual, age, age_group, female, education) |>
  distinct() |>
  left_join(choice_table, by = "id_individual")
```

The code chunk below summarises the tibble created to explore the number of SQ and non-SQ choices.

```
choice_table |>
  count(choice, frequency, name = "number_of_choices") |>
  mutate(
    share_of_choices = number_of_choices / sum(number_of_choices)
  ) |>
  pivot_wider(names_from = choice, values_from = c(number_of_choices, share_of_choices), names
_glue = "{.value}_{choice}") |>
  gt() |>
  tab_spanner(label = "Number of choices", columns = vars(starts_with("number_of_choices"))) |
>
  tab_spanner(label = "Share of choices", columns = vars(starts_with("share_of_choices"))) |>
  cols_label(
    frequency = "Frequency",
    number_of_choices_1 = "SQ",
    number_of_choices_2 = "Programme B",
    number_of_choices_3 = "Programme C",
    share_of_choices_1 = "SQ",
    share_of_choices_2 = "Programme B",
    share_of_choices_3 = "Programme C"
  ) |>
  fmt_number(columns = vars(starts_with("share")), decimals = 2)
```

In Table 7.4, we show the choice patterns of individuals in the dataset. Eight individuals never chose the SQ alternative (Programme A), whereas 175 individuals never chose the first non-SQ alternative (Programme B). The most common frequency for choosing the SQ option was four times. Additionally, the findings reveal that just over one-quarter of individuals chose the SQ option three times or less, while slightly more than one-third selected the SQ option six times or more. These findings underscore significant variability in how often individuals favour the SQ, pointing to potential differences in preferences or decision-making processes within the sample.

**Table 7.4** Choice patterns

| Frequency | Number of choices | | | Share of choices | | |
|---|---|---|---|---|---|---|
| | SQ | Programme B | Programme C | SQ | Programme B | Programme C |
| 0 | 8 | 175 | 139 | 0.00 | 0.06 | 0.05 |
| 1 | 27 | 258 | 285 | 0.01 | 0.09 | 0.10 |
| 2 | 72 | 253 | 285 | 0.02 | 0.08 | 0.10 |
| 3 | 148 | 191 | 169 | 0.05 | 0.06 | 0.06 |
| 4 | 199 | 80 | 84 | 0.07 | 0.03 | 0.03 |
| 5 | 192 | 33 | 29 | 0.06 | 0.01 | 0.01 |
| 6 | 157 | 7 | 8 | 0.05 | 0.00 | 0.00 |
| 7 | 110 | 3 | 1 | 0.04 | 0.00 | 0.00 |
| 8 | 44 | NA | NA | 0.01 | NA | NA |
| 9 | 15 | NA | NA | 0.01 | NA | NA |
| 10 | 28 | NA | NA | 0.01 | NA | NA |

Note that in Table 7.7.4, 28 of the individuals who completed all ten choice tasks can be identified as "serial non-participants", referring to those who consistently choose the status quo throughout the entire choice sequence (as discussed in Von Haefen et al. 2005; Thiene et al. 2012). It is important to consider the missing choice observations when calculating the share of serial non-participants. For example, an individual who only answered eight choice tasks and always chose the SQ alternative would be among the 44 individuals who chose this alternative eight times and would classify as a serial non-participant. A quick method to extend the analysis and create a dataset of serial non-participants is shown below, revealing that 51 individuals consistently chose the SQ in all of their recorded choices.

```
choice_table |>
  group_by(id_individual) |>
  mutate(
    number_of_choices = sum(frequency)
  ) |>
  filter(choice == 1 & frequency == number_of_choices)

# A tibble: 51 × 8
# Groups:   id_individual [51]
   id_individual   age age_group female education choice frequency
           <dbl> <dbl> <fct>     <fct>  <fct>     <fct>      <int>
 1            39    76 (75,90]   0      1         1             10
 2            43    41 (30,45]   0      1         1              9
 3            47    69 (60,75]   0      1         1             10
 4            77    57 (45,60]   0      1         1             10
 5            81    73 (60,75]   0      2         1             10
 6            83    25 (15,30]   0      1         1              9
 7            88    77 (75,90]   0      1         1             10
 8           107    81 (75,90]   0      1         1             10
 9           134    46 (45,60]   1      2         1              7
10           170    82 (75,90]   1      1         1             10
# ℹ 41 more rows
# ℹ 1 more variable: number_of_choices <int>
```

To explore the relationship between demographic variables and the likelihood of choosing the status quo versus other alternatives, we can use the `tibble` created to examine the choice shares across genders, using the variable `female`. We generate a bar plot in the script below, with three panels representing each of the three alternatives, to visually compare the distribution of choices.

```
choice_table |>
  count(choice, frequency, female, name = "number_of_choices") |>
  ggplot(mapping = aes(x = frequency, y = number_of_choices, fill = female)) +
  geom_bar(stat = "identity", position = "dodge") +
  facet_wrap(~choice) +
  labs(
    x = "Frequency",
    y = "Number of respondents",
    fill = "Female"
  ) +
  scale_x_continuous(breaks = seq(0, 10, by = 1)) +
  theme_bw() +
  theme(
    legend.position = "bottom"
  )
```

Figure 7.4 consists of three panels, corresponding to choices of Alternative 1, 2, and 3 (Programme A, B and C, respectively) and displaying the distribution of the frequency of responses for male and female individuals. The x-axis represents the frequency (0 to 10), and the y-axis shows the number of respondents. The bars are colour-coded, with red representing males (coded as "0") and blue representing females (coded as "1").

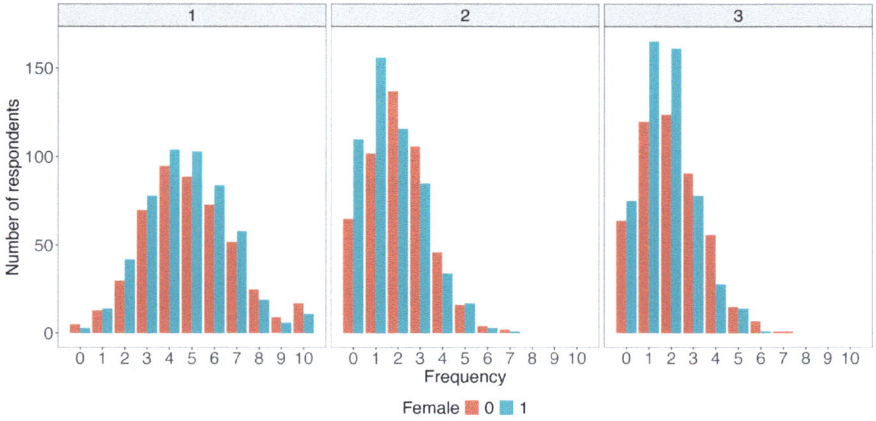


**Fig. 7.4** Response frequency by alternative and gender

In the first panel, the distribution is roughly symmetric, with the highest concentration of individuals around the middle frequencies. The other two panels show distributions centred on frequencies of two to three. The overall distribution in each panel is similar between males and females, with both genders showing similar trends in the number of respondents across different frequencies. In some specific bins, the counts for males and females differ slightly, but no substantial difference is evident between genders across the three groups.

The plot above allows us to examine differences in the shares of SQ and non-SQ choices that can be attributed to gender. While more rigorous statistical tests will follow, these simple visualisations and data summaries provide an initial, yet rich, understanding of how preferences and choice behaviours might vary between different subgroups in the sample. Such insights are crucial in informing and enhancing subsequent analytical processes, helping ensure that the models account for relevant demographic factors and better reflect the underlying choice dynamics.

### 7.2.4 Attribute Effects

An essential step in exploring choice data is understanding how different attribute levels impact individual decisions. The objective is to identify factors influencing individual choices and examine how varying levels of each attribute affect these selections. For example, we might be interested in whether people are more likely to choose alternatives with a specific feature (e.g. turbine height).

Comparing choice shares for different levels of a specific attribute can reveal the relative importance of each level in influencing choice behaviour. If the choice shares are similar or show minimal variation, this suggests that the different attribute levels have comparable marginal utilities. Since, as mentioned in Chap. 3, only differences in utility matter, their impact on choice outcomes will be approximately equal. This pattern might also indicate attribute non-attendance, a phenomenon in which individuals ignore or disregard one or more attributes of the alternatives when making their choices, as discussed by Campbell et al. (2011) and Weller et al. (2014).

For attributes with a predicted effect (like cost, where economic theory suggests individuals should have a negative preference), analysing choice patterns allows for a preliminary assessment of internal validity, ensuring the data reflects the intended relationships. It is important to remember that internal validity checks in DCEs (where hypothetical scenarios are used) cannot fully substitute other forms of validation, as hypothetical bias is always a concern. Nonetheless, the more internal validity checks you can pass, the more confident you can be in the data's reliability, even if it does not guarantee external validity. For attributes with numerical levels, comparing the proportion of choices made for each level can also guide your choice of functional forms to use in the models. While the standard assumption is a linear relationship in the utility function, observing how choice shares change with attribute levels can indicate a better fit of non-linear forms like quadratic, exponential, logarithmic, or higher-order polynomials for specific attributes. Note that the utility function itself remains linear additive.

The code chunk below extracts a `tibble` that outlines the attribute levels for each alternative to be analysed in subsequent steps. The code can be applied to numeric attributes (such as `redkite`, `distance` and `cost` in this dataset) and categorical variables with two levels. In this example, we demonstrate the process for the `redkite` attribute, showing how its numeric levels are handled across the different alternatives.

```
# Retrieve the attribute levels in each alternative for the "redkite" attribute
redkite_levels <- data_wind |>
  filter(!is.na(choice)) |>
  select(choice, choice_task, contains("redkite"), female) |>
  pivot_longer(
    cols = contains("redkite"),
    names_to = "alternative",
    values_to = "level"
  ) |>
  mutate(
    alternative = parse_number(alternative)
  )

redkite_levels
```

```
# A tibble: 25,899 × 4
   choice choice_task alternative level
   <fct>  <fct>             <dbl> <dbl>
 1 1      1                     1   0
 2 1      1                     2   2.5
 3 1      1                     3  -2.5
 4 1      2                     1   0
 5 1      2                     2   0
 6 1      2                     3  -2.5
 7 3      3                     1   0
 8 3      3                     2   0
 9 3      3                     3  -5
10 1      4                     1   0
# ℹ 25,889 more rows
```

For categorical variables with more than two levels (such as `farm` and `height`), which are represented by separate dummy-coded columns for each level (excluding the baseline level) in the dataset, a similar `tibble` is created. However, this process is a bit more complex since the individual columns for each level must be properly accounted for to ensure correct representation. Below, we illustrate this for the `farm` attribute.

```
# The same exercise for a dummy-coded attribute is a little trickier
farm_levels <- data_wind |>
  filter(!is.na(choice)) |>
  select(choice, choice_task, contains("farm"), female) |>
  pivot_longer(
    cols = contains("farm"),
    names_to = c("alternative", ".value"),
    names_sep = "_"
  ) |>
  mutate(
    alternative = parse_number(alternative),
    farm = farm2 * 2 + farm3 * 3,
    farm = ifelse(farm == 0, 1, farm)
  ) |>
  select(-farm2, -farm3)

farm_levels

# A tibble: 25,899 × 4
   choice choice_task alternative  farm
   <fct>  <fct>             <dbl> <dbl>
 1 1      1                     1     1
 2 1      1                     2     1
 3 1      1                     3     2
 4 1      2                     1     1
 5 1      2                     2     3
 6 1      2                     3     2
 7 3      3                     1     1
 8 3      3                     2     3
 9 3      3                     3     3
10 1      4                     1     1
# ℹ 25,889 more rows
```

With these data frames created (`redkite_levels` and `farm_levels`), generating summary tables and visualisations to explore the number of times each attribute level is chosen is straightforward. The code chunk below demonstrates how to create bar plots: first, for `redkite_levels`, and then for `farm_levels`.

```r
# Figure 7.5 ----
## Figure 7.5a ----
p1 <- redkite_levels |>
  group_by(level) |>
  summarize(
    share_chosen = mean(choice == alternative)
  ) |>
  ggplot(mapping = aes(x = level, y = share_chosen)) +
  geom_bar(stat = "summary") +
  scale_y_continuous(labels = scales::percent_format()) +
  scale_x_continuous(breaks = seq(-5, 5, by = 2.5)) +
  labs(
    title = "Including SQ choices",
    x = "Attribute (Redkite) level",
    y = "Choice share (%) for level when available"
  ) +
  theme_bw() +
  theme(
    axis.title.x = element_text(size = 10),
    axis.title.y = element_text(size = 10),
    legend.title = element_text(size = 10),
    axis.text = element_text(size = 10),
    legend.text = element_text(size = 10)
  )

## Figure 7.5b ----
p2 <- redkite_levels |>
  filter(alternative != sq_alt & choice != sq_alt) |>
  group_by(level) |>
  summarize(
    share_chosen = mean(choice == alternative)
  ) |>
  ggplot(mapping = aes(x = level, y = share_chosen)) +
  geom_bar(stat = "summary") +
  scale_y_continuous(labels = scales::percent_format()) +
  scale_x_continuous(breaks = seq(-5, 5, by = 2.5)) +
  labs(
    title = "Excluding SQ choices",
    x = "Attribute (Redkite) level",
    y = "Choice share (%) for level when available"
  ) +
  theme_bw() +
  theme(
    axis.title.x = element_text(size = 10),
    axis.title.y = element_text(size = 10),
    legend.title = element_text(size = 10),
    axis.text = element_text(size = 10),
    legend.text = element_text(size = 10)
  )

p1 + p2 + plot_layout(ncol = 2)
```

Figure 7.5 consists of two bar charts that compare choice shares across attribute levels. The left panel displays this relationship across all alternatives, while the right panel focuses solely on non-SQ alternatives. Recall that the `redkite` attribute levels range from −5.0 to 5.0 in increments of 2.5, resulting in five possible values. These charts illustrate the proportion of positive choices for each level, indicating how frequently a given level was selected when it was available.

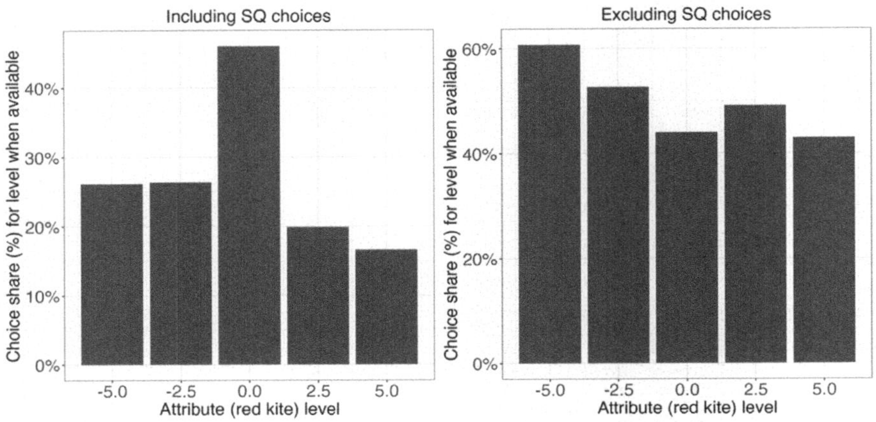


**Fig. 7.5** Choice shares by attribute level (red kite)

Starting with the left panel, the highest choice share is observed at the attribute level of 0.0, capturing over 45% of the share. However, this is primarily driven by SQ choices, as 0.0 is the attribute level associated with the SQ alternative. This is a common feature of DCEs, particularly in environmental and applied economics, where all attributes in the SQ option—the baseline option representing no change—are set to the same level across all choices. This can make it challenging to distinguish a genuine preference for a specific attribute level from the general tendency to stick with the status quo, a phenomenon known as SQ bias (as discussed by Scarpa et al. 2005; Oehlmann et al. 2017).

Turning to the right panel provides a clearer picture of preferences for the redkite attribute, independent of any potential SQ bias. Here, we observe a noticeable decline in choice shares as the attribute level increases from −5.0 to 5.0. Although this trend is somewhat visible in the left panel, the peak at 0.0 distorts the pattern. Since we can expect to see a higher share for preferred levels, this suggests that individuals tend to favour lower values of this attribute, all else being equal. The right panel also suggests that the decline from −5.0 to 5.0 is relatively linear, which offers initial guidance on how to specify this attribute in the utility function. While this assumption may need revision during the modelling stage, having a clear starting point based on empirical evidence is highly valuable.

```r
## Figure 7.6 ----
## Figure 7.6a ----
p1 <- farm_levels |>
  group_by(farm) |>
  summarize(
    share_chosen = mean(choice == alternative)
  ) |>
  ggplot(mapping = aes(x = farm, y = share_chosen)) +
  geom_bar(stat = "summary") +
  scale_y_continuous(labels = scales::percent_format()) +
  labs(
    title = "Including SQ choices",
    x = "Attribute (Farm) level",
    y = "Choice share (%) for level when available"
  ) +
  theme_bw() +
  theme(
    axis.title.x = element_text(size = 10),
    axis.title.y = element_text(size = 10),
    legend.title = element_text(size = 10),
    axis.text = element_text(size = 10),
    legend.text = element_text(size = 10)
  )

## Figure 7.6b ----
p2 <- farm_levels |>
  filter(alternative != sq_alt & choice != sq_alt) |>
  group_by(farm) |>
  summarize(
    share_chosen = mean(choice == alternative)
  ) |>
  ggplot(mapping = aes(x = farm, y = share_chosen)) +
  geom_bar(stat = "summary") +
  scale_y_continuous(labels = scales::percent_format()) +
  labs(
    title = "Excluding SQ choices",
    x = "Attribute (Farm) level",
    y = "Choice share (%) for level when available"
  ) +
  theme_bw() +
  theme(
    axis.title.x = element_text(size = 10),
    axis.title.y = element_text(size = 10),
    legend.title = element_text(size = 10),
    axis.text = element_text(size = 10),
    legend.text = element_text(size = 10)
  )

p1 + p2 + plot_layout(ncol = 2)
```

Similar to Figs. 7.5 and 7.6 displays choice shares for different levels of the `farm` attribute. In the left panel, which includes SQ choices, attribute level 1 (*LargeFarms*, see Table 4.2) has the highest choice share, exceeding 40%, while attribute levels 2 (*MediumFarms*) and 3 (*SmallFarms*) have lower shares, around 20%. In the right panel, which excludes SQ choices, the shares for levels 1, 2, and 3 are more balanced. However, it remains evident that large farms are preferred over medium and small farms, which are more or less equally preferred, all else being equal.

To explore how the choice shares across the `redkite` attribute levels differ by gender, we have included a column representing gender (named `female`) in the `redkite_levels` and `farm_levels` data frames. It would be straightforward to add additional variables such as age and education level, which are both available in this dataset, in this analysis. Here, we have selected `female` purely for demonstration purposes.

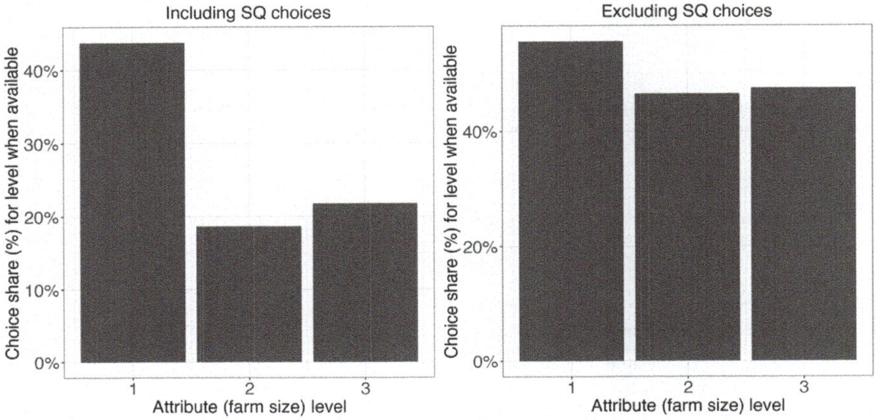


**Fig. 7.6** Choice shares by attribute level (farm size)

Including such variables is essential, as it enables the exploration of potential sources of heterogeneity in the data. If these variables reveal differences in how different groups choose based on attribute levels, it can provide valuable clues about the interactions to include in the utility function. Accounting for these interactions is important in building an accurate and predictive choice model, while identifying these differences among sample subgroups early on may help you arrive at a more appropriate model specification sooner, saving valuable time in the long run. To illustrate this, we reproduce the right panel of Fig. 7.5 to reveal how the choice shares across the `redkite` attribute levels among the non-SQ alternatives differ between males and females.

```
# Figure 7.7 ----
redkite_levels |>
  filter(alternative != sq_alt & choice != sq_alt) |>
  group_by(level, female) |>
  summarize(
    share_chosen = mean(choice == alternative)
  ) |>
  ggplot(mapping = aes(x = level, y = share_chosen, fill = female)) +
  geom_bar(stat = "summary", position = "dodge") +
  scale_y_continuous(labels = scales::percent_format()) +
  scale_x_continuous(breaks = seq(-5, 5, by = 2.5)) +
  labs(
    title = "Excluding SQ choices",
    x = "Attribute (red kite) level",
    y = "Choice share (%) for level when available"
  ) +
  theme_bw() +
  theme(
    axis.title.x = element_text(size = 10),
    axis.title.y = element_text(size = 10),
    legend.title = element_text(size = 10),
    axis.text = element_text(size = 10),
    legend.text = element_text(size = 10)
  )
```

Figure 7.7 shows that choice shares for each level of the `redkite` attribute among the non-SQ alternatives do not differ substantially between males and females. At

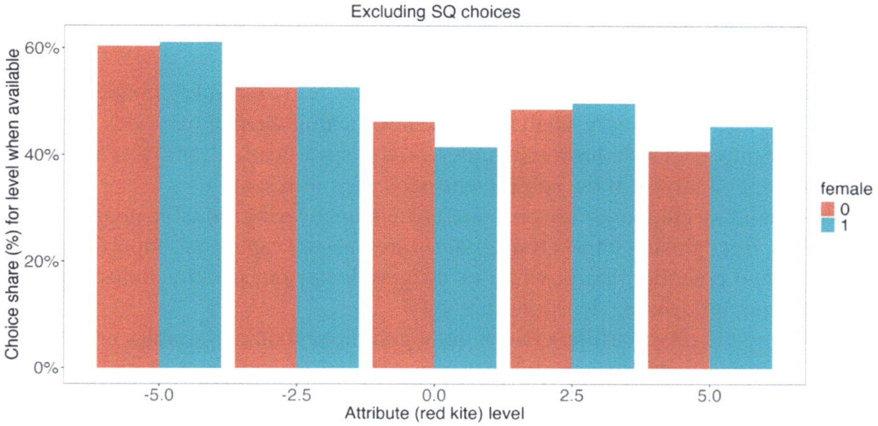


**Fig. 7.7** Choice shares by attribute level (red kite) and gender

first glance, this may suggest that preferences for this attribute are similar between males and females, however more rigorous and thorough testing during the modelling phase will be needed to confirm this observation.

## 7.3 Preliminary Analysis: An Ongoing Process

The goal of this chapter is to introduce you to the types of preliminary analysis you can perform when you first obtain your DCE data. While this chapter showcases several valuable techniques, it does not represent an exhaustive list, as the methods you choose to explore will depend heavily on the nature of your data and the specific research questions you seek to answer. The primary takeaway from this chapter is that the initial phase of analysis is just as critical as the modelling stage, if not more so, in laying the groundwork for robust and accurate results. Conducting a thorough preliminary analysis allows you to gain a deeper understanding of your data and helps you identify patterns, relationships, and potential issues early on. This can significantly impact the direction and success of the subsequent analysis stages.

It is essential not to think of this stage as occurring only at the start of your analysis. On the contrary, revisiting preliminary analyses throughout your research can yield significant insights, particularly as you refine your research questions, adapt your modelling approach, and interpret your findings. Simple comparisons, descriptive statistics, and exploratory data analysis are all invaluable tools that will help you frame your questions more effectively, guide your decisions on model specification, and validate the trends or relationships you uncover. Continually revisiting these initial analyses as your research evolves can help ensure your research remains rooted in the data, leading to more accurate, meaningful, and credible results.

## 7.4 Key Takeaways

- Thoroughly exploring your data is essential before diving into complex choice models. The preliminary analysis presented in this chapter provides valuable insights into choice behaviour, guides model specification, and sets the stage for a deeper analysis in the subsequent steps of your research.
- Understanding choice patterns is imperative in uncovering valuable insights from the data. Recognising why certain choices are missing can reveal important information and potential biases, while identifying behaviour patterns helps pinpoint key factors influencing decision-making.
- Analysing the relationship between demographic and other variables and choice behaviour can help you uncover sources of heterogeneity and provide a more nuanced understanding of the data.
- Understanding how different attribute levels affect choices is crucial for identifying key drivers of decisions, assessing the relative importance of each attribute in the choice process, and getting insights into the functional form most suited for each attribute.
- Exploratory data analysis is not just a starting point; it is an ongoing process. Iterative exploration is essential for refining research questions, guiding model decisions, and ensuring robust, meaningful results.

## References

Bradley M, Daly A (1994) Use of the logit scaling approach to test for rank-order and fatigue effects in stated preference data. Transportation 21(2):167–184. https://doi.org/10.1007/BF01098791

Campbell D, Erdem S (2019) Including opt-out options in discrete choice experiments: issues to consider. Patient 12(1):1–14. https://doi.org/10.1007/s40271-018-0324-6

Campbell D, Hensher DA, Scarpa R (2011) Non-attendance to attributes in environmental choice analysis: a latent class specification. J Environ Plann Man 54(8):1061–1076. https://doi.org/10.1080/09640568.2010.549367

Firke S (2023) Janitor: simple tools for examining and cleaning dirty data. R package version 2.2.0.9000. https://sfirke.github.io/janitor/

Hess S, Palma D (2019) Apollo: a flexible, powerful and customisable freeware package for choice model estimation and application. J Choice Model 32:100170. https://doi.org/10.1016/j.jocm.2019.100170

Iannone R, Cheng J, Schloerke B et al. (2023) gt: easily create presentation-ready display tables. https://CRAN.R-project.org/package=gt

Müller K, Wickham H (2023) tibble: simple data frames. https://CRAN.R-project.org/package=tibble

Oehlmann M, Meyerhoff J, Mariel P, Weller P (2017) Uncovering context-induced status quo effects in choice experiments. J Environ Econ and Manag 81:59–73. https://doi.org/10.1016/j.jeem.2016.09.002

Pedersen T (2024) patchwork: the composer of plots. R package version 1.3.0. https://CRAN.R-project.org/package=patchwork

Scarpa R, Ferrini S, Willis K (2005) Performance of error component models for status-quo effects in choice experiments. In: Scarpa R, Alberini A (eds) Applications of simulation methods in environmental and resource economics. The economics of non-market goods and resources. Springer Netherlands, Dordrecht, pp 247–273. https://doi.org/10.1007/1-4020-3684-1_13

Thiene M, Meyerhoff J, De Salvo M (2012) Scale and taste heterogeneity for forest biodiversity: models of serial nonparticipation and their effects. J Forest Econ 18(4):355–369. https://doi.org/10.1016/j.jfe.2012.06.005

Von Haefen RH, Massey DM, Adamowicz WL (2005) Serial nonparticipation in repeated discrete choice models. Am J Agric Econ 87(4):1061–1076. https://doi.org/10.1111/j.1467-8276.2005.00794.x

Weller P, Oehlmann M, Mariel P, Meyerhoff J (2014) Stated and inferred attribute non-attendance in a design of designs approach. J Choice Model 11:43–56. https://doi.org/10.1016/j.jocm.2014.04.002

Wickham H (2016) ggplot2: elegant graphics for data analysis. Springer-Verlag, New York. https://ggplot2.tidyverse.org

Wickham H, Averick M, Bryan J et al (2019) Welcome to the tidyverse. J Open Source Softw 4(43):1686. https://doi.org/10.21105/joss.01686

Wickham H, François R, Henry L et al. (2023) dplyr: a grammar of data manipulation. https://CRAN.R-project.org/package=dplyr

Wickham H, Vaughan D, Girlich M (2024) tidyr: tidy messy data. R package version 1.3.1. https://tidyr.tidyverse.org

# Chapter 8
# Maximum Likelihood and Related Issues

**Abstract** This chapter explores Maximum Likelihood (ML) estimation, a statistical method used to estimate parameters of a given probability distribution. We begin with an introduction to the fundamental components of ML estimation, including the likelihood function, the density function, and the process of identifying parameter values that maximise the likelihood of the observed data. This chapter also covers numerical optimisation methods, both gradient-based and non-gradient, for situations where analytical solutions are impractical. We address sample variation in statistical estimation, highlighting the issues that may arise when relying on a single sample to infer population parameters, and review the use of simulation techniques, such as generating artificial datasets, to evaluate the reliability of these estimates.

## 8.1 Maximum Likelihood

Maximum likelihood (ML) estimation is a widely used technique for analysing discrete choice data. ML estimators are under general conditions asymptotically normal, allowing for the use of many standard techniques for statistical inference. This versatility makes the ML estimator a popular choice for modelling a broad range of discrete choice models. The ML estimation process involves formulating a likelihood function, optimising it to find parameter values that maximise this likelihood, and performing statistical inferences based on the obtained estimates.

Understanding the challenges associated with these issues is essential for ensuring robust and accurate parameter estimates. Even if you do not delve into the finer details of optimisation, a brief exploration of the content in this chapter is highly recommended to comprehend its potential impact on your DCE project. The insights gained will significantly enhance your ability to navigate and troubleshoot challenges in the estimation process.

 
P. Mariel et al., *Environmental Valuation with Discrete Choice Experiments in R*, The Economics of Non-Market Goods and Resources 17,
https://doi.org/10.1007/978-3-031-89338-4_8

We have tried to lighten the technical burden of this chapter by using easy-to-understand examples outside the field of statistics to bring these concepts closer to readers, at the expense of not describing some technical aspects in detail. We hope this approach will make the content more accessible and engaging, even for those less familiar with statistical theory. In the following section, we provide a summary of the fundamental concepts underlying the ML estimation method.

Let us assume that we have a set of $N$ observations of a single explained variable in a $N \times 1$ vector

$$\mathbf{y} = \begin{bmatrix} y_1 \\ \vdots \\ y_N \end{bmatrix},$$

and $N$ observations of $K$ explanatory variables represented in a $N \times K$ matrix

$$\mathbf{X} = \begin{bmatrix} \mathbf{x}_1{}' \\ \vdots \\ \mathbf{x}_N{}' \end{bmatrix} = \begin{bmatrix} x_{11} & \cdots & x_{1K} \\ \vdots & \ddots & \vdots \\ x_{N1} & \cdots & x_{NK} \end{bmatrix}.$$

A joint probability mass function or density function depends on a set of parameters $\boldsymbol{\zeta}$:

$$f(\mathbf{y}, \mathbf{X}|, \boldsymbol{\zeta}). \tag{8.1}$$

The specification of the density function Eq. (8.1) defines a likelihood function

$$L(\boldsymbol{\zeta}|\mathbf{y}, \mathbf{X}) = f(\mathbf{y}, \mathbf{X}|, \boldsymbol{\zeta}). \tag{8.2}$$

The density function $f$ describes the data-generating process and gives the likelihood of observing $\mathbf{y}$ and $\mathbf{X}$ given $\boldsymbol{\zeta}$. The likelihood function $L$ reinterprets the density function as a function of the parameters $\boldsymbol{\zeta}$ given observed data $\mathbf{y}$ and $\mathbf{X}$.

The likelihood function $L(\boldsymbol{\zeta}|\mathbf{y}, \mathbf{X})$ defined in Eq. (8.2) requires specifying both the conditional density $f(\mathbf{y}|\mathbf{X}, \boldsymbol{\theta})$ and the marginal density $f(\mathbf{X}|\boldsymbol{\psi})$, where $\boldsymbol{\theta}$ and $\boldsymbol{\psi}$ are distinct subsets of the parameter vector $\boldsymbol{\zeta}$. This is because the joint (unconditional) likelihood function can be factorised as

$$f(\mathbf{y}, \mathbf{X}|, \boldsymbol{\zeta}) = f(\mathbf{y}|\mathbf{X}, \boldsymbol{\theta}) f(\mathbf{X}|\boldsymbol{\psi}).$$

In typical applications, estimation is based on the conditional likelihood $L(\boldsymbol{\theta}) = f(\mathbf{y}|\mathbf{X}, \boldsymbol{\theta})$ since the primary interest usually lies in modelling how the response variable $\mathbf{y}$ behaves conditional on the explanatory variables $\mathbf{X}$. When $\boldsymbol{\theta}$ and $\boldsymbol{\psi}$ are disjoint subsets of parameters, an assumption commonly satisfied in standard modelling frameworks, this approach is unproblematic. However, in situations like endogenous sampling, this condition does not hold. In such cases, it is necessary to use the full joint density $f(\mathbf{y}, \mathbf{X}|, \boldsymbol{\zeta})$ rather than relying solely on the conditional likelihood.

The term maximum likelihood estimator (MLE) is often used to mean two different things:

(1) The value of $\boldsymbol{\theta}$ that globally maximises the likelihood function $L(\boldsymbol{\theta}) = f(\mathbf{y}|\mathbf{X}, \boldsymbol{\theta})$ over the entire parameter space $\boldsymbol{\Theta}$.
(2) Any solution (root) of the likelihood equation $\partial L(\boldsymbol{\theta})/\partial \boldsymbol{\theta} = 0$ that corresponds to a local maximum.

We refer to the first concept as the global maximum likelihood estimator and may use the term local maximum likelihood estimator for the second concept when needed (Amemiya 1985, Sect. 4.2.1). Strictly speaking, the MLE should identify the parameter value that gives the highest likelihood. While the desired definition of an MLE is the parameter that globally maximises the likelihood, real-world statistical practice and the complexity of many likelihood functions lead some authors to relax this usage.

To employ analogy to describe the global maximum likelihood estimator, imagine you are climbing a mountain, and each point on the surface of the mountain represents a different set of parameter values $\boldsymbol{\theta}$ (coordinates of the points) that we are trying to estimate. Our goal is to find the highest peak of the mountain, which corresponds to the parameter values that make our observed data most likely.

Since the logarithm of $L(\boldsymbol{\theta})$ is a monotonically increasing transformation, taking $\ln L(\boldsymbol{\theta})$ does not alter the locations of global or local maxima, so we proceed by maximising $\ln L(\boldsymbol{\theta})$. According to the principle of the maximum likelihood estimator, the estimator of $\boldsymbol{\theta}_0$, denoted $\widehat{\boldsymbol{\theta}}$, is obtained by solving the following maximisation problem:

$$\max_{\theta \in \boldsymbol{\Theta}} \ln L(\boldsymbol{\theta}) .$$

The vector $\widehat{\boldsymbol{\theta}}$ satisfies the standard conditions for a maximum defined as

$$\begin{aligned} \underbrace{\boldsymbol{S}(\hat{\boldsymbol{\theta}})}_{\ell \times 1} &= \left. \frac{\partial \ln L(\boldsymbol{\theta})}{\partial \boldsymbol{\theta}} \right|_{\theta = \hat{\theta}} = 0 \\ \underbrace{\boldsymbol{H}(\hat{\boldsymbol{\theta}})}_{\ell \times \ell} &= \left. \frac{\partial^2 \ln L(\boldsymbol{\theta})}{\partial \boldsymbol{\theta}\, \partial \boldsymbol{\theta}'} \right|_{\theta = \hat{\theta}} \quad \text{is a negative definite matrix,} \end{aligned} \tag{8.3}$$

here $\boldsymbol{S}(\cdot)$ is the gradient vector or *Score* and $\boldsymbol{H}(\cdot)$ the *Hessian matrix* of the $\ln L(\boldsymbol{\theta})$ function. This does not guarantee that $\widehat{\boldsymbol{\theta}}$ is the global maximum of the function, only that it is a local maximum, unless there is a unique solution within the interior of $\boldsymbol{\Theta}$, meaning that the function $\ln L$ is globally concave.

Using the mountain climber analogy, if we are in a landscape with only one mountain and stand at its summit, we can be certain we are on the highest peak. However, in a landscape with multiple mountains, we must verify that none of the other summits is higher than the one we are on.

The *Fisher Information Matrix* denoted as $\boldsymbol{I}(\boldsymbol{\theta})$ is the variance of $\partial \ln L(\boldsymbol{\theta})/\partial \boldsymbol{\theta}$ and it is defined as the expectation of the outer product of the score vector, that is

$$\boldsymbol{I}(\boldsymbol{\theta}) = E\left[\frac{\partial \ln L(\boldsymbol{\theta})}{\partial \boldsymbol{\theta}} \frac{\partial \ln L(\boldsymbol{\theta})}{\partial \boldsymbol{\theta}\prime}\right].$$

Large values of $\boldsymbol{I}(\boldsymbol{\theta})$ indicate that small changes in $\boldsymbol{\theta}$ result in significant variations in the log-likelihood, suggesting that the log-likelihood contains substantial information about $\boldsymbol{\theta}$. Under the regularity conditions (Cameron and Trivedi 2005, p 141), the following relationship, known as the information matrix equality, holds:

$$E\left[\frac{\partial \ln L(\boldsymbol{\theta})}{\partial \boldsymbol{\theta}} \frac{\partial \ln L(\boldsymbol{\theta})}{\partial \boldsymbol{\theta}'}\bigg|_{\boldsymbol{\theta}=\boldsymbol{\theta}_0}\right] = -E\left[\frac{\partial^2 \ln L(\boldsymbol{\theta})}{\partial \boldsymbol{\theta}\, \partial \boldsymbol{\theta}'}\bigg|_{\boldsymbol{\theta}=\boldsymbol{\theta}_0}\right].$$

That is why the *Fisher Information Matrix* is in many textbooks defined as

$$\boldsymbol{I}(\boldsymbol{\theta}_0) = -E\left[\frac{\partial^2 \ln L(\boldsymbol{\theta})}{\partial \boldsymbol{\theta}\, \partial \boldsymbol{\theta}'}\bigg|_{\boldsymbol{\theta}=\boldsymbol{\theta}_0}\right], \tag{8.4}$$

and interpreted as the amount of information about $\boldsymbol{\theta}$ that, on average, a sample provides.

The Hessian (based on second partial derivatives) provides information about the curvature of the function. Specifically, it tells us about the curvature of the log-likelihood function, which is a measure of how curved or flat the function is apart from indicating concavity or convexity.

The Hessian matrix helps us understand how the likelihood function is curving at a specific point (at different values of $\mathbf{X}$), while the *Fisher Information Matrix* (Eq. (8.4)) tells us the amount of information about $\boldsymbol{\theta}_0$, we get, on average, from our observations about the parameters we are estimating. That is why it is used to indicate the precision of our estimates.

In general, under a specific set of conditions (see Amemiya 1985, p. 121)

$$\sqrt{N}\left(\widehat{\boldsymbol{\theta}} - \boldsymbol{\theta}_0\right) \xrightarrow{d} N\left(0, [\boldsymbol{I}_A(\boldsymbol{\theta}_0)]^{-1}\right), \tag{8.5}$$

where $\widehat{\boldsymbol{\theta}}$ is the maximum likelihood estimator and

$$\boldsymbol{I}_A(\boldsymbol{\theta}_0) = -\lim_{N\to\infty} E\left[\frac{1}{N}\frac{\partial^2 \ln L(\boldsymbol{\theta})}{\partial\boldsymbol{\theta}\,\partial\boldsymbol{\theta}'}\bigg|_{\theta=\theta_0}\right].$$

This means that under certain conditions, the maximum likelihood estimator of a parameter $\boldsymbol{\theta}_0$ is asymptotically normally distributed with mean $\boldsymbol{\theta}_0$ and an asymptotic variance–covariance matrix defined as

$$\boldsymbol{V}_A\left(\widehat{\boldsymbol{\theta}}\right) = \frac{1}{N}[\boldsymbol{I}_A(\boldsymbol{\theta}_0)]^{-1}.$$

Note that:

- the variance–covariance matrix of the maximum likelihood estimator is inversely proportional to the sample size $N$. This means that as the sample size increases, the variance of the estimator decreases, and the estimation becomes more precise.
- the variance–covariance matrix of the maximum likelihood estimator is inversely proportional to the information matrix $\boldsymbol{I}_A(\boldsymbol{\theta}_0)$. This means that the more information we have about the parameters, the more precise our estimates will be.

For a given finite sample size $N$, the maximum likelihood estimator of $\boldsymbol{V}_A\left(\widehat{\boldsymbol{\theta}}\right)$ is

$$\hat{\boldsymbol{V}}(\hat{\boldsymbol{\theta}}) = -\left(E\left[\boldsymbol{H}(\hat{\boldsymbol{\theta}})\right]\right)^{-1} = -\left(E\left[\frac{\partial^2 \ln L(\boldsymbol{\theta})}{\partial\boldsymbol{\theta}\,\partial\boldsymbol{\theta}'}\bigg|_{\theta=\hat{\theta}}\right]\right)^{-1} = [I(\boldsymbol{\theta})]^{-1}_{\theta=\hat{\theta}}. \tag{8.6}$$

Sometimes, the calculation of this estimator can be difficult to perform. In such cases, we can use alternative estimators that are consistent with and represent approximations of the maximum likelihood estimators of $\boldsymbol{V}_A\left(\widehat{\boldsymbol{\theta}}\right)$.

The first approximation, $\widehat{\boldsymbol{V}}_1\left(\widehat{\boldsymbol{\theta}}\right)$, is based on the inverse of the Hessian matrix evaluated at the value of the maximum likelihood estimator $\widehat{\boldsymbol{\theta}}$, that is

$$\widehat{\boldsymbol{V}}_1\left(\widehat{\boldsymbol{\theta}}\right) = -\left(\boldsymbol{H}\left(\widehat{\boldsymbol{\theta}}\right)\right)^{-1} = -\left(\frac{\partial^2 \ln L(\boldsymbol{\theta})}{\partial\boldsymbol{\theta}\,\partial\boldsymbol{\theta}'}\right)^{-1}_{\theta=\hat{\theta}}.$$

The second approximation is based on the Berndt-Hall-Hall-Hausman (BHHH) matrix (Berndt et al. 1974), defined as the sum of outer products of gradients of the individual likelihood functions evaluated at the value of the maximum likelihood estimator $\widehat{\boldsymbol{\theta}}$:

$$B(\hat{\theta}) = \sum_{n=1}^{N} \left( \frac{\partial \ln L(\boldsymbol{\theta}; y_n, \mathbf{x}_n)}{\partial \boldsymbol{\theta}} \right) \left( \frac{\partial \ln L(\boldsymbol{\theta}; y_n, \mathbf{x}_n)}{\partial \boldsymbol{\theta}'} \right) \Bigg|_{\theta=\hat{\theta}}. \tag{8.7}$$

Thus, the second approximation of the theoretical variance–covariance matrix defined in Eq. (8.6) is:

$$\widehat{V}_2\left(\widehat{\theta}\right) = \left(B\left(\widehat{\theta}\right)\right)^{-1} = \left[\sum_{n=1}^{N} \left(\frac{\partial \ln L(\boldsymbol{\theta}; y_n, \mathbf{x}_n)}{\partial \boldsymbol{\theta}}\right)\left(\frac{\partial \ln L(\boldsymbol{\theta}; y_n, \mathbf{x}_n)}{\partial \boldsymbol{\theta}'}\right)\Big|_{\theta=\hat{\theta}}\right]^{-1}. \tag{8.8}$$

All three estimators ($\widehat{V}\left(\widehat{\theta}\right)$, $\widehat{V}_1\left(\widehat{\theta}\right)$, $\widehat{V}_2\left(\widehat{\theta}\right)$) are consistent estimators of $V_A\left(\widehat{\theta}\right)$. In specific cases, they may coincide, but if they differ, the choice of which one to use is generally determined by considerations of computational convenience. For instance, some numerical optimisation methods for obtaining maximum likelihood estimates, which are discussed in the next section, employ the matrices defined in Eqs. (8.7) and (8.8) at each iteration. Once the iterative estimation process concludes, the matrix from Eqs. (8.7) or (8.8) (depending on which method was used) in the final iteration is used to estimate $V_A\left(\widehat{\theta}\right)$.

The assumptions regarding the error terms in the model are crucial for the validity of the maximum likelihood estimator. The most common assumptions are that the error terms are independent and identically distributed and follow a specific distribution, such as the normal distribution. However, in practice, these assumptions are frequently not met. Violations of these assumptions can lead to biased and inconsistent estimates. One of the strategies to solve some of these issues related to the estimation of the variance–covariance matrix is to use a robust covariance matrix.

The *robust covariance matrix* is based on the definition of the *sandwich* estimator (Huber 1967) defined as:

$$\widehat{V}_{robust}\left(\widehat{\theta}\right) = \left(-H\left(\widehat{\theta}\right)\right)^{-1} B\left(\widehat{\theta}\right)\left(-H\left(\widehat{\theta}\right)\right)^{-1}. \tag{8.9}$$

The calculation of the robust covariance matrix is commonly integrated into standard statistical and econometric software packages. It is a preferred option over the standard estimators ($\widehat{V}\left(\widehat{\theta}\right)$, $\widehat{V}_1\left(\widehat{\theta}\right)$, $\widehat{V}_2\left(\widehat{\theta}\right)$) due to its robustness against violations of certain model assumptions mentioned above, such as heteroscedasticity (when the variability of the errors is not constant across individuals) or the lack of independence of errors.

## 8.2 Numerical Optimisation Methods

Finding the global maximum and, consequently, the maximum likelihood estimates of a simple likelihood function is a relatively straightforward process. However, as models become more complex, the process of maximising the likelihood function becomes more involved. In fact, for some of the models presented in this book, there is no explicit solution for the system of equations based on the first-order conditions (Eq. (8.3)). Therefore, maximising the likelihood function in such cases must be carried out numerically. This is accomplished by employing iterative numerical optimisation methods.

Numerical optimisation methods are mathematical techniques used to find the maximum or minimum of a function when an analytical solution is either difficult or impossible to obtain. They have a wide range of applications, including economics and econometrics, where they are particularly valuable for estimating parameters in discrete choice models. In the context of econometrics, numerical optimisation methods can be classified into several categories.

*Gradient-Based* methods (e.g. Gradient Descent, Newton–Raphson, Gauss–Newton, BFGS) involve using information about the gradient of the objective function. *Non-Gradient* methods include, for example, Nelder-Mead, which is based on repeated adjustments of a shape (simplex) made of points by reflecting, expanding, contracting, or shrinking its shape, or Simulated Annealing (SANN), inspired by the annealing process in metallurgy. *Metaheuristic Methods* like Genetic Algorithms and Particle Swarm Optimisation are inspired by natural processes and iteratively evolve potential solutions.

Another effective non-gradient optimisation method implemented in the R package *Apollo* (Hess and Palma 2019) and used throughout this book is the *Bunch-Gay-Welsch* (BGW) method (Bunch et al. 1993). A key feature of BGW is that it exploits the special structure of statistical estimation problems by maintaining a secant approximation of the second-order part of the Hessian, and adaptively switches between a Gauss–Newton and an augmented Hessian approximation.

Turning our attention to *Gradient-Based Methods*, they initiate their iterative process with initial parameter values $\widehat{\boldsymbol{\theta}}_0$. This process relies on the gradient and a weight matrix $\boldsymbol{A}$ and proceeds as follows:

$$\widehat{\boldsymbol{\theta}}_{i+1} = \widehat{\boldsymbol{\theta}}_i + \boldsymbol{A}\left[\left.\frac{\partial \ln L(\boldsymbol{\theta})}{\partial \boldsymbol{\theta}}\right|_{\boldsymbol{\theta}=\widehat{\boldsymbol{\theta}}_i}\right], \quad i = 0, 1, 2, \ldots \tag{8.10}$$

To better understand how numerical gradient-based optimisation methods work, we can compare this to the situation of a blindfolded climber trying to ascend the highest mountain in a complex mountain terrain. The climber, unable to see the terrain, relies on the gradient, i.e. the direction with the steepest slope, and a weight matrix $\boldsymbol{A}$ which helps adjust each step based on the curvature of the terrain. By adjusting their position based on the gradient and curvature of the terrain, the climber gradually approaches the summit and reaches a point where further steps do not lead to a significant increase in height. This point represents the summit of the mountain and the (local) maximum of our likelihood function. The coordinates of this point are the parameter estimates.

There are several modifications of the basic gradient-based methods defined in Eq. (8.10) that have been developed to improve their performance. One of the oldest algorithms is the Newton–Raphson method, which is based on a quadratic approximation via Taylor series of the log-likelihood function. In this case, the weight matrix $\boldsymbol{A}$ is represented by the Hessian matrix and takes the following form:

$$\widehat{\boldsymbol{\theta}}_{i+1} = \widehat{\boldsymbol{\theta}}_i - \left[ \left. \frac{\partial^2 \ln L(\boldsymbol{\theta})}{\partial \boldsymbol{\theta}\, \partial \boldsymbol{\theta}'} \right|_{\boldsymbol{\theta}=\hat{\boldsymbol{\theta}}_i} \right]^{-1} \left[ \left. \frac{\partial \ln L(\boldsymbol{\theta})}{\partial \boldsymbol{\theta}} \right|_{\boldsymbol{\theta}=\hat{\boldsymbol{\theta}}_i} \right].$$

Another approach is applied by the Berndt, Hall, Hall and Hausman (BHHH) algorithm, which substitutes the second derivatives of the Hessian by the matrix defined in Eq. (8.7). It is defined as

$$\begin{aligned} \hat{\boldsymbol{\theta}}_{i+1} &= \hat{\boldsymbol{\theta}}_i + \boldsymbol{B}^{-1}(\hat{\boldsymbol{\theta}}_i) \left[ \left. \frac{\partial \ln L(\boldsymbol{\theta})}{\partial \boldsymbol{\theta}} \right|_{\boldsymbol{\theta}=\hat{\boldsymbol{\theta}}_i} \right] \\ &= \hat{\boldsymbol{\theta}}_i + \left[ \sum_{n=1}^{N} \left. \left( \frac{\partial \ln L(\boldsymbol{\theta}; y_n, \mathbf{x}_n)}{\partial \boldsymbol{\theta}} \right) \left( \frac{\partial \ln L(\boldsymbol{\theta}; y_n, \mathbf{x}_n)}{\partial \boldsymbol{\theta}'} \right) \right|_{\boldsymbol{\theta}=\hat{\boldsymbol{\theta}}_i} \right]^{-1} \left[ \left. \frac{\partial \ln L(\boldsymbol{\theta})}{\partial \boldsymbol{\theta}} \right|_{\boldsymbol{\theta}=\hat{\boldsymbol{\theta}}_i} \right] \end{aligned} \quad (8.11)$$

The Newton–Raphson method and the BHHH algorithm are both gradient-based optimisation techniques. The Newton–Raphson method updates the parameter estimates by inverting the Hessian matrix and multiplying it by the gradient of the log-likelihood function. In contrast, the BHHH algorithm approximates the Hessian matrix constructed from the outer products of gradients. The Newton–Raphson method tends to converge faster near the solution due to its use of exact second derivatives but requires computing and inverting the full Hessian, which can be computationally expensive. On the other hand, BHHH avoids the full Hessian computation, potentially reducing the computational burden, but may converge more slowly.

Other gradient-based methods include gradient descent, conjugate gradient, quasi-Newton methods like BFGS, and stochastic gradient descent, each offering different trade-offs in terms of computational efficiency and convergence properties depending on the optimisation problem at hand (Hare et al. 2013; Nash and Varadhan 2011; Nash 2020).

## 8.3 An Example in R

In the R programming language, numerical optimisation methods are implemented by the use of a variety of libraries and functions designed to locate the minimum or maximum of a given function. We will illustrate the application of numerical optimisation methods in the context of maximum likelihood estimation using a simple example of a Multinomial Logit (MNL) model. To do this, we will generate a hypothetical dataset and estimate the model parameters using the *maxLik* package (Henningsen and Toomet 2011). This example will provide insights into the challenges associated with numerical optimisation methods and the importance of understanding the shape of the likelihood function in the estimation process.

Let us consider a simple MNL model (as defined in Sect. 3.2) with one choice task per individual $T = 1$ and only two alternatives and one attribute ($attr$) defined as

$$\begin{aligned} U_{n1} &= ASC_1 + \beta_1\, attr_{n1} + \varepsilon_{n1} \\ U_{n2} &= \qquad\quad\; \beta_1\, attr_{n2} + \varepsilon_{n2} \end{aligned}, \tag{8.12}$$

where ASC stands for alternative specific constant. To identify the model, we can only estimate a maximum of $J - 1$ constants and, therefore, we set $ASC_2 = 0$. Consequently, we only have two parameters we need to estimate.

$$\boldsymbol{\theta} = \begin{bmatrix} ASC_1 \\ \beta_1 \end{bmatrix} \boldsymbol{\Theta} = \{ASC_1, \beta_1 | \boldsymbol{\theta} \in \mathbb{R}^2\}.$$

This example may seem overly simple, but it has a great advantage because the likelihood function depends only on two parameters, $ASC_1$ and $\beta_1$. This allows for a graphical representation that provides information on how the shape of the log-likelihood function $\ln L$ affects the process of numerical optimisation.

If $i_n$ is the chosen alternative by individual $n$, the $\ln L$ function defined in Eq. (3.14) simplifies in our case to

$$\ln L(\boldsymbol{\theta}) = \sum_{n=1}^{N} \ln\left( \frac{\exp(ASC_{i_n} + \beta_1\, attr_{ni_n})}{\sum_{j=1}^{2} \exp(ASC_j + \beta_1\, attr_{nj})} \right). \tag{8.13}$$

To illustrate the process of numerical optimisation, we will create an artificial dataset of 20 observations based on the model defined in Eq. (8.12). The values of $attr_{n1}$ and $attr_{n2}$ will be generated as random draws from a uniform distribution between zero and ten. We will also introduce a parameter corr that controls for the correlation between $attr_{n1}$ and $attr_{n2}$, which will have a critical impact on the shape of the log-likelihood function defined in Eq. (8.13).

```r
# Load R packages
library(tidyverse)
library(patchwork)
library(janitor)
library(purrr)
library(maxLik)
library(evd)

# Function for data generation
generate_data_mnl <- function(asc1, beta1, nobs, corr, seed = NULL){
  # Set seed if specified
  if (!is.null(seed)) {
    set.seed(seed)
  }

  # The data frame
  data_mnl <- tibble(
    alt1_attr1 = runif(nobs, 0, 10),
    alt2_attr1 = corr * alt1_attr1 + (1 - corr) * runif(nobs, 0, 10),
    utility1   = asc1 + beta1 * alt1_attr1 + rgumbel(nobs),
    utility2   =        beta1 * alt2_attr1 + rgumbel(nobs)
  ) |>
    rowwise() |>
    mutate(
      choice = which.max(c_across(starts_with("utility")))
    )

  return(data_mnl)
}

# Generate data
data_mnl <- generate_data_mnl(
  asc1 = 0.5,
  beta1 = 0.5,
  nobs = 20,
  corr = 0.0,
  seed = 1234
)
```

As can be seen in the code chunk above, the population values of the parameters are set to $ASC_1 = 0.50$ and $\beta_1 = 0.50$. The ln$L$ function (Eq. (8.13)) for an MNL model is globally concave and its maximisation through a numerical optimisation method (BHHH in our case) is a straightforward task. This is shown in the script below.

```r
# Define the log-likelihood function
ll <- function(parameters){
  # Parameters of the function ll
  estimation_asc1 <- parameters[1]
  estimation_beta1 <- parameters[2]

  # Utility functions
  est_utility1 <- estimation_asc1 + estimation_beta1 * data_mnl$alt1_attr1
  est_utility2 <-                   estimation_beta1 * data_mnl$alt2_attr1

  # Save the utility chosen by each individual
  chosen_utility <- est_utility1 * (ifelse(data_mnl$choice == 1,1,0)) +
                    est_utility2 * (ifelse(data_mnl$choice == 2,1,0))

  # Compute the probability of each individual's chosen utility
  prob_chosen_alternative <- exp(chosen_utility) / (exp(est_utility1) + exp(est_utility2))

  ll <- log(prob_chosen_alternative)

  return(ll)
}

# Estimate the model
ll_max <- maxLik(ll, start = c(2.0, -2.0), print.level = 2, method = "BHHH")
```

The object ll_max contains the result of the optimisation procedure:

```
summary(ll_max)
--------------------------------------------
Maximum Likelihood estimation
BHHH maximisation, 19 iterations
Return code 8: successive function values within relative tolerance limit (reltol)
Log-Likelihood: -9.878913
2  free parameters
Estimates:
     Estimate Std. error t value Pr(> t)
[1,]   0.9820     0.5643   1.740  0.0818 .
[2,]   0.2806     0.1490   1.884  0.0596 .
---
Signif. codes:  0 '***' 0.001 '**' 0.01 '*' 0.05 '.' 0.1 ' ' 1
--------------------------------------------
```

The output of the maxLik function provides information on the estimated parameters, the value of the log-likelihood function at the maximum, and the convergence status of the optimisation algorithm. The estimated values of the parameters are $\widehat{ASC}_1 =$ 0.98 and $\widehat{\beta}_1 = 0.28$.

Figure 8.1 presents this optimisation process graphically. The optimisation algorithm used here is the BHHH algorithm, as defined in Eq. (8.11). The contour plot in Fig. 8.1 displays both the initial values ($ASC_1 = 2.00$ and $\beta_1 = -2.00$) and the global maximum. The estimated parameter values ( $\widehat{ASC}_1 = 0.98$, $\widehat{\beta}_1 = 0.28$) represent the coordinates of the summit and the maximum value of the optimised function (–9.88) represents the altitude of the mountain. In the climber analogy, our case corresponds to a landscape with only one mountain (global concavity) and after the optimisation process, the climber is standing at its summit.

In this case, there is a very low correlation between $attr_{n1}$ and $attr_{n2}$. The population correlation is set to zero (corr < –– 0) and the sample correlation in our data set of 20 observations is –0.10.

Due to the global concavity of the maximised ln$L$ function that can be observed in Fig. 8.1, the selection of initial values becomes inconsequential. However, in functions with local maxima, the choice of initial values becomes a critical factor.

Given the small sample size, there are notable differences between the population values $ASC_1 = 0.5$, $\beta_1 = 0.5$ and the estimated values $\widehat{ASC}_1 = 0.98$, $\widehat{\beta}_1 = 0.28$. Recall that the ML estimator has asymptotic properties, meaning the estimate will converge to the true value as the sample size increases. However, a single draw from the estimator distribution (representing our parameter estimates: $\widehat{ASC}_1 = 0.98$, $\widehat{\beta}_1 = 0.28$) may be either close to or far from the true value. When the sample size is small and, subsequently, the variability of the estimator is high, the probability of the estimate being far from the true value increases. The next section on sample variation provides more details on this topic.

The Hessian matrix, computed at the estimated parameter values and approximated in the BHHH algorithm by Eq. (8.7) can be obtained by

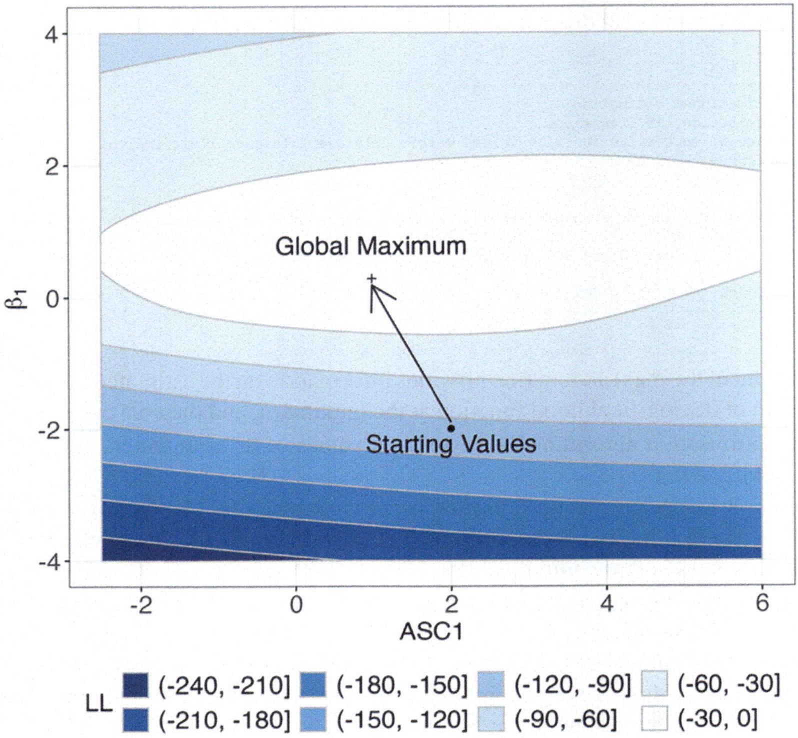


**Fig. 8.1** $ln\,L(\boldsymbol{\theta})$ function with low correlation of attributes

```
ll_max$hessian

           [,1]        [,2]
[1,] -3.1542612   0.7780652
[2,]  0.7780652 -45.2491605
attr(,"type")
[1] "BHHH"
```

The variance–covariance matrix of the estimated parameters defined by Eq. (8.6) is approximated in this case by Eq. (8.8) and can be computed as

```
-solve(ll_max$hessian)

            [,1]        [,2]
[1,] 0.318381876 0.005474618
[2,] 0.005474618 0.022193994
```

Thus, the estimated $\widehat{\mathrm{Var}}\left(\widehat{ASC}_1\right) = 0.32$ and $\widehat{\mathrm{Var}}\left(\widehat{\beta}_1\right) = 0.02$.

Note that the square root of these variances ($\sqrt{\widehat{\text{Var}}\left(\widehat{ASC}_1\right)} = 0.56$ and $\sqrt{\widehat{\text{Var}}\left(\widehat{\beta}_1\right)} = 0.15$) coincides with the standard errors of the estimated parameters shown in the second column of the output of the summary(ll_max) command presented in the R code chunk above. The functional form of $\ln L(\boldsymbol{\theta})$ is shaped by the model type to be estimated, as well as by the characteristics of the explanatory variables, here $attr_{n1}$ and $attr_{n2}$. The impact of the relationship between these variables on the shape of $\ln L(\boldsymbol{\theta})$ and consequently on the behaviour of numerical optimisation algorithms, is illustrated in the example below.

Let us increase the correlation between our explanatory variables $attr_{n1}$ and $attr_{n2}$. This introduces the well-known issue called multicollinearity (when two or more explanatory variables are highly correlated) in linear regression (Gujarati and Porter 2009). In a maximum likelihood estimation, this corresponds to the creation of flat regions in the $\ln L(\boldsymbol{\theta})$ function.

```r
# Generate the data
data_mnl <- generate_data_mnl(
  asc1 = 0.5,
  beta1 = 0.5,
  nobs = 20,
  corr = 0.95,
  seed = 1234
)

# Estimate the model
ll_max <- maxLik(ll, start = c(2.0, -2.0), print.level = 2, method = "BHHH")
```

Specifically, we increase the parameter corr in the script to 0.95. In this specific artificial dataset, the new value of corr results in an exceptionally high correlation of 0.99 between $attr_{n1}$ and $attr_{n2}$.

The results of the optimisation procedure in this case are

```
summary(ll_max)

--------------------------------------------
Maximum Likelihood estimation
BHHH maximisation, 5 iterations
Return code 2: successive function values within tolerance limit (tol)
Log-Likelihood: -9.849363
2  free parameters
Estimates:
     Estimate Std. error t value Pr(> t)
[1,]    1.395      0.568   2.455  0.0141 *
[2,]    1.502      2.740   0.548  0.5836
---
Signif. codes:  0 '***' 0.001 '**' 0.01 '*' 0.05 '.' 0.1 ' ' 1
--------------------------------------------
```

The output of the maxLik function shows a successful convergence status of the optimisation algorithm and the estimated values of the parameters in this second artificial data set (with a high correlation between $attr_{n1}$ and $attr_{n2}$) are $\widehat{ASC}_1 = 1.40$ and $\widehat{\beta}_1 = 1.50$. As evident in Fig. 8.2, the impact of the correlation between $attr_{n1}$ and $attr_{n2}$ is substantial and the functional form of the log-likelihood function

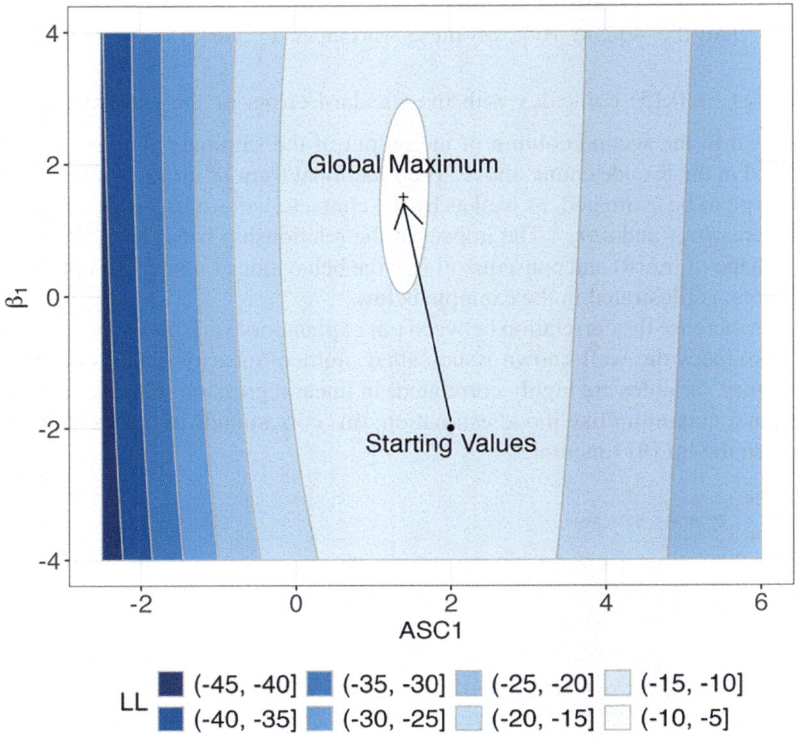


**Fig. 8.2** $ln\,L(\boldsymbol{\theta})$ function with high correlation of attributes

undergoes a significant change, displaying an almost flat region around the global maximum.

Maximising such a nearly flat function results in decreased estimation precision, leading to greater variances in the estimated parameters. It is straightforward to see that by increasing the correlation between $attr_{n1}$ and $attr_{n2}$, the values of the Hessian matrix have decreased to

```
ll_max$hessian

           [,1]        [,2]
[1,] -3.15067918  0.08341137
[2,]  0.08341137 -0.13537325
attr(,"type")
[1] "BHHH"
```

Subsequently, the values of variance–covariance matrix of the estimated parameters changed to

```
-solve(ll_max$hessian)

          [,1]      [,2]
[1,] 0.3226551 0.1988067
[2,] 0.1988067 7.5094803
```

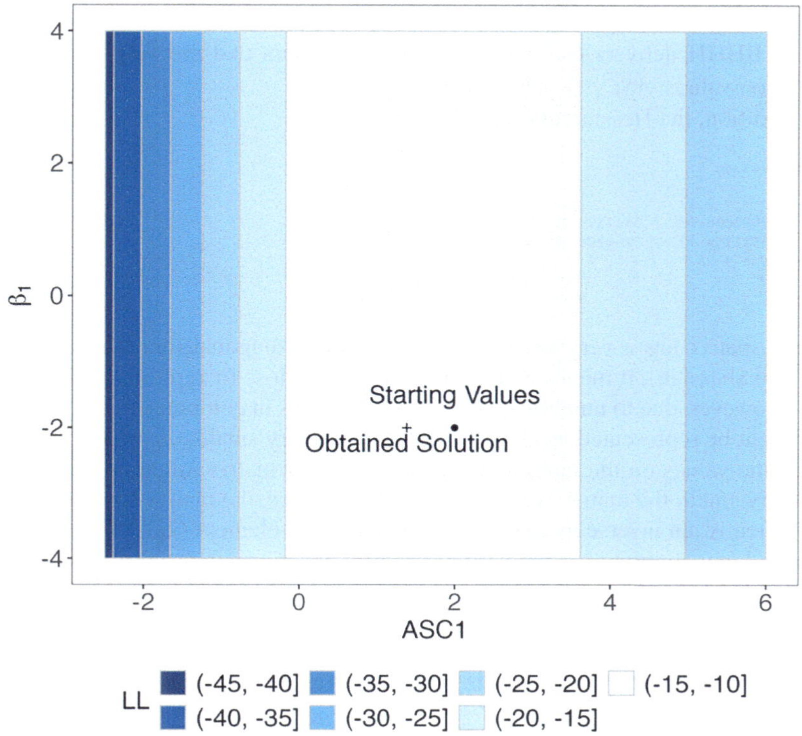


**Fig. 8.3** $ln\, L(\boldsymbol{\theta})$ function with perfect correlation of attributes

This implies $\widehat{\mathrm{Var}}\left(\widehat{ASC}_1\right) = 0.32$ and $\widehat{\mathrm{Var}}\left(\widehat{\beta}_1\right) = 7.51$. This represents a substantial increase in the estimated variances, resulting in lower precision of the estimated parameters. This outcome is also associated with a much larger difference between the population values of the parameters $ASC_1 = 0.5$, $\beta_1 = 0.5$ and the estimated values $\widehat{ASC}_1 = 1.39$, $\widehat{\beta}_1 = 1.50$.

We will conclude this example by showing an extreme case of perfect multi-collinearity, that is, $attr_{n1} = attr_{n2}$ achieved by corr $= 1.0$.

```
# Generate the data
data_mnl <- generate_data_mnl(
  asc1 = 0.5,
  beta1 = 0.5,
  nobs = 20,
  corr = 1,
  seed = 1234
)

# Estimate the model
ll_max <- maxLik(ll, start = c(2.0, -2.0), print.level = 2, method = "BHHH")
```

The $\ln L(\boldsymbol{\theta})$ function is completely flat in this case and the numerical optimisation method BHHH delivers estimations of the parameters that are very far from the population values: $\widehat{ASC}_1 = 1.39$ and $\widehat{\beta}_1 = -2.00$.

In addition, the Hessian matrix is singular.

```
ll_max$hessian

              [,1]          [,2]
[1,] -3.200000e+00 -5.551115e-11
[2,] -5.551115e-11 -2.526820e-19
attr(,"type")
[1] "BHHH"
```

When a matrix has a very small value on the main diagonal (here, element (2,2) of ll_max$hessian), it means that its determinant is close to zero, indicating singularity. However, due to numerical precision limitations in computers, values close to zero might be represented as non-zero values with very small magnitudes. So, even though the values on the main diagonal of a singular matrix might not be zero but extremely small, the matrix is still singular. In this case, the matrix is not invertible. Consequently, an inverse matrix does not exist (since element (2,2) of the matrix is zero), and any attempt to compute the variance–covariance matrix of the estimated parameters by inverting this singular matrix results in an error message. The exact message depends on the type of optimisation method applied, but in our case was.

```
Error in solve.default(ll_max$hessian): system is computationally singular.
```

Figure 8.3 shows this case graphically by means of a contour plot.

The issue of perfect multicollinearity frequently arises in discrete choice models, especially when incorporating several dummy variables. In such cases, a common error occurs when a linear combination of a subset of these variables becomes identical to one of them.

When dealing with real data collected from surveys and employing more complex discrete choice models, the probability of encountering flat regions within the likelihood function is considerably higher. This can occur due to either the model's inherent structure or the characteristics of the collected data.

**Standardising Explanatory Variables**

To mitigate the issue of flat regions within the likelihood function, it is considered good practice to standardise or rescale the explanatory variables in our models (such as dividing monthly income by 1000). This practice simplifies the task for numerical optimisation algorithms and helps ensure that parameter values are within a similar range. Consequently, when the explanatory variables within our model are rescaled so that the corresponding estimated parameters will have a similar range, an estimated parameter that significantly differs from the estimates of other parameters (e.g. the estimated value is in the hundreds rather than single digits) and exhibits an exceedingly high standard error serves as a clear indicator of a flat region within the log-likelihood function.

We also recommend carefully reviewing all dummy attributes incorporated in the model, along with socio-demographic variables coded as dummy variables. Dummy variables may readily generate flat regions in the log-likelihood function.

The challenge of encountering flat regions in the log-likelihood function is one of many pitfalls that numerical optimisation methods may face. In more complex discrete choice models, log-likelihood functions often exhibit local maxima. To illustrate this concern, we will use a two-variable function that deviates from the likelihood function of a discrete choice model but finds relevance in mathematical literature due to its distinctive functional shape. This function is known as the Ackley function and is defined as follows:

$$f_{Ackley}(\beta_1, \beta_2) = -a\,e^{-b\sqrt{\frac{\beta_1^2+\beta_2^2}{2}}} - e^{\left(\frac{cos(c\,\beta_1)+cos(c\,\beta_2)}{2}\right)+a+e}.$$

Its functional form for the value of parameters $a = 20$, $b = 0.2$, and $c = 2\pi$ is represented by the 3D plot below (Fig. 8.4).

The value of its global maximum is zero and corresponds to the parameter values of $\beta_1 = 0$ and $\beta_2 = 0$, that is $f_{Ackley}(0, 0) = 0$. Nevertheless, as can easily be seen in the contour plot, there are several local maxima. For example, $f_{Ackley}(0, -1) \approx -2.64$ or $f_{Ackley}(0, 1) \approx -2.64$.

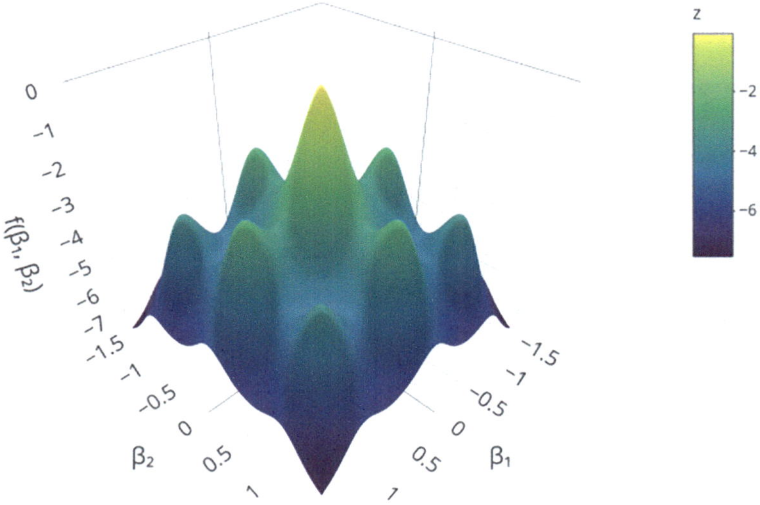


**Fig. 8.4** The Ackley function

The subsequent contour plots illustrate how distinct numerical optimisation techniques can yield disparate outcomes, even when using identical starting values. In this particular scenario, the starting values are $\beta_1 = 0$ and $\beta_2 = -1.5$, and the employed numerical optimisation methods are BFGS, Nelder-Mead, and SANN.

Figure 8.5 illustrates the performance of three optimisation methods—BFGS, Nelder-Mead, and SANN—each starting from the same initial point, marked as "Starting Values," and attempting to locate the global maximum, with their respective solution indicated by a " $+$ " symbol in each plot. In the case of BFGS, the method begins at the initial point but does not reach the global maximum $\beta_1 = 0$, $\beta_2 = 0$. Instead, it converges to a local maximum $\beta_1 = 0$, $\beta_2 = 1$, labelled as "Obtained Solution". The contours surrounding the obtained solution suggest that the method becomes trapped in a local optimum, ending up in a region away from the true global maximum.

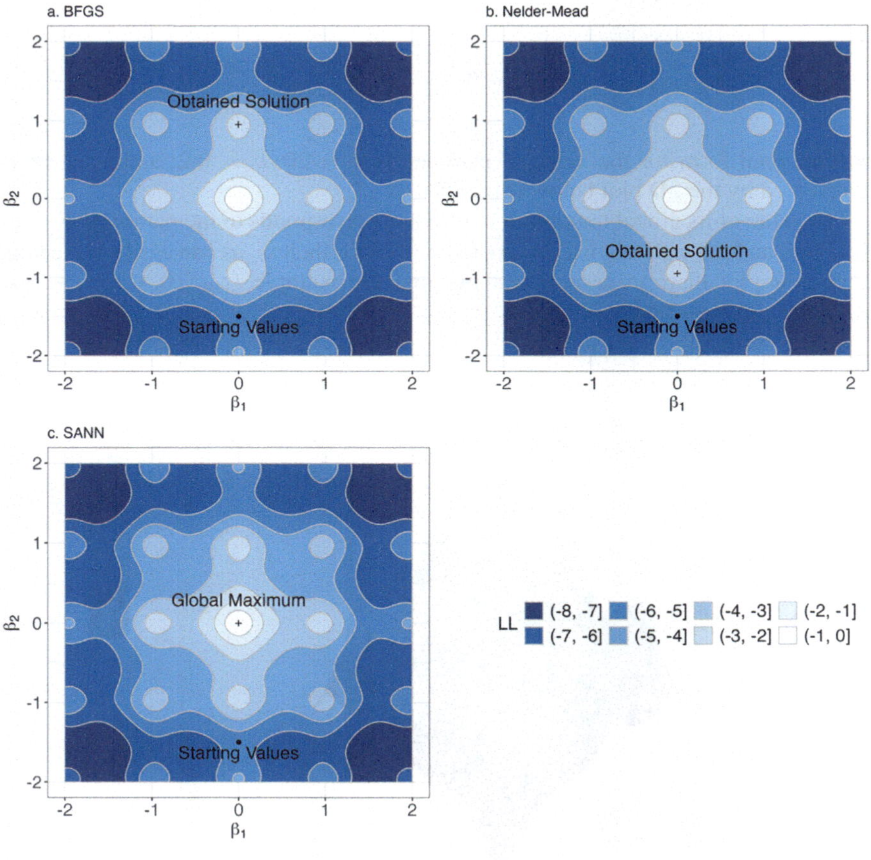


**Fig. 8.5** Starting values and solutions with different algorithms

For the Nelder-Mead method, a similar outcome is observed. Although the algorithm starts from the same point and finds a solution ($\beta_1 = 0, \beta_2 = -1$), also labelled "Obtained Solution", it too gets stuck in a local maximum and fails to converge to the global maximum.

In contrast, the SANN method, starting from the same point, successfully navigates the contours and converges to the global maximum ($\beta_1 = 0, \beta_2 = 0$), labelled "Global Maximum". This indicates that SANN is the only method of the three that effectively finds the optimal solution of the Ackley function, reaching the global peak of the objective function.

This diversity in results underscores the distinct characteristics and behaviours of these algorithms. The BFGS algorithm, a quasi-Newton method, and the Nelder-Mead method, which is gradient-independent, are both prone to converging to local maxima because of their reliance on immediate gradient information and heuristic search steps, respectively. On the other hand, SANN, with its probabilistic approach, has a mechanism for escaping local maxima, thereby increasing the likelihood of discovering the global maximum in a complex landscape such as the one represented by the Ackley function. However, this conclusion cannot be generalised and depends on the specific function to be optimised.

The outcome of numerical optimisation can also be affected by the choice of initial values. Going back to our blindfolded climber analogy, think of the starting values as the coordinates where we drop the climber to start her search for the summit. Sometimes, we may start in the vicinity of the highest peak, but other times we might be far away from it, surrounded by lower peaks. We do not know where the highest peak is, but have to rely on the climber to tell us.

The subsequent graphs illustrate the varying results achieved using the same BFGS optimisation algorithm but with different starting points. These variations highlight the sensitivity of the optimisation process to its initial conditions, demonstrating how the path to the final result can diverge significantly based on where the algorithm begins its search.

Figure 8.6 illustrates that when initiated at $\beta_1 = 0.5$, $\beta_2 = -1.5$, the BFGS algorithm tends to settle at a local maximum situated at $\beta_1 = 0$, $\beta_2 = 1$. Starting the algorithm at $\beta_1 = 0.5$, $\beta_2 = 1.5$ leads to convergence to another local maximum, this time at $\beta_1 = 0$, $\beta_2 = -1$. The BFGS algorithm reaches the global maximum at $\beta_1 = 0$, $\beta_2 = 0$ when it commences within a vicinity proximate to this peak, such as in the lower panel of Fig. 8.6, where the starting point is set at $\beta_1 = 0.5$, $\beta_2 = 0.5$. The selection of the appropriate optimisation procedure and the use of multiple starting values are crucial components of numerical optimisation, especially when the objective is to locate the global maximum of a function while avoiding local maxima.

Starting an optimisation algorithm from several different points increases the likelihood of finding the global maximum. If a method consistently converges to the same point from various starting values, there is a stronger case for that point being the global maximum. Hole and Yoo (2017) present a method for searching for initial values in a more systematic manner.

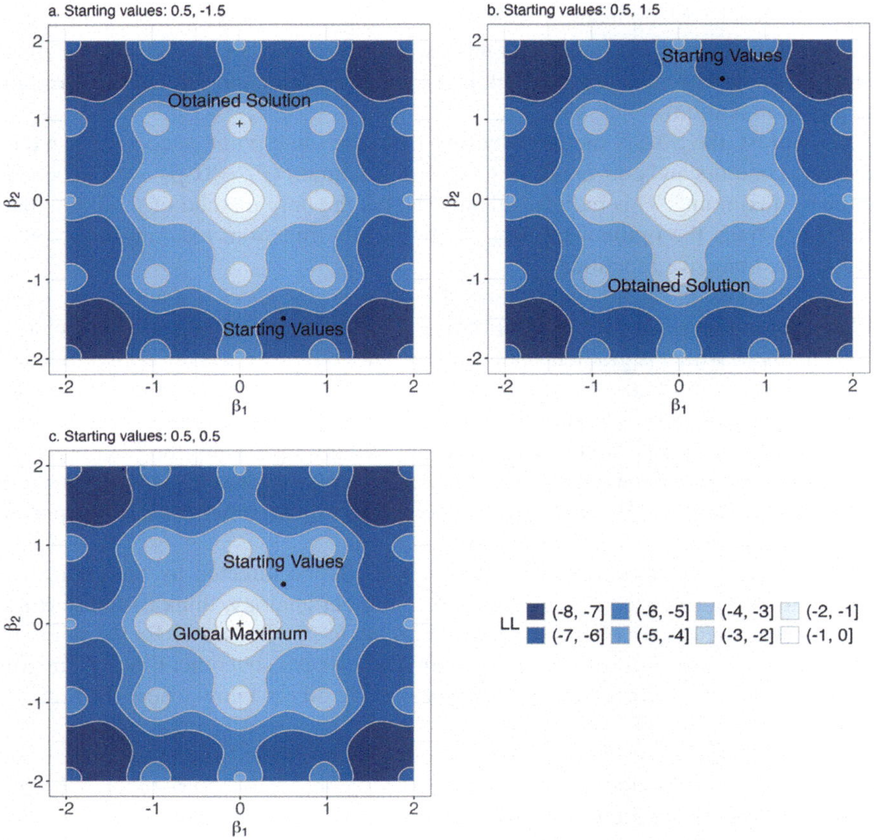


**Fig. 8.6** Solutions with different starting values using the BFGS algorithm

> **ⓘ Use different optimisation algorithms**
>
> Different optimisation algorithms are designed with various underlying mechanisms, making some more suited for certain types of problems than others. For example, algorithms that use gradient information might be more efficient for smooth, continuous functions, while others that use probabilistic steps might be better for discontinuous or rugged functions
>
> **Only when various numerical optimisation methods and multiple sets of initial values consistently converge to the same maximum can we have some confidence that it is indeed a global maximum**

The examples provided here involve only two parameters, facilitating a two-dimensional graphical representation of the log-likelihood function. However, in case studies involving dozens of parameters (as is typical in environmental valuation studies), these challenges are amplified. Researchers need to recognise this and allocate adequate time to address these complexities in the estimation phase of their research.

Avoiding local optima in maximum likelihood estimation is crucial to obtain accurate parameter estimates for your choice models. Here are some practical tips to help mitigate the risk of falling into local optima:

**Practical tips**

1. **Rescale variables:** Consider rescaling your input variables. Rescaling can prevent certain parameters from dominating the optimisation process and allows the parameter space to be explored more evenly.
2. **Initialisation of parameters:** Start the optimisation process with sensible parameter values. You can use estimations from other studies or use a specific method (Bliemer and Collins 2016; Hole and Yoo 2017).
3. **Multiple starting points:** Run the optimisation algorithm from multiple initial parameter sets. This increases the likelihood of finding the global optimum.
4. **Use different optimisation algorithms:** Choose different optimisation algorithms if possible based on different principles. For example, use a gradient-based algorithm and a heuristic algorithm to compare results.
5. **Ensemble methods:** Combine results from multiple optimisation runs. Ensemble methods, such as averaging or selecting the most common parameter values, can mitigate the impact of local optima.
6. **Diagnostic tools:** Use diagnostic tools to visualise the optimisation process. Plotting the likelihood function or monitoring parameter trajectories can offer insights into the optimisation process.

## 8.4 Sample Variation

Researchers usually work with data collected from a single sample representing the target population. To make inferences about this population, they use statistical methods to estimate unknown parameters from the sample. Since researchers typically only have one sample to work with, they cannot repeat the estimation process multiple times. However, if they were to collect another dataset and apply the same estimator, they would likely end up with a different estimate due to sample variation. Essentially, estimations are like random draws of a random variable (the estimator). For this one draw to be trustworthy, the distribution from which it is drawn should be narrow and centred on the true population value of the parameter.

If the distribution is not centred on this value, the estimator is said to be biased. To try and judge whether or not an estimator is biased, it can be useful to generate one or more artificial datasets in which the population values of the parameters (such as the preference for an environmental attribute) are known, and the results from these trustworthy draws can then be compared to the set of parameter values. These techniques are called simulation procedures or Monte Carlo.

Simulated data can also be used to explore the behaviour of complex systems that are difficult or impossible to study in the real world. For example, economists may use simulated data to study the behaviour of specific markets or the impact of policy interventions on the economy. Some examples of these approaches can be found in Greene (2018, Chapter 15).

In our context, the simulation approach is valuable as it enables repeated sampling from a specified model to examine the statistical properties of various estimation techniques. It can also assess the efficiency of experimental designs or verify sufficient variability in collected revealed preference (RP) data. The process involves generating multiple hypothetical datasets from the right-hand-side matrix that is based on the experimental design for stated preference (SP) data or explanatory variable values for RP data. Parameters are set to assumed true population values, with Gumbel errors added (see Sect. 8.3). Each dataset is then used for model estimation, and the resulting parameter estimates are saved. Analysing their empirical distribution determines whether the right-hand-side matrix supports unbiased parameter estimation. This approach should be applied in both SP and RP studies. An example of this approach in the context of discrete choice experiments can be found in Mariel et al. (2021), Sect. 3.3.

In this section we will use the simulation approach to explain the concept of sample variation and its implications for the estimation.

### 8.4.1 Sample Variation in Practice

To demonstrate the practicality of generating synthetic datasets, we will use the same simple example as before (Sect. 8.3) of a discrete choice model with two alternatives and one attribute in which the utilities are defined as:

$$
\begin{aligned}
U_{n1} &= ASC_1 + \beta_1\, attr_{n1} + \varepsilon_{n1} \\
U_{n2} &= \qquad\quad\;\; \beta_1\, attr_{n2} + \varepsilon_{n2}\,.
\end{aligned}
\tag{8.14}
$$

Similar to Sect. 8.3, we create a synthetic dataset with 50 observations, assuming population parameters of $ASC_1 = 0.50$ and $\beta_1 = 0.50$ and apply the ML estimator.

```
# Generate data
data_mnl <- generate_data_mnl(
  asc1 = 0.5,
  beta1 = 0.5,
  nobs = 50,
  corr = 0.0,
  seed = 1234
)
# Estimate the model
ll_max <- maxLik(ll, start = c(2.0, -2.0), print.level = 2, method = "BHHH")

summary(ll_max)
```

As shown below, this results in the following estimated values: $\widehat{ASC}_1 = 0.78$, $\widehat{\beta}_1 = 0.61$.

```
--------------------------------------------
Maximum Likelihood estimation
BHHH maximisation, 14 iterations
Return code 8: successive function values within relative tolerance limit (reltol)
Log-Likelihood: -20.41627
2  free parameters
Estimates:
     Estimate Std. error t value Pr(> t)
[1,]   0.7843     0.4036   1.944 0.05195 .
[2,]   0.6059     0.2335   2.595 0.00945 **
---
Signif. codes:  0 '***' 0.001 '**' 0.01 '*' 0.05 '.' 0.1 ' ' 1
--------------------------------------------
```

This is precisely the situation faced by a researcher whose goal is to estimate the preferences of a specific population regarding environmental goods or services through a DCE. The researcher assumes that there are certain population values for the model parameters (the preferences) that are not known (as our data are simulated, however, we know the population values are $ASC_1 = 0.50$ and $\beta_1 = 0.50$). Once the sample is collected, the researcher applies their chosen estimator to obtain the ML estimates (in our case $\widehat{ASC}_1 = 0.78$, $\widehat{\beta}_1 = 0.61$). The goal is for these estimates to be close to the population values, in other words, to be trustworthy. This is something that researchers cannot verify with a single sample, as they only have one draw from the estimator's distribution.

If there are any issues with the data, if any of the model assumptions are not met, or if our estimation method fails for any reason, these estimates may deviate from the population values and interpretations based on these estimates would be incorrect. Therefore, researchers must apply various statistical techniques to verify the validity of their estimates (for example cross-validation, residual analysis, goodness-of-fit tests, information criteria).

With simulated data, we can easily check the validity of our estimator and get an idea of the expected variability of the estimator through repeated sample generations and repeated model estimations. This is straightforward to carry out with statistical software by generating a set of synthetic data. Another sample can be generated by running the same R code chunk to generate new draws of the error terms $\varepsilon_{n1}$ and $\varepsilon_{n2}$ that will lead to different utilities in Eq. (8.14) and, subsequently, to different choices.

The following R code chunk generates a second synthetic data set of 50 observations and applies the ML estimator to it. Notice that we have not set a seed here because we want different realisations of the random draws used to generate new sample.

```
# Generate data
data_mnl <- generate_data_mnl(
  asc1 = 0.5,
  beta1 = 0.5,
  nobs = 50,
  corr = 0.0
)

# Estimate the model
ll_max <- maxLik(ll, start = c(2.0, -2.0), print.level = 2, method = "BHHH")

----- Initial parameters: -----
fcn value: -19.63417
     parameter initial gradient free
[1,]       0.5        0.04294345    1
[2,]       0.5        4.03371385    1
Condition number of the (active) hessian: 9.400661
-----Iteration 1 -----
-----Iteration 2 -----
-----Iteration 3 -----
-----Iteration 4 -----
--------------
successive function values within relative tolerance limit (reltol)
4  iterations
estimate: 0.5668042 0.5826055
Function value: -19.47365
```

As shown above, when we apply the ML estimator to this second synthetic data set based on the same population values $ASC_1 = 0.50$ and $\beta_1 = 0.50$, we get estimated values $\widehat{ASC}_1 = 0.57$ and $\widehat{\beta}_1 = 0.58$, which differ from the estimates we obtained previously. This process can be repeated several times. The estimated values of the parameters will vary from sample to sample.

If we generate 500 sets of synthetic data and apply the ML estimator to each of them, we will obtain 500 different parameter estimates. These estimates can be represented by a histogram and can serve as an approximation of the estimator's distribution (Eq. (8.5)). The upper section of Fig. 8.7 displays histograms generated from 500 estimations of $ASC_1$ and $\beta_1$, based on a dataset containing 50 observations created by the following R code chunk.

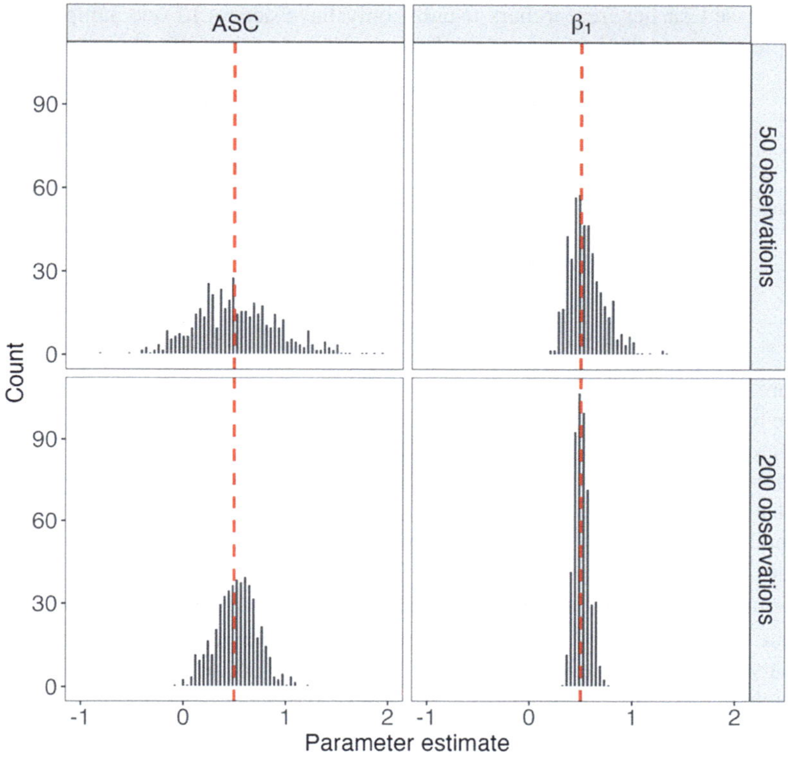


**Fig. 8.7** Histograms of $ASC_1$ and $\beta_1$ estimations for N = 50 and N = 200 observations

```
# Create an empty list
models <- vector(mode = "list", length = 500)

# Loop through each model index to generate data and estimate the model
for (i in seq_along(models)) {
  data_mnl <- generate_data_mnl(asc1 = 0.5,
                                beta1 = 0.5,
                                nobs = 50,
                                corr = 0.0)

  model <- maxLik(ll, start = c(0.5, 0.5), method = "BHHH")

  models[[i]] <- model
}

# Extract all parameter information in a data frame
estimates_1 <- map_df(models, tidy) |>
  mutate(
    simulation = "50 observations"
  )
```

As discussed earlier, researchers usually only have access to one sample. In our example using synthetic datasets, the first sample led to the following estimation.

```
--------------------------------------------
Maximum Likelihood estimation
BHHH maximisation, 14 iterations
Return code 8: successive function values within relative tolerance limit (reltol)
Log-Likelihood: -20.41627
2  free parameters
Estimates:
     Estimate Std. error t value Pr(> t)
[1,]   0.7843     0.4036   1.944 0.05195 .
[2,]   0.6059     0.2335   2.595 0.00945 **
---
Signif. codes:  0 '***' 0.001 '**' 0.01 '*' 0.05 '.' 0.1 ' ' 1
--------------------------------------------
```

The precision of these estimates is indicated by the standard error, defined as the square root of the variance, which represents the expected variability of the estimate in different samples. The standard error, in the context of ML, measures the variability or uncertainty associated with an estimator's point estimate when applied to different samples from the same population. It quantifies the expected variability of estimates obtained if the estimation process were repeated multiple times with different random samples from the population.

In our case, the standard error of $\widehat{ASC}_1$ is 0.40 and of $\widehat{\beta}_1$ is 0.23. These values indicate that the expected precision of the parameter estimate $\widehat{\beta}_1$ is better than that of the constant. This is due to the nature of the variables accompanying the estimated parameters. Generally, the greater the variability and range of values of the variable, the better the precision of the corresponding parameter estimate. Focusing only on the sample variability of the estimates, we can see that Fig. 8.7 provides similar information to the standard errors of the estimates.

If we were to repeat the process of generating synthetic data, this time for a larger sample of 200 observations, we would obtain a narrower distribution of estimates due to the consistency of the maximum likelihood estimator, as can be seen in the lower section of Fig. 8.7.

As mentioned earlier, a particular estimation of the parameter $ASC_1$ or $\beta_1$ corresponding to a specific sample size represents a draw from these plotted distributions. This single estimation is the only one a researcher obtains from the only dataset of collected observations they possess. Consequently, comparing the histograms in the two figures above, it is preferable to draw from the distributions presented in the lower panels of Fig. 8.7 corresponding to $N = 200$ observations than from the distributions in the upper panels, as the former is narrower and centred on the population value, indicating a lower probability of obtaining an estimate significantly distant from the population value.

ⓘ **Employ consistent estimators on large datasets**

Employing **consistent** and **efficient** estimators in properly defined models and on datasets with **larger sample sizes** generally enhances the likelihood of our estimation aligning closely with the population value, even when drawing only once from the estimator's distribution.

## 8.5 Key Takeaways

- Log-likelihood functions for estimating complex models beyond MNL models tend not to be globally concave, leading optimisation algorithms to frequently converge on local maxima rather than the global maximum.
- Employing different optimisation algorithms and experimenting with diverse starting values can help you explore different regions of the parameter space and improve the chances of finding the global maximum.
- Sample variation is a common issue due to the inherent randomness in the sampling process. This variability means that estimates from a single sample might not perfectly represent the true population parameters.
- The precision of parameter estimates depends on the variability and range of the associated values in the data. More extensive variability and a broader range of data typically lead to more accurate and reliable estimates.
- Consistent and efficient estimators applied to large datasets enhance the alignment of estimates with true population values. Even with only one sample, using such estimators reduces the impact of sample variability, improving the reliability of the estimates and making them more representative of the population values.

## References

Amemiya T (1985) Advanced econometrics. Harvard University Press, Cambridge, Massachusetts

Berndt EK, Hall BH, Hall RE, Hausman JA (1974) Estimation and inference in non-linear structural models. Ann Econ and Soc Meas 3(4):653–665

Bliemer MCJ, Collins AT (2016) On determining priors for the generation of efficient stated choice experimental designs. J Choice Model 21:10–14. https://doi.org/10.1016/j.jocm.2016.03.001

Bunch DS, Gay DM, Welsch RE (1993) Algorithm 717: subroutines for maximum likelihood and quasi-likelihood estimation of parameters in nonlinear regression models. ACM Trans Math Softw 19(1):109–130. https://doi.org/10.1145/151271.151279

Cameron AC, Trivedi PK (2005) Microeconometrics: methods and applications. Cambridge University Press, Cambridge

Greene WH (2018) Econometric analysis, 8th edn. Pearson India

Gujarati DN, Porter DC (2009) Basic econometrics, 5th edn. McGraw-Hill, New York
Hare W, Nutini J, Tesfamariam S (2013) A survey of non-gradient optimization methods in structural engineering. Adv Eng Softw 59:19–28
Henningsen A, Toomet O (2011) MaxLik: a package for maximum likelihood estimation in R. Comput Stat 26(3):443–458. https://doi.org/10.1007/s00180-010-0217-1
Hess S, Palma D (2019) Apollo: a flexible, powerful and customisable freeware package for choice model estimation and application. J Choice Model 32:100170. https://doi.org/10.1016/j.jocm.2019.100170
Hole AR, Yoo HI (2017) The use of heuristic optimization algorithms to facilitate maximum simulated likelihood estimation of random parameter logit models. J R Stat Soc c: Appl Stat 66(5):997–1013. https://doi.org/10.1111/rssc.12209
Huber P (1967) The behavior of maximum likelihood estimation under nonstandard conditions. In: LeCam L, Neyman J (eds) Proceedings of the fifth Berkeley symposium on mathematical statistics and probability. University of California Press
Mariel P, Hoyos D, Meyerhoff J et al (2021) Environmental valuation with discrete choice experiments: guidance on design, implementation and data analysis. Springer Nature. https://doi.org/10.1007/978-3-030-62669-3
Nash JC (2020) Provenance of R's gradient optimizers. R J 12(1)
Nash JC, Varadhan R (2011) Unifying optimization algorithms to aid software system users: optimx for R. J Stat Softw 43:1–14

# Chapter 9
# Estimation

**Abstract** This chapter covers the estimation of discrete choice models. We begin with a simple Multinomial Logit (MNL) model (with and without unobserved preference heterogeneity) and highlight the importance of optimisation diagnostics, review goodness-of-fit indicators and the identification of outliers, and provide insights into the interpretation of estimates. Progressing to more advanced topics, we continue with the Random Parameters Mixed Logit (RP-MXL) model, addressing both uncorrelated and correlated coefficients, and discuss different parameterisation approaches such as the preference space and the willingness-to-pay space. We conclude with an analysis of Latent Class Mixed Logit (LC-MXL) models and a discussion of extensions of RP-MXL and LC-MXL models.

## 9.1 Introduction

This chapter outlines the estimation of the most common models used in discrete choice analysis. We begin with a standard MNL model, comprised of only the attributes and alternative specific constants. To investigate *observed preference heterogeneity*, we extend the model to include socio-demographic variables and interact these with the attributes. We then review parameter estimates, model diagnostics, and goodness of fit measures for the MNL model.

To capture *unobserved preference heterogeneity*, we move to the Random Parameters Mixed Logit (RP-MXL) model, which is the most frequently used model in environmental valuation. We begin with an RP-MXL model in preference space and walk you through its estimation with the *Apollo* package in R. We discuss the output for an RP-MXL model with both uncorrelated and correlated coefficients, as well as a WTP space with correlated random coefficients. Finally, we present the Latent Class Mixed Logit (LC-MXL) model, which captures unobserved preference heterogeneity via discrete classes, and review extensions of the RP-MXL and LC-MXL models.

These models represent the most frequently used models to estimate DCE data in environmental valuation. It is common practice to use these models as a starting



P. Mariel et al., *Environmental Valuation with Discrete Choice Experiments in R*,
The Economics of Non-Market Goods and Resources 17,
https://doi.org/10.1007/978-3-031-89338-4_9

point, and subsequently compare the results with more complex models such as hybrid choice models (Mariel et al. 2024). Due to space constraints in this book, a complete review of extensions of these models cannot be presented and discussed here, however, you can find *Apollo* scripts for a number of extended models on the accompanying website (http://www.apollochoicemodelling.com) of Hess and Palma (2019).

In this chapter, we review mixed logit models in detail, specifically, RP-MXL and LC-MXL models. Which mixed logit model specification is most suitable for your study depends on its objectives, hypotheses, and data, and importantly, the distributional assumptions regarding unobserved preference heterogeneity.

An RP-MXL model is better suited when individual preferences are believed to vary smoothly and continuously, as it assumes continuous distributions of preferences across individuals. This is particularly useful when preferences are expected to change gradually across a population without distinct groupings. Conversely, an LC-MXL model is preferable when clear, identifiable segments are believed to exist within the population, with relatively homogeneous preferences within classes but distinct differences between them.

Thus, RP-MXL and LC-MXL models provide different perspectives on how unobserved preference heterogeneity is distributed among individuals in a stated choice dataset. Both models have their strengths and weaknesses, and determining the best model in advance is challenging: it depends entirely on the context and the data. In a recent study in health economics comparing both approaches (Boeri et al. 2020), the authors found that the RP-MXL and LC-MXL models revealed similar mean preference weights and attribute importance across models. When conducting subgroup analyses, however, the models could lead to different implications.

Overall, there is no compelling reason to believe that any single (RP-MXL or LC-MXL) model will consistently outperform others across all samples. For empirical data with unknown parameters, a "perfect" model is unlikely to exist. Furthermore, if our goal is to capture sample-level averages, we would expect mean preferences to be similar regardless of the model specification. To ensure that you find the best model for your specific research context, we recommend testing both RP-MXL and LC-MXL specifications under a range of distributional assumptions.

We recommend beginning the analysis with a simple MNL model before delving into mixed logit models, which capture unobserved heterogeneity. Starting simple and gradually adding more complexity allows us to detect potential errors stemming from the data, variable definitions, or model specifications during the modelling process.

Chapter 3 provides an example of discrete choice model estimation using an MNL model with two alternatives and one attribute with a manually defined log-likelihood function. This approach can be expanded to estimate more complex models; however, it is usually more effective to use specialised software packages specifically designed for these analyses. There are several R packages designed to estimate discrete choice models.[1] In this chapter, we will use the *Apollo* R package (Hess and Palma 2019), which is comprehensive and highly versatile. This package can be used to estimate a wide array of models, provides various post-estimation analyses, and allows for full customisation according to your specific research needs.

> **Custom vs. package-based approaches**
>
> In addition to using specialised R packages to estimate DCE models, you can also write your own log-likelihood function and use one of R's built-in optimisers to estimate the model parameters. Another option for optimisation is to utilise specialised R packages designed for maximum likelihood estimation, such as the widely used `maxLik` package (Henningsen and Toomet 2011), a popular library among choice modellers. Writing your own code to estimate a model in R provides greater flexibility and customisation, allowing you to tailor the model precisely to your specific research needs and experiment with non-standard methods. However, it can be time-consuming, requires a deep understanding of the underlying algorithms, and increases the risk of coding errors. Relying on pre-existing packages is often faster, more reliable, and includes community support, but it may limit your ability to deviate from the package's standard functionalities

## 9.2 Multinomial Logit Model

The MNL model is widely used to analyse discrete choice data because of its simplicity, intuitive structure, and ease of estimation and interpretation. The MNL model provides a straightforward approach to understanding how individuals make choices among a finite set of alternatives and has key advantages related to its estimation: (1) it can be estimated using Maximum Likelihood (ML), and (2) its log-likelihood function is globally concave, meaning that no issues associated with local maxima will arise during the estimation process. Researchers often begin their analysis with the MNL model to gain initial insights into their data, and we will do the same in this chapter.

This section outlines the estimation process for the model defined in Eq. (4.1) (chap. 4). We will detail the steps to estimate and interpret the MNL model, which serves as the foundation for our analysis of discrete choice data. The model to be estimated is

[1] The long-standing packages offered for estimating DCE models in R are: *mlogit* (Croissant 2013) and *mnlogit* (Hasan et al. 2016). More recent packages include *mixl* (Molloy 2020), which specialises in large-scale models, *RSGHB* (Dumont et al. 2019), offering estimation of MNL, RP-MXL, Error components mixed logit, LC-MXL, and nested logit models using the Hierarchical Bayesian framework, and *gmnl* (Sarrias and Daziano 2017), which is a comprehensive package that supports a wide range of models such as MNL, MXL, and G-MXL models.

$$
\begin{aligned}
U_{n1t} = \quad & \beta_{mf} MediumFarms_{n1t} + \beta_{sf} SmallFarms_{n1t} \\
& + \beta_{mh} MediumHeight_{n1t} + \beta_{lh} LowHeight_{n1t} \\
& + \beta_{rk} RedKite_{n1t} + \beta_{md} MinDistance_{n1t} \\
& + \beta_{cost} Cost_{n1t} + \varepsilon_{n1t} \\
U_{n2t} = ASC_2 & + \beta_{mf} MediumFarms_{n2t} + \beta_{sf} SmallFarms_{n2t} \\
& + \beta_{mh} MediumHeight_{n2t} + \beta_{lh} LowHeight_{n2t} \\
& + \beta_{rk} RedKite_{n2t} + \beta_{md} MinDistance_{n2t} \\
& + \beta_{cost} Cost_{n2t} + \varepsilon_{n2t} \\
U_{n3t} = ASC_3 & + \beta_{mf} MediumFarms_{n3t} + \beta_{sf} SmallFarms_{n3t} \\
& + \beta_{mh} MediumHeight_{n3t} + \beta_{lh} LowHeight_{n3t} \\
& + \beta_{rk} RedKite_{n3t} + \beta_{md} MinDistance_{n3t} \\
& + \beta_{cost} Cost_{n3t} + \varepsilon_{n3t}
\end{aligned}
\tag{9.1}
$$

The abbreviations $sf$, $mf$, $lh$, $mh$, $rk$, $md$, and $cost$ in the subscripts in Eq. (9.1) correspond to the attributes *SmallFarms*, *MediumFarms*, *LowHeight*, *MediumHeight*, *RedKite*, *MinDistance*, and *Cost*, respectively.

> ⓘ **Limitations of MNL models**
>
> While the MNL model offers a useful starting point for understanding the data collected in discrete choice experiments, its estimates should be interpreted with caution due to its restrictive assumptions. A simple MNL (presented in Sect. 9.2.1) is restrictive because it does not account for any type of preference heterogeneity. It implies proportional substitution across alternatives (IIA) and does not properly treat repeated choice situations
>
> An MNL accounting for observed heterogeneity (presented in Sect. 9.2.2) addresses the first limitation by introducing interactions with socio-demographic variables. The RP-MXL model (Sect. 9.3.1) also addresses the second and third limitations by including unobserved preference heterogeneity and accounting for panel effects
>
> Despite its limitations, the MNL model remains a valuable tool for analysing choice data and is widely used as a baseline for comparison. By starting with the MNL model and progressing to more sophisticated models, you can gain a comprehensive understanding of your data and derive robust insights into the valuation of environmental goods or services

### *9.2.1 MNL Without Observed Heterogeneity*

We begin by estimating the MNL model as defined in Eq. (4.1) in *Apollo* (see the code chunk below). After some preliminaries, the *Apollo* library is initialised, core controls are configured, and the dataset is imported, with any *NA* choices being removed from the dataset. Subsequently, initial values for the optimisation procedure, denoted as `apollo_beta`, are defined. To ensure the identification of the model, certain parameters must be initialised and fixed at zero. The `apollo_fixed` object in the R chunk below contains the names of parameters that are fixed at their initial values and do not participate in the iterative maximisation process.

As discussed in Chap. 3, the likelihood function of an MNL model is globally concave, making the optimisation process during the estimation straightforward. Any initial values within reasonable ranges, matching the scale of attribute levels, will lead to convergence at the global maximum. For example, assigning a starting value of 0.5 to a coefficient of a dummy-coded attribute and 0.1 to a coefficient of quantitative attribute with levels 1 through 10 is more appropriate than assigning a starting value like 1000.

In more complex models like mixed logit models, the correct specification of initial parameter values becomes crucial to ensure convergence during estimation. In empirical studies, it is common to have a priori hypotheses indicating whether the effect of certain attributes on utility is expected to be positive or negative. Assigning a small, appropriately scaled value (prior) with the correct sign is a more effective strategy than initialising the value at zero.

Even with suitable priors, repeatedly estimating the model with different initial values is essential to test the robustness of the obtained estimate. Unfortunately, when estimating more complex models, researchers often neglect the necessity of performing repeated estimations using different sets of starting values and different optimisation methods. Section 8.3 of this book contains further details on this issue.

```r
## Initialise Apollo ----
apollo_initialise()

## Set core controls ----
apollo_control = list(
  modelName = "mnl",
  modelDescr = "Basic MNL model on the windmills dataset",
  indivID = "id_individual"
)

## Import data ----
# Read in the data and filter out missing choices
database <- read_csv(gzcon(url("https://raw.githubusercontent.com/edsandorf/evdce/refs/heads/m
ain/Data/data-windmills.csv"))) |> clean_names()

## Set the starting values of the parameters ----
apollo_beta <- c(
  b_asc_alt1 = 0.00,
  b_asc_alt2 = 0.50,
  b_asc_alt3 = 0.50,
  b_medium_farms = 0.25,
  b_small_farms = 0.50,
  b_medium_height = 0.25,
  b_low_height = 0.50,
  b_red_kite = -0.05,
  b_min_distance = 0.50,
  b_cost = -0.50
)

# Specify the vector of parameters to hold fixed at their starting values
```

```
apollo_fixed <- c("b_asc_alt1")

# Group and validate inputs
apollo_inputs <- apollo_validateInputs()
```

Next, we set up the primary function `apollo_probabilities`, the core function of the entire estimation script. It uses the `apollo_beta` object defined previously, and defines the utilities of all alternatives (`V[["alt1"]]` for Alternative 1, and so on), the codification of the chosen alternatives in the dataset (`alternatives`), and the availability of each alternative for each individual and each choice occasion. Finally, probabilities `P` defined in Eq. (3.13) in Chap. 3 are computed.

```
## Define the model and likelihood function ----
apollo_probabilities <- function(apollo_beta, apollo_inputs, functionality = "estimate") {
  ## Attach inputs and detach after function exit
  apollo_attach(apollo_beta, apollo_inputs)
  on.exit(apollo_detach(apollo_beta, apollo_inputs))

  # Define the list of utility functions
  V <- list(
    alt1 = c(
      b_asc_alt1 +
      b_medium_farms * alt1_farm2 +
      b_small_farms * alt1_farm3 +
      b_medium_height * alt1_height2 +
      b_low_height * alt1_height3 +
      b_red_kite * alt1_redkite +
      b_min_distance * alt1_distance +
      b_cost * alt1_cost
    ),
    alt2 = c(
      b_asc_alt2 +
      b_medium_farms * alt2_farm2 +
      b_small_farms * alt2_farm3 +
      b_medium_height * alt2_height2 +
      b_low_height * alt2_height3 +
      b_red_kite * alt2_redkite +
      b_min_distance * alt2_distance +
      b_cost * alt2_cost
    ),
    alt3 = c(
      b_asc_alt3 +
      b_medium_farms * alt3_farm2 +
      b_small_farms * alt3_farm3 +
      b_medium_height * alt3_height2 +
      b_low_height * alt3_height3 +
      b_red_kite * alt3_redkite +
      b_min_distance * alt3_distance +
      b_cost * alt3_cost
    )
  )

  # Define settings for MNL model component
  mnl_settings <- list(
    alternatives = c(alt1 = 1, alt2 = 2, alt3 = 3),
    avail = list(alt1 = 1, alt2 = 1, alt3 = 1),
    choiceVar = choice,
    V = V
  )

  # Calculate the probabilities
  P <- list(
```

```
    model = apollo_mnl(mnl_settings, functionality)
  )

  # Take the product across observations
  P <- apollo_panelProd(P, apollo_inputs, functionality)

  # Prepare and return the outputs
  P <- apollo_prepareProb(P, apollo_inputs, functionality)

  # Return the probabilities
  return(
    P
  )
}
```

Finally, the model is estimated. The optimisation procedure can be chosen from *bfgs*, *bgw*, *bhhh*, or *nr*, as described in Chap. 3.

```
## Estimate the model  ----
model <- apollo_estimate(
  apollo_beta,
  apollo_fixed,
  apollo_probabilities,
  apollo_inputs,
  estimate_settings = list(
    writeIter = FALSE,
    silent = TRUE,
    estimationRoutine = "bgw"
  )
)
```

Following the estimation, the results can either be displayed on-screen (`apollo_modelOutput`) or saved to the hard disk (`apollo_saveOutput`). Please note that the model was estimated using responses from 1,000 individuals. However, since they did not, on average, complete all 10 choice tasks, the dataset contains 8,633 rows (observations).

```
## Print model output to console ----
apollo_modelOutput(
  model,
  modelOutput_settings = list(
    printOutliers = 10
  )
)

Model run by user using Apollo 0.3.4 on R 4.4.1 for Darwin.
Please acknowledge the use of Apollo by citing Hess & Palma (2019)
  DOI 10.1016/j.jocm.2019.100170
  www.ApolloChoiceModelling.com

Model name                                  : MNL
Model description                           : MNL windmills
Model run at                                : 2024-10-22 09:58:01.490184
Estimation method                           : bgw
Model diagnosis                             : Relative function convergence
Optimisation diagnosis                      : Maximum found
     hessian properties                     : Negative definite
     maximum eigenvalue                     : -79.768651
     reciprocal of condition number         : 0.00180258
Number of individuals                       : 1000
Number of rows in database                  : 8633
Number of modelled outcomes                 : 8633
```

```
Number of cores used                        :  20
Model without mixing

LL(start)                                   : -7097.83
LL at equal shares, LL(0)                   : -9484.32
LL at observed shares, LL(C)                : -8539.99
LL(final)                                   : -6904.38
Rho-squared vs equal shares                  :  0.272
Adj.Rho-squared vs equal shares              :  0.2711
Rho-squared vs observed shares               :  0.1915
Adj.Rho-squared vs observed shares           :  0.1907
AIC                                         :  13826.77
BIC                                         :  13890.34

Estimated parameters                        : 9
Time taken (hh:mm:ss)                       :  00:00:10.51
     pre-estimation                         :  00:00:9.63
     estimation                             :  00:00:0.21
     post-estimation                        :  00:00:0.67
Iterations                                  :  6

Unconstrained optimisation.

Estimates:
                   Estimate        s.e.   t.rat.(0)    Rob.s.e. Rob.t.rat.(0)
b_asc_alt1          0.00000          NA          NA          NA            NA
b_asc_alt2          0.75585    0.070255      10.759    0.072545        10.419
b_asc_alt3          0.77974    0.071594      10.891    0.075151        10.376
b_medium_farms     -0.23558    0.051550      -4.570    0.052113        -4.520
b_small_farms       0.16667    0.050880       3.276    0.049945         3.337
b_medium_height    -0.27738    0.053133      -5.220    0.054950        -5.048
b_low_height        0.54463    0.050369      10.813    0.052212        10.431
b_red_kite         -0.05314    0.005870      -9.053    0.005810        -9.147
b_min_distance      0.30925    0.056191       5.504    0.054001         5.727
b_cost             -0.41783    0.008978     -46.539    0.012074       -34.605

 10 most extreme outliers in terms of lowest average per choice prediction:
  ID Avg prob per choice
  55          0.05925056
 364          0.06601088
 823          0.07548937
 192          0.09845133
 685          0.10018138
 516          0.11212739
 601          0.15379231
 328          0.16114760
 753          0.16385559
  56          0.16987244
```

#### 9.2.1.1 Optimisation Diagnostics

Before looking at the estimates of the parameters, the convergence of the optimisation method must be checked. If the optimisation method fails, the interpretation of coefficient estimates becomes meaningless. The `Model diagnosis` section of the output contains several indicators that inform the researcher about the optimisation process.

In our case, the optimisation was completed successfully, as indicated by the "`Relative function convergence`" message, which is specific to the *bgw* optimisation method. Relative function convergence happens when there is a very small relative change in the objective function, defined by a tolerance level where any further search would result in changes too small to be significant.

The Hessian (see Eq. (8.3)) is expected to be negative definite after a successful convergence, which we can see in the `Optimisation diagnosis` section of the *Apollo* output. The `maximum eigenvalue` is another indicator of the optimisation process. We typically expect a very low negative number (a high absolute value) for the maximum eigenvalue, and small absolute values can indicate convergence issues. This is because the maximum eigenvalue provides information about the curvature of the likelihood function at the estimated maximum point. A high absolute value indicates a steep curvature, suggesting a well-defined maximum.

After a successful maximisation process, all eigenvalues of the Hessian should be negative. Positive values can indicate problems such as saddle points. The eigenvalues can be displayed as follows:

```
round(model$hessianEigenValue, digits = 3)

[1] -44252.388 -29228.780  -1488.477   -992.258   -815.473   -631.314   -321.062
[8]   -267.196    -79.769
```

The `reciprocal of condition number` is a measure of the sensitivity of the optimisation problem to changes in the objective function or parameters. A small reciprocal of the condition value suggests that the optimisation problem is well-conditioned, meaning that small changes in parameters lead to proportionally small changes in the objective function. This indicates stability and robustness in the optimisation process, which is desirable for obtaining reliable parameter estimates.

As we are estimating an MNL model, whose likelihood function is globally concave, we do not expect any issues with the optimisation. Therefore, all optimisation indicators here are indicative of a successful optimisation.

#### 9.2.1.2 Goodness of Fit

Several goodness of fit measures are included in the MNL output. These include $\rho^2$ measures based on the original definition of $\rho^2$ presented in Sect. 3.4.

`Rho-squared vs equal shares` is a goodness of fit criterion that compares the estimated model to a model in which all coefficients (including constants) are set to zero, implying equal shares for all alternatives. The criterion is defined as follows:

$$\rho^2(0) = 1 - \frac{\ln \widehat{L}(\beta)}{\ln \widehat{L}(0)},$$

where $\ln \widehat{L}(\beta)$ is the log-likelihood of the full (estimated) model and $\ln \widehat{L}(0)$ is the log-likelihood of the model where all coefficients (including constants) are set to zero.

The formula for the adjusted $\rho^2(0)$ is defined as

$$\rho^2_{adj}(0) = 1 - \frac{\ln \widehat{L}(\beta) - K_\beta}{\ln \widehat{L}(0)},$$

where $K_\beta$ is the number of parameters in the full model.

In contrast, `Rho-squared vs observed shares` ($\rho^2(C)$) defined in Eq. (3.25) is a goodness of fit criterion that compares the estimated model to a model that only includes alternative-specific constants (with the remaining coefficients are set to zero), with the log-likelihood for this restricted model denoted as $\ln \widehat{L}(C)$:

$$\rho^2(C) = 1 - \frac{\ln \widehat{L}(\beta)}{\ln \widehat{L}(C)}.$$

The adjusted $\rho^2_{adj}(C)$ delivered by *Apollo* is computed as:

$$\rho^2_{adj}(C) = 1 - \frac{\ln \widehat{L}(\beta) - K_\beta}{\ln \widehat{L}(C) - K_c},$$

where $K_\beta$ represents the number of parameters in the full model, and $K_c$ denotes the number of parameters in the constants-only model, with its definition being closely aligned with Eq. (3.26).

Values of $\rho^2$ can be compared across different models to determine which model provides the best fit for the data, however there is no general consensus on the interpretation of the absolute values of $\rho^2$. Note that the *same* data has to be used for the estimation of the models: you cannot compare model fit of models estimated on two different subsets of the data. According to Mokhtarian (2016), the value of $\rho^2$ depends on the benchmark used ($\ln L(C)$ or $\ln L(0)$), meaning that $\rho^2(C)$ can deliver completely different value than $\rho^2(0)$. Therefore, we recommend using $\rho^2(C)$ *or* $\rho^2(0)$ and sticking to the measure chosen.

Among the goodness-of-fit measures defined in Eq. (3.27), Eq. (3.28), Eq. (3.29), and Eq. (3.30), the *Apollo* output includes only the Akaike Information Criterion (AIC) defined in Eq. (3.27) and the Bayesian Information Criterion (BIC) defined in Eq. (3.30). These measures are used to compare the relative performance of different models, with lower values indicating better model performance. The AIC and BIC are both penalised log-likelihood functions, with the penalty term increasing with the number of parameters in the model. They are particularly useful when comparing models with a different number of parameters, as they balance model fit and complexity.

**ⓘ Limitations of goodness of fit measures**

Goodness of fit measures, such as AIC, BIC, and $\rho^2$ are effective tools for model comparison, but only when used within the confines of a single dataset. Their values are intrinsically linked to the specific data on which the models are estimated. Comparing goodness of fit values across different datasets does not provide meaningful insights, as the criteria are highly sensitive to the data-specific likelihoods, sample sizes, and underlying data characteristics. Such comparisons would not only be misleading but also violate the fundamental principles upon which these criteria are based

#### 9.2.1.3 Interpreting Parameter Estimates

Given that our utility functions are specified as linear in parameters, the estimated $\beta_k$ parameters presented in the output table above represent the marginal utility of each attribute (all else being equal), adjusted by the scale of the error term. In most instances, the coefficients lack direct interpretability; however, the signs and ratios of these coefficients carry significant meaning.

**ⓘ Synthetic data**

It is important to note that the models are based on data specifically generated for this book, rather than data from a real survey. Therefore, the following sections illustrate how to interpret results from DCE models, rather than providing insights into how individuals value wind farms

The signs of the estimated coefficients tell us whether an attribute contributes to an increase or decrease in utility, while the ratio of two coefficients reveals the relative importance of one attribute compared to another in influencing the utility of an alternative. For instance, if the ratio of two coefficients is 2, this indicates that the attribute associated with the numerator is twice as influential as the attribute corresponding to the denominator in determining the choice between the proposed alternatives. This is closely related to the definition of the mWTP (see Eq. (3.15), chap. 3).

As discussed in Chap. 8, maximum likelihood estimates are asymptotically unbiased and normally distributed, allowing us to compute standard errors and assess statistical significance. The robust standard errors (Eq. (8.9)) are preferred over the classical ones due to their robustness against violations of certain model assumptions, such as heteroscedasticity and the lack of independence of errors. Robust standard errors consider these violations and provide more accurate and reliable estimates of variance, resulting in more robust and valid confidence intervals and hypothesis tests.

According to the robust $t$-statistics labelled as `Rob.t.rat.(0)`, the coefficients of attributes *SmallFarms*, *MediumFarms*, *LowHeight*, *MediumHeight*, *RedKite*, *MinDistance*, and *Cost* are all statistically significant at the 5% level.

The signs of the estimated coefficients can be interpreted as follows:

- The coefficient for *MediumFarms* represents the differential effect of a medium-sized wind farm compared to a large wind farm (the benchmark category). The negative estimated coefficient suggests that respondents prefer wind farms with a larger number of turbines when comparing medium and large wind farms. This result seems counter-intuitive, as smaller wind farms are generally preferred due to their lower visual impact and potential noise pollution.
- The coefficient for *SmallFarms* represents the differential effect of a small wind farm compared to a large wind farm. The positive estimated coefficient indicates that respondents prefer wind farms with fewer turbines when comparing small and large wind farms. This result is consistent with our expectations.
- Similar conclusions can be drawn for the coefficients of *LowHeight* and *MediumHeight*. The estimated coefficient for *MediumHeight* is negative, suggesting that respondents favour wind farms with taller turbines, which is counter-intuitive since people generally prefer lower turbines due to their reduced visual impact and noise. The estimated coefficient for *LowHeight*, however, indicates that respondents prefer wind farms with lower turbines, which is an expected result.
- The *RedKite* attribute represents the reduction of the red kite population that may take place due to deadly encounters of red kites with turbines. The estimated coefficient is negative, suggesting that an increased reduction of the red kite population causes disutility. This result is consistent with the expectation that people are averse to the reduction of bird populations, especially those of endangered species.
- The estimated coefficient of *MinDistance* is positive, indicating that respondents prefer wind farms located farther from residential areas. This result aligns with the expectation that a greater distance from residential areas reduces the visual impact of wind farms, potentially improving their acceptance among the local population.
- The estimated coefficient of the *Cost* attribute is negative, indicating that a surcharge to the electricity bill causes disutility. This result is consistent with the expectation that people are averse to additional costs, even if they are associated with positive outcomes such as environmental conservation or renewable energy production.

Estimation outputs with positive coefficients for the cost attribute are usually an indication of an error in the data coding or model specification, wrong convergence of the optimisation procedure, or other issues. In some rare cases, however, a positive cost coefficient may align with expectations. This is the case for a Giffen good, defined by increased demand as its price rises and decreased demand as the price falls (He 2021), making a positive cost coefficient plausible. Additionally, certain behavioural biases in environmental economics can also result in positive cost coefficients. Examples of these include "warm glow" and "yeah-saying" biases, which can distort responses, potentially leading to an unexpected positive cost coefficient (see Chaps. 2 and 8 in Mariel et al. 2021 for more details).

The estimated coefficients of the alternative-specific constants (ASCs) are not directly interpretable, as they capture the average effect on the utility of all factors not included in the set of attributes. However, they can indicate if any of the alternatives have been selected more frequently (on average) than the others. In our case, the ASCs for alternatives 2 and 3 are positive and significant at the 5% significance level. This indicates that individuals, on average, prefer selecting Programme B or C over the future status quo option (Programme A—Alternative 1). This finding was already indicated in Chap. 7 when analysing the raw data.

#### 9.2.1.4 Outliers

According to Sarkar et al. (2011), an observation can be considered (statistically) unusual in three ways: as an outlier, an influential point, or a point with high leverage. Outliers are observations with values of the explained variable that deviate significantly from the expected range, resulting in large residuals. Outliers can be caused by various factors, such as data entry errors, respondent misunderstanding of the choice task, or genuine extreme preferences.

An observation is termed influential if its removal significantly alters the coefficient estimates, while a point with high leverage is one where the explanatory variable value is significantly distant from the mean, indicating a greater potential to affect the model's fit. Influence can thus be seen as the combination of leverage and outliers.

Detecting outliers in an MNL model can be challenging due to the categorical nature of the dependent variable. In linear regressions, outliers are observations where the predicted values significantly deviate from the actual values, resulting in unusually large residuals. However, in an MNL model, we work with latent, unobserved utilities rather than an observed dependent variable. The concept of outliers, as understood in linear regressions, cannot be directly applied to the multinomial logit model.

The detection of outliers based on *predicted probabilities* is implemented in *Apollo*, where outliers are defined by the lowest average probability per choice prediction. The final section of the *Apollo* output presents the ID and the average probability per choice task of the 10 "worst" outliers: those with the lowest average per choice prediction. The number of outliers printed is set in `modelOutput_settings` (in our case, `printOutliers = 10`). These individuals are considered outliers, and their responses may have a significant impact on the estimation results. That is, their preferences (or choices) are not well described by the current model.

We can also compute the predicted probabilities for all individuals in the sample using the `apollo_predict` function and calculate the average predicted probability for the chosen alternatives for each individual (see the code chunk below).

Individuals with the lowest average predicted probabilities can be considered outliers and should be carefully examined to determine the cause of their extreme preferences.

If the model is correctly specified and represents the data well, the probabilities of the chosen alternative are expected to be high. For example, the table below shows the probabilities of choosing alternatives 1, 2, and 3 for the first individual in the sample. The last column contains the probabilities of the chosen alternatives in the sequence of choices 1, 1, 3, 1, 3, 2, 1, 2, 2.

```
# Calculate the predicted probabilities
predicted_probabilities <- apollo_prediction(model, apollo_probabilities, apollo_inputs)

predicted_probabilities[predicted_probabilities$ID == 1, ]

  ID Observation      alt1       alt2       alt3    chosen
1 1            1 0.6054823 0.36588807 0.02862959 0.6054823
2 1            2 0.6965618 0.22394516 0.07949305 0.6965618
3 1            3 0.2327838 0.24262930 0.52458692 0.5245869
4 1            4 0.7083386 0.10333129 0.18833010 0.7083386
5 1            5 0.3502641 0.51545074 0.13428512 0.1342851
6 1            6 0.4696864 0.35791922 0.17239439 0.3579192
7 1            7 0.5488156 0.05139848 0.39978596 0.5488156
8 1            8 0.3350414 0.43765072 0.22730787 0.4376507
9 1            9 0.4104606 0.49808396 0.09145548 0.4980840

# Calculate the average predicted probability by individual
avg_chosen <- predicted_probabilities |>
  group_by(ID) |>
  summarise(
    avg_prob = mean(chosen)
  ) |>
  arrange(avg_prob)

# Get the ID of the first outlier
first_outlier <- avg_chosen |>
  slice(1) |>
  pull(ID)
```

If the probabilities are low, this may indicate that the model does not fit the data well or that the individual has extreme preferences. The table of the ten worst outliers in the output table above indicates that the worst outlier is the individual with ID 55, exhibiting the lowest average predicted probabilities across all choices. The implication is that this individual's choices deviate from what the estimated model predicts, possibly due to data entry errors, misinterpretation of the choice task, or other factors. It is essential to carefully review the entries for this individual to identify any potential data entry errors.

The predicted probabilities for the individual with ID 55 are presented in the table below.

```
predicted_probabilities[predicted_probabilities$ID == first_outlier, ]

    ID Observation      alt1       alt2       alt3     chosen
475 55           1 0.5488156 0.05139848 0.39978596 0.05139848
476 55           2 0.6073351 0.04881240 0.34385250 0.04881240
477 55           3 0.4104606 0.49808396 0.09145548 0.41046056
478 55           4 0.8572168 0.02858856 0.11419461 0.02858856
479 55           5 0.4402074 0.02444058 0.53535205 0.02444058
480 55           6 0.8617692 0.07163949 0.06659133 0.06659133
481 55           7 0.5832286 0.30688639 0.10988500 0.10988500
482 55           8 0.5549730 0.41048347 0.03454351 0.03454351
```

```
483 55          9 0.5144685 0.02699141 0.45854009 0.02699141
484 55         10 0.6822877 0.10862281 0.20908952 0.10862281
```

Note that the average of the last column `chosen` is 0.091, which does not exactly match the number indicated in the `Avg prob per choice` column in the outlier section of the MNL output presented above. This discrepancy is due to the panel data structure. *Apollo* calculates the exponent of the log of the probability of the sequence of choices and assumes that all choice tasks of an individual have the same probability of the chosen alternative, which is why this average is an approximation. However, whether you use this method or the manual computation presented above, the same individuals are identified as potential outliers.

The presence of outliers may require treatment. The first step is to carefully check the rows corresponding to these outliers in the data. Some form of treatment for these outliers should be proposed (Campbell et al. 2010b; Donald and Maddala 1993). In our study, we will not implement specific treatments for outliers. However, in a real-world study, it is important to carefully examine outliers in order to identify the potential causes of their extreme preferences, and to decide whether they should be excluded from the analysis or if adjustments to the model or data are necessary.

Our primary objective should always be to preserve data integrity. Removing outliers can introduce bias and diminish the representativeness of the sample, potentially resulting in a model that fits the remaining data well but fails to generalise to the broader population. Retaining all observations helps ensure that the model reflects the full diversity of the data. Additionally, numerous or extreme outliers often signal that the current model is not capturing some underlying variation or complexity. Pursuing a more appropriate model is likely to yield a more accurate and robust understanding of the relationships within the data.

### 9.2.2 MNL with Observed Heterogeneity

In this section, we will build upon our initial MNL model by introducing additional complexity. Before transitioning to RP-MXL or LC-MXL models, which account for unobserved preference heterogeneity stemming from individual characteristics not captured in the data (e.g. personal values or experiences), we should assess how much of the observed heterogeneity among individuals can be explained by the socio-demographic variables included in the dataset. Observed heterogeneity refers to differences in preferences that can be explained by measurable characteristics. To analyse the observed heterogeneity, we will select the socio-demographic variables that, according to our a priori hypotheses, may cause differences in preferences, and interact these variables with the relevant attributes.

Incorporating observed sources of heterogeneity into a model is generally preferred over modelling only unobserved heterogeneity, because it allows us to directly see how specific factors such as age, income, or education influence marginal utilities, thus enhancing the interpretability of the results. This approach offers actionable insights, is easier to communicate to stakeholders, and reduces the dependence on assumptions about unmeasured factors, which can be difficult to verify and may lead to biased estimates if those assumptions are incorrect.

While variables like age, gender, and education are typically exogenous and can be included in the model without concerns of endogeneity, some socio-demographic variables (e.g. choice of residential location) may be endogenous in certain contexts. Other variables collected at the individual level, such as responses to attitudinal questions, are inherently endogenous, and cannot be directly included in the model without addressing this endogeneity. The treatment of endogeneity lies beyond the scope of this book, but we encourage you to refer to Guevara (2015), Guevara and Polanco (2016), or Rose et al. (2023) for more details on this topic.

In the simulated data used in our study, we only have three demographic variables: *age*, *female*, and *education*. To account for a possible observed heterogeneity (see Sect. 3.1), we will interact these three variables with all attributes and alternative specific constants. With data from a real survey, the number of socio-demographic variables is likely to be much higher. Determining which variables to interact should be guided by the preliminary analyses (as presented in Chap. 7) and our a priori hypotheses about their expected effects. Socio-demographic variables that exhibit an effect on individuals' choice sequences or the frequency with which a specific attribute level is selected should be included as interactions. In our case the $j$-th ($j = 1, 2, 3$) utility that includes the interactions is defined as follows:

$$
\begin{aligned}
U_{njt} = {} & ASC_j + \delta_{asc_j,age} age_n + \delta_{asc_j,female} female_n + \delta_{asc_j,educ} education_n \\
& + \left(\beta_{sf} + \delta_{sf,age} age_n + \delta_{sf,female} female_n + \delta_{sf,educ} education_n\right) SmallFarms_{njt} \\
& + \left(\beta_{mf} + \delta_{mf,age} age_n + \delta_{mf,female} female_n + \delta_{mf,educ} education_n\right) MediumFarms_{njt} \\
& + \left(\beta_{lh} + \delta_{lh,age} age_n + \delta_{lh,female} female_n + \delta_{lh,educ} education_n\right) LowHeight_{njt} \\
& + \left(\beta_{mh} + \delta_{mh,age} age_n + \delta_{mh,female} female_n + \delta_{mh,educ} education_n\right) MediumHeight_{njt} \\
& + \left(\beta_{rk} + \delta_{rk,age} age_n + \delta_{rk,female} female_n + \delta_{rk,educ} education_n\right) RedKite_{njt} \\
& + \left(\beta_{md} + \delta_{md,age} age_n + \delta_{md,female} female_n + \delta_{md,educ} education_n\right) MinDistance_{njt} \\
& + \left(\beta_{cost} + \delta_{cost,age} age_n + \delta_{cost,female} female_n + \delta_{cost,educ} education_n\right) Cost_{njt} + \varepsilon_{njt}
\end{aligned} \tag{9.2}
$$

The abbreviations $sf$, $mf$, $lh$, $mh$, $rk$, $md$, and $cost$ in the subscripts correspond to the attributes *SmallFarms*, *MediumFarms*, *LowHeight*, *MediumHeight*, *RedKite*, *MinDistance*, and *Cost*, respectively. They are used in the R script to define the interaction terms in the utility function, facilitating the connection between the mathematical notation and the script.

The MNL model defined in Eq. (9.2) can be estimated in the *Apollo* package by making small changes with respect to the previous script. Specifically, we must add the coefficients corresponding to the interactions into the vector of coefficients to be estimated. The name of the coefficients starts with `b_` for coefficients $\beta_k$, $k \in (sf, mf, lh, mh, rk, md, cost)$ and `delta_` for coefficients $\delta_{k,m}$, $k \in (sf, mf, lh, mh, rk, md, cost)$ and $m \in (age, female, education)$.

```
# Starting values of the parameters
apollo_beta <- c(
  b_asc_alt1 = 0.00,
  b_asc_alt2 = 0.50,
  b_asc_alt3 = 0.50,
  b_medium_farm = 0.25,
  b_small_farms = 0.50,
  b_medium_height = 0.25,
  b_low_height = 0.50,
  b_red_kite = -0.05,
  b_min_distance = 0.50,
  b_cost = -0.50,
  delta_asc2_age = 0.00,
  delta_asc2_female = 0.00,
  delta_asc2_educ = 0.00,
  delta_asc3_age = 0.00,
  delta_asc3_female = 0.00,
  delta_asc3_educ = 0.00,
  delta_mf_age = 0.00,
  delta_mf_female = 0.00,
  delta_mf_educ = 0.00,
  delta_sf_age = 0.00,
  delta_sf_female = 0.00,
  delta_sf_educ = 0.00,
  delta_mh_age = 0.00,
  delta_mh_female = 0.00,


  delta_mh_educ = 0.00,
  delta_lh_age = 0.00,
  delta_lh_female = 0.00,
  delta_lh_educ = 0.00,
  delta_rk_age = 0.00,
  delta_rk_female = 0.00,
  delta_rk_educ = 0.00,
  delta_md_age = 0.00,
  delta_md_female = 0.00,
  delta_md_educ = 0.00,
  delta_ct_age = 0.00,
  delta_ct_female = 0.00,
  delta_ct_educ = 0.00
)
```

To save space, we will show you how to introduce these interactions in the representative utilities for only one of the alternatives (Alternative 2). In the remaining two alternatives, the incorporation of these interactions is identical.

```
V <- list(
  alt1 = …,
  alt2 = (
    b_asc_alt2 + delta_asc2_age * age + delta_asc2_female * female + delta_asc2_educ * educati
on +
      (b_medium_farms + delta_mf_age * age + delta_mf_female * female + delta_mf_educ * educat
ion) * alt2_farm2 +
      (b_small_farms  + delta_sf_age * age + delta_sf_female * female + delta_sf_educ * educat
ion) * alt2_farm3 +
      (b_medium_height + delta_mh_age * age + delta_mh_female * female + delta_mh_educ * educa
tion) * alt2_height2 +
      (b_low_height  + delta_lh_age * age + delta_lh_female * female + delta_lh_educ * educati
on) * alt2_height3 +
      (b_red_kite + delta_rk_age * age + delta_rk_female * female + delta_rk_educ * education)
 * alt2_redkite +
      (b_min_distance + delta_md_age * age + delta_md_female * female + delta_md_educ * educat
ion) * alt2_distance +
      (b_cost + delta_ct_age * age + delta_ct_female * female + delta_ct_educ * education) * a
lt2_cost
  ),
  alt3 = …
)
```

The interpretation of the coefficients interacting with the socio-demographic variables changes radically in this model: in the model without interactions, the coefficients $\beta_k$ represent the marginal utility of each attribute, adjusted by the scale of the error term. In the presence of interactions, the estimated $\beta_k$ coefficients represent the marginal utility of each attribute for an individual whose age, gender, and education level are all equal to zero, which may not correspond to any real individual.

The $\delta_{k,m}$ coefficients represent the change in the marginal utility of each attribute associated with a change in the corresponding socio-demographic variable. For example, the coefficient $\delta_{sf,age}$ represents the change in the marginal utility of the *SmallFarms* attribute associated with a change in the individual's age. The preferences of individuals with different socio-demographic characteristics can be inferred from the joint interpretation of the $\beta_k$ and $\delta_{k,m}$ coefficients. Individuals with different observed socio-demographic characteristics will have different preferences for the attributes, which is why we say that we are able to model observed preference heterogeneity in this model.

The inclusion of interactions also impacts the interpretation of the significance of the $\beta_k$ coefficients. The coefficient $\beta_k$ may not be significant in the model without interactions, but some of the interaction coefficients $\delta_{k,m}$ might be significant, indicating a significant impact of the corresponding attribute on utility. Therefore, it is important to interpret the $\beta_k$ and $\delta_{k,m}$ coefficients jointly.

The output below presents the results of the MNL model with socio-demographic interactions. The final section presents the 10 worst outliers, defined by the lowest average predicted probabilities for the chosen alternative.

```
Model run by user using Apollo 0.3.4 on R 4.4.1 for Darwin.
Please acknowledge the use of Apollo by citing Hess & Palma (2019)
  DOI 10.1016/j.jocm.2019.100170
  www.ApolloChoiceModelling.com

Model name                                  : MNL_socdem_ASC
Model description                           : MNL windmills
Model run at                                : 2024-10-30 13:10:16.9677
Estimation method                           : bgw
Model diagnosis                             : Relative function convergence
Optimisation diagnosis                      : Maximum found
     hessian properties                     : Negative definite
     maximum eigenvalue                     : -4.427732
     reciprocal of condition number         : 4.077e-08
Number of individuals                       : 1000
Number of rows in database                  : 8633
Number of modelled outcomes                 : 8633

Number of cores used                        :  20
Model without mixing

LL(start)                                   : -7097.83
LL at equal shares, LL(0)                   : -9484.32
LL at observed shares, LL(C)                : -8539.99
LL(final)                                   : -6838.93
Rho-squared vs equal shares                  :  0.2789
Adj.Rho-squared vs equal shares              :  0.2751
Rho-squared vs observed shares               :  0.1992
Adj.Rho-squared vs observed shares           :  0.1952
AIC                                         :  13749.86
BIC                                         :  14004.14

Estimated parameters                        : 36
Time taken (hh:mm:ss)                       :  00:00:9.14
     pre-estimation                         :  00:00:1.47
     estimation                             :  00:00:0.74
     post-estimation                        :  00:00:6.93
Iterations                                  :  8

Unconstrained optimisation.

Estimates:
                     Estimate        s.e.   t.rat.(0)    Rob.s.e. Rob.t.rat.(0)
b_asc_alt1           0.000000          NA          NA          NA            NA
b_asc_alt2           0.630471    0.293661     2.14694    0.312594       2.01690
b_asc_alt3           0.425055    0.298966     1.42175    0.315873       1.34565
b_medium_farms      -0.136680    0.217268    -0.62908    0.221380      -0.61740
b_small_farms        0.513285    0.213187     2.40767    0.199575       2.57189
b_medium_height     -0.085668    0.221074    -0.38751    0.227899      -0.37590
b_low_height         0.609917    0.210970     2.89102    0.219417       2.77972
b_red_kite          -0.055401    0.024633    -2.24907    0.023442      -2.36336
b_min_distance       0.633531    0.236071     2.68364    0.222121       2.85219
b_cost              -0.420934    0.037422   -11.24843    0.049816      -8.44974
delta_asc2_age      -0.001724    0.004871    -0.35386    0.005461      -0.31567
delta_asc2_female    0.286675    0.142174     2.01637    0.147897       1.93834
delta_asc2_educ      0.049980    0.085685     0.58330    0.088728       0.56330
delta_asc3_age     -2.7092e-04   0.004954    -0.05468    0.005566      -0.04867
delta_asc3_female    0.350865    0.145072     2.41855    0.152643       2.29859
delta_asc3_educ      0.118721    0.087310     1.35977    0.091324       1.30000
delta_mf_age        -0.004842    0.003582    -1.35173    0.003584      -1.35094
delta_mf_female      0.042415    0.104188     0.40710    0.105926       0.40042
delta_mf_educ        0.051688    0.062707     0.82428    0.063557       0.81325
```

```
delta_sf_age         -0.003436    0.003520    -0.97626    0.003318     -1.03565
delta_sf_female      -0.074899    0.102646    -0.72968    0.101408     -0.73859
delta_sf_educ        -0.084418    0.061559    -1.37135    0.059969     -1.40769
delta_mh_age         -0.010267    0.003670    -2.79772    0.003701     -2.77397
delta_mh_female       0.071962    0.107432     0.66984    0.111154      0.64741
delta_mh_educ         0.131051    0.064367     2.03599    0.064058      2.04580
delta_lh_age         -0.005033    0.003481    -1.44602    0.003537     -1.42312
delta_lh_female      -0.027038    0.101707    -0.26584    0.105607     -0.25602
delta_lh_educ         0.102068    0.061227     1.66703    0.063172      1.61570
delta_rk_age        2.9974e-04  4.0707e-04     0.73634  3.7590e-04      0.79740
delta_rk_female       0.012575    0.011842     1.06194    0.011814      1.06448
delta_rk_educ        -0.010256    0.007138    -1.43677    0.007217     -1.42107
delta_md_age         -0.003405    0.003900    -0.87315    0.003534     -0.96340
delta_md_female      2.654e-05    0.113379  2.3409e-04    0.109508   2.4237e-04
delta_md_educ        -0.088214    0.068155    -1.29431    0.066228     -1.33196
delta_ct_age          0.002525  6.1544e-04     4.10309  7.6074e-04      3.31939
delta_ct_female      -0.118681    0.018329    -6.47500    0.024019     -4.94109
delta_ct_educ        -0.034648    0.010830    -3.19932    0.013774     -2.51548

 10 most extreme outliers in terms of lowest average per choice prediction:
  ID Avg prob per choice
 823          0.05276481
 364          0.07965293
  55          0.08036387
 685          0.09127360
 192          0.11321424
 516          0.11994649
 601          0.15046427
 428          0.15773333
 328          0.15932958
  56          0.16289777
```

The interactions included in this model are a very simple and effective way to capture heterogeneity in preferences among different population subgroups. We can see that the coefficient $\delta_{mh,age}$ (`delta_mh_age` in the R-script) is negative and significant at the 5% level, indicating that the marginal utility of the *MediumHeight* attribute is lower for older individuals. The coefficient $\delta_{mh,educ}$ (`delta_mh_educ` in the R-script) is positive and significant at the 5% level, indicating that the marginal utility of the *MediumHeight* attribute is higher for individuals with a higher level of education.

Many researchers apply models capable of capturing unobserved heterogeneity (RP-MXL, LC-MXL) without first analysing the observed heterogeneity in detail using different respondent characteristics. We recommend first analysing the observed preference heterogeneity before moving on to more complex models.

**ⓘ Incorporating determinants of preference heterogeneity**

To be able to include potential determinants of preference heterogeneity in your models, variables of interest must be identified and included in the questionnaire. This requires a thorough analysis of both the good or service to be valued as well as population characteristics during the design phase of the DCE, and may necessitate comprehensive focus groups. Spatial data can be added after the survey, using geographical information systems (GIS), if the location of the place of residence, the place visited for recreation, etc. is recorded in the survey (postal code or coordinates)

It is important to note that interacting individual socio-demographic variables with all attributes significantly increases the number of parameters in the model. In our case, the initial 9 parameters in the simplest MNL model have increased to 36 in the MNL model with socio-demographic interactions. To estimate the parameters of all interactions, we need a sufficiently large experimental design (and sample), with enough variability in the attributes and collected characteristics.

The model estimated in this section can be compared in terms of model fit to the MNL model without interactions presented in Sect. 9.2.1, based on the log-likelihood value, AIC, BIC and the LR (likelihood ratio) test.

| | ln $L$ | $\rho^2$ | AIC | BIC |
|---|---|---|---|---|
| simple MNL | −6904.38 | 0.272 | 13,826.77 | 13,890.34 |
| MNL with interactions | −6838.93 | 0.279 | 13,749.86 | 14,004.14 |

As expected, an increased number of parameters in the model with interactions improved the value of ln $L$ from −6904.38 to −6838.93. The $\rho^2$ value increased from 0.272 in the simple MNL model to 0.279 in the MNL model with observed heterogeneity, suggesting that the model with observed heterogeneity explains the data slightly better than the simple MNL model. The model with observed heterogeneity has a lower AIC value (13749.86) compared to the simple MNL model (13826.77), indicating that the model with observed heterogeneity finds a better balance between goodness of fit and model complexity. In contrast, the BIC value is higher for the MNL model with observed heterogeneity (14004.14) compared to the simple MNL model (13890.34). This indicates that the penalty for adding more parameters in the model with observed heterogeneity outweighs the improvement in fit, according to the BIC criterion. The BIC generally favours simpler models more heavily compared to the AIC criterion, due to its higher penalty for increased complexity caused by an increased number of parameters.

The LR test compares the log-likelihoods of two nested models to determine if the more complex model significantly improves the model fit. The null hypothesis is that the simpler model (in which all coefficients of the interaction terms are zero) is adequate, while the alternative hypothesis is that the more complex model provides a better fit. The degrees of freedom for the LR test is the difference in the number of estimated parameters between the two models (36 − 9 = 27).

$$
\begin{aligned}
LR &= -2 \times (\text{LL(simple MNL)} - \text{LL(MNL with interactions)}) \\
&= -2 \times (-6904.38 - (-6838.93)) \\
&= 130.09
\end{aligned}
$$

The null hypothesis is clearly rejected as $130.09 > \chi^2_{27,0.05} = 40.11$. This indicates that the MNL model with observed heterogeneity provides a significantly better fit to the data compared to the simple MNL model. The *Apollo* package offers the function `apollo_lrTest` to carry out this test.

## 9.3 Mixed Logit Model

As discussed in Chap. 3, a mixed logit model is defined as any model where the unconditional probability of the sequence of choices $\mathbf{i}_n^\star$ is given by the mixed logit probability formula:

$$P_n(\mathbf{i}_n^\star|\mathbf{\Omega}) = \int P_n(\mathbf{i}_n^\star|\boldsymbol{\beta})f(\boldsymbol{\beta}|\mathbf{\Omega})d\boldsymbol{\beta} ,$$

where the coefficients are assumed to be distributed according to a density function $f(\boldsymbol{\beta}|\mathbf{\Omega})$, which is unknown and depends on parameters $\mathbf{\Omega}$. The distribution of each element of $\boldsymbol{\beta}$ can be continuous or discrete, these elements can be correlated, and some elements can even be fixed.

McFadden and Train (2000) demonstrate that a mixed logit model can approximate any choice model with any desired level of accuracy, regardless of the distribution of preferences. However, in practice, the specification of a particular $f(\boldsymbol{\beta}|\mathbf{\Omega})$, imposes certain constraints on the model.

Mixed logit (MXL) models, which include random parameters MXL (RP-MXL), error components MXL, discrete-mixture MXL, and latent class MXL (LC-MXL) models, among others, expand upon the MNL model by accounting for unobserved heterogeneity in the estimated coefficients. In MXLs, unobserved heterogeneity is presumed to conform to either a continuous (RP-MXL) or discrete distribution (LC-MXL) across the population.

### *9.3.1 Random Parameters Mixed Logit Model (RP-MXL)*

In the early applications of MXLs, the continuous distributions were primarily limited to univariate normal densities, but nowadays the distributional assumptions are much more flexible (Train and Sonnier 2005; Daly et al. 2012). With the growing computational power of today's computers, multivariate distributions are frequently applied, allowing for the correlation of random coefficients.

The standard application of mixed logit models with uncorrelated coefficients typically imposes constraints by assuming that the variance–covariance matrix of the coefficients is diagonal. However, from a theoretical point of view, a specification with correlated random coefficients is more flexible than a specification with uncorrelated coefficients (Train and Weeks 2005). Note, however, that even this type of model still imposes restrictions due to the distributional assumption.

The use of correlated random coefficients has also garnered significant attention in the discussion surrounding scale heterogeneity. Scale heterogeneity is defined by individuals having coefficients with different scales, with some having larger (or smaller) coefficients relative to the rest of individuals. Therefore, scale heterogeneity induces correlation among coefficients, as a respondent's choice may be more random (with all coefficients being smaller in magnitude and closer to zero) or more deterministic (with all coefficients being larger in magnitude). The scale of utility, reflecting the magnitude of all utility coefficients, typically varies across individuals.

Hess and Train (2017) drew the following highly relevant conclusions related to this issue. First, mixed logit models can accommodate various forms of correlation, including scale heterogeneity. Second, Generalised mixed logit (G-MNL) models (see Fiebig et al. 2010) represent a constrained version of mixed logit models that, with proper implementation, can address scale heterogeneity but typically exclude other forms of correlation. Third, none of these models can separate scale heterogeneity from other correlation sources, and fourth, models assuming that scale heterogeneity is the sole source of correlation unavoidably include other correlation sources in the estimated scale parameter.

Based on the discussion above, we should employ a random parameter model with correlated coefficients to avoid imposing any restrictions on the correlations. Given that these models typically involve many parameters and are difficult to estimate, we recommend first estimating a model with uncorrelated coefficients. This approach can provide initial insights into the data, and this preliminary step helps us obtain estimates that may provide starting values for the RP-MXL model with correlated coefficients.

RP-MXL models generally keep the interactions with socio-demographic variables we included in the extended MNL model in Sect. 9.2.2 to investigate observed heterogeneity. As indicated above, the observed heterogeneity refers to differences in preferences that can be explained by measurable characteristics. Unobserved heterogeneity, which stems from individual characteristics not captured in the data (e.g. personal values, experiences), is inherently more challenging to identify and model.

**ⓘ Prioritising observed heterogeneity**

Your analysis should first explore observed heterogeneity before moving on to unobserved heterogeneity. This is because the observed heterogeneity provides a foundational understanding of preference variations and sets a baseline that can be expanded upon by exploring unobserved heterogeneity. By first analysing observed heterogeneity, you can avoid misattributing variation in preferences to unobserved factors that might actually be caused by observable variables not included in the model

#### 9.3.1.1 Uncorrelated Coefficients

The utilities of the RP-MXL model with uncorrelated coefficients corresponding to Eq. (9.2) are defined as follows:

$$\begin{aligned} U_{njt} = ASC_{nj} &+ \beta_{sf,n} SmallFarms_{njt} \\ &+ \beta_{mf,n} MediumFarms_{njt} \\ &+ \beta_{lh,n} LowHeight_{njt} \\ &+ \beta_{mh,n} MediumHeight_{njt} \\ &+ \beta_{rk,n} RedKite_{njt} \\ &+ \beta_{md,n} MinDistance_{njt} \\ &+ \beta_{cost,n} Cost_{njt} + \varepsilon_{njt} \end{aligned} \tag{9.3}$$

The difference with respect to the MNL model defined in Eq. (9.2) is that the $\beta_{k,n}$ coefficients are now random and follow a specific distribution. In our case, the coefficients of the non-cost attributes are assumed to be distributed normally, while the cost attribute is distributed log-normally (with a reversed sign) to avoid problems with the finite moments of the WTP (Daly et al. 2012).

Selecting the appropriate distribution to model the diversity in underlying population preferences has emerged as a key focus of DCE research in recent years. However, it remains a challenge, and despite the wealth of literature on this topic (Daly et al. 2012; Train 2016), the issue of selecting the optimal distribution remains unresolved.

The choice of distribution for a random coefficient in a mixed logit model is fundamentally an empirical decision that depends entirely on the data—specifically, what distributions are believed or observed to best represent the variation in preferences among individuals. Since different distributions can capture different types of heterogeneity, the selection should reflect the underlying patterns in the data, rather than relying on theoretical assumptions alone. Key considerations include whether the distribution should be unimodal or bimodal, symmetrical or asymmetrical, and whether it should be bounded.

As in the MNL model, all attributes are interacted with the socio-demographic variables by the use of non-random coefficients $\delta_{km}$. These interactions affect the mean of the distribution, which is why these coefficients are sometimes called *mean-shifters*. Specifically, we assume that

$$\beta_{k,n} \sim N\left(\mu_k + \delta_{k,age} age_n + \delta_{k,female} female_n + \delta_{k,educ} education_n, \sigma_k\right),$$
$$k \in (sf, mf, lh, mh, rk, md, cost), \qquad (9.4)$$

and

$$\beta_{cost,n} \sim -exp(N(\mu_{cost} + \delta_{cost,age} age_n + \delta_{cost,female} female_n$$
$$+\delta_{cost,educ} education_n, \sigma_{cost})), \qquad (9.5)$$

The alternative specific constants are defined as

$$ASC_{nj} = ASC_j + \delta_{asc_j,age} age_n + \delta_{asc_j,female} female_n + \delta_{asc_j,educ} education_n\,. \qquad (9.6)$$

This case, represented by interactions of the socio-demographic variables defined in Eqs. (9.4, 9.5, and 9.6) represents just one of many potential specifications for the RP-MXL model. A commonly used variation involves adding interactions with socio-demographic variables to the standard deviations of the assumed distributions (Greene and Hensher 2007). This approach is suitable when preference heterogeneity is believed to vary across different subgroups defined by socio-demographic characteristics.

The script below begins with preliminary steps to establish the initial parameter values for the estimation. Starting values used in this chapter are chosen arbitrarily and for the reasons explained in Sect. 8.3, it is crucial to use a variety of starting values.

Next, the estimation of the RP-MXL model with uncorrelated coefficients is carried out. The additional parameters with respect to the MNL model are the standard deviations of assumed normal distributions of the random coefficients $\beta_{k,n}$.

> **Interpreting parameters of a log-normal distributed cost coefficient**
>
> It is important to note that the parameters $\mu_{ct}$ and $\sigma_{ct}$ of the log-normal distributed cost coefficient defined in the code chunk below do not represent the mean and standard deviation of the distribution. The mean and standard deviation of a log-normal distribution obtained as $\exp(N(\mu_{ct}, \sigma_{ct}))$ are $\exp\left(\mu_{ct} + \sigma_{ct}^2/2\right)$ and $\exp\left(\mu_{ct} + \sigma_{ct}^2\right) \cdot \sqrt{\exp\left(\sigma_{ct}^2 - 1\right)}$, respectively. Thus, if $\mu_{ct} = -0.5$ and $\sigma_{ct} = 0.1$, the mean of the log-normal distribution is $\exp\left(-0.5 + 0.1^2/2\right) = 0.61$ and the standard deviation is $\exp\left(-0.5 + 0.1^2/2\right) \cdot \sqrt{\exp(0.1^2 - 1)} = 0.37$. We reverse the sign of the log-normal distribution of the cost coefficient in our models in order to obtain a negative coefficient for the cost attribute

```r
# Loading R packages
## Apollo: choice models in R
library(apollo)

## Initialize Apollo ----
apollo_initialise()

## Set core controls ----
apollo_control = list(
  modelName = "rpl-mixl-uncorrelated",
  modelDescr = "RP-MIXL with uncorrelated coefficients on the windmills dataset",
  indivID = "id_individual",
  nCores = 20
)

## Import data ----
# Read in the data and filter out missing choices
database <- read_csv(gzcon(url("https://raw.githubusercontent.com/edsandorf/evdce/refs/heads/m
ain/Data/data-windmills.csv"))) |> clean_names()


## Set the starting values of the parameters ----
apollo_beta <- c(
  asc_alt1 = 0.00,
  asc_alt2 = 0.50,
  asc_alt3 = 0.50,
  mu_mf    =  0.25,
  sd_mf =0.1,
  mu_sf =  0.50,
  sd_sf = 0.2,
  mu_mh = 0.25,
  sd_mh = 0.1,
  mu_lh = 0.50,
  sd_lh = 0.2,
  mu_rk = -0.05,
  sd_rk = 0.01,
  mu_md = 0.50,
  sd_md = 0.2,
  mu_ct = -0.50,
  sd_ct = 0.1,
```

```
    delta_asc2_age = 0.00,
    delta_asc2_female = 0.00,
    delta_asc2_educ = 0.00,
    delta_asc3_age = 0.00,
    delta_asc3_female = 0.00,
    delta_asc3_educ = 0.00,
    delta_mf_age = -0.01,
    delta_sf_age = -0.01,
    delta_mf_female = -0.18,
    delta_sf_female = -0.06,
    delta_mf_educ = -0.04,
    delta_sf_educ = -0.02,
    delta_mh_age = -0.01,
    delta_lh_age = -0.01,
    delta_mh_female = 0.01,
    delta_lh_female = 0.04,
    delta_mh_educ = 0.02,
    delta_lh_educ = 0.12,
    delta_rk_age = -0.01,
    delta_md_age = -0.01,
    delta_rk_female = 0.01,
    delta_md_female = 0.01,
```

```
    delta_rk_educ = 0.12,
    delta_md_educ = -0.01,
    delta_ct_age = 0.01,
    delta_ct_female = -0.01,
    delta_ct_educ = -0.01
)

apollo_fixed = c("asc_alt1")
```

The `apollo_draws` and `apollo_randCoeff` functions define the type of random draws used to approximate the integral of the ln $L$ function (see Eq. (3.20), chap. 3) and the distributions assumed for the random coefficients. As stated above, we assume normal distributions for the non-cost attributes and a log-normal distribution with a reversed sign for the cost attribute. The mean coefficients of all attributes are interacted with the socio-demographic variables age, gender, and education.

Note that we are using random inter-draws to capture variations between respondents, thereby reflecting the heterogeneity of preferences across individuals. These draws provide different realisations of the random parameters for each respondent. In contrast, intra-draws (not used in our example) pertain to variations within the choices made by a single respondent (Hess and Giergiczny 2015). They can account for additional randomness across different decisions made by the same individual. Depending on the data and the assumptions about the decision-making process, both inter- and intra-draws can be used either together or separately to enhance model accuracy.

> **ⓘ What type of draw should I use?**
>
> Typically, Halton draws are employed in RP-MXL models. They are a suitable option for models with a limited number of random coefficients, but using Halton draws with more than approximately five random components can introduce issues related to multicollinearity. In the *Apollo* package, a range of alternative random sampling methods

are available, including pseudo-Monte Carlo sampling, Modified Latin Hypercube Sampling (MLHS), Sobol sequences, and Sobol sequences with Faure-Tezuka and/or Owen scrambling. Czajkowski and Budziński (2019) compared various sampling methods including Halton, Sobol, and MLHS across a wide range of experimental conditions and showed that a scrambled Sobol sequence exhibited the lowest simulation error across all experimental conditions

The precision of the approximation of the integral to be maximised (Eq. (3.20), chap. 3) depends crucially on the number and quality of random draws employed for the approximation. Determining the optimal number of draws to estimate models with random components is a critical aspect of statistical modelling, but it lacks a definitive recommendation. More draws tend to yield more reliable results because they provide a better approximation of the multidimensional integral that is your log-likelihood function. Generally, several thousand random draws should be used instead of the few hundred draws usually found in the literature. Using a limited number of draws results in a poor approximation of the integral, essentially causing that the model being estimated diverges from the intended model specification. Parameter estimates obtained this way will be biased.

Occasionally, we may find that our model converges with a low number of draws but fails to do so with a high number. This discrepancy points to a problem within the model itself, and in no case should we rely on the estimation with a low number of draws. To reduce estimation costs, many researchers use a low number of draws during the specification search and then re-estimate the final model with a larger number of draws. This practice, though common, is not advisable. The use of a low number of draws during the specification search results in a poor approximation of the integral, potentially introducing bias into the decision-making process that shapes the final model specification. It is essential to use the same number of draws in the specification stage as in the final model.

```
## Define the random components ----
apollo_draws <- list(
  interDrawsType = "sobol",
  interNDraws = 5000,
  interUnifDraws = c(),
  interNormDraws = c(
    "draws_mf",
    "draws_sf",
    "draws_mh",
    "draws_lh",
    "draws_rk",
    "draws_md",
    "draws_ct"
  ),
  intraDrawsType = "halton",
  intraNDraws = 0,
  intraUnifDraws = c(),
  intraNormDraws = c()
)

apollo_randCoeff <- function(apollo_beta, apollo_inputs) {
  randcoeff <- list(
    r_mf = mu_mf + sd_mf * draws_mf + delta_mf_age * age + delta_mf_female * female + delta_mf
_educ * education,
    r_sf = mu_sf + sd_sf * draws_sf + delta_sf_age * age + delta_sf_female * female + delta_sf
_educ * education,
    r_mh = mu_mh + sd_mh * draws_mh + delta_mh_age * age + delta_mh_female * female + delta_mh
_educ * education,
    r_lh = mu_lh + sd_lh * draws_lh + delta_lh_age * age + delta_lh_female * female + delta_lh
_educ * education,
    r_rk = mu_rk + sd_rk * draws_rk + delta_rk_age * age + delta_rk_female * female + delta_rk
_educ * education,
    r_md = mu_md + sd_md * draws_md + delta_md_age * age + delta_md_female * female + delta_md
_educ * education,
    r_ct = -exp(mu_ct + sd_ct * draws_ct + delta_ct_age * age + delta_ct_female * female + del
ta_ct_educ * education)
  )

  return(
    randcoeff
  )
}

## Group and validate inputs ----
apollo_inputs <- apollo_validateInputs()
```

Next, the utilities are defined and the model is estimated. Recall that the random coefficients in the utility functions have been defined previously in the `apollo_randCoeff` function.

```
## Define the model and likelihood function ----
apollo_probabilities <- function(apollo_beta, apollo_inputs, functionality = "estimate") {
  ## Attach inputs and detach after function exit
  apollo_attach(apollo_beta, apollo_inputs)
  on.exit(apollo_detach(apollo_beta, apollo_inputs))

  # Define the list of utility functions
  V <- list(
    alt1 = (
      asc_alt1 +
        r_mf * alt1_farm2 +
        r_sf * alt1_farm3 +
        r_mh * alt1_height2 +
        r_lh * alt1_height3 +
        r_rk * alt1_redkite +
        r_md * alt1_distance +
        r_ct * alt1_cost
    ),
    alt2 = (
      asc_alt2 +
```

```
        delta_asc2_age * age +
        delta_asc2_female * female +
        delta_asc2_educ * education +
        r_mf * alt2_farm2 +
        r_sf * alt2_farm3 +
        r_mh * alt2_height2 +
        r_lh * alt2_height3 +
        r_rk * alt2_redkite +
        r_md * alt2_distance +
        r_ct * alt2_cost
    ),
    alt3 = (
      asc_alt3 +
        delta_asc3_age * age +
        delta_asc3_female * female +
        delta_asc3_educ * education +
        r_mf * alt3_farm2 +
        r_sf * alt3_farm3 +
        r_mh * alt3_height2 +
        r_lh * alt3_height3 +
        r_rk * alt3_redkite +
        r_md * alt3_distance +
        r_ct * alt3_cost
    )
  )

  # Define settings for MNL model component
  mnl_settings <- list(
    alternatives = c(alt1 = 1, alt2 = 2, alt3 = 3),
    avail = list(alt1 = 1, alt2 = 1, alt3 = 1),
    choiceVar = choice,
    V = V
  )

  # Calculate the probabilities
  P <- list(
    model = apollo_mnl(mnl_settings, functionality)
  )

  # Take the product across observations
  P <- apollo_panelProd(P, apollo_inputs, functionality)

  # Average across inter-individual draws
  P <- apollo_avgInterDraws(P, apollo_inputs, functionality)

  # Prepare and return the outputs
  P <- apollo_prepareProb(P, apollo_inputs, functionality)

  # Return the probabilities
  return(
    P
  )
}

## Estimate the model ----
model <- apollo_estimate(
  apollo_beta,
  apollo_fixed,
  apollo_probabilities,
  apollo_inputs,
  estimate_settings = list(
    writeIter = FALSE,
    silent = FALSE,
    estimationRoutine = "bgw"
  )
)
```

The time required to estimate an RP-MXL model is highly dependent on three key factors (aside from the capacity of the computer): the number of parameters, the sample size, and the number of random draws employed in the estimation process. Depending on these factors, the estimation process can take between several minutes and several hours to complete.

In our case, the model estimation was conducted on a Dell Precision 7920 Tower workstation equipped with dual Intel Xeon Scalable processors, providing a total of 20 cores (the number of cores can be indicated in *Apollo* in `apollo_control`). The system also featured 256 GB of DDR4 ECC RAM. The estimation took approximately 5 h.

```
Model run by user using Apollo 0.3.4 on R 4.4.1 for Darwin.
Please acknowledge the use of Apollo by citing Hess & Palma (2019)
  DOI 10.1016/j.jocm.2019.100170
  www.ApolloChoiceModelling.com

Model name                                  : RP_MXL_uncorrelated_ASC
Model description                           : RP MXL uncorrelated_ASC
Model run at                                : 2024-10-23 07:54:25.503884
Estimation method                           : bgw
Model diagnosis                             : Relative function convergence
Optimisation diagnosis                      : Maximum found
     hessian properties                     : Negative definite
     maximum eigenvalue                     : -3.648296
     reciprocal of condition number         : 5.89505e-08
Number of individuals                       : 1000
Number of rows in database                  : 8633
Number of modelled outcomes                 : 8633

Number of cores used                        :  20
Number of inter-individual draws            : 5000 (sobol)

LL(start)                                   : -11223.22
LL at equal shares, LL(0)                   : -9484.32
LL at observed shares, LL(C)                : -8539.99
LL(final)                                   : -6629.72
Rho-squared vs equal shares                  :  0.301
Adj.Rho-squared vs equal shares              :  0.2964
Rho-squared vs observed shares               :  0.2237
Adj.Rho-squared vs observed shares           :  0.2189
AIC                                         :  13345.44
BIC                                         :  13649.17

Estimated parameters                        : 43
Time taken (hh:mm:ss)                       :  05:04:23.33
     pre-estimation                         :  00:02:18.85
     estimation                             :  00:39:21.30
     post-estimation                        :  04:22:43.18
Iterations                                  :  32

Unconstrained optimisation.

Estimates:
                     Estimate        s.e.   t.rat.(0)    Rob.s.e. Rob.t.rat.(0)
asc_alt1             0.000000          NA          NA          NA            NA
asc_alt2             0.888053    0.332088    2.674147    0.350722      2.532070
asc_alt3             0.660792    0.335043    1.972260    0.341033      1.937616
```

```
mu_mf               -0.106326    0.232523   -0.457271    0.239890    -0.443228
sd_mf               -0.075288    0.211953   -0.355212    0.102262    -0.736231
mu_sf                0.544692    0.229987    2.368364    0.218442     2.493535
sd_sf                0.035975    0.182728    0.196876    0.033284     1.080829
mu_mh               -0.056492    0.236044   -0.239326    0.247812    -0.227961
sd_mh                0.220451    0.187164    1.177851    0.197559     1.115872
mu_lh                0.671154    0.234830    2.858042    0.238613     2.812725
sd_lh               -0.405961    0.104374   -3.889468    0.107756    -3.767418
mu_rk               -0.056683    0.026447   -2.143292    0.025170    -2.252036
sd_rk               -0.003439    0.054015   -0.063676    0.018319    -0.187758
mu_md                0.671188    0.250730    2.676938    0.239239     2.805514
sd_md                0.012836    0.184714    0.069491    0.021359     0.600974
mu_ct               -0.724175    0.120437   -6.012898    0.142243    -5.091114
sd_ct               -0.434625    0.021765  -19.968970    0.027441   -15.838248
delta_asc2_age       0.001448    0.006060    0.238998    0.006865     0.210964
delta_asc2_female    0.344519    0.153944    2.237953    0.156381     2.203083
delta_asc2_educ    5.7619e-04    0.093128    0.006187    0.094325     0.006109
delta_asc3_age       0.003188    0.006111    0.521600    0.006788     0.469594
delta_asc3_female    0.406054    0.156912    2.587783    0.158068     2.568859
delta_asc3_educ      0.074513    0.094589    0.787754    0.095689     0.778703
delta_mf_age        -0.006023    0.003953   -1.523703    0.004044    -1.489316
delta_sf_age        -0.003445    0.003924   -0.878075    0.003788    -0.909535
delta_mf_female      0.034284    0.109892    0.311981    0.111935     0.306288
delta_sf_female     -0.060944    0.109009   -0.559074    0.106704    -0.571148
delta_mf_educ        0.052123    0.066025    0.789444    0.066924     0.778843
delta_sf_educ       -0.092817    0.065306   -1.421278    0.063152    -1.469746
delta_mh_age        -0.012866    0.004079   -3.154070    0.004214    -3.053438
delta_lh_age        -0.006292    0.004012   -1.568408    0.004103    -1.533412
delta_mh_female      0.079799    0.112756    0.707715    0.116306     0.686113
delta_lh_female      0.003658    0.111147    0.032914    0.111659     0.032763
delta_mh_educ        0.155202    0.067551    2.297546    0.066959     2.317863
delta_lh_educ        0.102999    0.066842    1.540934    0.066592     1.546719
delta_rk_age       2.4704e-04  4.4922e-04    0.549932  4.2395e-04     0.582714
delta_md_age        -0.004784    0.004271   -1.120104    0.003980    -1.202019
delta_rk_female      0.012416    0.012569    0.987878    0.012541     0.990044
delta_md_female     -0.025449    0.119032   -0.213799    0.115011    -0.221273
delta_rk_educ       -0.009618    0.007565   -1.271371    0.007633    -1.260077
delta_md_educ       -0.074403    0.071502   -1.040572    0.069263    -1.074220
delta_ct_age        -0.004655    0.002305   -2.019429    0.003008    -1.547648
delta_ct_female      0.306227    0.054080    5.662469    0.057267     5.347340
delta_ct_educ        0.061434    0.032280    1.903192    0.034325     1.789771

 10 most extreme outliers in terms of lowest average per choice prediction:
  ID Avg prob per choice
 364           0.1676696
 823           0.1702922
 685           0.1763564
 516           0.1813155
 518           0.1823856
  55           0.1896258
 328           0.1903052
 601           0.1950062
 192           0.2040892
 896           0.2131087
```

First, we have to check the convergence of the model, as in the MNL model. If the model does not converge, the estimation process needs to be repeated with different starting values and/or different maximisation procedures. If the model converges successfully, the next step is to check the sign and significance of the estimated parameters. The sign of the estimated coefficients should be consistent with the expected sign of the attribute. We will not delve into a detailed analysis of convergence, as it is outlined in the MNL section above. We will move directly to specific issues related to the RP-MXL model.

> ### ⓘ Handling negative signs of standard deviations
>
> The output of the RP_MXL model may contain negative signs for some standard deviations. These negative signs should be ignored, since the internal function used to estimate these coefficients does not distinguish between deviations to the left or right, and the sign is therefore meaningless. In any reported output table, the sign of the estimated standard deviations should always be positive, independent of which sign the software reports for a standard deviation

In more complex models, NA values for standard errors can appear in the output table, which can be attributed to various factors. First, the model may have theoretical identification issues, which are challenging to pinpoint because requirements vary based on the model's structure. Second, the model may be too complex to model with the available data, resulting in empirical identification problems. If NA values are present for standard errors in a model, the estimated parameters cannot be interpreted.

```
Model name                              : RP_MXL_uncorrelated_ASC_no_convergence
Model description                       : RP MXL uncorrelated
Model run at                            : 2024-09-17 15:13:48.1975
Estimation method                       : bgw
Model diagnosis                         : Iteration limit
Number of individuals                   : 5
Number of rows in database              : 47
Number of modelled outcomes             : 47

Number of cores used                    :  20
Number of inter-individual draws        : 5000 (sobol)

LL(start)                               : -186.61
LL at equal shares, LL(0)               : -51.63
LL at observed shares, LL(C)            : -43.64
LL(final)                               : -4.47
Rho-squared vs equal shares              :  0.9135
Adj.Rho-squared vs equal shares          :  0.0807
Rho-squared vs observed shares           :  0.8976
Adj.Rho-squared vs observed shares       :  -0.0418
AIC                                     :  94.94
BIC                                     :  174.49

Estimated parameters                    : 43
Time taken (hh:mm:ss)                   :  00:00:44.15
     pre-estimation                     :  00:00:6.51
     estimation                         :  00:00:37.33
     post-estimation                    :  00:00:0.31
Iterations                              :  200 (Iteration limit)

Unconstrained optimisation.

Estimates:
                     Estimate        s.e.   t.rat.(0)    Rob.s.e. Rob.t.rat.(0)
asc_alt1              0.00000          NA          NA          NA            NA
asc_alt2           -116.89110          NA          NA          NA            NA
asc_alt3           -164.34715          NA          NA          NA            NA
```

```
mu_mf               323.16883      NA       NA       NA       NA
sd_mf               8.114e-06      NA       NA       NA       NA
mu_sf               273.74846      NA       NA       NA       NA
sd_sf              -4.132e-05      NA       NA       NA       NA
mu_mh              -636.31324      NA       NA       NA       NA
sd_mh              -3.108e-05      NA       NA       NA       NA
mu_lh              -392.51146      NA       NA       NA       NA
sd_lh              -3.206e-05      NA       NA       NA       NA
mu_rk               -43.69824      NA       NA       NA       NA
sd_rk              -4.748e-06      NA       NA       NA       NA
mu_md              -136.12819      NA       NA       NA       NA
sd_md               5.553e-05      NA       NA       NA       NA
mu_ct               -23.40758      NA       NA       NA       NA
sd_ct              -2.448e-06      NA       NA       NA       NA
delta_asc2_age       -1.03204      NA       NA       NA       NA
delta_asc2_female  -192.69803      NA       NA       NA       NA
delta_asc2_educ      93.27692      NA       NA       NA       NA
delta_asc3_age        3.81150      NA       NA       NA       NA
delta_asc3_female   102.81802      NA       NA       NA       NA
delta_asc3_educ     -82.31368      NA       NA       NA       NA
delta_mf_age        -14.39692      NA       NA       NA       NA
delta_sf_age        -13.25869      NA       NA       NA       NA
delta_mf_female      23.51976      NA       NA       NA       NA
delta_sf_female    -186.69593      NA       NA       NA       NA
delta_mf_educ       167.08470      NA       NA       NA       NA
delta_sf_educ       231.61049      NA       NA       NA       NA
delta_mh_age          7.13318      NA       NA       NA       NA
delta_lh_age          5.98390      NA       NA       NA       NA
delta_mh_female     232.96394      NA       NA       NA       NA
delta_lh_female      60.03318      NA       NA       NA       NA
delta_mh_educ        19.93970      NA       NA       NA       NA
delta_lh_educ        17.80249      NA       NA       NA       NA
delta_rk_age          0.03765      NA       NA       NA       NA
delta_md_age         11.88717      NA       NA       NA       NA
delta_rk_female      20.23079      NA       NA       NA       NA
delta_md_female      77.90125      NA       NA       NA       NA
delta_rk_educ         6.95355      NA       NA       NA       NA
delta_md_educ      -207.09940      NA       NA       NA       NA
delta_ct_age          0.45870      NA       NA       NA       NA
delta_ct_female       1.14214      NA       NA       NA       NA
delta_ct_educ        -1.81272      NA       NA       NA       NA
```

For example, if we attempt to estimate our model using only 50 observations from the first five individuals, convergence cannot be achieved due to insufficient information in the dataset to estimate such a complex model. The output of this unsuccessful estimation process is shown below.

### Interpreting Coefficient Estimates

The interpretation of the estimated coefficients here is similar to the interpretation of the coefficients in the MNL model. Focusing on the normally distributed coefficients, the mean parameters represent the average population preferences, while the standard deviations represent the variability of the preferences across the population.

Due the presence of mean-shifters, the interpretation of all coefficients must take into account the interactions with socio-demographic variables. For example, the coefficient $\beta_{sf,n}$ represents the utility of the *SmallFarms* attribute and is distributed normally. Its estimated distribution is $N(0.545 + (-0.003)\ age_n + (-0.061)\ female_n + (-0.093)\ education_n, 0.036)$.

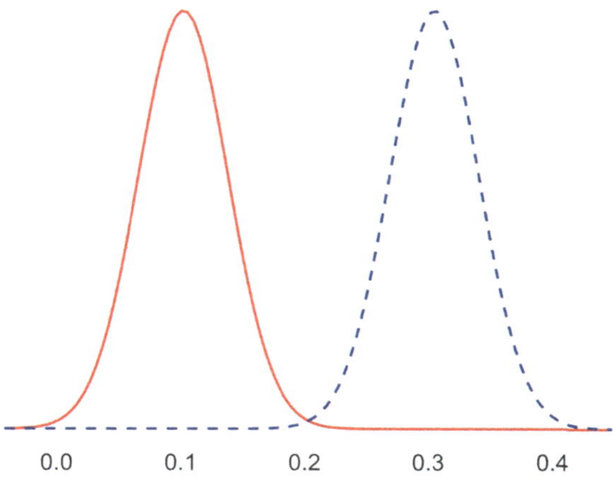


**Fig. 9.1** Estimated distributions of the coefficient of the attribute *SmallFarms* across different socio-demographic profiles

This means that its estimated distribution for a 30-year-old female with a high level of education is $N$ $(0.545 + (-0.003) \cdot 30 + (-0.061) \cdot 1 + (-0.093) \cdot 3, 0.036)$, that is $N$ $(0.102, 0.036)$.

Similarly, the estimated distribution for a 25-year-old female with a mid-level education is $N(0.545 + (-0.003) \cdot 25 + (-0.061) \cdot 1 + (-0.093) \cdot 1, 0.036)$, that is $N$ $(0.305, 0.036)$.

Figure 9.1 displays these two distributions: the solid red line represents the estimated distribution for a 30-year-old female with a high level of education and the dashed blue line represents the estimated distribution for a 25-year-old female with a low level of education. The distributions share the same standard deviation but differ in their mean values, as assumed in Eq. (9.4).

The estimated distributions should be checked for all coefficients, as they can serve as a valuable indicator of model misspecification. For instance, if the estimated standard deviation is excessively wide and the distribution encompasses negative and positive values, the adequacy of the assumed distribution and the suitability of the specified RP-MXL model should be questioned. This can occur if individual preferences are contentious among respondents and the true distribution is bimodal, with one peak in the negative range and another in the positive range. If such preferences are modelled by an incorrectly assumed normal distribution, this distribution will be excessively broad and centred around a value close to zero. This is not a rare occurrence in the environmental valuation field, where attributes can be highly polarising, leading to a bimodal distribution of preferences.

An example of this case is shown in Fig. 9.2 below. In such situations, you may want to explore alternatives, such as an LC-MXL model (Sect. 9.3.2) or a semi-parametric method (Train 2016), as these might be more suitable. Train (2016) represents a recent advancement in choice modelling by introducing a logit-mixed logit

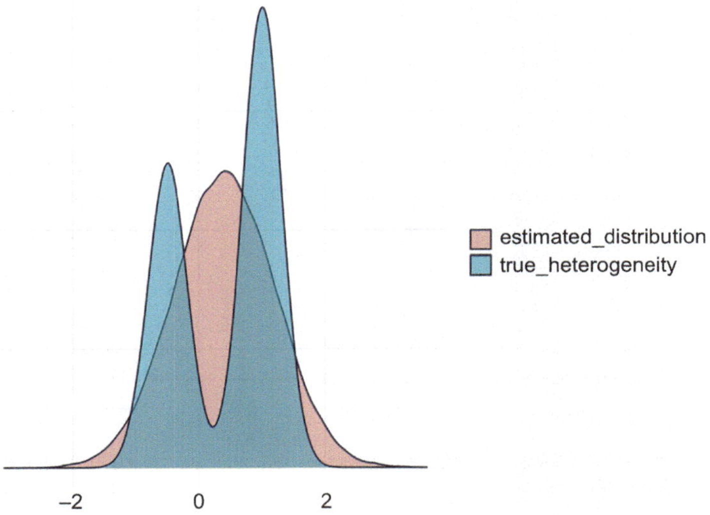


**Fig. 9.2** Polarised preferences

(LML) model, which uses the logit formula not only for the choice probabilities but for specifying the mixing distribution. However, this approach lies beyond the scope of this text.

Wide standard deviations can also be suggestive of other issues in the data. For instance, if some participants have lexicographic preferences (Hess et al. 2010), such as always choosing the alternative with the lowest level of a specific attribute, the corresponding coefficient of this attribute for this subgroup of participants will be very low (let us say 0.3). If other participants have preferences corresponding to a coefficient close to 1.5, the preference distribution will become bimodal with one peak over 0.3 and another over 1.5, as illustrated in Fig. 9.3. If we incorrectly assume that the underlying distribution is normal, the estimated standard deviation will be very high, because the incorrectly assumed normal distribution will take on a broad shape trying to represent the underlying two peaks. The solution in this case is to try to identify the lexicographic preferences and to model them adequately (see Campbell et al. 2006).

Another special case is attribute non-attendance, where respondents simplify choice tasks by consistently disregarding one or more attributes of the alternatives (Campbell et al. 2011; Hess and Hensher 2010). Keep an eye out for high standard deviations and wide distributions that include positive and negative values, as this can indicate that a normal distribution is not appropriate for the given scenario.

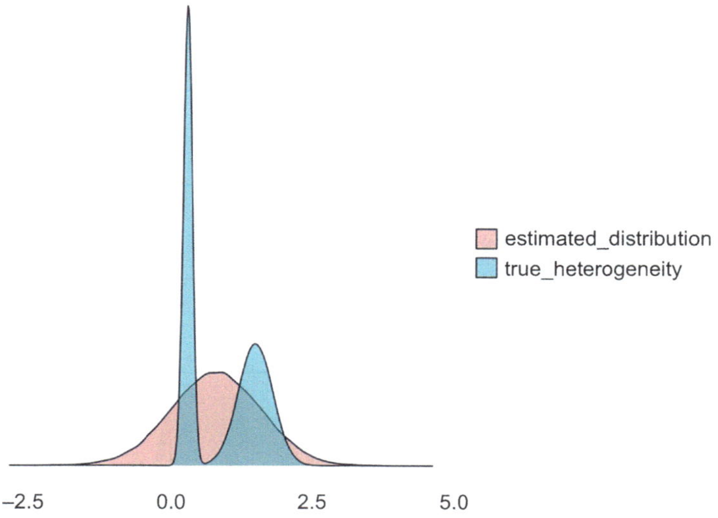


**Fig. 9.3** Lexicographic preferences

> **ⓘ Risks of misspecified distributions in RP-MXL models**
>
> Assuming the wrong distribution in an RP-MXL model does not necessarily result in incorrect estimates of the first and second moments (i.e. the mean and variance), which are typically of greatest concern. The main risk lies in the missed opportunities for deeper insights and the potential misrepresentation of preferences within the population. A misspecified distribution may obscure important patterns, such as skewness or multimodality, leading to a less accurate portrayal of the heterogeneity of preferences. Therefore, while the core statistics may still be accurate, the nuanced understanding of how preferences vary across individuals could be compromised

Let us now consider the cost coefficient, whose distribution is assumed to be log-normal with a reversed sign. Since the cost coefficient is used in the denominator of the WTP equation, values of zero cause problems (Daly et al. 2012). According to Eq. (9.5), the estimated cost coefficient distribution of a 30-year-old female with a high level of education is $-exp(N($ -0.724 $+ (-0.005) \cdot 30 + (0.306) \cdot 1 + (0.061) \cdot 3, -0.435))$, i.e. $-exp(N(-0.373, 0.435))$. Similarly, the estimated cost coefficient distribution of a 25-year-old female with a low level of education is $-exp(N(-0.724 + (-0.005) \cdot 25 + (0.306) \cdot 1 + (0.061) \cdot 1, -0.435))$, i.e. $-exp(N(-0.473, 0.435))$

Figure 9.4 below displays these two distributions, with the pink curve representing the estimated cost distribution for a 30-year-old female with a high level of education

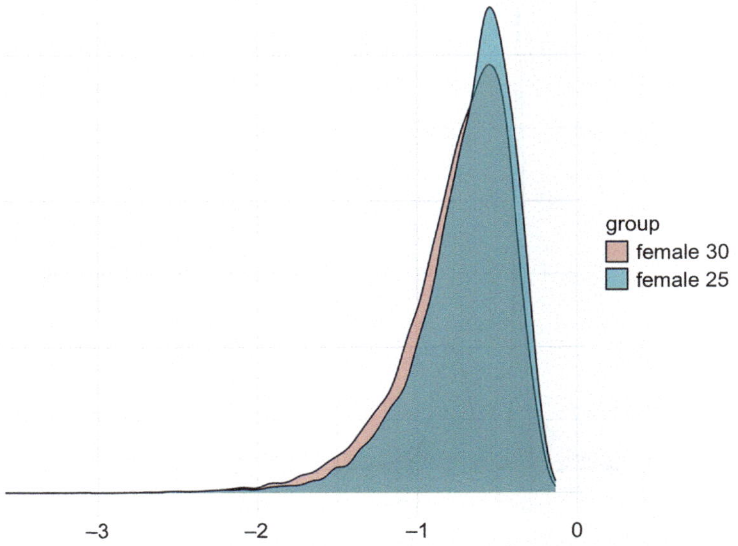


**Fig. 9.4** Estimated distributions of the coefficient of the cost attribute across different socio-demographic profiles

and the turquoise curve illustrating the estimated cost distribution for a 25-year-old female with a low level of education.

The RP-MXL model with uncorrelated utility coefficients is a commonly used model in environmental valuation, despite its restrictive nature. This is because these models assume that scale is constant across all utilities, resulting in the corresponding WTP values being correlated in a very particular way (Train and Weeks 2005). Similarly, a model specified in WTP space (Sect. 9.3.1.2.2) with uncorrelated coefficients implies a specific pattern of correlation in utility coefficients. Sarkar et al. (2011) demonstrate that the RP-MXL model with uncorrelated utility coefficients may exhibit bias stemming from the omission of their correlation.

Researchers often refer to McFadden and Train (2000)'s work showing that any choice model, regardless of preference distribution, can be closely approximated by a mixed logit model with random coefficients, to support their use of the RP-MXL model. However, this approximation does not hold true when the assumed distribution of the utility coefficients is not appropriate and/or the utility coefficients' variance–covariance matrix in the RP-MXL model is restricted in a specific way, as is the case with uncorrelated utility coefficients.

#### 9.3.1.2 Correlated Coefficients

This section focuses on the RP-MXL model with correlated coefficients, expanding on the previous section that addressed the RP-MXL model with uncorrelated coefficients. The key difference lies in the covariance structure of the random coefficients: RP-MXL models with uncorrelated coefficients assume independent random coefficients with a diagonal covariance matrix, while RP-MXL models with correlated coefficients allow interdependencies through off-diagonal elements. This section aims to offer practical guidance on their implementation in preference and WTP spaces and to evaluate their impact on model outputs.

**RP-MXL: Preference Space**

The utility specifications in the RP-MXL model, as defined in Eq. (9.3), are referred to as being in *preference space* because the model is defined in terms of the coefficients that represent individual preferences. In RP-MXL preference space models, a suitable distribution is assigned to these coefficients, and the parameters of this distribution, such as the mean and variance, are estimated to capture the variation in preferences across individuals.

The RP-MXL model with correlated utility coefficients offers greater flexibility than the uncorrelated RP-MXL model but is used less frequently, likely because of challenges related to its estimation (requiring a significantly higher number of parameters) and the complexity of its interpretation. This flexible approach accounts for both individual scale heterogeneity and correlation between coefficients caused by behavioural phenomena. However, recall that the correlation matrix reflects both scale heterogeneity *and* behavioural phenomena, and that these two effects cannot be separately identified empirically (Hess and Train 2017; Mariel and Artabe 2020).

Despite this, researchers frequently interpret coefficient correlations as solely stemming from behavioural phenomena. For example, a researcher might interpret a positive correlation between random coefficients for the size of farms and height of the turbines as reflecting the expectation that individuals in favour of wind power tend to support large wind farms with high turbines. This behavioural effect can indeed by expressed by the data, but we cannot say that this is supported by the positive correlation between random coefficients, as the correlation (apart from the behavioural phenomenon) also reflects also the correlation caused by scale heterogeneity. If interpreting the correlation matrix is relevant to the research question, a two-step procedure, as outlined in Mariel and Artabe (2020), can be employed to interpret specific estimated correlations, helping us disentangle unobserved preference heterogeneity.

According to Eq. (3.19) in Chap. 3, an RP-MXL model is based on the following definition of the utilities:

$$U_{njt} = \mathbf{x'}_{njt}\boldsymbol{\beta}_n + \varepsilon_{njt}, \tag{9.7}$$

where coefficients $\boldsymbol{\beta}_n$ are distributed according to the density function $f(\boldsymbol{\beta}|\boldsymbol{\Omega})$. Assuming a multivariate normal distribution, the vector of random coefficients can be decomposed into

$$\boldsymbol{\beta}_n = \boldsymbol{\beta} + \boldsymbol{\Delta} z_n + \boldsymbol{\Gamma}\boldsymbol{v}_n, \tag{9.8}$$

where $\boldsymbol{\beta}$ denotes a parameter vector representing the fixed means of the random coefficient distribution, $z_n$ represents the vector of observed individual-specific characteristics influencing the mean of the random coefficient distribution (*mean-shifters*), and $\boldsymbol{\Delta}$ is the associated parameter matrix. The variation due to random, unobserved preferences is denoted by $\boldsymbol{v}_n$, a vector of uncorrelated random variables with a mean of zero and a covariance matrix $\boldsymbol{\Sigma}$ with known values on the diagonal, determined by identification constraints. The parameter matrix $\boldsymbol{\Delta}$ allows for distinct mean shifts among the means $\boldsymbol{\beta}$, while the lower triangular matrix $\boldsymbol{\Gamma}$ permits various covariance structures among $K$ random coefficients.

As stated above, most published papers employing the RP-MXL model assume $\boldsymbol{\Gamma} = diag(\gamma_{11}, \gamma_{22}, \ldots, \gamma_{KK})$, i.e. that the random coefficients are uncorrelated. In cases involving freely correlated coefficients, the full variance–covariance matrix of the random coefficients is defined as follows:

$$Var(\boldsymbol{\beta}_n) = \boldsymbol{\Gamma}\,\boldsymbol{\Sigma}\boldsymbol{\Gamma}'. \tag{9.9}$$

The estimated standard deviations of the random coefficients usually presented in output tables of the estimated models are computed as square roots of the main diagonal of this matrix. The standard errors for these estimators can be computed using the Delta method (Oehlert 1992) that will be explained in detail in Chap. 10. The script below outlines the estimation of the model defined in Eq. (9.3), now assuming correlated $\boldsymbol{\beta}_n$ coefficients.

To estimate the RP-MXL model with correlated coefficients, we begin with preliminary steps, similar the script from the previous section detailing the estimation of an RP-MXL model with uncorrelated coefficients.

The first difference in the script arises from the augmented number of parameters. In addition to the ASCs, mean coefficients (denoted as starting with *mu_*), and *mean-shifters* (denoted as starting with *delta_*), the elements of the lower triangular matrix **Γ** (beginning with ch_) specified in Eq. (9.8) have to be estimated. Consequently, the total count of coefficients to be estimated reaches 58, further increasing the complexity of an already intricate estimation procedure.

```
# Starting values of the parameters
apollo_beta <- c(
  asc_alt1 = 0,
  asc_alt2 = 0.5,
  asc_alt3 = 0.5,
  mu_mf = 0.25,
  mu_sf = 0.5,
  mu_mh = 0.25,
  mu_lh = 0.5,
  mu_rk = -0.05,
  mu_md = 0.5,
  mu_ct = -1.2,
  ch_mf = 0.1,
  ch_mf_sf = 0,
  ch_sf = 0.2,
  ch_mf_mh = 0,
  ch_sf_mh = 0,
  ch_mh = 0.1,
  ch_mf_lh = 0,
  ch_sf_lh = 0,
  ch_mh_lh = 0,
  ch_lh = 0.2,
  ch_mf_rk = 0,
  ch_sf_rk = 0,
  ch_mh_rk = 0,
  ch_lh_rk = 0,
  ch_rk = 0.01,
  ch_mf_md = 0,
  ch_sf_md = 0,
  ch_mh_md = 0,
  ch_lh_md = 0,
  ch_rk_md = 0,
  ch_md = 0.2,
  ch_mf_ct = 0,
  ch_sf_ct = 0,
  ch_mh_ct = 0,
  ch_lh_ct = 0,
  ch_rk_ct = 0,
  ch_md_ct = 0,
  ch_ct = 1,
  delta_asc2_age = 0,
  delta_asc2_female = 0,
  delta_asc2_educ = 0,
  delta_asc3_age = 0,
  delta_asc3_female = 0,
```

```
  delta_asc3_educ = 0,
  delta_mf_age = -0.01,
  delta_sf_age = -0.01,
  delta_mf_female = -0.18,
  delta_sf_female = -0.06,
  delta_mf_educ = -0.04,
  delta_sf_educ = -0.02,
  delta_mh_age = -0.01,
  delta_lh_age = -0.01,
  delta_mh_female = 0.01,
  delta_lh_female = 0.04,
  delta_mh_educ = 0.02,
  delta_lh_educ = 0.12,
  delta_rk_age = -0.01,
  delta_md_age = -0.01,
  delta_rk_female = 0.01,
  delta_md_female = 0.01,
  delta_rk_educ = 0.12,
  delta_md_educ = -0.01,
  delta_ct_age = 0.01,
  delta_ct_female = -0.01,
  delta_ct_educ = -0.01
)

# Vector of parameters to be kept fixed at their starting value
apollo_fixed = c("asc_alt1")
```

The definition of the random coefficients is presented below. For each coefficient, it includes the mean coefficients (mu_), mean-shifters (delta_) multiplied by the corresponding socio-demographic variable, and the elements of the lower triangular matrix $\mathbf{\Gamma}$ (ch_) multiplied in a very specific way by random (*Sobol*) draws denoted as draws_ such that the ch_ coefficients become the elements of the Cholesky (Rencher 2002) related to the variance–covariance matrix of the random coefficients.

```
## Define the random components ----
apollo_draws <- list(
  interDrawsType = "sobol",
  interNDraws = 5000,
  interUnifDraws = c(),
  interNormDraws = c(
    "draws_mf",
    "draws_sf",
    "draws_mh",
    "draws_lh",
    "draws_rk",
    "draws_md",
    "draws_ct"
  ),
  intraDrawsType = "sobol",
  intraNDraws = 0,
  intraUnifDraws = c(),
  intraNormDraws = c()
)

apollo_randCoeff <- function(apollo_beta, apollo_inputs) {
  randcoeff <- list(
    r_mf = mu_mf + ch_mf * draws_mf + delta_mf_age * age + delta_mf_female * female + delta_mf
_educ * education,
    r_sf = mu_sf + ch_mf_sf * draws_mf + ch_sf * draws_sf + delta_sf_age * age + delta_sf_fema
le * female + delta_sf_educ * education,
    r_mh = mu_mh + ch_mf_mh * draws_mf + ch_sf_mh * draws_sf + ch_mh * draws_mh + delta_mh_age
* age + delta_mh_female * female + delta_mh_educ * education,
    r_lh = mu_lh + ch_mf_lh * draws_mf + ch_sf_lh * draws_sf + ch_mh_lh * draws_mh + ch_lh * d
raws_lh + delta_lh_age * age + delta_lh_female * female + delta_lh_educ * education,
    r_rk = mu_rk + ch_mf_rk * draws_mf + ch_sf_rk * draws_sf + ch_mh_rk * draws_mh + ch_lh_rk
```

```
* draws_lh  + ch_rk * draws_rk + delta_rk_age * age + delta_rk_female * female + delta_rk_educ
* education,
    r_md = mu_md + ch_mf_md * draws_mf + ch_sf_md * draws_sf + ch_mh_md * draws_mh + ch_lh_md
* draws_lh + ch_rk_md * draws_rk + ch_md * draws_md + delta_md_age * age + delta_md_female * f
emale + delta_md_educ * education,
    r_ct = -exp(mu_ct + ch_mf_ct * draws_mf + ch_sf_ct * draws_sf + ch_mh_ct * draws_mh + ch_l
h_ct * draws_lh + ch_rk_ct * draws_rk + ch_md_ct * draws_md + ch_ct * draws_ct + delta_ct_age
* age + delta_ct_female * female + delta_ct_educ * education)
  )

  return(
    randcoeff
  )
}
```

The function `apollo_probabilities` is defined in the same way as in the case of uncorrelated coefficients, with the only difference being the different definition of the random coefficients (`randcoeff`). The utilities (`V[["alt1"]]`, `V[["alt2"]]` and `V[["alt3"]]`) are defined in the same way as in Sect. 9.2.1.

The output of the estimation procedure is shown below.

```
Model run by user using Apollo 0.3.4 on R 4.4.1 for Darwin.
Please acknowledge the use of Apollo by citing Hess & Palma (2019)
  DOI 10.1016/j.jocm.2019.100170
  www.ApolloChoiceModelling.com

Model name                                  : RP_MXL_correlated_ASC
Model description                           : RP MXL correlated_ASC
Model run at                                : 2024-10-23 16:40:37.425295
Estimation method                           : bgw
Model diagnosis                             : Relative function convergence
Optimisation diagnosis                      : Maximum found
     hessian properties                     : Negative definite
     maximum eigenvalue                     : -3.470042
     reciprocal of condition number         : 6.17811e-08
Number of individuals                       : 1000
Number of rows in database                  : 8633
Number of modelled outcomes                 : 8633

Number of cores used                        :  20
Number of inter-individual draws            : 5000 (sobol)

LL(start)                                   : -7923.19
LL at equal shares, LL(0)                   : -9484.32
LL at observed shares, LL(C)                : -8539.99
LL(final)                                   : -6590.23
Rho-squared vs equal shares                  :  0.3051
Adj.Rho-squared vs equal shares              :  0.2984
Rho-squared vs observed shares               :  0.2283
Adj.Rho-squared vs observed shares           :  0.221
AIC                                         :  13308.47
BIC                                         :  13760.52

Estimated parameters                        : 64
Time taken (hh:mm:ss)                       :  05:58:34.12
     pre-estimation                         :  00:02:43.56
     estimation                             :  00:46:21.60
     post-estimation                        :  05:09:28.96
Iterations                                  :  42

Unconstrained optimisation.

Estimates:
                     Estimate        s.e.   t.rat.(0)    Rob.s.e. Rob.t.rat.(0)
```

| | | | | | |
|---|---|---|---|---|---|
| asc_alt1 | 0.000000 | NA | NA | NA | NA |
| asc_alt2 | 0.535014 | 0.338837 | 1.578973 | 0.362648 | 1.475301 |
| asc_alt3 | 0.303428 | 0.342031 | 0.887134 | 0.348380 | 0.870967 |
| mu_mf | 0.002963 | 0.250623 | 0.011824 | 0.248096 | 0.011945 |
| mu_sf | 0.598634 | 0.240060 | 2.493685 | 0.222404 | 2.691649 |
| mu_mh | 0.094414 | 0.256931 | 0.367468 | 0.259948 | 0.363203 |
| mu_lh | 0.741278 | 0.247542 | 2.994554 | 0.247383 | 2.996478 |
| mu_rk | -0.053295 | 0.027664 | -1.926495 | 0.026248 | -2.030402 |
| mu_md | 0.714672 | 0.263532 | 2.711894 | 0.248310 | 2.878137 |
| mu_ct | -0.841893 | 0.137903 | -6.104954 | 0.155661 | -5.408516 |
| ch_mf | 0.490235 | 0.103345 | 4.743674 | 0.097425 | 5.031951 |
| ch_mf_sf | 0.176308 | 0.114024 | 1.546242 | 0.113691 | 1.550763 |
| ch_sf | 0.172869 | 0.126860 | 1.362681 | 0.107043 | 1.614952 |
| ch_mf_mh | 0.486711 | 0.152934 | 3.182488 | 0.148215 | 3.283807 |
| ch_sf_mh | -0.144612 | 0.245872 | -0.588160 | 0.262795 | -0.550285 |
| ch_mh | 0.316287 | 0.221808 | 1.425949 | 0.220668 | 1.433314 |
| ch_mf_lh | 0.251800 | 0.177202 | 1.420978 | 0.198264 | 1.270025 |
| ch_sf_lh | 0.137092 | 0.293094 | 0.467742 | 0.324314 | 0.422715 |
| ch_mh_lh | 0.106585 | 0.295636 | 0.360527 | 0.301888 | 0.353060 |
| ch_lh | 0.418328 | 0.153809 | 2.719792 | 0.150570 | 2.778300 |
| ch_mf_rk | 0.023628 | 0.014234 | 1.659945 | 0.012790 | 1.847424 |
| ch_sf_rk | -0.016555 | 0.019942 | -0.830169 | 0.015126 | -1.094489 |
| ch_mh_rk | -0.014733 | 0.020735 | -0.710550 | 0.014059 | -1.047970 |
| ch_lh_rk | 1.5291e-04 | 0.021129 | 0.007237 | 0.016360 | 0.009347 |
| ch_rk | 0.001591 | 0.032735 | 0.048607 | 0.012106 | 0.131430 |
| ch_mf_md | 0.004970 | 0.153176 | 0.032448 | 0.155153 | 0.032034 |
| ch_sf_md | 0.214155 | 0.181372 | 1.180750 | 0.173300 | 1.235749 |
| ch_mh_md | -0.011233 | 0.216112 | -0.051976 | 0.194806 | -0.057661 |
| ch_lh_md | -0.182648 | 0.183823 | -0.993608 | 0.150082 | -1.216985 |
| ch_rk_md | 0.063685 | 0.263271 | 0.241898 | 0.084218 | 0.756186 |
| ch_md | -0.034142 | 0.294210 | -0.116047 | 0.138115 | -0.247201 |
| ch_mf_ct | 0.494859 | 0.082030 | 6.032644 | 0.078945 | 6.268394 |
| ch_sf_ct | 0.257626 | 0.166296 | 1.549208 | 0.163444 | 1.576236 |
| ch_mh_ct | 0.308969 | 0.139615 | 2.213007 | 0.097312 | 3.175024 |
| ch_lh_ct | -0.018202 | 0.153552 | -0.118537 | 0.115245 | -0.157938 |
| ch_rk_ct | 0.091379 | 0.149493 | 0.611261 | 0.084871 | 1.076685 |
| ch_md_ct | -0.016603 | 0.190697 | -0.087068 | 0.184307 | -0.090086 |
| ch_ct | 0.071605 | 0.131021 | 0.546515 | 0.079062 | 0.905683 |
| delta_asc2_age | 0.013081 | 0.006310 | 2.072968 | 0.007502 | 1.743767 |
| delta_asc2_female | 0.296190 | 0.157663 | 1.878630 | 0.162978 | 1.817364 |
| delta_asc2_educ | -0.094243 | 0.095923 | -0.982494 | 0.099538 | -0.946813 |
| delta_asc3_age | 0.014686 | 0.006383 | 2.300871 | 0.007361 | 1.995265 |
| delta_asc3_female | 0.333260 | 0.160644 | 2.074527 | 0.163370 | 2.039910 |
| delta_asc3_educ | -0.012678 | 0.097301 | -0.130299 | 0.100011 | -0.126768 |
| delta_mf_age | -0.005781 | 0.004307 | -1.342420 | 0.004339 | -1.332377 |
| delta_sf_age | -0.001172 | 0.004184 | -0.280109 | 0.004150 | -0.282435 |
| delta_mf_female | 0.059304 | 0.118137 | 0.501998 | 0.116145 | 0.510604 |
| delta_sf_female | -0.046371 | 0.112970 | -0.410471 | 0.109487 | -0.423531 |
| delta_mf_educ | 0.045787 | 0.070853 | 0.646223 | 0.069139 | 0.662248 |
| delta_sf_educ | -0.126757 | 0.067901 | -1.866796 | 0.065273 | -1.941973 |
| delta_mh_age | -0.013628 | 0.004444 | -3.066653 | 0.004462 | -3.054418 |
| delta_lh_age | -0.003907 | 0.004338 | -0.900543 | 0.004514 | -0.865425 |
| delta_mh_female | 0.109314 | 0.122229 | 0.894341 | 0.121878 | 0.896918 |
| delta_lh_female | 0.012187 | 0.116334 | 0.104761 | 0.115147 | 0.105842 |
| delta_mh_educ | 0.165991 | 0.073110 | 2.270441 | 0.069274 | 2.396151 |
| delta_lh_educ | 0.080063 | 0.070061 | 1.142772 | 0.068998 | 1.160381 |
| delta_rk_age | 2.0278e-04 | 4.7504e-04 | 0.426875 | 4.4835e-04 | 0.452284 |
| delta_md_age | -0.004576 | 0.004547 | -1.006431 | 0.004238 | -1.079798 |
| delta_rk_female | 0.011816 | 0.013087 | 0.902865 | 0.012882 | 0.917258 |
| delta_md_female | -0.014124 | 0.124150 | -0.113764 | 0.119169 | -0.118518 |
| delta_rk_educ | -0.009823 | 0.007863 | -1.249278 | 0.007745 | -1.268193 |
| delta_md_educ | -0.083483 | 0.074468 | -1.121068 | 0.070813 | -1.178919 |
| delta_ct_age | 0.001362 | 0.002642 | 0.515545 | 0.003826 | 0.356024 |
| delta_ct_female | 0.288478 | 0.063338 | 4.554558 | 0.065011 | 4.437344 |
| delta_ct_educ | 0.009620 | 0.038989 | 0.246725 | 0.042524 | 0.226217 |

The main complexity of this model lies in recovering the variance–covariance matrix of the random coefficients, especially the estimated standard deviations. The mean parameters $\mu$ related to normal distributions represent the mean of the distribution, but the estimated elements of the matrix $\mathbf{\Gamma}$ displayed in the output table (`ch_`) do not have a direct interpretation or meaning.

The standard deviations of the underlying assumed distributions of the random coefficients must be recovered through the following procedure based on Eq. (9.9), with the code chunk in R shown below.

The estimated matrix $\mathbf{\Gamma}$ is defined as

$$\widehat{\Gamma} = \begin{bmatrix} 0.490 & 0 & 0 & 0 & 0 & 0 & 0 \\ 0.176 & 0.173 & 0 & 0 & 0 & 0 & 0 \\ 0.487 & -0.145 & 0.316 & 0 & 0 & 0 & 0 \\ 0.252 & 0.137 & 0.107 & 0.418 & 0 & 0 & 0 \\ 0.024 & -0.017 & -0.015 & 0.000 & 0.002 & 0 & 0 \\ 0.005 & 0.214 & -0.011 & -0.183 & 0.064 & -0.034 & 0 \\ 0.495 & 0.258 & 0.309 & -0.018 & 0.091 & -0.017 & 0.072 \end{bmatrix}.$$

According to Eq. (9.9), the full variance–covariance matrix of the random coefficients is:

$$Var(\boldsymbol{\beta}_n) = \mathbf{\Gamma}\,\mathbf{\Sigma}\,\mathbf{\Gamma}'.$$

As $\mathbf{\Sigma} = \boldsymbol{I}$, because of the identification restriction imposed by our RP-MXL model, the estimated variance–covariance matrix of the random coefficients is defined as:

$$\widehat{Var}\left(\widehat{\boldsymbol{\beta}}_n\right) = \widehat{\mathbf{\Gamma}}\widehat{\mathbf{\Gamma}}'$$

We will carry out this computation in R with the code chunk below.

```
# Create a zero matrix
gamma <- matrix(0, nrow = 7, ncol = 7)

# Given how we have stored the parameters, we can fill the upper triangular of
# a zero matrix.
cholesky_elements <- model$estimate[str_detect(names(model$estimate), "ch_.*")]
gamma[upper.tri(gamma, diag = TRUE)] <- cholesky_elements

# Variance-covariance of the betas
vcov_beta <- t(gamma) %*% gamma

# Correlation of the betas
corr_beta <- cov2cor(vcov_beta)
```

Therefore, in our case

$$\widehat{Var}\left(\hat{\boldsymbol{\beta}}_n\right) = \hat{\Gamma}\hat{\Gamma}' = \begin{bmatrix} 0.240 & 0.086 & 0.239 & 0.123 & 0.012 & 0.002 & 0.243 \\ 0.086 & 0.061 & 0.061 & 0.068 & 0.001 & 0.038 & 0.132 \\ 0.239 & 0.061 & 0.358 & 0.136 & 0.009 & -0.032 & 0.301 \\ 0.123 & 0.068 & 0.136 & 0.269 & 0.002 & -0.047 & 0.185 \\ 0.012 & 0.001 & 0.009 & 0.002 & 0.001 & -0.003 & 0.003 \\ 0.002 & 0.038 & -0.032 & -0.047 & -0.003 & 0.085 & 0.064 \\ 0.243 & 0.132 & 0.301 & 0.185 & 0.003 & 0.064 & 0.421 \end{bmatrix}.$$

The corresponding correlation matrix is.

$$\begin{bmatrix} 1.000 & 0.714 & 0.814 & 0.486 & 0.728 & 0.017 & 0.763 \\ 0.714 & 1.000 & 0.412 & 0.532 & 0.163 & 0.528 & 0.823 \\ 0.814 & 0.412 & 1.000 & 0.440 & 0.476 & -0.185 & 0.777 \\ 0.486 & 0.532 & 0.440 & 1.000 & 0.129 & -0.312 & 0.551 \\ 0.728 & 0.163 & 0.476 & 0.129 & 1.000 & -0.338 & 0.143 \\ 0.017 & 0.528 & -0.185 & -0.312 & -0.338 & 1.000 & 0.339 \\ 0.763 & 0.823 & 0.777 & 0.551 & 0.143 & 0.339 & 1.000 \end{bmatrix}.$$

Recall that the correlations in this matrix include not only behavioural correlations but also scale heterogeneity (Mariel and Artabe 2020). Scale heterogeneity implies that for some individuals, all coefficients are either consistently larger or smaller than average, resulting in correlated coefficients. This correlation arises because a person's choices may appear more random (if all coefficients are smaller and closer to zero) or more deterministic (if all coefficients are larger) as seen from the econometrician's perspective.

The estimated standard deviations of the random coefficients are represented by the square roots of the main diagonal of $\widehat{Var}\left(\hat{\boldsymbol{\beta}}_n\right)$. To compute their standard errors, which reflect the sample variation of these standard deviations, the Delta method must be employed. This is necessary because the estimation procedure only provides standard errors for the elements of the matrix $\boldsymbol{\Gamma}$.

If $\gamma_{ij}$ denotes the elements of the lower triangular matrix $\mathbf{\Gamma}$, and given that $\widehat{Var}\left(\widehat{\boldsymbol{\beta}}_n\right) = \widehat{\mathbf{\Gamma}}\widehat{\mathbf{\Gamma}}'$, the element (1,1) of $\widehat{Var}\left(\widehat{\boldsymbol{\beta}}_n\right)$ is $\widehat{\gamma}_{11}^2$, the element (2,2) is $\widehat{\gamma}_{21}^2 + \widehat{\gamma}_{22}^2$, the element (3,3) is $\widehat{\gamma}_{31}^2 + \widehat{\gamma}_{32}^2 + \widehat{\gamma}_{33}^2$, and so on. The estimated standard deviations of the random coefficients with their robust standard errors are computed in the R chunk below.

```
## Standard deviation of the random parameters
deltaMethod_settings <-
  list(
    expression = c(
      rob_se_ch_mf = "sqrt(ch_mf^2)",
      rob_se_ch_sf = "sqrt(ch_mf_sf^2 + ch_sf^2)",
      rob_se_ch_mh = "sqrt(ch_mf_mh^2 + ch_sf_mh^2 + ch_mh^2)",
      rob_se_ch_lh = "sqrt(ch_mf_lh^2 + ch_sf_lh^2 + ch_mh_lh^2 + ch_lh^2)",
      rob_se_ch_rk = "sqrt(ch_mf_rk^2 + ch_sf_rk^2 + ch_mh_rk^2 + ch_lh_rk^2 +ch_rk^2)",
      rob_se_ch_md = "sqrt(ch_mf_md^2 + ch_sf_md^2 + ch_mh_md^2 + ch_lh_md^2 +ch_rk_md^2 +ch_m
d^2)",
      rob_se_ch_ct = "sqrt(ch_mf_ct^2 + ch_sf_ct^2 + ch_mh_ct^2 + ch_lh_ct^2 +ch_rk_ct^2 +ch_m
d_ct^2 + ch_ct^2)"
    ),
    varcov="robust"
  )

est_sd <- apollo_deltaMethod(model, deltaMethod_settings)

Running Delta method computation for user-defined function using robust standard errors

   Expression  Value   s.e. t-ratio (0)
 rob_se_ch_mf 0.4902 0.0974        5.03
 rob_se_ch_sf 0.2469 0.1111        2.22
 rob_se_ch_mh 0.5982 0.1031        5.80
 rob_se_ch_lh 0.5182 0.1095        4.73
 rob_se_ch_rk 0.0324 0.0147        2.20
 rob_se_ch_md 0.2909 0.1422        2.05
 rob_se_ch_ct 0.6487 0.0600       10.80
INFORMATION: The results of the Delta method calculations are returned invisibly as
  an output from this function. Calling the function via


  result=apollo_deltaMethod(...) will save this output in an object
  called result (or otherwise named object).
```

The output table above shows the robust standard errors of the estimated standard deviations, estimated as square roots of the main diagonal of $\widehat{Var}\left(\widehat{\boldsymbol{\beta}}_n\right)$.

Turning our attention to the parameters of the normal distributions for the coefficients of the non-cost attributes, the estimated means and standard deviations ($\sigma_k, k = 1, 2, \ldots, 6$) of the random coefficients defined in Eq. (9.7) and Eq. (9.8) are shown in Table 9.1.

**Table 9.1** Estimated means and standard deviations of the random parameters

| | mean | rob_se_mean | std_dev | rob_se_std_dev |
|---|---|---|---|---|
| Medium farms | 0.003 | 0.248 | 0.490 | 0.097 |
| Small farms | 0.599 | 0.222 | 0.247 | 0.111 |
| Medium turbines | 0.094 | 0.260 | 0.598 | 0.103 |
| Low turbines | 0.741 | 0.247 | 0.518 | 0.110 |
| Red kite | −0.053 | 0.026 | 0.032 | 0.015 |
| Minimum distance | 0.715 | 0.248 | 0.291 | 0.142 |
| Cost | −0.842 | 0.156 | 0.649 | 0.060 |

Standard errors are robust and calculated using the Delta method

```
# Create a nice output table with the means and standard deviations using the gt() package
tibble(
  attribute = c("Medium farms", "Small farms", "Medium turbines", "Low turbines", "Red kite",
"Minimum distance", "Cost"),
  mean = model$estimate[str_detect(names(model$estimate), "mu_.*")],
  rob_se_mean = model$robse[str_detect(names(model$robse), "mu_.*")],
  std_dev = est_sd[, 2],
  rob_se_std_dev = est_sd[, 3]
) |>
  gt(
    rowname_col = "attribute"
  ) |>
  tab_header(
    title = "Estimated mean and standard deviation of the random parameters"
  ) |>
  fmt_number(
    columns = c(mean, rob_se_mean, std_dev, rob_se_std_dev),
    decimals = 3
  ) |>
  tab_footnote(
    "Standard errors are robust and calculated using the Delta method."
  )
```

The first column presents the means ($\mu_k, k = 1, 2, ..., 6$) of the random coefficients, while the second column shows the robust standard errors of these means representing the sample variability (as explained in Sect. 8.4) of these means. The third column displays the estimated standard deviations ($\sigma_k, k = 1, 2, ..., 6$) of the random coefficients, i.e. the unexplained preference variability among the participants (unobserved heterogeneity). The fourth column shows the robust standard errors of these standard deviations, i.e. the sample variation of this preference variability.

The estimations coming from the model with correlated random coefficients do not differ significantly from the results obtained from the RP-MXL model with uncorrelated coefficients in Sect. 9.3.1.1 presented in the R-output of the model called `RP_MXL_uncorrelated_ASC`. From a theoretical perspective, the RP-MXL model with correlated coefficients is more flexible, as it does not impose any restrictions on the correlation structure or the scale parameter, unlike the RP-MXL model with uncorrelated coefficients, but even so, the RP-MXL model with correlated coefficients can remain restrictive due to the assumed distributions of preferences and the cost coefficient.

Even if the numerical results from the correlated and uncorrelated RP-MXL models appear similar, allowing for correlation among taste coefficients can, in principle, accommodate more flexible forms of unobserved heterogeneity, including certain aspects of scale heterogeneity, and failing to account for it can lead to biased inferences about true preference heterogeneity (Train 2009; Hensher et al. 2015). Nevertheless, this additional flexibility is not limitless, because the correlated RP-MXL model still relies on specific parametric assumptions (e.g. normal or lognormal distributions for random coefficients), which can remain restrictive. Consequently, if correlation in the data is weak or the sample size is insufficient to identify a richer covariance structure, the correlated model may converge to similar results as the uncorrelated model while requiring more computational effort and imposing higher data demands (Hensher et al. 2015). Thus, in practice, the decision to use a correlated specification depends on whether the data plausibly exhibit pronounced correlation or differential scale patterns that warrant the added model complexity and cost.

**RP-MXL: Willingness to Pay Space**

As shown in Chap. 3, the mWTP is the ratio of marginal utilities of the non-cost and cost attributes. In the case of the RP-MXL model, this is the ratio of two randomly distributed coefficients, i.e. a ratio of distributions, not a ratio of coefficients as in the MNL model. Thus, deriving the distribution of mWTP values for RP-MXL models becomes more complex unless certain restrictions apply (see below). See Chap. 10 for approaches to obtain the mWTP in RP-MXL models.

Daly et al. (2012) demonstrate that some popular distributions used for the monetary coefficient in RP-MXL models, including the normal, truncated normal, uniform, and triangular distributions, can imply infinite moments for the distribution of WTP. Although any distribution that bounds away from zero can be used for the cost coefficient, the log-normal distribution is the most common choice.

If (1) the model in preference space without mean-shifters and uncorrelated coefficients is estimated, (2) the coefficient of the non-monetary attribute (e.g. $\beta_{sf,n}$ in Eq. (9.3)) is normally distributed, and (3) the coefficient of the cost attribute (e.g. $\beta_{cost,n}$ in Eq. (9.3)) is log-normally distributed (with a reversed sign), the distribution of the mWTP values can be derived as follows:

$$\widehat{mWTP} = -\frac{\widehat{\mu}_{sf} + \widehat{\sigma}_{sf} \nu_{sf}}{-\exp\left(\widehat{\mu}_{cost} + \widehat{\sigma}_{cost} \nu_{cost}\right)},$$

where $\widehat{\mu}_{sf}$ and $\widehat{\sigma}_{sf}$ are estimated parameters of the non-cost attribute (*SmallFarms*), $\widehat{\mu}_{cost}$ and $\widehat{\sigma}_{cost}$ are estimated parameters of the log-normal distribution corresponding to the cost, and $\nu_{sf} \sim N(0, 1)$, $\nu_{cost} \sim N(0, 1)$.

A problem arises when the denominator values are close to zero. In such cases, the resulting ratio becomes extremely large, leading to an unrealistic distribution of mWTP characterised by a long upper tail (Train and Weeks 2005). One of the newest proposals to solve this problem, based on a shifted negative log-normal distribution for the cost coefficient, can be found in Crastes dit Sourd (2024).

An alternative approach to solve this problem are models in *WTP space* that avoid this issue by directly specifying a distribution for the mWTP values. Train and Weeks (2005) compare these two approaches and conclude that models using convenient distributions in preference space demonstrate a better fit to the data (both within the sample and in out-of-sample scenarios) compared to models employing convenient distributions in WTP space. However, the mWTP distributions derived from these preference-based models exhibit unreasonably large variances, implying that many individuals are willing to pay exorbitant amounts of money to obtain or avoid a particular attribute.

The utility of the model estimated in Sect. 9.3.1.2.1 is a model in *preference space*. Following Train and Weeks (2005), let us assume explicitly that the cost coefficient is negative:

$$\begin{aligned} U_{njt} = ASC_{nj} &+ \beta_{sf,n} SmallFarms_{njt} \\ &+ \beta_{mf,n} MediumFarms_{njt} \\ &+ \beta_{lh,n} LowHeight_{njt} \\ &+ \beta_{mh,n} MediumHeight_{njt} \\ &+ \beta_{rk,n} RedKite_{njt} \\ &+ \beta_{md,n} MinDistance_{njt} \\ &- \beta_{cost,n} Cost_{njt} + \varepsilon_{njt} \end{aligned} \tag{9.10}$$

In this *preference space* definition, the coefficients $\beta_{k,n}$ are assumed to follow a specific distribution. In our case, the non-cost attributes are assumed to be distributed normally, while the cost attribute is distributed log-normally (with a reversed sign, as defined in Eq. (9.5) to avoid problems with the finite moments of the mWTP (Daly et al. 2012). We also add the socio-demographic variables to the model as mean-shifters and assume that

$$\beta_{k,n} \sim N\big(\mu_k + \delta_{k,age} age_n + \delta_{k,female} female_n + \delta_{k,educ} education_n, \sigma_k\big),$$
$$k \in (sf, mf, lh, mh, rk, md, cost),$$

and

$$\beta_{cost,n} \sim exp(N\big(\mu_{cost} + \delta_{cost,age} age_n + \delta_{cost,female} female_n + \delta_{cost,educ} education_n, \sigma_{cost}\big)),$$

As the reversed sign is implemented in the model definition Eq. (9.10).

The non-random alternative specific constants are defined as

$$ASC_{nj} = ASC_j + \delta_{asc_j,age} age_n + \delta_{asc_j,female} female_n + \delta_{asc_j,educ} education_n .$$

This model in *preference space* can be transformed into a model in *WTP space* by a simple redefinition of the utilities (Train and Weeks 2005):

$$\begin{aligned} U_{njt} = ASC_{nj} + \beta_{cost,n} (&wtp_{sf,n} SmallFarms_{njt} \\ &+wtp_{mf,n} MediumFarms_{njt} \\ &+wtp_{lh,n} LowHeight_{njt} \\ &+wtp_{mh,n} MediumHeight_{njt}, \\ &+wtp_{rk,n} RedKite_{njt} \\ &+wtp_{md,n} MinDistance_{njt} \\ &-Cost_{njt}) + \varepsilon_{njt} , \end{aligned} \tag{9.11}$$

where the cost coefficient $\beta_{cost,n}$ multiplies the linear combination of mWTP and non-monetary attributes. Equation (9.10) is identical to Eq. (9.11) because

$$wtp_{k,n} = \frac{\beta_{k,n}}{\beta_{cost,n}}, \quad k \in (sf, mf, lh, mh, rk, md).$$

If in the model defined by Eq. (9.10), the price coefficient follows a log-normal distribution and the coefficients related to non-price attributes are normally distributed, the mWTP does not follow any standard distribution because it becomes the ratio of a normal term to a log-normal term. Likewise, when mWTP is normally distributed in Eq. (9.11) and the price coefficient follows a log-normal distribution, the utility coefficients are assumed to follow a non-standard distribution determined by the product of a normal term and a log-normal term. The imposition of restrictions in this context is asymmetric.

Under the parameterisation defined in Eq. (9.11), the variation in mWTP, which is independent of scale, is distinguished from the variation in the price coefficient, which incorporates scale. See Train and Weeks (2005) for more details.

We have now estimated two RP-MXL models: one in preference space with correlated coefficients (Sect. 9.3.1.2.1), and one in WTP space with correlated mWTPs (this section). For both of these models, neither coefficients nor mWTPs are independent. Given that we allow for the correlation of the random coefficients and mWTP values, both models account for the random scale, but they differ in how they handle the distributions of coefficients and mWTP. In both cases, the price coefficient follows a log-normal distribution. In the preference space model, we assume that non-price coefficients have a normal distribution, which makes the mWTPs the ratio of a normal to a log-normal distribution. On the other hand, in the WTP space model, we assume that mWTPs are normally distributed, leading to coefficients that are a combination of a log-normal and a normal distribution.

Overall, the WTP space model is more intuitive and easier to interpret, but is less flexible than the preference space model. The preference space model allows for more complex relationships between the coefficients and the mWTPs, but it is more difficult to interpret. The choice between the two models depends on your research question and the assumptions about the underlying preferences of decision-makers.

The R script for estimating the model in Eq. (9.3) in WTP space closely resembles the one used for the model in preference space. The primary difference lies in the definition of the random coefficients and the utilities. The random coefficients are defined in the code chunk below. Note that the cost coefficient is now log-normally distributed, and its sign is not reversed, as per the model definition in Eq. (9.11).

```
# ################################################################# #
#### DEFINE MODEL AND LIKELIHOOD FUNCTION                       ####
# ################################################################# #

apollo_probabilities=function(apollo_beta, apollo_inputs, functionality="estimate"){

  ### Function initialisation: do not change the following three commands

  ### Attach inputs and detach after function exit
  apollo_attach(apollo_beta, apollo_inputs)
  on.exit(apollo_detach(apollo_beta, apollo_inputs))

  ### Create list of probabilities P
  P = list()

  ### List of utilities: these must use the same names as in mnl_settings, order is irrelevant
  V = list()
  V[["alt1"]] = (    asc_alt1 + r_ct *
                           (+ r_mf * alt1_farm2
                            + r_sf * alt1_farm3
                            + r_mh * alt1_height2
                            + r_lh * alt1_height3
                            + r_rk * alt1_redkite
                            + r_md * alt1_distance
```

```
                              -         alt1_cost      ))

  V[["alt2"]] =  (      asc_alt2
                      + delta_asc2_age     * age
                      + delta_asc2_female  * female
                      + delta_asc2_educ    * education
                             + r_ct *
                           ( + r_mf * alt2_farm2
                             + r_sf * alt2_farm3
                             + r_mh * alt2_height2
                             + r_lh * alt2_height3
                             + r_rk * alt2_redkite
                             + r_md * alt2_distance
                             -        alt2_cost      ))

  V[["alt3"]] = (   asc_alt3
                  + delta_asc3_age     * age
                  + delta_asc3_female  * female
                  + delta_asc3_educ    * education
                         + r_ct *
                        (+ r_mf * alt3_farm2
                         + r_sf * alt3_farm3
                         + r_mh * alt3_height2
                         + r_lh * alt3_height3
                         + r_rk * alt3_redkite
                         + r_md * alt3_distance
                         -        alt3_cost      ))

  ### Define settings for MNL model component
  mnl_settings = list(
    alternatives  = c(alt1=1, alt2=2, alt3=3),
    avail         = list(alt1=1, alt2=1, alt3=1),
    choiceVar     = choice,
    utilities     = V
  )

  ### Compute probabilities using MNL model
  P[["model"]] = apollo_mnl(mnl_settings, functionality)

  ### Take product across observations for same individual
  P = apollo_panelProd(P, apollo_inputs, functionality)

  ### Average across inter-individual draws
  P = apollo_avgInterDraws(P, apollo_inputs, functionality)

  ### Prepare and return outputs of function
  P = apollo_prepareProb(P, apollo_inputs, functionality)
  return(P)
}
```

The output of the model is presented below.

```
Model run by user using Apollo 0.3.4 on R 4.4.1 for Darwin.
Please acknowledge the use of Apollo by citing Hess & Palma (2019)
  DOI 10.1016/j.jocm.2019.100170
  www.ApolloChoiceModelling.com

Model name                                : RP_MXL_correlated_WTPspace_ASC
Model description                         : RPL MXL correlated WTP space_ASC
Model run at                              : 2024-10-26 20:29:09.250105
Estimation method                         : bgw
Model diagnosis                           : Relative function convergence
```

```
Optimisation diagnosis                         : Maximum found
     hessian properties                        : Negative definite
     maximum eigenvalue                        : -2.415914
     reciprocal of condition number            : 1.41845e-07
Number of individuals                          : 1000
Number of rows in database                     : 8633
Number of modelled outcomes                    : 8633

Number of cores used                           :  20
Number of inter-individual draws               : 5000 (sobol)

LL(start)                                      : -7213.25
LL at equal shares, LL(0)                      : -9484.32
LL at observed shares, LL(C)                   : -8539.99
LL(final)                                      : -6575.25
Rho-squared vs equal shares                    :  0.3067
Adj.Rho-squared vs equal shares                :  0.3
Rho-squared vs observed shares                 :  0.2301
Adj.Rho-squared vs observed shares             :  0.2228
AIC                                            :  13278.5
BIC                                            :  13730.56

Estimated parameters                           : 64
Time taken (hh:mm:ss)                          :  06:04:22.67
     pre-estimation                            :  00:02:46.21
     estimation                                :  00:47:06.66
     post-estimation                           :  05:14:29.80
Iterations                                     :  70

Unconstrained optimisation.

Estimates:
                     Estimate        s.e.   t.rat.(0)    Rob.s.e. Rob.t.rat.(0)
asc_alt1             0.000000          NA          NA          NA            NA
asc_alt2             0.232499    0.304340    0.763945    0.373038      0.623259
asc_alt3            -0.027710    0.306424   -0.090432    0.359747     -0.077028
mu_mf               -0.625631    0.454325   -1.377057    0.438702     -1.426095
mu_sf                1.074452    0.430390    2.496461    0.405953      2.646742
mu_mh               -0.249598    0.443276   -0.563077    0.464317     -0.537560
mu_lh                1.819301    0.461973    3.938112    0.502778      3.618498
mu_rk               -0.158599    0.054513   -2.909356    0.055375     -2.864087
mu_md                1.674561    0.457772    3.658065    0.456816      3.665726
mu_ct               -0.956726    0.132796   -7.204487    0.153862     -6.218068
ch_mf                0.990486    0.145246    6.819370    0.125356      7.901357
ch_mf_sf             0.004603    0.169657    0.027133    0.151069      0.030471
ch_sf                0.312924    0.209379    1.494538    0.172174      1.817488
ch_mf_mh             1.122099    0.169059    6.637333    0.180912      6.202454
ch_sf_mh             0.015236    0.282886    0.053859    0.253162      0.060183
ch_mh               -0.142536    0.454070   -0.313907    0.201376     -0.707808
ch_mf_lh            -0.009983    0.191867   -0.052031    0.173349     -0.057590
ch_sf_lh             0.840806    0.245628    3.423083    0.185489      4.532921
ch_mh_lh             0.001810    0.512770    0.003530    0.210236      0.008609
ch_lh                0.289826    0.502983    0.576214    0.234705      1.234849
ch_mf_rk             0.073144    0.021752    3.362587    0.021150      3.458360
ch_sf_rk            -0.015497    0.039540   -0.391929    0.030826     -0.502725
ch_mh_rk             0.017919    0.059089    0.303257    0.032177      0.556901
ch_lh_rk             0.004949    0.066039    0.074935    0.033148      0.149291
ch_rk               -0.005966    0.053097   -0.112354    0.027990     -0.213137
ch_mf_md            -0.365776    0.160366   -2.280876    0.138730     -2.636594
ch_sf_md             0.034590    0.200391    0.172615    0.139690      0.247623
ch_mh_md            -0.041861    0.305492   -0.137029    0.107765     -0.388448
ch_lh_md            -0.010292    0.313409   -0.032838    0.115692     -0.088957
```

| | | | | | |
|---|---|---|---|---|---|
| ch_rk_md | 0.086303 | 0.299050 | 0.288590 | 0.143793 | 0.600185 |
| ch_md | 0.011129 | 0.276561 | 0.040242 | 0.044630 | 0.249365 |
| ch_mf_ct | 0.515079 | 0.050589 | 10.181680 | 0.047226 | 10.906719 |
| ch_sf_ct | -0.122419 | 0.101681 | -1.203951 | 0.071691 | -1.707592 |
| ch_mh_ct | -0.028040 | 0.205705 | -0.136314 | 0.106640 | -0.262945 |
| ch_lh_ct | -0.094497 | 0.170012 | -0.555824 | 0.096243 | -0.981852 |
| ch_rk_ct | 0.137187 | 0.134933 | 1.016706 | 0.073346 | 1.870415 |
| ch_md_ct | 0.009639 | 0.177799 | 0.054214 | 0.069271 | 0.139154 |
| ch_ct | -0.158872 | 0.111608 | -1.423479 | 0.056117 | -2.831095 |
| delta_asc2_age | 0.025312 | 0.005764 | 4.391638 | 0.007927 | 3.193385 |
| delta_asc2_female | 0.089655 | 0.136593 | 0.656366 | 0.151944 | 0.590052 |
| delta_asc2_educ | -0.213497 | 0.081984 | -2.604138 | 0.087803 | -2.431546 |
| delta_asc3_age | 0.028269 | 0.005848 | 4.834207 | 0.007864 | 3.594943 |
| delta_asc3_female | 0.122678 | 0.138774 | 0.884016 | 0.151438 | 0.810087 |
| delta_asc3_educ | -0.146802 | 0.082958 | -1.769580 | 0.088626 | -1.656417 |
| delta_mf_age | -0.014603 | 0.006994 | -2.088058 | 0.006538 | -2.233485 |
| delta_sf_age | -0.009611 | 0.006537 | -1.470264 | 0.006202 | -1.549728 |
| delta_mf_female | 0.503333 | 0.216327 | 2.326722 | 0.212493 | 2.368699 |
| delta_sf_female | -0.111548 | 0.203102 | -0.549221 | 0.197409 | -0.565058 |
| delta_mf_educ | 0.192979 | 0.127776 | 1.510294 | 0.123540 | 1.562071 |
| delta_sf_educ | -0.077213 | 0.121729 | -0.634304 | 0.119492 | -0.646176 |
| delta_mh_age | -0.035519 | 0.006836 | -5.196030 | 0.006912 | -5.138737 |
| delta_lh_age | -0.021563 | 0.007287 | -2.958982 | 0.008584 | -2.512105 |
| delta_mh_female | 0.428105 | 0.209788 | 2.040658 | 0.215891 | 1.982965 |
| delta_lh_female | -0.215496 | 0.212862 | -1.012371 | 0.218161 | -0.987784 |
| delta_mh_educ | 0.487053 | 0.123930 | 3.930063 | 0.122492 | 3.976220 |
| delta_lh_educ | 0.290281 | 0.127534 | 2.276107 | 0.128413 | 2.260532 |
| delta_rk_age | 9.3861e-04 | 8.5323e-04 | 1.100072 | 8.5546e-04 | 1.097194 |
| delta_md_age | -0.019974 | 0.007100 | -2.813240 | 0.007483 | -2.669104 |
| delta_rk_female | 0.060717 | 0.025688 | 2.363629 | 0.025409 | 2.389549 |
| delta_md_female | -0.026003 | 0.215336 | -0.120755 | 0.211772 | -0.122787 |
| delta_rk_educ | -0.023858 | 0.015184 | -1.571224 | 0.015635 | -1.525930 |
| delta_md_educ | -0.002766 | 0.128707 | -0.021489 | 0.128346 | -0.021549 |
| delta_ct_age | 0.002796 | 0.002356 | 1.186863 | 0.003250 | 0.860238 |
| delta_ct_female | 0.267026 | 0.060355 | 4.424235 | 0.064773 | 4.122501 |
| delta_ct_educ | 0.026211 | 0.036201 | 0.724050 | 0.038212 | 0.685944 |

The variance–covariance matrix of the random coefficients, along with the standard errors of its elements, must be derived from the estimated parameters following the same method as described in the previous section. According to Eq. (9.9), the full variance–covariance matrix of the random coefficients is defined as:

$$\widehat{Var}\left(\widehat{\boldsymbol{\beta}}_n\right) = \widehat{\boldsymbol{\Gamma}}\widehat{\boldsymbol{\Gamma}}'.$$

Therefore, in our case

$$\widehat{Var}\left(\widehat{\boldsymbol{\beta}}_n\right) = \widehat{\boldsymbol{\Gamma}}\,\widehat{\boldsymbol{\Gamma}}' = \begin{bmatrix} 0.981 & 0.005 & 1.111 & -0.010 & 0.072 & -0.362 & 0.510 \\ 0.005 & 0.098 & 0.010 & 0.263 & -0.005 & 0.009 & -0.036 \\ 1.111 & 0.010 & 1.280 & 0.001 & 0.079 & -0.404 & 0.580 \\ -0.010 & 0.263 & 0.001 & 0.791 & -0.012 & 0.030 & -0.136 \\ 0.072 & -0.005 & 0.079 & -0.012 & 0.006 & -0.029 & 0.038 \\ -0.362 & 0.009 & -0.404 & 0.030 & -0.029 & 0.144 & -0.179 \\ 0.510 & -0.036 & 0.580 & -0.136 & 0.038 & -0.179 & 0.334 \end{bmatrix}.$$

**Table 9.2** Estimated mean and standard deviation of the random parameters

| | mean | rob_se_mean | std_dev | rob_se_std_dev |
|---|---|---|---|---|
| Medium farms | −0.626 | 0.439 | 0.991 | 0.125 |
| Small farms | 1.074 | 0.406 | 0.313 | 0.173 |
| Medium turbines | −0.250 | 0.464 | 1.131 | 0.182 |
| Low turbines | 1.819 | 0.503 | 0.889 | 0.181 |
| Red kite | −0.159 | 0.055 | 0.077 | 0.023 |
| Minimum distance | 1.675 | 0.457 | 0.380 | 0.144 |
| Cost | −0.957 | 0.154 | 0.578 | 0.035 |

*Note* Standard errors are robust and calculated using the Delta method

As detailed in Sect. 9.3.1.2.1, the standard errors of the estimated standard deviations of the random coefficients (i.e. the square roots of the main diagonal of $\widehat{Var}\left(\widehat{\boldsymbol{\beta}}_n\right)$) are computed using the Delta method.

The estimated means and standard deviations ($\sigma_k$, $k = 1, 2, ..., 6$) of the random WTP coefficients, as defined in Eq. (9.11) and assumed to be normally distributed, are presented in Table 9.2.

There are many different ways to model observed and unobserved heterogeneity in the context of mixed logit models assuming random coefficients with a continuous distribution. These are some recommendations based on the recent and relevant literature, mainly Daly et al. (2012), Hess and Rose (2012), Train and Weeks (2005), and Hess and Train (2017):

1. ***Estimate a correlated RP-MXL model.*** To explore all forms of correlation among utility coefficients, implement an RP-MXL model with a full correlation structure. Start by estimating the model with uncorrelated coefficients and use these estimates as initial values for the full covariance model.
2. ***Specify a distribution for the price coefficient in WTP analysis.*** When estimating mWTP or conducting welfare analyses, ensure that the price coefficient's distribution does not overlap with zero to avoid undefined mean mWTPs. Consider using a model in WTP space for more direct estimation of mWTP distributions.
3. ***Consider restricting covariance terms.*** After considering full covariance, evaluate the need to restrict covariance terms in your model. Keane and Wasi (2013) indicate that in some cases, restrictions on full covariance are justified and lead to better model fit. However, we recommend testing multiple specifications (full covariance, scale-heterogeneity-only covariance, no covariance) to identify the most appropriate model for your data, as the best fit can vary by data.

4. ***Interpret scale heterogeneity models carefully.*** If your model accounts only for scale heterogeneity, ensure that your interpretations align with this limitation. Keep in mind that the estimated scale parameter will capture various correlations in the data, not just scale heterogeneity. Do not claim that significant scale heterogeneity exists solely based on statistical significance, as this could arise from other unmodeled correlations. Additionally, avoid asserting that scale heterogeneity is disentangled from preference heterogeneity, as they are not separately identifiable.
5. ***Correct the interpretation of models with unscaled coefficients.*** If your model includes scale heterogeneity but excludes scaling for certain coefficients (e.g. alternative specific constants), refrain from interpreting it as accommodating scale heterogeneity. While the model may still be valid for its intended analysis, it does not accurately reflect scale heterogeneity.
6. ***Implications of uncorrelated utility coefficients.*** When restricting your model to uncorrelated utility coefficients, recognise that this precludes accounting for scale heterogeneity or other forms of correlation. Be cautious in interpreting the distribution of coefficient ratios, such as mWTP, as the absence of correlations may lead to biased estimates

### 9.3.2 Latent Class Model (LC-MXL)

In contrast to the RP-MXL model, the LC-MXL approach assumes that the unobserved heterogeneity in the population can be captured by a discrete distribution. A certain number of classes, as specified by the analyst, accommodates the heterogeneity, with each class having a separate vector of coefficients.

The LC-MXL model is often misunderstood as a classification method. However, it is essential to keep in mind that class membership is known only in terms of probabilities, making LC-MXL models distinct from a classification method. Due to the probabilistic class allocation model that is part of the LC-MXL model, each respondent in the sample belongs to each class with a certain probability. An excellent discussion of different treatments of unobserved heterogeneity with a specific focus on LC-MXL models can be found in Hess (2024).

**Parametric and non-parametric distributions**

Parametric and non-parametric distributions are two approaches used to capture the unobserved heterogeneity in individuals' preferences in RUM models. Parametric distributions assume that the random coefficients follow a specific distribution defined by a set of parameters. This approach offers a clear and interpretable functional form, with fewer parameters needed due to its fixed structure. However, a major drawback is the risk of bias or misleading results if the chosen distribution does not accurately reflect the true underlying preferences

In contrast, non-parametric distributions do not impose a specific functional form on the random coefficients. Instead, they allow the data to dictate the shape of the distribution. An example of a non-parametric approach are discrete distributions (used in the LC-MXL model in this section), which represent preferences using a finite number of mass points. Non-parametric distributions are highly flexible, capable of modelling any distribution shape, and can capture complex patterns in the data. However, this flexibility comes at the cost of greater computational intensity, as non-parametric models typically require the estimation of many parameters

In a continuous mixture model like the RP-MXL model, correlation between coefficients can be explicitly accounted for by specifying a joint distribution for the random taste coefficients. In an LC-MXL model, however, correlation between coefficients is intrinsic to the model's structure, as long as the coefficients in question vary across the different classes. The distribution of preferences in an LC-MXL model depends on both the estimates of the class-specific coefficients and the individual-specific class membership probabilities

We will start by estimating a two-class LC-MXL model with the following utility functions ($q = 1, 2$). The syntax can easily be extended to models with more classes. Later in this section, we will also present guidance on selecting the number of classes when estimating latent class models.

$$
\begin{aligned}
U_{c_s,n1t} = \quad & \beta_{c_s,mf} MediumFarms_{n1t} + \beta_{c_s,sf} SmallFarms_{n1t} \\
& + \beta_{c_s,mh} MediumHeight_{n1t} + \beta_{c_s,lh} LowHeight_{n1t} \\
& + \beta_{c_s,rk} RedKite_{n1t} + \beta_{c_s,md} MinDistance_{n1t} \\
& + \beta_{c_s,cost} Cost_{n1t} + \varepsilon_{n1t} \\
U_{c_s,n2t} = ASC_{c_s,2} & + \beta_{c_s,mf} MediumFarms_{n2t} + \beta_{c_s,sf} SmallFarms_{n2t} \\
& + \beta_{c_s,mh} MediumHeight_{n2t} + \beta_{c_s,lh} LowHeight_{n2t} \\
& + \beta_{c_s,rk} RedKite_{n2t} + \beta_{c_s,md} MinDistance_{n2t} \\
& + \beta_{c_s,cost} Cost_{n2t} + \varepsilon_{n2t}
\end{aligned}
$$

$$
\begin{aligned}
U_{c_s,n3t} = ASC_{c_s,3} &+ \beta_{c_s,mf} MediumFarms_{n3t} + \beta_{c_s,sf} SmallFarms_{n3t} \\
&+ \beta_{c_s,mh} MediumHeight_{n3t} + \beta_{c_s,lh} LowHeight_{n3t} \\
&+ \beta_{c_s,rk} RedKite_{n3t} + \beta_{c_s,md} MinDistance_{n3t} \\
&+ \beta_{c_s,cost} Cost_{n3t} + \varepsilon_{n3t}
\end{aligned}
\quad (9.12)
$$

Let $\pi_{c_q,n}$ be the allocation probability for class $q = 1, 2$ for individual $n$. We assume that these probabilities depend on the socio-demographic variables *age*, *female* and *education*. The class allocation probabilities are then given as

$$
\pi_{c_q,n} = \frac{exp\left(\mu_{c_q} + \lambda_{c_q,age} age_n + \lambda_{c_q,female} female_n + \lambda_{c_q,educ} education_n\right)}{\sum_{s=1}^{C} exp(\mu_{c_s} + \lambda_{c_q,age} age_n + \lambda_{c_q,female} female_n + \lambda_{c_q,educ} education_n}. \quad (9.13)
$$

The set of parameters $\left(\mu_{c_1}, \lambda_{c_1,age}, \lambda_{c_1,female}, \lambda_{c_1,educ}\right)$ is normalised to zero to ensure the identification of the model.

The estimation script begins with preliminary steps, loading the *Apollo* library, and importing the data in the same way as in the estimation for the MNL and RP-MXL models. We will not repeat these steps here.

Next, the starting values are established. The alternative-specific constant and the parameters of the allocation function associated with the first class are set to zero and fixed at their starting values during the optimisation process by `apollo_fixed` to ensure the model identification.

```
## Starting values ----
apollo_beta <- c(
  cl1_asc_alt1 = 0,
  cl1_asc_alt2 = 0.5,
  cl1_asc_alt3 = 0.5,
  cl1_b_medium_farms = 0.25,
  cl1_b_small_farms = 0.5,
  cl1_b_medium_height = 0.5,
  cl1_b_low_height = 1,
  cl1_b_red_kite = -0.05,
  cl1_b_min_distance = 0.5,
  cl1_b_cost = -0.9,
  cl2_asc_alt1 = 0,
  cl2_asc_alt2 = 0.5,
  cl2_asc_alt3 = 0.5,
  cl2_b_medium_farms = -0.5,
  cl2_b_small_farms = 0.2,
  cl2_b_medium_height = -0.7,
  cl2_b_low_height = 0.5,
```

```
  cl2_b_red_kite = -0.07,
  cl2_b_min_distance = -0.2,
  cl2_b_cost = -0.3,
  cl1_cst_alloc_fun = 0,
  cl1_b_age = 0,
  cl1_b_female = 0,
  cl1_b_educ = 0,
  cl2_cst_alloc_fun = -1.5,
  cl2_b_age = 0.55,
  cl2_b_female = 1.5,
  cl2_b_educ = 2.25
)

# Vector of parameters to be kept fixed at their starting value
apollo_fixed = c(
  "cl1_asc_alt1",
  "cl2_asc_alt1",
  "cl1_cst_alloc_fun",
  "cl1_b_age",
  "cl1_b_female",
  "cl1_b_educ"
)
```

In the following steps, the necessary latent class components are defined, including the utility parameters and the allocation function of all classes.

```
## Define the latent class components ----
apollo_lcPars <- function(apollo_beta, apollo_inputs) {

  lcpars = list(
    asc_alt1 = list(cl1_asc_alt1, cl2_asc_alt1),
    asc_alt2 = list(cl1_asc_alt2, cl2_asc_alt2),
    asc_alt3 = list(cl1_asc_alt3, cl2_asc_alt3),
    b_medium_farms = list(cl1_b_medium_farms, cl2_b_medium_farms),
    b_small_farms = list(cl1_b_small_farms, cl2_b_small_farms),
    b_medium_height = list(cl1_b_medium_height, cl2_b_medium_height),
    b_low_height = list(cl1_b_low_height, cl2_b_low_height),
    b_red_kite = list(cl1_b_red_kite, cl2_b_red_kite),
    b_min_distance = list(cl1_b_min_distance, cl2_b_min_distance),
    b_cost = list(cl1_b_cost, cl2_b_cost)
  )

  ### Utilities of class allocation model
  V=list(
    class_a = cl1_cst_alloc_fun  + cl1_b_age * age + cl1_b_female * female + cl1_b_educ * educ
ation,
    class_b = cl2_cst_alloc_fun  + cl2_b_age * age + cl2_b_female * female + cl2_b_educ * educ
ation
  )

  ### Settings for class allocation models
  classAlloc_settings = list(
    classes = c(class_a = 1, class_b = 2),
    utilities = V
  )

  lcpars[["pi_values"]] = apollo_classAlloc(classAlloc_settings)

  return(lcpars)
}

# ################################################################# #
#### GROUP AND VALIDATE INPUTS                                   ####
# ################################################################# #

apollo_inputs = apollo_validateInputs()
```

In the final step, the utilities are defined and the model is estimated. Although the estimation process does not rely on maximising a simulated log-likelihood function, LC-MXL models exhibit a high susceptibility to encountering local maxima and convergence challenges. The Expectation Maximisation (EM) algorithm, developed by Dempster et al. (1977), has gained popularity as a tool for statistical estimation in problems involving incomplete data, and also performs well in the context of LC-MXL models (McLachlan and Krishnan 1996; McLachlan and Peel 2000). Regardless of the iterative optimisation procedure used, it is essential to perform robustness checks by estimating several models with various sets of starting values to ensure you have reliable results.

```
# ################################################################# #
#### DEFINE MODEL AND LIKELIHOOD FUNCTION                        ####
# ################################################################# #

apollo_probabilities=function(apollo_beta, apollo_inputs, functionality="estimate"){

  ### Attach inputs and detach after function exit
  apollo_attach(apollo_beta, apollo_inputs)
  on.exit(apollo_detach(apollo_beta, apollo_inputs))

  ### Create list of probabilities P
  P = list()

  ### Define settings for MNL model component that are generic across classes
  mnl_settings = list(
    alternatives = c(alt1=1, alt2=2, alt3=3),
    avail        = list(alt1=1, alt2=1, alt3=1),
    choiceVar    = choice
  )

  ### Loop over classes
  for(s in 1:length(pi_values)){

    ### Compute class-specific utilities
    V=list()

    V[["alt1"]] = (     asc_alt1         [[s]]
                      + b_medium_farms   [[s]] * alt1_farm2
                      + b_small_farms    [[s]] * alt1_farm3
                      + b_medium_height  [[s]] * alt1_height2
                      + b_low_height     [[s]] * alt1_height3
                      + b_red_kite       [[s]] * alt1_redkite
                      + b_min_distance   [[s]] * alt1_distance
                      + b_cost           [[s]] * alt1_cost      )

    V[["alt2"]] = (     asc_alt2         [[s]]
                      + b_medium_farms   [[s]] * alt2_farm2
                      + b_small_farms    [[s]] * alt2_farm3
                      + b_medium_height  [[s]] * alt2_height2
                      + b_low_height     [[s]] * alt2_height3
                      + b_red_kite       [[s]] * alt2_redkite
                      + b_min_distance   [[s]] * alt2_distance
                      + b_cost           [[s]] * alt2_cost      )

    V[["alt3"]] = (     asc_alt3         [[s]]
                      + b_medium_farms   [[s]] * alt3_farm2
                      + b_small_farms    [[s]] * alt3_farm3
                      + b_medium_height  [[s]] * alt3_height2
                      + b_low_height     [[s]] * alt3_height3
```

```
                + b_red_kite       [[s]] * alt3_redkite
                + b_min_distance   [[s]] * alt3_distance
                + b_cost           [[s]] * alt3_cost     )

    mnl_settings$utilities          = V
    mnl_settings$componentName = paste0("Class_",s)

    ### Compute within-class choice probabilities using MNL model
    P[[paste0("Class_",s)]] = apollo_mnl(mnl_settings, functionality)

    ### Take product across observation for same individual
    P[[paste0("Class_",s)]] = apollo_panelProd(P[[paste0("Class_",s)]], apollo_inputs ,functio
nality)

  }

  ### Compute latent class model probabilities
  lc_settings  = list(inClassProb = P, classProb=pi_values)
  P[["model"]] = apollo_lc(lc_settings, apollo_inputs, functionality)

  ### Prepare and return outputs of function
  P = apollo_prepareProb(P, apollo_inputs, functionality)
  return(P)
}
```

Finally, we estimate the model. The syntax based on the *bgw* algorithm is shown below.

```
## Estimate the model ----
model = apollo_estimate(
  apollo_beta,
  apollo_fixed,
  apollo_probabilities,
  apollo_inputs,
  estimate_settings = list(
    writeIter = FALSE,
    silent    = FALSE,
    iterMax   = 500,
    estimationRoutine = "bgw"
    )
  )
```

To use the *EM* algorithm for estimation, these syntax lines must be modified as follows. Note that the EM algorithm is applied in our case in combination with the *bfgs* maximum likelihood algorithm, as the EM algorithm does not provide standard errors.

```
model <- apollo_lcEM(
  apollo_beta,
  apollo_fixed,
  apollo_probabilities,
  apollo_inputs,
  lcEM_settings = list(
    EMmaxIterations = 500
    )
  )
```

The output of the model that has been estimated by the *EM* and *bfgs* algorithms is presented below.

```
Model run by user using Apollo 0.3.4 on R 4.4.1 for Darwin.
Please acknowledge the use of Apollo by citing Hess & Palma (2019)
  DOI 10.1016/j.jocm.2019.100170
  www.ApolloChoiceModelling.com
```

```
Model name                                      : LC_MXL_2Class
Model description                               : LC MXL_2Class
Model run at                                    : 2024-10-22 10:00:10.816887
Estimation method                               : EM algorithm (bfgs) -> Maximum likelihood (bfgs)
Model diagnosis                                 : successful convergence
Optimisation diagnosis                          : Maximum found
     hessian properties                         : Negative definite
     maximum eigenvalue                         : -8.200799
     reciprocal of condition number             : 2.32102e-05
Number of individuals                           : 1000
Number of rows in database                      : 8633
Number of modelled outcomes                     : 8633

Number of cores used                            :  20
Model without mixing

LL(start)                                       : -6618.81
LL (whole model) at equal shares, LL(0)         : -9484.32
LL (whole model) at observed shares, LL(C)      : -8539.99
LL(final, whole model)                          : -6618.81
Rho-squared vs equal shares                      :  0.3021
Adj.Rho-squared vs equal shares                  :  0.2998
Rho-squared vs observed shares                   :  0.225
Adj.Rho-squared vs observed shares               :  0.225
AIC                                             :  13281.61
BIC                                             :  13437.01

LL(0,Class_1)                       : -9484.32
LL(final,Class_1)                   : -7968.88
LL(0,Class_2)                       : -9484.32
LL(final,Class_2)                   : -7452.67

Estimated parameters                            : 22
Time taken (hh:mm:ss)                           :  00:01:35.68
     pre-estimation                             :  00:00:3.88
     estimation                                 :  00:00:1.66
     post-estimation                            :  00:01:30.14
Iterations                                      :  2 (EM) & 3 (bfgs)

Unconstrained optimisation.

Estimates:
                       Estimate        s.e.   t.rat.(0)    Rob.s.e.
cl1_asc_alt1            0.00000          NA          NA          NA
cl1_asc_alt2            0.59421    0.142374      4.1736    0.016786
cl1_asc_alt3            0.58880    0.144783      4.0668    0.023902
cl1_b_medium_farms      0.24017    0.101946      2.3559    0.027322
cl1_b_small_farms       0.31629    0.097610      3.2403    0.007398
cl1_b_medium_height     0.44283    0.109366      4.0491    0.036966
cl1_b_low_height        0.92817    0.109043      8.5120    0.020267
cl1_b_red_kite         -0.04578    0.010988     -4.1662  4.4170e-04
cl1_b_min_distance      0.49279    0.107172      4.5981    0.018942
cl1_b_cost             -0.74607    0.029103    -25.6356    0.017738
cl2_asc_alt1            0.00000          NA          NA          NA
cl2_asc_alt2            1.22439    0.106236     11.5252    0.013600
cl2_asc_alt3            1.22716    0.107047     11.4638    0.009984
cl2_b_medium_farms     -0.53437    0.075490     -7.0787    0.011635
cl2_b_small_farms       0.12809    0.072273      1.7723    0.005534
cl2_b_medium_height    -0.76882    0.081118     -9.4778    0.021397
cl2_b_low_height        0.41064    0.068972      5.9537    0.006477
cl2_b_red_kite         -0.05939    0.008422     -7.0521  4.0274e-04
cl2_b_min_distance      0.19309    0.080178      2.4083    0.001919
```

```
cl2_b_cost              -0.30010    0.013329    -22.5151    0.006341
cl1_cst_alloc_fun        0.00000          NA          NA          NA
cl1_b_age                0.00000          NA          NA          NA
cl1_b_female             0.00000          NA          NA          NA
cl1_b_educ               0.00000          NA          NA          NA
cl2_cst_alloc_fun       -0.15449    0.343181     -0.4502    0.354290
cl2_b_age                0.02047    0.005723      3.5771    0.006171
cl2_b_female            -0.85126    0.165067     -5.1570    0.165968
cl2_b_educ              -0.30545    0.099045     -3.0839    0.097742
                     Rob.t.rat.(0)
cl1_asc_alt1                  NA
cl1_asc_alt2             35.3986
cl1_asc_alt3             24.6341
cl1_b_medium_farms        8.7902
cl1_b_small_farms        42.7561
cl1_b_medium_height      11.9792
cl1_b_low_height         45.7970
cl1_b_red_kite         -103.6456
cl1_b_min_distance       26.0159
cl1_b_cost              -42.0606
cl2_asc_alt1                  NA
cl2_asc_alt2             90.0285
cl2_asc_alt3            122.9132
cl2_b_medium_farms      -45.9297
cl2_b_small_farms        23.1478
cl2_b_medium_height     -35.9314
cl2_b_low_height         63.3985
cl2_b_red_kite         -147.4769
cl2_b_min_distance      100.6007
cl2_b_cost              -47.3288
cl1_cst_alloc_fun             NA
cl1_b_age                     NA
cl1_b_female                  NA
cl1_b_educ                    NA
cl2_cst_alloc_fun        -0.4361
cl2_b_age                 3.3175
cl2_b_female             -5.1291
cl2_b_educ               -3.1251


Summary of class allocation for model component :
         Mean prob.
Class_1      0.5467
Class_2      0.4533
```

Given the functional form of the log-likelihood function of an LC-MXL model, finding the maximum of the function is generally more complicated for an LC-MXL model than for an RP-MXL model. Therefore, it is essential to thoroughly examine the indicators of the maximisation algorithm in the model output. As in previous models, the LC-MXL model should also be estimated using various different initial values and optimisation methods to ensure robust results. As noted earlier, the EM algorithm, here in combination with the *bfgs* algorithm, generally performs well with LC-MXL models, but its effectiveness can vary depending on the specific case.

We recommend beginning your modelling with a smaller number of classes and gradually increasing them (if necessary) to gain a more progressive understanding of preferences in the data. The probability of belonging to a specific class varies according to the socio-demographic variables included in the allocation function defined in Eq. (9.13). For example, the coefficient for *age* in the second class (`cl2_b_age`) is positive, indicating that older participants have a higher probability of belonging to class two. Conversely, being female (`cl2_b_female`) and having higher education levels (`cl2_b_educ`) decreases the probability of belonging to class two.

The last lines of the LC-MXL model output show averages of the class allocation probabilities, giving us an idea of the estimated sizes of the probabilistic classes. In our case, the classes are fairly balanced, with average probabilities around 50% for each class. However, if there is an extreme imbalance in probabilities between classes—such as one class having an average probability of 0.02% while the other has 99.98%, this could be a warning sign. Such an extreme imbalance may indicate convergence to a local maximum or saddle point, or it could be suggestive of a model misspecification.

Other indicators of potential model misspecification include the significance of the attributes and their signs, which should align with our a priori hypotheses. For the first class, all coefficients have the expected sign (identical to the MNL estimation) and are significant. In the second class, the signs of some attributes differ from those in the first class. For example, the coefficient of *MediumFarms*, representing the differential effect of a medium-sized wind farm compared to a large wind farm, is negative and significant at the 5% level in the second class. However, the coefficient of *SmallFarms* is positive (and significant at 10%), indicating positive preferences for a change from a large to a small wind farm. This is the same case as in the MNL model, and also applies to the height attribute: the estimated coefficient of the *LowHeight* attribute is significant at the 5% level and has a positive sign, indicating that respondents prefer low turbines to high turbines, but the estimated coefficient of *MediumHeight* is negative, indicating that respondents prefer large turbines to medium turbines.

ⓘ **Avoiding misinterpretation**

Do not compare the size of the coefficients between classes. The scale of utilities in the two classes is different, and thus cannot be compared. Comparisons between attributes should be made based on mWTP, not based on the coefficients

#### 9.3.2.1 Number of Classes

In an LC-MXL model, the number of classes is not directly estimated as a model parameter. Instead, it is determined through a model selection process. Typically, we recommend beginning with a two-class model and incrementally adding classes until there is no significant improvement in model fit or the model becomes inestimable due to insufficient information in the dataset. The choice of the number of classes is based on a combination of statistical criteria, classification quality, interpretability, and practical considerations.

In this process, information criteria such as the Akaike Information Criterion (AIC), Bayesian Information Criterion (BIC), or Consistent AIC (CAIC) are used to compare models with a different number of classes. These criteria help balance model fit with model complexity by penalising the inclusion of additional parameters.

However, we should always remember that the interpretability of the model and the practical implications of the number of classes are paramount: the selected model should provide meaningful and interpretable classes. Some authors suggest that the AIC over-estimates the number of classes and others document that the BIC tends to favour a small number of classes, especially for small sample sizes (McLachlan and Peel 2000). Scarpa and Thiene (2005) and Hynes and Scarpa (2008) indicate that, in choosing the number of classes, the statistical criteria and the significance of the parameter estimates should be taken into account, but should be contrasted with the researcher's own judgement of the suitability of the model.

The following output compares LC-MXL models with two, three, and four classes. The output includes the log-likelihood, the number of observations, the number of parameters, and the AIC, BIC, and CAIC values for each model. It also shows the estimated coefficients and stars that indicate significance at the 1% (***), 5%(**) and 10%(*) level.

```
---------------------------------------------------------------------
                 4 classes        3 classes        2 classes
---------------------------------------------------------------------
LogL              -6556.3          -6571.2          -6618.8
Num. of obser.     8633             8633             8633
Num. of param.      48               35               22
AIC               13208.6          13212.3          13281.6
BIC               13547.6          13459.5          13437.0
CAIC              13595.6          13494.5          13459.0
---------------------------------------------------------------------
Class 1       Size: 0.524              0.526            0.547
                    -----              -----            -----
 medium farms       0.292    ***       0.276    ***     0.240    ***
 small farms        0.329    ***       0.317    ***     0.316    ***
 medium turbines    0.487    ***       0.483    ***     0.443    ***
 low turbines       0.928    ***       0.935    ***     0.928    ***
 red kite          -0.043    ***      -0.045    ***    -0.046    ***
 minimum distance   0.502    ***       0.509    ***     0.493    ***
 cost              -0.757    ***      -0.755    ***    -0.746    ***
---------------------------------------------------------------------
Class 2       Size: 0.236              0.467            0.453
                    -----              -----            -----
 medium farms      -0.539    ***      -0.565    ***    -0.534    ***
 small farms        -0.018              0.154    ***     0.128    ***
 medium height     -0.587    **       -0.780    ***    -0.769    ***
 low height         0.651              0.444    ***     0.411    ***
 red kite          -0.074    **       -0.064    ***    -0.059    ***
 minimum distance   0.014              0.200    ***     0.193    ***
 cost              -0.326    ***      -0.326    ***    -0.300    ***
---------------------------------------------------------------------
Class 3       Size: 0.007              0.007
                    -----              -----
 medium farms       0.022              0.028    ***
 small farms       -0.624    ***      -0.625    ***
 medium height      0.332    ***       0.327    ***
 low height        -0.274    ***      -0.264    ***
 red kite           0.061    ***       0.062    ***
 minimum distance -0.962     ***      -0.947    ***
 cost               0.585    ***       0.583    ***
---------------------------------------------------------------------
Class 4       Size: 0.233
                    -----
 medium farms      -0.602    ***
 small farms        0.306
 medium height     -0.970
 low height         0.264
 red kite          -0.057    ***
 minimum distance   0.391
 cost              -0.331    ***
```

We will begin our comparison of the models with the first row of the table, the log-likelihood. We observe that the four-class model has the highest log-likelihood value, followed by the three-class and then the two-class model. This outcome is expected, as more parameters generally allow for a better fit. However, increasing the number of parameters with additional classes can lead to overfitting. While the four-class model has the lowest AIC value, the two-class model has the lowest BIC and CAIC values, as these information criteria include greater penalisations for an increased number of parameters.

Next, we turn our attention to the estimated coefficients. The two-class model shows signs of having two balanced classes, such as coefficients for all classes being significant and exhibiting the expected signs. In contrast, the three-class model includes a very small third class (see `Size` in the output table, indicating the percentage of the sample included in this class) as well as an unexpected positive sign for the cost attribute, indicating overfitting. The four-class model also includes a very small third class, and retains the problematic positive cost coefficient for this class.

Therefore, considering both the interpretability of the classes and the BIC and CAIC information criteria, the two-class model emerges as the most appropriate for our data.

## 9.4 Extensions of the RP-MXL and the LC-MXL Model

In this chapter, we have introduced the standard modelling approaches that account for observed and unobserved heterogeneity, based on RP-MXL and LC-MXL models. There are many different extensions of these models as well as different modelling approaches that can be applied to different research questions and data structures to fit your specific research context.

The most direct extension of these two approaches involves a model that assumes a latent class structure for unobserved heterogeneity, while also permitting heterogeneity within each class. This is accomplished by allowing the coefficients within each latent class to follow a continuous distribution. See Campbell et al. (2010b) for more details on this approach.

The LC-MXL model has seen an increasing number of applications that do not aim to explore unobserved heterogeneity, but reveal information processing and decision rule heterogeneity instead. This approach is called a confirmatory approach (Hess 2024), as a priori restrictions are imposed on the model and parameters are subsequently estimated given these constraints, which can be applied to the class membership model or the class-specific choice probabilities (Hess 2024). Prominent examples of this type of application include models aiming to attribute processing strategies, such as attribute non-attendance (Scarpa et al. 2009).

Another family of models coming from the extension of RP-MXL and LC-MXL models is known as hybrid choice models (HCM), or integrated choice and latent variable (ICLV) models. The goal of HCMs, as outlined by Ben-Akiva and McFadden (2002), is to extend the traditional random utility maximisation (RUM) model by incorporating a behavioural approach, thus enhancing the predictive power of choice models. HCMs provide a promising framework for including factors like attitudes, which are often measured in environmental valuation studies. Although the application of HCMs has become more common in environmental valuation, the debate regarding their suitability has mainly occurred in the transportation literature. Chorus and Kroesen (2017) offered a pointed critique of the HCM, while Vij and Walker (2016) discussed the conditions under which hybrid models might be beneficial. See Mariel et al. (2024) for a review of recent applications of this model in environmental valuation studies.

The recently introduced logit-mixed logit (LML) model by Train (2016) represents a significant advancement in choice modelling. It generalises many earlier parametric and semi- or nonparametric methods to better capture preference heterogeneity. This approach provides a flexible method for representing the distribution of random coefficients in mixed logit models. In the LML model, a logit formula is used not only for the choice probabilities but also to specify the mixing distribution.

These are just a few examples of the extensions of the RP-MXL and LC-MXL models, but there are many more extensions that can be applied to different research questions and data structures, which we do not have space to cover here. Remember that this is a continuously evolving field—make sure to consult the most recent literature to stay informed about the latest developments, and check to see if they are advantageous for your research context before delving into your next DCE project.

## 9.5 Key Takeaways

- The MNL model should be the initial model used to estimate discrete choice behaviour. It helps us understand individuals' choices and preferences and reveals basic patterns in choice behaviour, providing a critical foundation before moving on to more complex models.
- It is important to explore both observed and unobserved preference heterogeneity in your analysis. Start by examining observed heterogeneity to capture variations that can be directly measured, and then consider unobserved heterogeneity to account for differences that are not immediately visible.
- When modelling unobserved heterogeneity, keep the variables used to analyse observed heterogeneity in the model. It is crucial to incorporate both types of heterogeneity to ensure that the model accurately reflects all sources of variation and provides a comprehensive understanding of choice behaviour.
- Employing different optimisation algorithms and experimenting with diverse starting values can help you explore different regions of the parameter space and improve the chances of finding the global maximum.
- Evaluate a wide range of model specifications before finalising your model. Although no model perfectly captures the recorded choice data, testing various specifications helps identify the best model by comparing how well different models fit the data and addressing their limitations.
- Finding the best choice model for your data involves more than just statistical indicators. Consider your specific research context, including the research questions and assumptions about decision-makers' preferences, as these factors influence the model selection process. Ensure that the selected model aligns with the study's objectives and underlying assumptions.

## Bibliography

Ben-Akiva M, McFadden D (2002) Hybrid choice models: progress and challenges. Mark Lett 13:163–175. https://doi.org/10.1023/A:1020254301302

Boeri M, Saure D, Schacht A et al (2020) Modeling heterogeneity in patients' preferences for psoriasis treatments in a multicountry study: a comparison between random-parameters logit and latent class approaches. Pharmacoeconomics 38(6):593–606. https://doi.org/10.1007/s40273-020-00894-7

Campbell D, Boeri M, Longo A (2010a) Accommodating heterogeneity for reducing traffic pollution: a 'mixed' latent class approach. https://api.semanticscholar.org/CorpusID:127482608

Campbell D, Hess S, Scarpa R, Rose JM (2010b) Accommodating coefficient outliers in discrete choice modelling: a comparison of discrete and continuous mixing approaches. In: Hess S, Daly A (eds) Choice modelling: the state-of-the-art and the state-of-practice. Emerald Group Publishing Limited, Leeds, pp 331–352. https://doi.org/10.1108/9781849507738-015

Campbell D, Hensher DA, Scarpa R (2011) Non-attendance to attributes in environmental choice analysis: a latent class specification. J Environ Plan Manag 54(8):1061–1076. https://doi.org/10.1080/09640568.2010.549367

Campbell D, Hutchinson WG, Scarpa R (2006) Lexicographic preferences in discrete choice experiments: consequences on individual-specific willingness to pay estimates. FEEM working paper 128.06:1–22. https://doi.org/10.2139/ssrn.936933

Chorus CG, Kroesen M (2017) On the (im-)possibility of deriving transport policy implications from hybrid choice models. Transp Policy 36:217–222. https://doi.org/10.1016/j.tranpol.2014.09.001

Crastes dit Sourd R (2024) A new empirical approach for mitigating exploding implicit prices in mixed multinomial logit models. Am J Agric Econ 106(1):76–95. https://doi.org/10.1111/ajae.12367

Croissant Y (2013) Mlogit: multinomial logit models. https://CRAN.R-project.org/package=mlogit

Czajkowski M, Budziński W (2019) Simulation error in maximum likelihood estimation of discrete choice models. J Choice Model 31:73–85. https://doi.org/10.1016/j.jocm.2019.04.003

Daly A, Hess S, Train K (2012) Assuring finite moments for willingness to pay in random coefficient models. Transportation 39(1):19–31. https://doi.org/10.1007/s11116-011-9331-3

Dempster AP, Laird NM, Rubin DB (1977) Maximum likelihood from incomplete data via the em algorithm. J R Stat Soc: Ser B 39(1):1–38. https://doi.org/10.1111/j.2517-6161.1977.tb01600.x

Donald SG, Maddala GS (1993) Identifying outliers and influential observations in econometric models. In: Handbook of Statistics, 11th edn. Elsevier, pp 663–701. https://doi.org/10.1016/S0169-7161(05)80059-8

Dumont J, Keller J, Carpenter C (2019) RSGHB: functions for hierarchical bayesian estimation: a flexible approach. https://CRAN.R-project.org/package=RSGHB

Fiebig DG, Keane MP, Louviere J, Wasi N (2010) The generalized multinomial logit model: accounting for scale and coefficient heterogeneity. Mark Sci 29(3):393–421. https://doi.org/10.1287/mksc.1090.0508

Greene WH, Hensher DA (2007) Heteroscedastic control for random coefficients and error components in mixed logit. Transp Res E: Logist Transp Rev 43(5):610–623. https://doi.org/10.1016/j.tre.2006.02.001

Guevara CA (2015) Critical assessment of five methods to correct for endogeneity in discrete-choice models. Transp Res a: Policy Pract 82:240–254. https://doi.org/10.1016/j.tra.2015.10.005

Guevara CA, Polanco D (2016) Correcting for endogeneity due to omitted attributes in discrete-choice models: the multiple indicator solution. Transp a: Transp Sci 12(5):458–478. https://doi.org/10.1080/23249935.2016.1147504

Hasan A, Wang Z, Mahani AS (2016) Fast estimation of multinomial logit models: r package mnlogit. J Statistical Softw 75(1):1–24. https://doi.org/10.18637/jss.v075.i03

He Y (2021) A general theory of giffen goods. SSRN. https://doi.org/10.2139/ssrn.3984159

Henningsen A, Toomet O (2011) MaxLik: a package for maximum likelihood estimation in R. Comput Stat 26(3):443–458. https://doi.org/10.1007/s00180-010-0217-1

Hensher DA, Rose JM, Greene WH (2015) Applied choice analysis: a primer, 2nd edn. Cambridge University Press

Hess S (2024) Latent class structures: taste heterogeneity and beyond. In Handbook of choice modelling. Edward Elgar Publishing, pp 372–391

Hess S, Rose JM, Polak J (2010) Non-trading, lexicographic and inconsistent behaviour in stated choice data. Transp Res Part d: Transp Environ 15(7):405–417. https://doi.org/10.1016/j.trd.2010.04.008

Hess S, Giergiczny M (2015) Intra-respondent heterogeneity in a stated choice survey on wetland conservation in Belarus: first steps towards creating a link with uncertainty in contingent valuation. Environ and Resour Econ 60:327–347. https://doi.org/10.1007/s10640-014-9769-9

Hess S, Hensher DA (2010) Using conditioning on observed choices to retrieve individual-specific attribute processing strategies. Transp Res B Methodol 44(6):781–790. https://doi.org/10.1016/j.trb.2009.12.001

Hess S, Palma D (2019) Apollo: a flexible, powerful and customisable freeware package for choice model estimation and application. J Choice Model 32:100170. https://doi.org/10.1016/j.jocm.2019.100170

Hess S, Rose JM (2012) Can scale and coefficient heterogeneity be separated in random coefficients models? Transportation 39(6):1225–12239. https://doi.org/10.1007/s11116-012-9394-9

Hess S, Train K (2017) Correlation and scale in mixed logit models. J Choice Model 23:1–8. https://doi.org/10.1016/j.jocm.2017.03.001

Hynes HS, Scarpa R (2008) Effects on welfare measures of alternative means of accounting for preference heterogeneity in recreational demand models. Am J Agric Econ 90:1011–1027. https://doi.org//10.1111/j.1467-8276.2008.01148.x

Keane M, Wasi N (2013) Comparing alternative models of heterogeneity in consumer choice behavior. J Appl Econom 28(6):1018–1045. https://doi.org/10.1002/jae.2304

Mariel P, Artabe A (2020) Interpreting correlated random parameters in choice experiments. J Environ Econ Manag 103:102363. https://doi.org/10.1016/j.jeem.2020.102363

Mariel P, Hoyos D, Meyerhoff J et al (2021) Environmental valuation with discrete choice experiments: guidance on design, implementation and data analysis. Springer Nature. https://doi.org/10.1007/978-3-030-62669-3

Mariel P, Artabe A, Liebe U, Meyerhoff J (2024) An assessment of the current use of hybrid choice models in environmental economics, and considerations for future applications. J Choice Model 34:100520. https://doi.org/10.1016/j.jocm.2024.100520

McFadden D, Train K (2000) Mixed MNL models for discrete response. J Appl Econom 15(5):447–470. https://doi.org/10.1002/1099-1255(200009/10)15:5%3c447::AID-JAE570%3e3.0.CO;2-1

McLachlan G, Krishnan T (1996) The EM algorithm and extensions. John Wiley & Sons, New York

McLachlan G, Peel D (2000) Finite mixture models. Jon Wiley & Sons, New York. https://doi.org//10.1002/0471721182

Mokhtarian PL (2016) Discrete choice models' $\rho^2$: a reintroduction to an old friend. J Choice Model 21:60–65. https://doi.org/10.1016/j.jocm.2016.02.001

Molloy J (2020) Mixl: simulated maximum likelihood estimation of mixed logit models for large datasets. https://CRAN.R-project.org/package=mixl

Oehlert GW (1992) A note on the delta method. Am Stat 46(1):27–29. https://doi.org/10.2307/2684406

Rencher AC (2002) The multivariate normal distribution. In: Rencher AC (ed) Methods of multivariate analysis. https://doi.org/10.1002/0471271357.ch4

Rose JM, Borriello A, Pellegrini A (2023) Formative versus reflective attitude measures: extending the hybrid choice model. J Choice Model 48:100412. https://doi.org/10.1016/j.jocm.2023.100412

Sarkar SK, Midi H, Rana S (2011) Detection of outliers and influential observations in binary logistic regression: an empirical study. J Appl Sci 11(1):26–35. https://doi.org/10.3923/jas.2011.26.35
Sarrias M, Daziano R (2017) Multinomial logit models with continuous and discrete individual heterogeneity in R: the GMNL package. J Stat Softw 79(1):1–46. https://doi.org/10.18637/jss.v079.i02
Scarpa R, Gilbride TJ, Campbell D, Hensher DA (2009) Modelling attribute non-attendance in choice experiments for rural landscape valuation. Eur Rev Agric Econ 36(2):151–174. https://doi.org/10.1093/erae/jbp012
Scarpa R, Thiene M (2005) Destination choice models for rock climbing in the Northeastern Alps: a latent-class approach based on intensity of preferences. Land Econ 81:426–444. https://doi.org/10.3368/le.81.3.426
Train K (2009) Discrete choice methods with simulation (2nd edn). Cambridge University Press
Train K (2016) Mixed logit with a flexible mixing distribution. J Choice Model 19:40–53. https://doi.org/10.1016/j.jocm.2016.07.004
Train K, Sonnier G (2005) Mixed logit with bounded distributions of correlated partworths. In: Scarpa R, Alberini A (eds) Applications of simulation methods in environmental and resource economics. Springer, Dordrecht, pp 117–134
Train K, Weeks M (2005) Discrete choice models in preference space and willingness-to-pay space. In: Scarpa R, Alberini A (eds) Applications of simulation methods in environmental and resource economics. Springer, Dordrecht, pp 1–16. https://doi.org/10.1007/1-4020-3684-1_1
Vij A, Walker JL (2016) How, when and why integrated choice and latent variable models are latently useful. Transp Res B Methodol 90:192–217. https://doi.org/10.1016/j.trb.2016.04.021

# Chapter 10
# Post-Estimation Analysis

**Abstract** This chapter highlights the importance of the post-estimation analysis in extracting meaningful insights from discrete choice models. While constructing and estimating a model is an essential step, the true value of a DCE-based model lies in interpreting and applying its results. This chapter demonstrates how to translate model outputs, such as marginal willingness to pay and changes in consumer surplus, into practical, policy-relevant insights that enhance decision-making. We explore issues relevant to these outputs and provide guidance on how to accurately report uncertainty in your results.

## 10.1 Introduction

Constructing and estimating an econometric model is just the first step in the analytical process. While these models alone provide valuable insights, their true value lies in our ability to effectively interpret and apply their results. The insights gained from the model estimation are meaningful only when understood within the context of the model's assumptions and structure. Different models require different interpretations, and this is particularly true for discrete choice models. Even the most sophisticated model is of little use without a clear understanding of how to interpret its results.

The post-estimation analysis in discrete choice experiments (DCEs) plays a crucial role in extracting meaningful information from model outputs, and involves several key steps to ensure that results are both interpretable and applicable. First, it is important to examine the estimation performance and goodness-of-fit of the model by evaluating the estimated coefficients. This allows us to understand the impact of each attribute on choice probabilities, focusing on the significance and direction of these coefficients.

Robustness checks are necessary to test different model specifications and to confirm the stability of the results, while assessing the validity of the model is another critical step. External validity involves comparing findings with other studies or data sources to validate and reinforce the credibility of the results, while internal validity

 
P. Mariel et al., *Environmental Valuation with Discrete Choice Experiments in R*,
The Economics of Non-Market Goods and Resources 17,
https://doi.org/10.1007/978-3-031-89338-4_10

requires checking the consistency within the dataset and model outcomes. Sensitivity analyses should also be conducted to explore how changes in model assumptions or parameters affect the results. All of these steps are crucial for deriving meaningful insights and making informed decisions based on the DCE results.

In this chapter, we will concentrate on translating the outputs from DCE-based models into practical and policy-relevant insights. In fields like environmental economics, deriving estimates of marginal willingness to pay (mWTP) and predicting changes in consumer surplus due to policy shifts are usually of primary importance. By fully utilising the post-estimation analysis, we can maximise the practical impact of our models, ensuring that they contribute meaningfully to decision-making processes.

## 10.2 mWTP and Consumer Surplus

As detailed in Sect. 3.2.2, calculating the mWTP for a discrete choice model with a linear-in-parameters utility function is relatively straightforward. Assuming homogeneous preferences across individuals, alternatives, and choice situations, the mWTP is defined as the negative ratio of two marginal utility coefficients: the coefficient $\beta_k$ for a non-cost attribute in the numerator and the cost coefficient $\beta_c$ in the denominator.

$$WTP_k = -\frac{\partial U_{njt}/\partial non\_cost\_attr_{njt}}{\partial U_{njt}/\partial cost_{njt}} = -\frac{\beta_k}{\beta_c} \tag{10.1}$$

For example, using the estimates from the simple multinomial logit (MNL) model presented in Sect. 9.2.1 (see Table 10.1), the mWTP for the small wind farm attribute *SmallFarms* is calculated as −0.16667/−0.41783=€0.40 per month. This represents the marginal rate of substitution, indicating how many units of one attribute individuals in the sample are, on average, willing to give up to gain one more unit of another, assuming all other factors remain constant (ceteris paribus).

In this case of mWTP, the attribute being sacrificed is money, while the attribute being gained is the change in wind farm size. Since wind farm size is represented as a dummy variable, with the large wind farm as the reference level, these results suggest that the sample is, on average, willing to sacrifice €0.40 per month to move from a scenario with a large wind farm to one with a small wind farm. This marginal rate of substitution is what we refer to as the mWTP. The mWTP is expressed in the same units as the cost attribute. Since it is a currency value, it is typically rounded to the smallest unit, in this case to two decimal places, as is common practice with other currencies.

**Table 10.1** MNL estimates

| | Estimate | Std_err | t_stat | p_value |
|---|---|---|---|---|
| b_asc_alt1 | 0.000 | NA | NA | NA |
| b_asc_alt2 | 0.756 | 0.073 | 10.419 | 0.000 |
| b_asc_alt3 | 0.780 | 0.075 | 10.376 | 0.000 |
| b_medium_farms | −0.236 | 0.052 | −4.520 | 0.000 |
| b_small_farms | 0.167 | 0.050 | 3.337 | 0.001 |
| b_medium_height | −0.277 | 0.055 | −5.048 | 0.000 |
| b_low_height | 0.545 | 0.052 | 10.431 | 0.000 |
| b_red_kite | −0.053 | 0.006 | −9.147 | 0.000 |
| b_min_distance | 0.309 | 0.054 | 5.727 | 0.000 |
| b_cost | −0.418 | 0.012 | −34.605 | 0.000 |

While the mWTP is a valuable measure, it only captures the trade-off between a single non-cost attribute and the cost. When assessing the welfare impact of simultaneous changes across multiple attribute levels, a more comprehensive approach is needed. This is where the log-sum for consumer surplus comes into play. The log-sum method uses the estimates from a discrete choice model to evaluate how consumer surplus changes in response to simultaneous shifts in multiple attribute levels.

Unlike mWTP, which isolates the effect of a single attribute, the log-sum approach considers the overall change in utility across all attributes. It relies on the inclusive value, which captures the total utility or attractiveness of a choice set by reflecting the expected maximum utility an individual can derive from all available alternatives. Essentially, it aggregates utility across the choice set, representing the total value consumers derive from their options. By comparing the log-sums before and after a change in attribute levels, we can estimate the resulting change in consumer surplus, providing a holistic measure of welfare change.

In environmental economics, this method is particularly useful for evaluating policy interventions that simultaneously affect multiple attributes, offering a broader and more nuanced assessment of welfare impacts than mWTP alone. By capturing the total utility change, the log-sum approach aligns closely with core principles of welfare economics, providing insights into how overall consumer well-being is influenced by complex, multi-faceted changes.

As explained in Sect. 3.2.2, if the model is an MNL and utility is linear in parameters, the change in expected consumer surplus resulting from a change in the alternatives and/or the choice set, $\Delta E(CS)$, can be calculated as follows:

$$\Delta E(CS) = \frac{1}{-\beta_c}\left[\ln\left(\sum_{j=1}^{J^1} \exp\left(V_{nj}^1\right)\right) - \ln\left(\sum_{j=1}^{J^0} \exp\left(V_{nj}^0\right)\right)\right] \tag{10.2}$$

where $J$ represents the set of all available alternatives, $V_j$ denotes the representative utility of alternative $j$, and the superscripts 0 and 1 correspond to conditions before and after the change, respectively. The log-sum terms in this equation weigh the utility of each alternative by the probability of its selection, making them interpretable as expected utilities.

The formula in Eq. (10.2) calculates the change in expected utility resulting from the policy change and converts this utility difference into a monetary measure by scaling it with the marginal utility of income. When direct income data is unavailable, the estimated coefficient of the cost attribute—representing the marginal disutility of cost—can be used as the negative of the marginal utility of income (which explains why $-\beta_c$ appears in the denominator of Eq. (10.2)). The calculation of the change in consumer surplus thus leverages the coefficients estimated from the DCE alongside the relevant attribute values.

To calculate non-marginal welfare measures, a reference alternative is essential. In contrast to marginal welfare measures, which only reflect a one-unit (marginal) change of the non-monetary attribute, non-marginal or comprehensive measures can reflect the value of multiple changes compared to the reference alternative. In environmental valuation, a status quo (SQ) alternative is usually incorporated in the choice sets, where attribute level values are typically maintained at their baseline values (i.e. business as usual) and no additional payment is required, meaning the cost attribute has a monetary value of zero. For DCEs without an SQ alternative—such as forced choice setups where respondents must choose between two or more non-SQ options—only marginal welfare estimates can generally be calculated, as there is no baseline reference to derive comprehensive welfare changes.

To illustrate this, let us consider a change from the SQ to a scenario where a policy option is implemented based on the estimations presented in Sect. 9.2.1.

- *Before the policy change*: Only the SQ is available. The SQ involves large wind farms with tall turbines, a 10% reduction in the red kite population, a minimum distance of 750 m from residential areas, and no monthly surcharge (€0). That means, the utility for SQ is:

$$
\begin{aligned}
V^0 &= \widehat{\beta}_{mf} MediumFarms + \widehat{\beta}_{sf} SmallFarms + \widehat{\beta}_{mh} MediumHeight \\
&\quad + \widehat{\beta}_{lh} LowHeight + \widehat{\beta}_{rk} RedKite + \widehat{\beta}_{md} MinDistance + \widehat{\beta}_{cost} Cost \\
&= \widehat{\beta}_{mf} \cdot 0 + \widehat{\beta}_{sf} \cdot 0 + \widehat{\beta}_{mh} \cdot 0 + \widehat{\beta}_{lh} \cdot 0 + \widehat{\beta}_{rk} \cdot 0 + \widehat{\beta}_{md} \cdot 0 + \widehat{\beta}_{cost} \cdot 0 \\
&= (-0.236) \cdot 0 + 0.167 \cdot 0 + (-0.277) \cdot 0 + 0.545 \cdot 0 + (-0.053) \cdot 0 \\
&\quad + 0.309 \cdot 0 + (-0.418) \cdot 0 = 0
\end{aligned}
$$

- *After the policy change*: Only the policy is available. The policy option features small wind farms with shorter turbines, a 5% reduction in the red kite population, a minimum distance of 1,750 m from residential areas, and a monthly surcharge of €4.50. The utility for the policy is[1]:

$$
\begin{aligned}
V^1 &= \widehat{ASC}_{2,3} + \widehat{\beta}_{mf} MediumFarms + \widehat{\beta}_{sf} SmallFarms + \widehat{\beta}_{mh} MediumHeight \\
&+ \widehat{\beta}_{lh} LowHeight + \widehat{\beta}_{rk} RedKite + \widehat{\beta}_{md} MinDistance + \widehat{\beta}_{cost} Cost \\
&= \widehat{ASC}_{2,3} + \widehat{\beta}_{mf} \cdot 0 + \widehat{\beta}_{sf} \cdot 1 + \widehat{\beta}_{mh} \cdot 0 + \widehat{\beta}_{lh} \cdot 1 + \widehat{\beta}_{rk} \cdot (-5) + \widehat{\beta}_{md} \cdot 11 \\
&+ \widehat{\beta}_{cost} \cdot 4.5 \\
&= 0.768 + (-0.236) \cdot 0 + 0.167 \cdot 1 + (-0.277) \cdot 0 + 0.545 \cdot 1 \\
&+ (-0.053) \cdot (-5) \\
&+ 0.309 \cdot 1 + (-0.418) \cdot 4.5 = 0.174
\end{aligned}
$$

Since only one option is available in each scenario, the log-sum simplifies to the utility of that option, leading to the calculation: $\Delta E(CS) = -\beta_c^{-1} \cdot \left(V^1 - V^0\right) = 0.418^{-1} \cdot (0.174 - 0) =$ €0.42 per month. This change in consumer surplus indicates that switching from the SQ to the policy option increases consumer welfare by €0.42 per month on average. This reflects the gain in utility as consumers move from a less preferred option (SQ) to a more preferred one (policy), based on the attributes of both scenarios and the estimated marginal utilities. The change in consumer surplus is also expressed in the same units as the cost attribute, and is typically rounded to two decimal places, reflecting the precision commonly used when reporting monetary values.

### *10.2.1 The Role of Sampling Variation in Estimating Uncertainty*

When we perform calculations like taking a ratio (for mWTP) or applying the log-sum formula (for expected changes in consumer surplus), we combine these estimates in a non-linear way, which complicates the calculation of uncertainty. Therefore, the estimated mWTP of €0.40 per month and change in consumer surplus of €0.42 per month is only part of the story. The model parameters, as shown in the table above, are merely point estimates. Each parameter is accompanied by a standard error, which quantifies the level of uncertainty associated with the estimate. Additionally, these parameters are interconnected, as indicated by their covariance.

---

[1] For our purposes, we define $\widehat{ASC}_{2,3}$ as the mean of $\widehat{ASC}_2$ and $\widehat{ASC}_3$. This is because, when considered together, they represent the average unobserved attributes or fixed differences between the non-SQ alternatives and the SQ alternative. Although it is useful to estimate these parameters separately in the model—since they may capture potential ordering effects when moving from left to right—such distinctions are less meaningful for this type of policy analysis.

This inherent uncertainty underscores the need for caution when interpreting and utilising the parameter estimates. Indeed, the parameter estimates are just that—they are estimates. As explained in Chap. 3, these are the parameters that best predict choices within the sample, identified by maximising the log-likelihood function, given the specified model and utility functions. The log-likelihood function measures how well the model, with its given set of parameters, explains the observed choices. Maximising this function ensures that the model provides the best possible fit to the data, but it does not eliminate the inherent uncertainty tied to sampling variability.

The standard errors play a key role in capturing this uncertainty. They reflect how much the parameter estimates might vary if we were to draw a different sample from the same population. Smaller standard errors indicate more precise estimates, suggesting that the observed relationship is more stable across different samples. Conversely, larger standard errors imply greater variability and less confidence in the precision of estimates. In summary, while the €0.40 mWTP and €0.42 change in consumer surplus offer valuable point estimates, it is essential to contextualise them within the broader framework of statistical uncertainty and the inherent variability that comes with a sample-based analysis.

When calculating the mWTP and change in consumer surplus, it is essential to consider not only the variances of the parameters that enter Eqs. (10.1) and (10.2), respectively, but also their covariances. The variance, with its square root representing the standard error, indicates the uncertainty in each parameter's estimate, while the covariance reflects how these estimates vary in relation to each other.

Ignoring these factors can lead to Type I and Type II errors in hypothesis testing, undermining the reliability and robustness of policy recommendations based on the mWTP and welfare change estimates. If either are overlooked, the resulting estimates will appear more precise than they actually are, which can lead to a false sense of confidence and a Type I error—incorrectly concluding that mWTP or welfare change is significant when they are not. On the other hand, failing to properly account for variance or covariance can lead to an underestimation of the true uncertainty, increasing the risk of a Type II error—missing a significant mWTP or welfare change that actually exists.

As highlighted in Sect. 8.4 of this book, it is crucial to recognise that the variability discussed here stems from the sampling error, not preference heterogeneity. These concepts are often conflated, leading to misinterpretations, especially with respect to the computation of uncertainty measures. Such confusion frequently arises from misunderstandings about the asymptotic properties of maximum likelihood estimates, as discussed by Daly et al. (2023). In a standard MNL model where preferences are assumed to be homogeneous (or fixed within sub-groups sharing the same observed characteristics when accommodating observed preference heterogeneity), the uncertainty reflected in the estimated standard errors pertains solely to sample variation. We will explore how accounting for preference heterogeneity introduces additional variability in mWTP and welfare change calculations later on, but for now, we maintain the homogeneity assumption.

The next crucial question is how to properly account for the variances and covariances when calculating the mWTP and welfare change. This is essential in order to accurately interpret the variation in these estimates that arises from the sampling error. Our goal is to explain how to recognise and handle this variability when reporting predictions of mWTP and expected changes in consumer surplus. The literature offers methods to translate the sample variation of estimated parameters into measures of uncertainty, such as standard errors and confidence intervals. For a comprehensive overview and detailed descriptions, refer to Daly et al. (2023). In this chapter, we will focus on two prominent methods commonly discussed in the environmental economics literature: the Delta method (Oehlert 1992) and the Krinsky-Robb method (Krinsky and Robb 1986; Krinsky and Robb 1990).[2] Both methods offer valuable tools for handling the uncertainties associated with estimations of mWTP and welfare change, each with its own strengths and considerations. The Delta method is often preferred for its analytical simplicity, while the Krinsky-Robb method is favoured for its ability to provide a more detailed distributional analysis. Understanding and applying these methods will enhance the robustness and reliability of mWTP estimates in empirical research.

#### 10.2.1.1 The Delta Method

The Delta method is a widely adopted statistical technique used to approximate the distribution of a function of an estimator, particularly when dealing with non-linear transformations. This approach is especially valuable in situations where deriving the exact distributions is complex or impractical, as it allows for the calculation of standard errors without resorting to simulation techniques. As a standard method in statistical analysis, the Delta method is typically employed to determine the standard errors for functions of estimated parameters. This allows us to quantify the uncertainty in our calculated mWTPs and changes in consumer surplus, based on the inherent uncertainties of the original parameter estimates.

At its core, the Delta Method relies on the idea that, for a given estimator, small changes in the estimator will result in small changes in any smooth function of that estimator. The method assumes that the original estimator is approximately normally distributed, a reasonable assumption, especially in large samples, thanks to the Central Limit Theorem. This theorem states that the distribution of the average

[2] Another approach that has been used in the literature is bootstrapping (Armstrong et al. 2001). Bootstrapping involves repeatedly drawing a fixed number of observations from the original dataset, with replacement. The rationale is that if the original data is a good representation of the population, then the bootstrap samples will approximate what might be obtained through repeated sampling. These bootstrap samples can therefore provide a reliable estimate of the sampling variance. Although this method offers a flexible and robust way to estimate standard errors, it can be computationally demanding, particularly with large datasets or complex models, due to the need for repeated resampling and model estimation. Despite its strengths, bootstrapping is not widely used in the analysis of DCE data within environmental economics. However, if you can manage the computational requirements, this approach is highly recommended.

of a large number of independent and identically distributed random variables tends toward a normal distribution, even if the underlying variables themselves are not normally distributed. This normality assumption is what allows the Delta Method to provide accurate approximations, even for nonlinear functions. By employing a first-order Taylor expansion of the function around the true parameter value, the method essentially linearises the function, making it possible to estimate the standard error of the transformed parameter using the standard error of the original estimator.

While the Delta Method is a powerful tool for statistical analysis, it is important to be aware of its limitations. Its accuracy depends on the assumption that the function being approximated is sufficiently smooth and that the estimator is asymptotically normal. If these conditions are not met, the approximations generated by the Delta Method may be inaccurate, leading to unreliable standard errors. Therefore, careful consideration of these assumptions is needed when applying the Delta Method to ensure the validity of the results.

Although applying the Delta method might seem challenging, the good news is that the *Apollo* package (Hess and Palma 2019) provides a built-in function, `apollo_deltaMethod`, to calculate standard errors for any transformation of the model parameters. This function requires two arguments: `model` and `deltaMethod_settings`. The `model` argument is the object returned by the `apollo_estimate` function. The `deltaMethod_settings` argument is a list that includes the settings for `apollo_deltaMethod`.

The most important element in this list is `expression`, which is specified as a character vector containing one or more functions of the estimated parameters, expressed as text. For instance, to calculate the mWTP for the small wind farm size attribute level *SmallFarms*, you would use `expression = c(wtp_small_farms = "-b_small_farms / b_cost")`. Each expression should only include model parameter names (either estimated or fixed), numeric values, and mathematical operators. While naming an expression is not strictly necessary, doing so is recommended to easily track the results, especially when defining multiple functions. The code chunk below demonstrates how to calculate mWTPs for all attributes. The output includes a column with the calculated values, along with columns for the corresponding robust standard errors and robust $t$-ratios (evaluated with respect to 0, meaning they test whether a parameter estimate is statistically significantly different from 0).

```
# Calculate standard errors using the Delta method function from the apollo package
deltaMethod_settings <- list(
  expression = c(
    wtp_medium_farms = "-b_medium_farms / b_cost",
                 wtp_small_farms = "-b_small_farms / b_cost",
                 wtp_medium_height = "-b_medium_height / b_cost",
                 wtp_low_height = "-b_low_height / b_cost",
                 wtp_red_kite = "-b_red_kite / b_cost",
                 wtp_min_distance = "-b_min_distance / b_cost"
  )
)

# Apply the Delta method to calculate the standard errors of marginal WTP
wtp_results_delta <- apollo_deltaMethod(model, deltaMethod_settings)
```

```
Running Delta method computation for user-defined function using robust standard errors

        Expression   Value   s.e. t-ratio (0)
  wtp_medium_farms -0.5638 0.1271       -4.44
   wtp_small_farms  0.3989 0.1181        3.38
 wtp_medium_height -0.6638 0.1333       -4.98
    wtp_low_height  1.3035 0.1232       10.58
      wtp_red_kite -0.1272 0.0142       -8.96
  wtp_min_distance  0.7401 0.1301        5.69
INFORMATION: The results of the Delta method calculations are returned invisibly as
  an output from this function. Calling the function via
  result=apollo_deltaMethod(...) will save this output in an object
  called result (or otherwise named object).
```

With the standard errors calculated, we now have an estimate of the uncertainty or variability associated with the mWTP estimates. But how should we interpret these standard errors? The standard error provides a measure of how much the mWTP estimate might vary due to sampling variability. A smaller standard error indicates a more precise estimate, while a larger standard error suggests greater uncertainty.

To illustrate this, let us focus on the mWTP for *SmallFarms*, which is estimated to be €0.40 per month based on the MNL model results. After applying the Delta method, the associated (robust) standard error is 0.12. What does this standard error tell us? It provides insight into the sampling distribution of the mWTP estimate. If we were to repeat the study many times, drawing different samples from the population each time, the standard error would help us understand how much the mWTP estimates could vary.

The distribution of this sampling variability can be represented as a normal distribution centred on the mean of 0.40, which is our best estimate of the true mWTP based on the available data. The standard deviation of this distribution is given by the standard error of 0.12, as the standard error is, by definition, the standard deviation of the sampling distribution of a statistic. With this understanding, we can use the standard error to test hypotheses about the parameter in question.

By standardising the estimate—by dividing the estimate by its standard error—we obtain the $t$-ratio (or $z$-value), which allows us to compare the estimate against the null hypothesis or other benchmarks. Typically, we compare the estimate to zero, but any value of interest can be used. For a one-tailed test, we assess whether the estimate is either greater or less than the reference value (e.g. positive or negative if the reference is zero). A two-tailed test evaluates whether the estimate differs from the reference value, regardless of direction.

For example, if the absolute value of this $t$-ratio exceeds a critical value, we can reject the null hypothesis that the parameter is zero in favour of the alternative hypothesis. The critical value of 1.96 is commonly used because it corresponds to the two-tailed 95% confidence level, where $Z_{1-(0.05/2)} = Z_{0.975} = 1.96$. In contrast, the critical value for a one-tailed test is 1.64, as $Z_{1-0.05} = Z_{0.95} = 1.64$. However, the use of the 1.96 critical value and two-tailed tests is often preferred due to their greater flexibility in interpreting results, allowing for a more robust evaluation of hypotheses.

It is important to note that the exact critical value can vary slightly depending on the degrees of freedom in a $t$-distribution. Nonetheless, 1.96 and 1.64 are commonly used approximations for larger sample sizes, as the quantiles of the $t$-distribution converge to those of the standard normal distribution, improving accuracy as the sample size increases. For the mWTP in question, the calculated $t$-ratio is 3.38 (i.e. 0.3989/0.1181), which is greater than the critical value 1.96, meaning that we can reject the null hypothesis that the mWTP is zero in favour of the alternative hypothesis that the mWTP is significantly different from zero. Therefore, we can be more than 95% confident that the true mWTP for this attribute level is not zero. This analysis of significance helps enhance the validity and credibility of our policy recommendations.

The R code chunk below simulates the sampling distribution of mWTPs for all attributes and displays them in Fig. 10.1. For each attribute, this is done by generating 10,000 random values from a normal distribution, centred on the mean mWTP calculated as the negative ratio of the parameter for the non-cost attribute to the cost attribute parameter, with the (robust) standard error of this ratio obtained using the Delta method. Additionally, the code calculates 95% confidence intervals, which will be explained next.

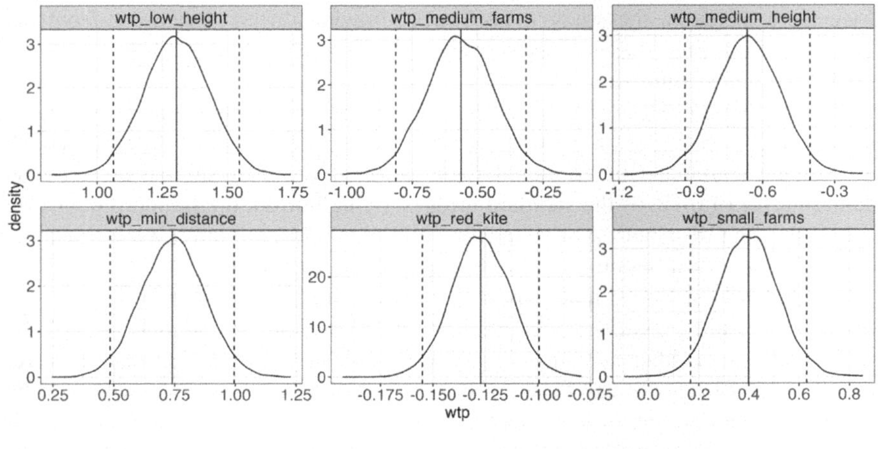


**Fig. 10.1** Confidence interval of the mWTP based on the Delta method

```
# Calculate the WTP values and confidence intervals (CIs)
wtp_results_delta <- wtp_results_delta |>
  clean_names() |>
  mutate(
    lower_ci = value - qnorm(0.975) * s_e,
    upper_ci = value + qnorm(0.975) * s_e
  )


# Plot results
wtp_results_delta |>
  group_by(expression) |>
  nest() |>
  mutate(
    wtp = map(data, ~ rnorm(10000, .x$value, .x$s_e)),
  ) |>
  unnest(cols = c(data, wtp)) |>
  ggplot() +
  geom_density(mapping = aes(x = wtp)) +
  geom_vline(data = wtp_results_delta, mapping = aes(xintercept = value)) +
  geom_vline(data = wtp_results_delta, mapping = aes(xintercept = lower_ci), lty = 2) +
  geom_vline(data = wtp_results_delta, mapping = aes(xintercept = upper_ci), lty = 2) +
  facet_wrap(vars(expression), nrow = 2, scales = "free") +
  theme_bw()
```

The standard errors can also be used to construct confidence intervals around the estimates. For example, a 95% confidence interval can be computed as:

$$\mathrm{CI} = \hat{\theta} \pm Z_{1-(\alpha/2)} \cdot \mathrm{SE}$$

where $\hat{\theta}$ is the estimated value, $Z_{1-(\alpha/2)}$ is the critical value from the standard normal distribution (specifically, $Z_{1-(0.05/2)} = Z_{0.975} = 1.96$), and SE is the standard error obtained through the Delta method. In repeated samplings, the confidence interval is expected to include the true value of the parameter in 95% of the cases. It is important to clarify that this does not reflect the distribution of the parameter in the population. The population parameter, such as the mean mWTP for this attribute level, is a fixed (unknown) value that does not vary. What the confidence interval tells us is that we are 95% confident that the calculated interval contains the population mean of the mWTP.

The code chunk below illustrates how to calculate this and displays the resulting confidence intervals. Inspecting the results, we can now say with a 95% level of confidence that the range of €0.17 to €0.63 contains the true monthly value of mWTP for *SmallFarms*. This can be summarised more concisely as €0.40 (95% CI: [€0.17, €0.63]).

```
# Print the table with CIs
wtp_results_delta |>
  gt(
    rowname_col = "expression",
    caption = "WTP estimates and 95% confidence intervals using the Delta method"
  ) |>
  fmt_number(
    decimals = 3
  )
```

The standard error for the predicted monthly change in consumer surplus associated with the scenarios can be calculated similarly. Although not shown, the code chunk below yields a robust standard error of 0.17, leading to €0.42 (95% CI: [€0.09, €0.74]) for the change in consumer surplus. Since this confidence interval does not include zero, we reject the null hypothesis that the change in consumer surplus is zero in favour of the alternative hypothesis that the change is significantly different from zero. This conclusion is further supported by the *t*-statistic of 2.49, which is above the threshold of 1.96.

```
# Settings for the function apollo_deltaMethod
deltaMethod_settings <- list(
  expression = c(
    welf_change = "-((b_asc_alt2 + b_asc_alt3)/2 +
                  b_small_farms + b_low_height + b_red_kite * -5 + b_min_distance +
                  b_cost * 4.5) / b_cost"
  )
)

# Calculate the standard errors using the Delta method
welf_results_delta <- apollo_deltaMethod(model, deltaMethod_settings) |>
  clean_names() |>
  mutate(
    lower_ci = value - qnorm(0.975) * s_e,
    upper_ci = value + qnorm(0.975) * s_e
  )
```

#### 10.2.1.2 The Krinsky-Robb Method

Krinsky and Robb (1986) and Krinsky and Robb (1990) describe a method originally proposed to assess uncertainty in non-linear transformations of maximum likelihood estimates. This approach exploits the asymptotic normality of these estimates (see Sect. 8.1) to generate random draws from a multivariate normal distribution centred on the estimated parameters, with a covariance matrix equal to the model's estimated covariance matrix. By repeatedly applying the non-linear function to these simulated parameter values, we obtain a distribution of the transformed values. While the direct calculation of uncertainty using the Delta method may oversimplify the variability of the estimated parameters, simulating draws can offer a more robust estimation by capturing the complete shape of the non-linear transformation.

In cases involving non-linear functions, the error structure can become complex, making first-order approximations like the Delta Method less effective, particularly when they assume symmetrical confidence intervals. Simulating a large number of draws allows for repeated derivations of quantities, generating a distribution for these quantities rather than a single point estimate—an approach that is especially important in the context of MXL models.

This method enhances our understanding of the variability and potential bias in our model estimates, ultimately leading to more reliable conclusions. It should be noted, however, that while the Krinsky-Robb method is effective for calculating standard errors for functions that do not involve ratios, it is not suitable for functions involving ratios, such as mWTP and consumer surplus. However, it remains useful for computing empirical confidence intervals.

The Krinsky-Robb method is commonly used in environmental economics for its simulation capabilities. While its application might seem complex, the underlying process is straightforward. First, a large number of random draws—often referred to as a simulated or bootstrap distribution—are generated from a multivariate normal distribution, where the mean vector corresponds to the estimated parameters and the covariance matrix matches the estimated variance–covariance matrix of the estimated parameters. Next, for each simulated parameter vector, the statistic of interest is calculated using the appropriate formula, resulting in an empirical distribution of that statistic. Finally, the desired confidence level (e.g. 95%) is applied to determine the corresponding percentiles of the simulated distribution, yielding the confidence interval.

The code chunk below carries out these steps by defining a function called `simulate_dist` to generate multivariate draws of estimated parameters. This function takes two arguments: `model` and `nsim`. The `model` argument is an output object from an *Apollo*-estimated model. For example, if you saved the result of `apollo_estimate` in an object named `model` (i.e. `model <- apollo_estimate(...)`), the model object will contain the parameter estimates in `estimates` and the robust variance–covariance matrix in `robse`. These are used to simulate a multivariate normal distribution centred on `model$estimates` with a covariance matrix equal to `model$robse`.

The `nsim` argument specifies the number of draws to generate from the multivariate normal distribution. The function utilises Cholesky decomposition to generate correlated multivariate normal variables by factorising the variance–covariance matrix into a lower triangular matrix, which then transforms independent standard normal variables into correlated ones.

With the `simulate_dist` function defined, we can now generate simulated distributions by calling it. Using the results from the MNL model stored in `model` and performing 10,000 multivariate normal draws (sufficient for demonstration purposes and suitable in most cases, though it is advisable to use as large a number as feasible), we conduct the simulation and store the resulting values in `sim_dists`. The resulting matrix has 10,000 rows, one for each draw, and a column for each parameter specified in the model, including those defined as fixed.

The next step is to perform the relevant calculations using the appropriate columns from the simulated distribution. For instance, to calculate mWTP, you would divide the negative of the simulated values of a non-cost attribute by the simulated values of the cost attribute for each draw. If you are interested in estimating the expected change in consumer surplus, you would apply the log-sum calculation to all of the relevant simulated columns. After computing the desired statistic across all simulations, you can then obtain the 95% confidence interval by extracting the 2.5th and 97.5th percentiles of the resulting distribution. To demonstrate this, we continue by calculating the mWTP for *SmallFarms* and the change in consumer surplus for the corresponding policy scenarios.

```
simulate_dist <- function(model, nsim){
  # Initialise matrix X to store simulated parameter estimates
  X <- matrix(model$estimate, nrow = nsim, ncol = length(model$estimate),
              byrow = TRUE, dimnames = list(NULL, names(model$estimate)))

  # Extract means and variance-covariance matrix for multivariate normal distribution
  mu <- model$estimate[!is.na(model$robse)]
  sigma <- model$robvarcov

  # Cholesky decomposition of the variance-covariance matrix
  L <- chol(sigma)

  # Generate matrix of standard normal random variables
  Z <- matrix(rnorm(nsim * model$numParams), ncol = model$numParams)

  # Transform standard normal variables to multivariate normal and update matrix X
  X[, !is.na(model$robse)] <- t(mu + L %*% t(Z))

  # Return the matrix 'X', which contains the simulated parameter estimates
   return(X)
}

# Generate 10,000 simulated distributions
sim_dists <- simulate_dist(model, 10000)

# Calculate the simulated marginal WTP for small wind farms
sim_wtp <- -sim_dists[, "b_small_farms"] / sim_dists[, "b_cost"]

# 95% confidence interval the simulated distribution
quantile(sim_wtp, c(0.025, 0.975))

     2.5%     97.5%
0.1931036 0.6080009

# Change in consumer surplus
# Compute the simulated distribution for V1
sim_V1 <- rowMeans(sim_dists[, c("b_asc_alt2", "b_asc_alt3")]) +
  sim_dists[, "b_small_farms"] +
  sim_dists[, "b_low_height"] +
  sim_dists[, "b_red_kite"] * -5 +
  sim_dists[, "b_min_distance"] +
  sim_dists[, "b_cost"] * 4.5

# Calculate the simulated welfare change (V1 divided by negative cost)
sim_welf <- sim_V1 / -sim_dists[, "b_cost"]

# 95% confidence interval the simulated distribution
quantile(sim_welf, c(0.025, 0.975))

      2.5%      97.5%
-0.0546138  0.9008859
```

We can now report the results with greater confidence, specifically that the monthly mWTP is €0.40 (95% CI: [€0.19, €0.61]). As observed when using the Delta method, this confidence interval does not include zero, meaning we can reject the null hypothesis that the mWTP is zero. From a policy perspective, this strengthens the validity of the analysis and supports the decision to implement these policies, as the mWTP is statistically significant and positive.

This implies that, on average, individuals in the population are willing to pay a positive amount for the reduction in wind farm size. Assuming the sample is representative, €0.40 remains our best estimate of the true value, and this estimate becomes more reliable as the sample size increases.

The confidence interval indicates the level of uncertainty around the estimate: a wider interval suggests greater uncertainty about the true value, whereas a narrower interval provides more confidence in the accuracy of the estimate. This is evident from the histogram of the simulated mWTP distribution presented in Fig. 10.2. The majority of the distribution's mass and the measures of central tendency are centred around the predicted value of €0.40 (marked by the green line). The distribution closely resembles a normal distribution, characterised by a single peak and symmetrical shape, with most values clustered near the mean. Values falling outside the confidence interval are shaded in red. As expected, only 5% of the values (2.5% in each tail) fall outside of the boundaries of the confidence interval (marked by the red lines).

Similarly, for our estimate of the change in consumer surplus for transitioning from the SQ to the policy scenario, we can state that the monthly change in consumer surplus is €0.42 (95% CI: [€-0.05, €0.90]). In contrast to the confidence interval found using the Delta method, this confidence interval includes zero, indicating that we cannot reject the null hypothesis that the change in consumer surplus is zero. From a policy perspective, this suggests that implementing the policy may not lead to a statistically significant positive change in societal welfare.

Assuming the sample is representative, €0.42 remains the best estimate of the true welfare change. However, we have less than 95% confidence that this estimate does not include zero. The histogram of the simulated welfare change distribution is

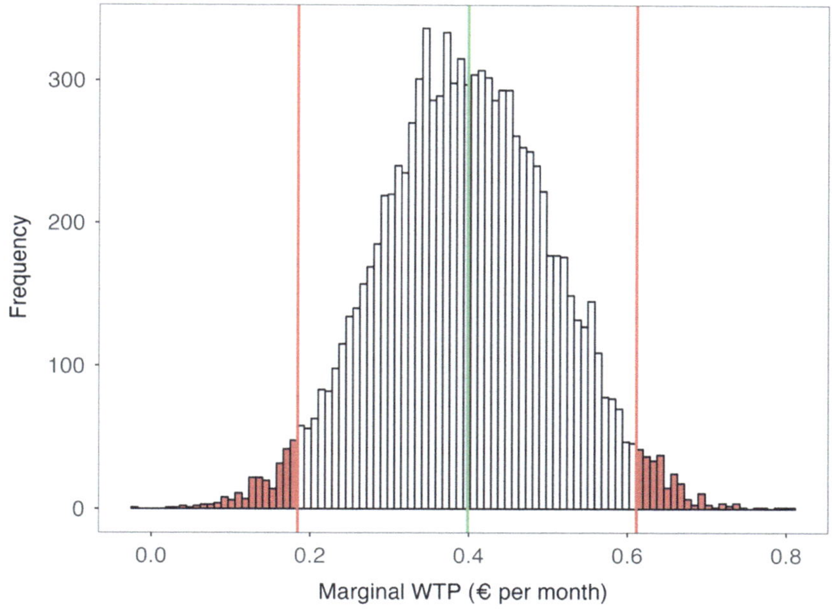


**Fig. 10.2** Histogram of the mWTP distribution for *SmallFarms*

shown in Fig. 10.3, where the majority of the distribution's mass and central tendency are centred around €0.42, though zero falls within the confidence interval.

Multiple mWTP values and their corresponding confidence intervals can be calculated simultaneously. The code chunk below demonstrates this process.

```
sim_dists |>
  as_tibble() |>
  pivot_longer(-b_cost, names_to = "attribute", values_to = "wtp") |>
  group_by(attribute) |>
  mutate(
    wtp = wtp / -b_cost,

  ) |>
  summarize(
    mean = mean(wtp),
    lower_ci = quantile(wtp, 0.025),
    upper_ci = quantile(wtp, 0.975)
  ) |>
  filter(!(attribute %in% c("b_cost", "b_asc_alt1"))) |>
  slice(1, 2, 8, 4, 3, 5, 6, 7) |>
  gt() |>
  fmt_number()
```

The output of this code chunk is shown in Table 10.3.

The code can be extended to evaluate a wider range of policy scenarios for assessing welfare changes. For instance, as part of the sensitivity analysis, it is valuable for policymakers to examine expected changes in consumer surplus under different assumptions, especially related to policy scenario costs.

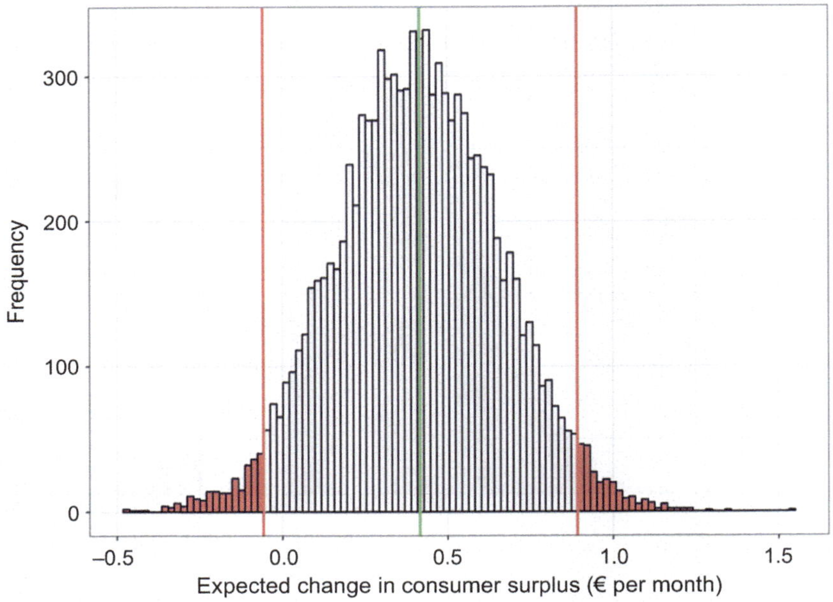


**Fig. 10.3** Consumer surplus change

Previously, the expected change in consumer surplus was calculated based on a fixed scenario with a policy cost of €4.50. Below, we demonstrate how to predict the expected change in consumer surplus for the same policy scenario, using all possible scenario costs between €0 and €7.50, in increments of €0.01 to provide additional insights for policymakers. Using the empirical distributions generated earlier via the Krinsky-Robb method, we then retrieve the confidence intervals for these predictions and visualise the results, with the confidence intervals displayed as an envelope, which is a graphical representation that shows the range of plausible values for a parameter at a given confidence level. Figure 10.4 presents the expected change in consumer surplus (in Euros per month) with confidence interval in pink.

We add vertical dashed lines to indicate the boundaries of statistical significance. If the cost is to the left of the leftmost dashed line (at €4.44), there is more than 95% confidence that the expected welfare change from the policy scenario will be positive. Conversely, if the cost is to the right of the rightmost dashed line (at €5.41), the expected welfare change is negative with the same level of confidence. For costs between these dashed lines, the null hypothesis that the expected change in consumer surplus is not statistically different from zero cannot be rejected.

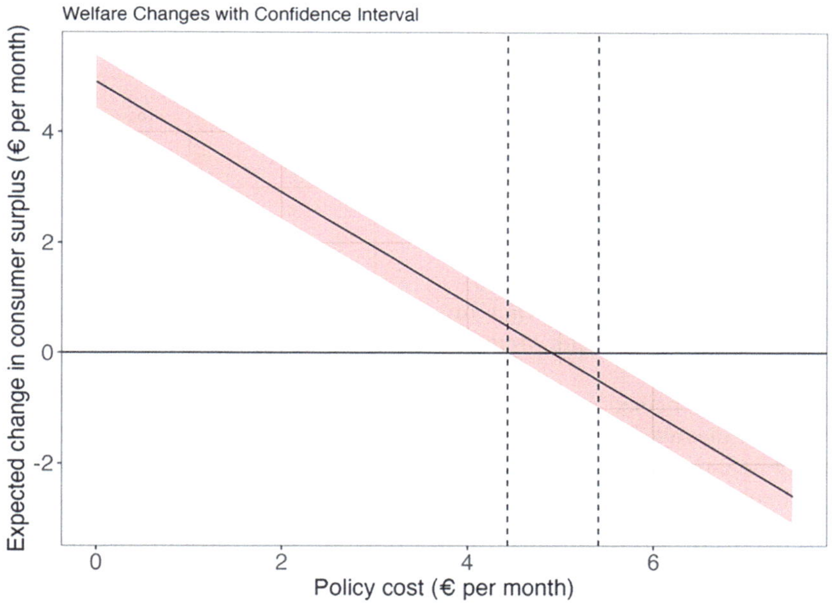


**Fig. 10.4** Welfare change with confidence intervals

```r
# Specify cost vector to simulate over
costs <- seq(0, 7.5, by = 0.01)

# Compute the mean welfare changes
welf <- (mean(model$estimate[c("b_asc_alt2", "b_asc_alt3")]) +
           model$estimate["b_small_farms"] +
           model$estimate["b_low_height"] +
           model$estimate["b_red_kite"] * -5 +
           model$estimate["b_min_distance"] +
           model$estimate["b_cost"] * costs) / -model$estimate["b_cost"]

# Compute the simulated welfare changes
sim_welf <- (rowMeans(sim_dists[, c("b_asc_alt2", "b_asc_alt3")]) +
               sim_dists[, "b_small_farms"] +
               sim_dists[, "b_low_height"] +
               sim_dists[, "b_red_kite"] * -5 +
               sim_dists[, "b_min_distance"] + sim_dists[, "b_cost"] %*% t(costs)) / -sim_d
ists[, "b_cost"]

# Plot the prediction (with confidence interval envelope)
tibble(
  costs = costs,
  welf = welf,
  lower = apply(sim_welf, 2, quantile, probs = 0.025),
  upper = apply(sim_welf, 2, quantile, probs = 0.975)
) |>
  ggplot(aes(x = costs)) +
  geom_line(aes(y = welf)) +
  geom_ribbon(aes(ymin = lower, ymax = upper), alpha = 0.2, fill = "red") +
  labs(
    x = "Policy cost (€ per month)",
    y = "Expected change in consumer surplus (€ per month)",
    title = "Welfare Changes with Confidence Interval"
  ) +
  geom_hline(yintercept = 0) +
  geom_vline(xintercept = max(costs[apply(sim_welf, 2, quantile, probs = 0.025) > 0]), line
type = "dashed") +
  geom_vline(xintercept = min(costs[apply(sim_welf, 2, quantile, probs = 0.975) < 0]), line
type = "dashed") +
  theme_bw()
```

#### 10.2.1.3 Comparing Confidence Intervals: Delta Method vs. Krinsky-Robb Method

While the Delta method and the Krinsky-Robb method produce similar confidence intervals for the mWTPs analysed here (i.e. Table 10.2 versus Table 10.3), the same does not hold true for the welfare estimate. In fact, the Delta method suggests that the welfare change is statistically significant, whereas the Krinsky-Robb method leads to the opposite conclusion. This discrepancy underscores the fact that the two methods do not always yield the same results. The differences arise from their distinct approaches to handling parameter transformations, distributional assumptions, and sample sizes. Therefore, it is essential to understand that these methods can lead to different conclusions, depending on the context.

The log-sum calculation for changes in consumer surplus is notably more complex and non-linear than the straightforward ratio used to determine the mWTPs. This complexity may explain why the confidence intervals for mWTPs were comparable in the two methods, while those for the welfare estimate differed. The Delta method

**Table 10.2** Confidence intervals of the mWTP estimates based on the Delta method

| | Value | st.err | t_ratio_0 | Lower_ci | Upper_ci |
|---|---|---|---|---|---|
| wtp_medium_farms | −0.56 | 0.13 | −4.44 | −0.81 | −0.32 |
| wtp_small_farms | 0.40 | 0.12 | 3.38 | 0.17 | 0.63 |
| wtp_medium_height | −0.66 | 0.13 | −4.98 | −0.93 | −0.40 |
| wtp_low_height | 1.30 | 0.12 | 10.58 | 1.06 | 1.55 |
| wtp_red_kite | −0.13 | 0.01 | −8.96 | −0.16 | −0.10 |
| wtp_min_distance | 0.74 | 0.13 | 5.69 | 0.49 | 1.00 |

**Table 10.3** Confidence interval for mWTP of estimates based on the Krinsky-Robb method

| Attribute | Mean | Lower_ci | Upper_ci |
|---|---|---|---|
| b_asc_alt2 | 1.81 | 1.31 | 2.32 |
| b_asc_alt3 | 1.87 | 1.69 | 2.06 |
| b_small_farms | 0.40 | 0.19 | 0.61 |
| b_medium_farms | −0.56 | −0.82 | −0.31 |
| b_low_height | 1.30 | 1.10 | 1.51 |
| b_medium_height | −0.66 | −0.91 | −0.42 |
| b_min_distance | 0.74 | 0.52 | 0.96 |
| b_red_kite | −0.13 | −0.16 | −0.10 |

approximates the variance of a non-linear function using a first-order Taylor expansion, which can be less accurate for highly non-linear functions, potentially leading to an underestimation or overestimation of the standard error and the confidence intervals. In contrast, the Krinsky-Robb method accounts for non-linearity by simulating the distribution of the function from the estimated parameter distribution, which can more accurately capture the true variability in non-linear settings.

Furthermore, the Delta method assumes an approximately normal distribution of the estimated parameters. If this assumption is violated (e.g. due to skewness or kurtosis), the resulting confidence intervals may be inaccurate. The Krinsky-Robb method on the other hand, does not rely on this assumption and uses the empirical distribution from simulations, providing more robust confidence intervals in such cases. The Delta method is generally well-suited for large samples and simpler models where the normality assumption and linear approximations hold. In these scenarios, the confidence intervals from both methods can be expected to be more closely aligned. The Krinsky-Robb method is particularly valuable for smaller samples or more complex models where the assumptions underlying the Delta method are more likely to be violated. In such cases, the confidence intervals from the Krinsky-Robb method may be wider, reflecting the increased uncertainty.

As a general rule, when working with smaller samples and more complex parameter transformations—such as those involved in applying the log-sum formula to estimate changes in consumer surplus—the Krinsky-Robb method tends to be more reliable for obtaining confidence intervals compared to the Delta method. Therefore, we recommend using the Krinsky-Robb method in these cases.

Ultimately, while differences between the two methods exist, they are often minor, especially when the sample size is large, and the parameter transformations are relatively straightforward. The key is to account for the variation due to the sampling error, which both the Delta and Krinsky-Robb methods handle effectively. In practice, the choice of method may not lead to materially significant differences in confidence intervals, but understanding their distinctions helps ensure that results are interpreted correctly.

## 10.3 Accounting for Preference Heterogeneity in mWTP and Welfare Estimation

So far, the analysis in this chapter assumes preference homogeneity within the sample, meaning that all individuals, and by extension the entire population, are presumed to share identical preferences for all attributes. These preferences are represented by the single estimate produced by the MNL model. The assumption of preference homogeneity extends to the calculation of mWTP and welfare changes, implying that all individuals are treated as having the same mWTP and welfare impacts.

However, this strong assumption may not hold in many empirical studies, and more flexible models have been developed to account for preference heterogeneity and to address other inherent limitations of the MNL model. Therefore, it is crucial to recognise the presence of observed or unobserved preference heterogeneity when using parameter estimates from such models in your post-estimation analysis.

> ⓘ **Preference heterogeneity**
>
> Considering preference heterogeneity introduces an additional layer of variability in the resulting estimates, which is distinct from the variability caused by the sampling error. These sources of variability are distinct and should not be conflated.

In the rest of this chapter, we discuss how to accurately retrieve and interpret mWTP and welfare estimates for models that capture preference heterogeneity. We begin with the MNL model, which explains preferences based on differences in socio-demographic characteristics, and then move to more complex models that capture both observed and unobserved preference heterogeneity, focusing on MXL models, specifically the RP-MXL and LC-MXL models.

### 10.3.1 MNL Model with Observed Heterogeneity

When the utility function includes interactions between socio-demographic variables and attributes, the model can account for observed sources of heterogeneity within the population. If any of the parameters in the expressions for mWTP or welfare change (as defined in Eqs. (10.1) and (10.2), respectively) involve such interactions, the resulting estimates will naturally vary according to the socio-demographic characteristics involved in these interactions. Omitting these interaction terms would result in estimates that reflect only a subset of the population—specifically, those individuals for whom the interacted socio-demographic variables are zero or at their baseline levels.

Consider the scenario where a single interaction term is present in the utility function, influencing one or more components of the mWTP or welfare change calculations. This implies that there is a distinct value of mWTP or welfare change for each level of the interaction variable. For example, if the interaction is with a binary indicator (such as gender, coded as female/male), the model will yield two separate estimates, one for each group. If the interaction involves a categorical variable (such as education), the model will produce estimates corresponding to each category level. If the interaction variable is continuous, the model results can be used to generate an infinite number of mWTP or welfare change estimates across the entire range of the variable. Estimates can also be extrapolated beyond the observed data range if such predictions are desired.

In cases where multiple interaction terms are present in the utility function affecting one or more of the attributes in the mWTP or welfare change calculations, the calculations become even more granular. Distinct estimates can be produced for each combination of the interacting socio-demographic variables. This means that for any given combination of socio-demographic characteristics within the data, or for any feasible combination that the analyst wishes to predict, the model can provide specific mWTP or welfare change estimates pertaining to each sub-group. This not only can better reflect the diversity in the population's preferences but also allows for a deeper understanding of how different groups value changes in attributes or policies, offering valuable insights for policymakers.

The next step is retrieving these estimates—here, we begin by calculating the mWTP. Recall from Sect. 9.2.2 that the utility function for alternative $j$ in the MNL model with observed heterogeneity is defined as follows:

$$
\begin{aligned}
U_{njt} = {} & ASC_j + \delta_{asc_j,age} age_n + \delta_{asc_j,female} female_n + \delta_{asc_j,educ} education_n \\
& + \left(\beta_{sf} + \delta_{sf,age} age_n + \delta_{sf,female} female_n + \delta_{sf,educ} education_n\right) \\
& SmallFarms_{njt} \\
& + \left(\beta_{mf} + \delta_{mf,age} age_n + \delta_{mf,female} female_n + \delta_{mf,educ} education_n\right) \\
& MediumFarms_{njt} \\
& + \left(\beta_{lh} + \delta_{lh,age} age_n + \delta_{lh,female} female_n + \delta_{lh,educ} education_n\right)
\end{aligned}
$$

$$
\begin{aligned}
&LowHeight_{njt}\\
&+ \left(\beta_{mh} + \delta_{mh,age} age_n + \delta_{mh,female} female_n + \delta_{mh,educ} education_n\right)\\
&MediumHeight_{njt}\\
&+ \left(\beta_{rk} + \delta_{rk,age} age_n + \delta_{rk,female} female_n + \delta_{rk,educ} education_n\right)\\
&RedKite_{njt}\\
&+ \left(\beta_{md} + \delta_{md,age} age_n + \delta_{md,female} female_n + \delta_{md,educ} education_n\right)\\
&MinDistance_{njt}\\
&+ \left(\beta_{cost} + \delta_{cost,age} age_n + \delta_{cost,female} female_n + \delta_{cost,educ} education_n\right)\\
&Cost_{njt} + \varepsilon_{njt}
\end{aligned}
\qquad (10.3)
$$

Let us focus again on the mWTP values associated with *SmallFarms*. The marginal utility for this attribute level includes interactions with *age*, *gender*, and *education*, and similar interactions are present for the cost attribute. In this dataset, *age* is a numerical variable that ranges from 18 to 89, representing an individual's age in years. Thus, the parameter $\delta_{sf,age}$ in Eq. (10.3) represents the ceteris paribus effect of a one-year increase in age on the marginal utility of *SmallFarms*. At the same time, $\delta_{cost,age}$ quantifies how a one-year increase in age affects the marginal utility of the cost attribute, holding all else constant.

The *gender* variable is a binary indicator, with 1 representing female individuals and 0 representing male individuals. Consequently, $\delta_{sf,female}$ and $\delta_{cost,female}$ capture the difference in marginal utilities that female individuals assign to the small wind farm and cost attributes, respectively, relative to male individuals with all else being equal. The *education* variable in this dataset is an ordinal variable ranging from 1 to 3, with 3 representing the highest level of education. Since this variable enters the utility function linearly, the parameters $\delta_{sf,educ}$ and $\delta_{cost,educ}$ are the ceteris paribus effect on the marginal utilities of the small wind farm and cost attributes, respectively, as one moves from one educational level to the next. Considering all three socio-demographic variables together, there are 432 possible sub-groups within the sample (72 age levels, 2 genders, and 3 levels of education). The interactions in the utility function allow us to retrieve a unique mWTP estimate for each of these sub-groups.

The code chunk below demonstrates how to calculate the mWTP for each of the 432 sub-groups. We begin by creating a data frame that contains all possible socio-demographic combinations. To do this, we use the built-in R function `expand.grid`, which generates a row for every unique permutation of the provided vectors. Next, we compute the marginal utility for the relevant parameters—specifically *SmallFarms* and the cost attribute—across these combinations.

The marginal utility calculation follows the expression outlined in Eq. (10.3) and applies the parameters estimated in the MNL model with observed heterogeneity. Note that `model` in the code chunk below now refers to this updated model, not the baseline MNL model referenced earlier in the chapter. With the marginal utilities calculated, deriving the mWTP for each combination becomes straightforward, as shown in the next step.

```
# Create a data frame with the desired socio-demographic combinations
soc_dem <- expand.grid(
  age = 18:89,
  female = 0:1,
  education = 1:3
)

# Calculate b_small_farms and b_cost
b_small_farms <- model$estimate["b_small_farms"] +
  colSums(t(soc_dem) * model$estimate[c("delta_sf_age", "delta_sf_female", "delta_sf_educ")
])

b_cost <- model$estimate["b_cost"] +
  colSums(t(soc_dem) * model$estimate[c("delta_ct_age", "delta_ct_female", "delta_ct_educ")
])

# Calculate marginal WTP
wtp <- -b_small_farms / b_cost
```

While examining mWTPs for each sub-group individually is possible, it is often more practical to focus on specific combinations. For instance, to retrieve the mWTP for an individual who is 20 years old, female, and has the highest level of education, you can use the code `wtp[soc_dem$age == 20 & soc_dem$female == 1 & soc_dem$education == 3]`. The mWTP for such an individual is predicted to be €0.20.

More commonly, the goal is to explore how mWTP varies with different levels of a particular socio-demographic variable while keeping other variables constant. The code chunk below demonstrates how to use the `wtp` vector to analyse how mWTP for this attribute changes with each level of the socio-demographic variables. For *age*, we achieve this by grouping the data by age and calculating the average mWTP within each age group.

This approach isolates the effect of age on mWTP, allowing us to observe that older individuals tend to have a lower mWTP for this attribute. As we can see in Fig. 10.5, the relationship is somewhat non-linear, showing slight concavity, with mWTP decreasing more rapidly as age increases. The observed pattern is driven by the estimated interaction terms and how their combined effect on both non-cost and cost attributes modifies the relationship. This means that the relationship between an explanatory variable and mWTP can be positive or negative and can become steeper or flatter depending on the magnitude of the variable (in this case, *age*) and the estimated parameters.

```
# Plot marginal WTP by age holding all else constant
soc_dem |>
  mutate(wtp)  |>
  group_by(age) |>
  summarise(
    mean_wtp = mean(wtp)
  ) |>
  ungroup() |>
  ggplot(aes(x = age, y = mean_wtp)) +
  geom_line() +
  labs(
    x = "Age (in years)",
    y = "Marginal WTP (€ per month)",
  ) +
  theme_bw()
```

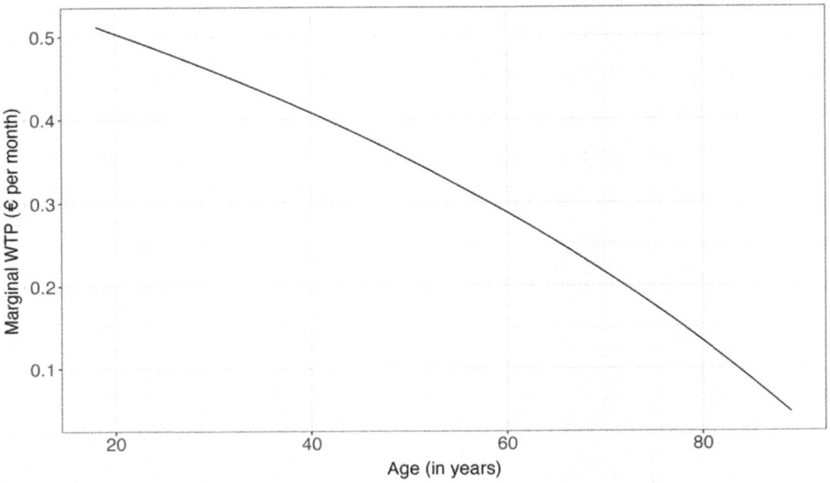


**Fig. 10.5** mWTP by age for *SmallFarms*

**Table 10.4** mWTP of *SmallFarms* by gender

| Female | Mean_marginal_wtp |
|---|---|
| 0 | 0.45 |
| 1 | 0.18 |

The resulting table (see Table 10.4) of mWTP differences by gender shows that, on average, females are willing to pay less than males. Similarly, the table (see Table 10.5) for *education* indicates that individuals with higher levels of education have a lower mWTP compared to those with lower levels of education. For *education*, the relationship is slightly convex, reflecting how the interaction terms influence the mWTP across both attributes.

**Table 10.5** mWTP of *SmallFarms* by education

| Education | Mean_marginal_wtp |
|---|---|
| 1 | 0.56 |
| 2 | 0.30 |
| 3 | 0.08 |

```
# Tabulate marginal WTP by gender holding all else constant
soc_dem |>
  mutate(
    wtp = wtp
  ) |>
  group_by(female) |>
  summarise(
    mean_marginal_wtp = mean(wtp)) |>
  ungroup() |>
  gt() |>
  fmt_number(
    columns = mean_marginal_wtp,
  )
```

```
# Tabulate marginal WTP by educational level holding all else constant
soc_dem |>
  mutate(
    wtp = wtp
  ) |>
  group_by(education) |>
  summarise(
    mean_marginal_wtp = mean(wtp)) |>
  ungroup() |>
  gt() |>
  fmt_number(
    columns = mean_marginal_wtp,
  )
```

As previously mentioned, we could analyse the mWTPs for each sub-group separately, but this approach may have limited practical value, as certain combinations of socio-demographic variables may be more prevalent in the sample (and, by extension, in the population). A more insightful approach involves replicating the respective mWTP estimates based on the share of each combination in your sample. By employing this approach, you gain a clearer understanding of how different socio-demographic factors interact and contribute to variations in mWTP, and you also better appreciate the observed heterogeneity within your sample.

The code chunk below demonstrates this process and generates a histogram to visualise the distribution. As we can see in Fig. 10.6, there is heterogeneity in how much the sampled individuals are willing to pay. Keep in mind that this heterogeneity is explainable by the variation in the three socio-demographic variables in the data, namely *age*, *gender* and *education*, which were interacted with both the non-cost and cost attributes.

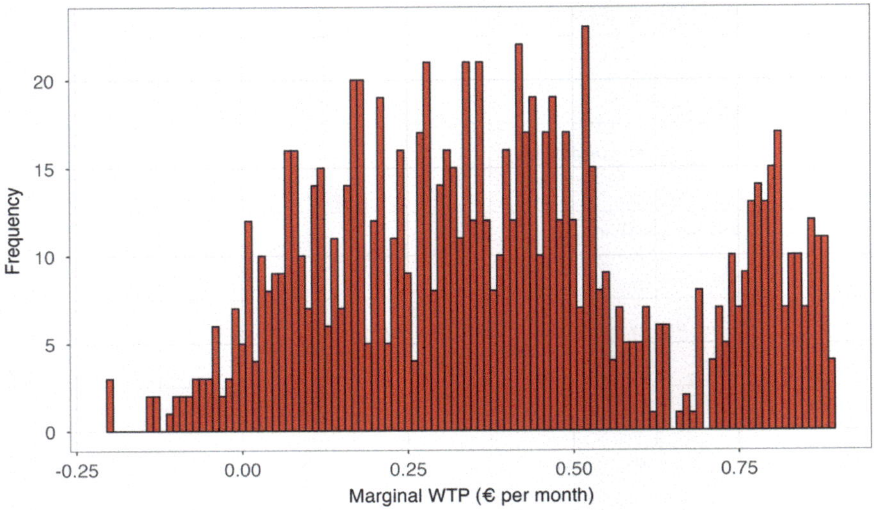


**Fig. 10.6** mWTP distribution by socio-demographic characteristics

```r
# Creating a count for each socio-demographic combination
counts <- database |>
  select(id_individual, age, female, education) |>
  distinct() |>
  count(age, female, education) |>
  full_join(soc_dem, by = c("age", "female", "education")) |>
  replace_na(
    list(
      n = 0
    )
  ) |>
  # This to match the sorting of soc_dem
  arrange(education, female, age) |>
  pull(n)

# Generate marginal WTP distribution using the count for each socio-demographic combination
tibble(
  wtp = rep(wtp, times = counts)
) |>
  ggplot(aes(x = wtp)) +
  geom_histogram(binwidth = 0.01, color = 1, fill = "red") +
  labs(
    x = "Marginal WTP (€ per month)",
    y = "Frequency",
    title = "Marginal WTP Distribution by Socio-demographic Characteristics"
  ) +
  theme_bw()
```

The histogram in Fig. 10.6 reveals that, based on the estimates from the MNL model with observed heterogeneity, the monthly mWTP for *SmallFarms* within the sample spans from €-0.20 (found for an 80-year-old female with the highest level of education) to €0.89 (observed for a 20-year-old male with the lowest level of education). However, this only provides a partial picture: we must also consider the variation stemming from the sampling error.

To be able to correctly and confidently interpret our results, we need not only the mWTP estimates but also an understanding of how much confidence we should have in these predictions for each subgroup. This raises two important questions:

1. Are the estimates for each subgroup statistically significant?
2. Are they statistically different from each other?

Without addressing these questions, we cannot determine if the mWTP for 20-year-old males with the lowest level of education is statistically distinct from that of 80-year-old females with the highest level of education. This distinction is vital for policymakers, as it allows them to tailor and target their policy decisions more effectively.

To address both questions, we can apply either the Delta method or the Krinsky-Robb method, as previously discussed. For brevity, we will demonstrate this using the Delta method.

The first entry in the expression list specifies the function to calculate the mWTP for the subgroup of 80-year-old females with the highest level of education (who had the lowest mWTP). The second entry calculates the equivalent mWTP for 20-year-old males with the lowest level of education (who had the highest mWTP). The final entry computes the difference between these two subgroups. Using the `apollo_deltaMethod` function, we obtain the corresponding robust standard errors and $t$-ratios for these estimates. The results are then supplemented with confidence intervals and displayed.

```
# Settings for the function apollo_deltaMethod
deltaMethod_settings <- list(
  expression = c(
    wtp_lowest = "-(b_small_farms + delta_sf_age * 80 + delta_sf_female * 1 + delta_sf_educ
* 3) /
                   (b_cost + delta_ct_age * 80 + delta_ct_female * 1 + delta_ct_educ * 3)",
    wtp_highest = "-(b_small_farms + delta_sf_age * 20 + delta_sf_female * 0 + delta_sf_edu
c * 1) /
                   (b_cost + delta_ct_age * 20 + delta_ct_female * 0 + delta_ct_educ * 1)",
    wtp_diff = "(-(b_small_farms + delta_sf_age * 20 + delta_sf_female * 0 + delta_sf_educ
* 1) /
                   (b_cost + delta_ct_age * 20 + delta_ct_female * 0 + delta_ct_educ * 1))
-
                 -(b_small_farms + delta_sf_age * 80 + delta_sf_female * 1 + delta_sf_educ
* 3) /
                   (b_cost + delta_ct_age * 80 + delta_ct_female * 1 + delta_ct_educ * 3)"
  )
)

# Apply the Delta method to calculate the standard errors of the marginal WTP
wtp_results_delta_dif <- apollo_deltaMethod(model, deltaMethod_settings)

Running Delta method computation for user-defined function using robust standard errors

  Expression    Value   s.e. t-ratio (0)
  wtp_lowest -0.2032 0.3440       -0.59
 wtp_highest  0.8891 0.2919        3.05
    wtp_diff  1.0923 0.5858        1.86
INFORMATION: The results of the Delta method calculations are returned invisibly as
  an output from this function. Calling the function via
  result=apollo_deltaMethod(...) will save this output in an object
  called result (or otherwise named object).

# Calculate the WTP values and CIs
wtp_results_delta_dif <- wtp_results_delta_dif |>
  clean_names() |>
  mutate(
    lower_ci = value - qnorm(0.975) * s_e,
    upper_ci = value + qnorm(0.975) * s_e
  )

wtp_results_delta_dif |>
  gt() |>
  fmt_number()
```

After applying the Delta method, we can conclude that only the higher of the two mWTP estimates—held by 20-year-old males with the lowest level of education—is statistically different from zero. The confidence interval for the lower estimate, associated with 80-year-old females with the highest level of education, includes zero. Statistically, this indicates that this subgroup is not willing to pay for the change in the attribute level. As a result, policymakers can gain a clearer insight into which demographic might benefit if this attribute level is implemented, which in this case is younger individuals with lower levels of education.

We can see in Table 10.6 that the confidence intervals for both groups overlap. Note that while non-overlapping intervals would confirm a statistically significant difference between the estimates, overlapping intervals do not necessarily indicate that the two values are statistically indistinguishable. To robustly assess whether the means are different, as we do here, it is better to test whether the mean of the difference between the two distributions is statistically significant. In this case, the test results show that we fail to reject the null hypothesis at a 95% significance level that the mean difference is zero, since its confidence interval includes zero. Thus, at a 95% significance level, we cannot claim that the subgroup with the highest mWTP is different from the subgroup with the lowest mWTP. Despite the apparent relative heterogeneity in mWTP among different subgroups, this observed variation is not statistically significant based on the analysis.

> ⓘ **Note**
>
> Interactions between different variables can influence the direction of effects, which can lead to varying outcomes when calculating mWTP or welfare changes. In some cases, the effects may counterbalance across interactions, resulting in a distribution of mWTP or welfare change that appears relatively homogeneous. Conversely, the combined effect of these interactions can amplify differences, leading to a more heterogeneous distributions. For example, while $\delta_{sf,age} < 0$ suggests that older individuals derive lower marginal utility from *SmallFarms*, whether this translates into a lower mWTP for older individuals depends on the sign and relative magnitude of $\delta_{cost,age}$, which captures how the marginal disutility of the cost attribute changes with age. These combined effects cannot be fully understood without simulating their joint impact across the range of the explanatory variable. This highlights the importance of moving beyond simply interpreting estimation results and undertaking a more comprehensive analysis to understand the broader implications of the estimated model parameters.
>
> An important but often overlooked consequence of interacting socio-demographic variables with multiple parameters is that it naturally introduces correlation among the derived marginal utilities. The extent of this correlation is influenced not only by the estimated values of the interaction terms (the $\delta$ parameters) but also by the correlation among the socio-demographic variables themselves within the sample. Capturing this correlation across multiple attributes via interactions is a significant yet frequently underestimated benefit of incorporating observed sources of heterogeneity.

So, when moving to more complex models such as MXL models to account for preference correlations, it is important to understand that these complex models primarily capture correlation in unobserved sources of heterogeneity. There is considerable value in explaining as much of this correlation as possible through individual (observable) characteristics. For policymakers, this approach is especially important, as it allows them to better understand how different sub-groups within the population support or are impacted by policy decisions. Thus, while MXL models are valuable, a thorough examination of observed heterogeneity using interactions can

**Table 10.6** Difference in mWTP between two subgroups

| Expression | Value | s_e | t_ratio_0 | Lower_ci | Upper_ci |
|---|---|---|---|---|---|
| wtp_lowest | −0.20 | 0.34 | −0.59 | −0.88 | 0.47 |
| wtp_highest | 0.89 | 0.29 | 3.05 | 0.32 | 1.46 |
| wtp_diff | 1.09 | 0.59 | 1.86 | −0.06 | 2.24 |

provide key insights into the distribution of preferences across socio-demographic groups—insights that are directly actionable in the policy-making process.

To illustrate the extent of the correlation among the predicted mWTP estimates for each individual across all attributes, we present the following correlation table. It reveals the relationships between mWTP estimates for different attributes, driven by the interaction of the same socio-demographic variables across these attributes. It is important to note that a high degree of correlation is anticipated because the cost parameter is a shared component in the denominator of all mWTP calculations.

```
              medium_farms small_farms medium_height low_height red_kite
medium_farms         1.000      -0.422         0.992     -0.004    0.323
small_farms         -0.422       1.000        -0.406      0.239   -0.312
medium_height        0.992      -0.406         1.000      0.124    0.198
low_height          -0.004       0.239         0.124      1.000   -0.946
red_kite             0.323      -0.312         0.198     -0.946    1.000
min_distance        -0.510       0.974        -0.519      0.031   -0.144
              min_distance
medium_farms        -0.510
small_farms          0.974
medium_height       -0.519
low_height           0.031
red_kite            -0.144
min_distance         1.000
```

## 10.3.2 RP-MXL Model

When interpreting the results from more complex MXL models, just as with simpler MNL models, the primary goal of the post-estimation analysis is to thoroughly understand what the model reveals. MXL models incorporate unobserved sources of preference heterogeneity, allowing us to assess what the distribution of each parameter tells us about preferences within the sample and the broader population. For the RP-MXL specification, it is important to recognise that the model estimates only the parameters that describe the distributions of the random coefficients.

For example, with independent normal distributions, the model retrieves the means and standard deviations of the distributions. When accounting for correlation, it also estimates the correlation structure, typically through a lower triangular Cholesky matrix (see Sect. 9.3.1 for more details). For uniform distributions, the model typically retrieves the upper and lower bounds. Various continuous random distributions can be used, including those with more than two parameters. Regardless of the distribution chosen, the model only retrieves its main parameters, and it can be challenging to interpret how these parameters translate into the actual distribution. This complexity becomes even more pronounced when calculating mWTP or welfare changes, as these involve one or more of the random parameters.

The best way to fully understand these results is to simulate the resulting distribution. There is really no substitute for this—simulation provides a complete picture of what the distribution looks like. When conducting the post-estimation analysis, it is essential to look beyond the mean, as it alone does not capture the full distribution of key variables like mWTP and welfare changes. The strength of the RP-MXL model lies in uncovering heterogeneity, so understanding the distribution's shape, variability, and key percentiles is crucial in providing policymakers with insights that account for the diverse effects of their decisions.

#### 10.3.2.1 Unconditional and Conditional Distributions

When considering the output from MXL models, it is helpful to distinguish between *unconditional* and *conditional* preference distributions. The distinction lies in how these models account for individual-specific information. The unconditional distribution of preferences represents the overall distribution across the sample, considering only the randomness in the model's parameters without incorporating individual-specific choices. It provides a broad view of how preferences are distributed across all individuals and, as discussed in Hess (2010), does not directly provide any information on the likely location of a given respondent on this distribution.

In contrast, the conditional distribution of preferences is derived by conditioning on the observed choices made by individuals. This distribution reflects the specific preferences of each individual based on their observed behaviour, thus offering insight into the likely position of each sampled individual on the distribution. The theoretical background of these distributions for RP-MXL models is presented in Sect. 3.3.1.

To gain a clearer understanding of the differences in these preference distributions, we will use the estimates obtained from the uncorrelated RP-MXL model defined in Eqs. (9.3), (9.4) and (9.5) in Sect. 9.3.1.1, which are presented in Table 10.7 below, and focus on the distribution of preferences for the low turbines attribute level *LowHeight*.

The coefficient of *LowHeight* was assumed to follow a normal distribution and, as we can see, was estimated as having a mean of 0.671, a standard deviation of 0.406, with mean shifters for *age* (-0.006), *female* (0.004) and *education* (0.103). We can calculate the mean for a specific subset of individuals as well. For example, the mean for individuals who are 40 years old, male, and have the lowest level of education is 0.522. The distribution this coefficient among this sub-sample can be visualised using the code below (see Fig. 10.7).

**Table 10.7** RP-MXL model with uncorrelated coefficients

| | Estimate | std_err | t_stat | p_value |
|---|---|---|---|---|
| asc_alt1 | 0.000 | NA | NA | NA |
| asc_alt2 | 0.888 | 0.351 | 2.532 | 0.011 |
| asc_alt3 | 0.661 | 0.341 | 1.938 | 0.053 |
| mu_mf | −0.106 | 0.240 | −0.443 | 0.658 |
| sd_mf | −0.075 | 0.102 | −0.736 | 0.462 |
| mu_sf | 0.545 | 0.218 | 2.494 | 0.013 |
| sd_sf | 0.036 | 0.033 | 1.081 | 0.280 |
| mu_mh | −0.056 | 0.248 | −0.228 | 0.820 |
| sd_mh | 0.220 | 0.198 | 1.116 | 0.265 |
| mu_lh | 0.671 | 0.239 | 2.813 | 0.005 |
| sd_lh | −0.406 | 0.108 | −3.767 | 0.000 |
| mu_rk | −0.057 | 0.025 | −2.252 | 0.024 |
| sd_rk | −0.003 | 0.018 | −0.188 | 0.851 |
| mu_md | 0.671 | 0.239 | 2.806 | 0.005 |
| sd_md | 0.013 | 0.021 | 0.601 | 0.548 |
| mu_ct | −0.724 | 0.142 | −5.091 | 0.000 |
| sd_ct | −0.435 | 0.027 | −15.838 | 0.000 |
| delta_asc2_age | 0.001 | 0.007 | 0.211 | 0.833 |
| delta_asc2_female | 0.345 | 0.156 | 2.203 | 0.028 |
| delta_asc2_educ | 0.001 | 0.094 | 0.006 | 0.995 |
| delta_asc3_age | 0.003 | 0.007 | 0.470 | 0.639 |
| delta_asc3_female | 0.406 | 0.158 | 2.569 | 0.010 |
| delta_asc3_educ | 0.075 | 0.096 | 0.779 | 0.436 |
| delta_mf_age | −0.006 | 0.004 | −1.489 | 0.136 |
| delta_sf_age | −0.003 | 0.004 | −0.910 | 0.363 |
| delta_mf_female | 0.034 | 0.112 | 0.306 | 0.759 |
| delta_sf_female | −0.061 | 0.107 | −0.571 | 0.568 |
| delta_mf_educ | 0.052 | 0.067 | 0.779 | 0.436 |
| delta_sf_educ | −0.093 | 0.063 | −1.470 | 0.142 |
| delta_mh_age | −0.013 | 0.004 | −3.053 | 0.002 |
| delta_lh_age | −0.006 | 0.004 | −1.533 | 0.125 |
| delta_mh_female | 0.080 | 0.116 | 0.686 | 0.493 |
| delta_lh_female | 0.004 | 0.112 | 0.033 | 0.974 |
| delta_mh_educ | 0.155 | 0.067 | 2.318 | 0.020 |
| delta_lh_educ | 0.103 | 0.067 | 1.547 | 0.122 |
| delta_rk_age | 0.000 | 0.000 | 0.583 | 0.560 |
| delta_md_age | −0.005 | 0.004 | −1.202 | 0.229 |

(continued)

**Table 10.7** (continued)

| | Estimate | std_err | t_stat | p_value |
|---|---|---|---|---|
| delta_rk_female | 0.012 | 0.013 | 0.990 | 0.322 |
| delta_md_female | −0.025 | 0.115 | −0.221 | 0.825 |
| delta_rk_educ | −0.010 | 0.008 | −1.260 | 0.208 |
| delta_md_educ | −0.074 | 0.069 | −1.074 | 0.283 |
| delta_ct_age | −0.005 | 0.003 | −1.548 | 0.122 |
| delta_ct_female | 0.306 | 0.057 | 5.347 | 0.000 |
| delta_ct_educ | 0.061 | 0.034 | 1.790 | 0.074 |

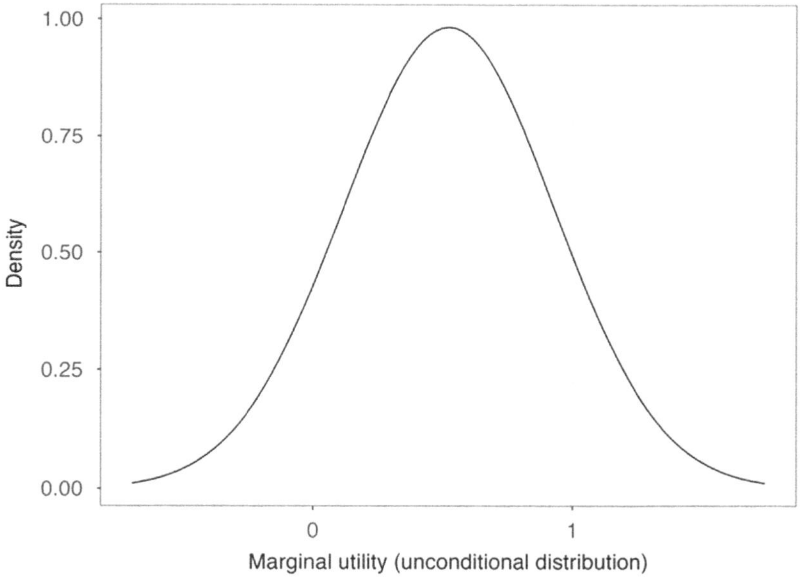


**Fig. 10.7** Distribution of the *LowHeight* coefficient for a specific sub-population

```r
# Define the mean and standard deviation of the normal distribution
mean_value <- model$estimate["mu_lh"] +
  model$estimate["delta_lh_age"] * 40 +
  model$estimate["delta_lh_female"] * 0 +
  model$estimate["delta_lh_educ"] * 1

sd_value <- abs(model$estimate["sd_lh"])

# Plot over the range given by 3 standard deviations from the mean
tibble(
  x_range = c(
    qnorm(pnorm(-3), mean = mean_value, sd = sd_value),
    qnorm(pnorm(3), mean = mean_value, sd = sd_value)
  )
) |>
  ggplot(mapping = aes(x = x_range)) +
  stat_function(fun = dnorm, args = list(mean = mean_value, sd = sd_value)) +
  labs(
    x = "Marginal utility (unconditional distribution)",
    y = "Density"
  ) +
  theme_bw()
```

Such an analysis provides valuable insights into sub-samples of the data (and, by extension, the sub-population if the sample is representative). Given the normal distribution, we can infer the following:

- About 50% of this sub-population has a marginal utility for this attribute level greater than 0.671.
- Approximately 68% of the sub-population's preferences fall within the range $[0.117, 0.928]$, which is the mean $\pm$ one standard deviation.
- Roughly 95% of the sub-population's preferences lie within $[-0.289, 1.334]$, corresponding to the mean $\pm$ two standard deviations.
- An estimated 10% of the sub-population exhibits disutility for this attribute, meaning their preferences are negative.

While these statistics offer substantial insights into the general sub-population, they do not reveal where a specific individual lies within this distribution. However, knowing an individual's specific location on the distribution can be highly informative. It allows for the comparison of different individuals' positions to assess if observable characteristics correlate with their place in the distribution. Individual-specific preference estimates provide a more detailed understanding of each individual's decision-making process, offering richer insights into their choices. This method captures the variation in preferences across individuals, accounting for the fact that each person has unique preferences shaped by their choices. Note that if multiple individuals within the sub-sample make the exact same choices across the same set of options, their individual-specific estimates will be identical.

To determine where a specific individual lies on the distribution, we refer to Eq. (3.21) from Chap. 3:

$$\bar{\boldsymbol{\beta}}_n \approx \sum_{r=1}^{R} \left( \frac{P_n\left(\mathbf{i}_n^\star | \boldsymbol{\beta}_{nr}\right)}{\sum_{r=1}^{R} P_n\left(\mathbf{i}_n^\star | \boldsymbol{\beta}_{nr}\right)} \right) \cdot \boldsymbol{\beta}_{nr} \tag{10.4}$$

This equation calculates the mean of the conditional distribution for individual $n$, denoted as $\overline{\boldsymbol{\beta}}_n$. Here, $\boldsymbol{\beta}_{nr}$ represents the $r$ th draw from the unconditional distribution, and $P_n(\mathbf{i}_n^\star|\boldsymbol{\beta}_{nr})$ is the probability of the observed sequence of choices given the data $\mathbf{x}_n$ and the value of $\boldsymbol{\beta}_{nr}$ from the $r$ th draw. To make this more intuitive, the equation can be rewritten as

$$\bar{\boldsymbol{\beta}}_n \approx \sum_{r=1}^{R} w_{nr}\boldsymbol{\beta}_{nr}$$

where $w_{nr}$ is the weight assigned to the $r$ th draw of $\boldsymbol{\beta}_{nr}$ for individual $n$, and it is proportional to $P_n(\mathbf{i}_n^\star|\boldsymbol{\beta}_{nr})$. The weight $w_{nr}$ is calculated as

$$w_{nr} = \frac{P_n(\mathbf{i}_n^\star|\boldsymbol{\beta}_{nr})}{\sum_{r=1}^{R} P_n(\mathbf{i}_n^\star|\boldsymbol{\beta}_{nr})} \tag{10.5}$$

which is the term inside the parenthesis in Eq. (10.4). Since $0 < w_{nr} < 1$ and $\sum_{r=1}^{R} w_{nr} = 1$, these weights are intuitive: they represent the likelihood that the $r$ th draw of $\boldsymbol{\beta}_n$ corresponds to individual $n$'s preferences, given their choices and the overall distribution of preferences. Recall that the conditional estimates for each individual follow a random distribution. Here, $\overline{\boldsymbol{\beta}}_n$ represents the expected value of this distribution. Similarly, the conditional standard deviations for individual $n$, denoted as $\breve{\overline{\boldsymbol{\beta}}}_n$, can be calculated as follows:

$$\breve{\bar{\boldsymbol{\beta}}}_n = \sqrt{\sum_{r=1}^{R} w_{nr}\left(\bar{\boldsymbol{\beta}}_n - \boldsymbol{\beta}_{nr}\right)^2}$$

This equation provides a measure of the variability in the individual's preferences, considering the likelihood of each draw.

To retrieve the unconditional and conditional distributions in *Apollo* after estimating a model, where the results are stored in an object named `model`, and `apollo_probabilities` and `apollo_inputs` remain the same as in the estimation, we use the code chunk below.

```
# Unconditional distributions
unconditionals <- apollo_unconditionals(
  model,
  apollo_probabilities,
  apollo_inputs
)

# Conditional distributions
conditionals <- apollo_conditionals(
  model,
  apollo_probabilities,
  apollo_inputs
)
```

These functions are applicable to models with random parameters, including continuous mixtures and latent class models. In the context of an RP-MXL model:

- The `apollo_unconditionals` function generates a list of matrices, each corresponding to a random parameter. Each matrix in this list contains draws from the distribution of the respective random parameter. The rows correspond to individual observations, and the columns represent the different draws.
- The `apollo_conditionals` function produces a list of matrices, each representing a random parameter. These matrices have three columns: the individual ID, the conditional mean of the parameter, and the conditional standard deviation.

For example, to access the element related to *LowHeight*, you would use `unconditionals$r_lh` for the unconditional distributions or `conditionals$r_lh` for the conditional distributions, depending on your needs. Note that the label `r_lh` corresponds to the name assigned to the distribution for this attribute level in the `apollo_randCoeff` function, which was specified in `apollo_inputs`.

While the `apollo_conditionals` function is invaluable on its own, there are situations in which deriving $w_r$ (the weight of each draw) is advantageous. This approach offers greater flexibility, allowing you to calculate expected values and standard deviations for various derived quantities (e.g. mWTP or consumer surplus) using more than one unconditional distribution.

To compute $w_r$, first you need to calculate the probability of the sequence of choices made by each individual for every set of random draws. This can be done using `apollo_probabilities`, with the model estimates (found in `model$estimate`), the same `apollo_inputs` as before, and setting `functionality = "conditionals"`. The weight $w_r$ for each draw is then calculated as the probability of that draw divided by the sum of the probabilities across all draws for the individual. The code to calculate $w_r$ for each draw and individual is shown below.

```
# Probabilities of choice sequences for every draw
P <- apollo_probabilities(
  model$estimate,
  apollo_inputs,
  functionality = "conditionals"
)

# Conditional weight for every draw
w <- P / rowSums(P)
```

Once `w` and the `unconditionals` are obtained, you can compute the conditional means and standard deviations of the individual-specific distributions. We illustrate this below by deriving the conditional distribution of marginal utilities for *LowHeight*. Additionally, you can validate these calculations by comparing them with the results from the `apollo_conditionals` function, confirming that they match to at least 10 decimal places (allowing for minor rounding differences). We present the first 10 rows side by side to visually confirm their equivalence (Table 10.8).

**Table 10.8** First 10 rows of the conditional distributions

| Generated using apollo_conditionals | | | Generated using $w_r$ | | |
|---|---|---|---|---|---|
| Id | Post_mean | Post_sd | Id_individual | Post_mean | Post_sd |
| 1 | 0.5325129261 | 0.3790540481 | 1 | 0.5325129261 | 0.3790540481 |
| 2 | 0.5795069678 | 0.3948245265 | 2 | 0.5795069678 | 0.3948245265 |
| 3 | 0.5867581023 | 0.3877814762 | 3 | 0.5867581023 | 0.3877814762 |
| 4 | 0.4997331590 | 0.3807392220 | 4 | 0.4997331590 | 0.3807392220 |
| 5 | 0.5837628038 | 0.3815403785 | 5 | 0.5837628038 | 0.3815403785 |
| 6 | 0.7853607731 | 0.3982633021 | 6 | 0.7853607731 | 0.3982633021 |
| 7 | 0.5935375977 | 0.3931974903 | 7 | 0.5935375977 | 0.3931974903 |
| 8 | 0.5342556675 | 0.3872762482 | 8 | 0.5342556675 | 0.3872762482 |
| 9 | 0.7059091483 | 0.3944318392 | 9 | 0.7059091483 | 0.3944318392 |
| 10 | 0.4461188589 | 0.3910808440 | 10 | 0.4461188589 | 0.3910808440 |

```
# Retrieve the parameters of the individual-specific conditional distributions
conditionals_lh <- tibble(
  id_individual = unique(database$id_individual),
  post_mean = rowSums(w * unconditionals$r_lh),
  post_sd = sqrt(rowSums(w * (rowSums(w * unconditionals$r_lh) - unconditionals$r_lh)^2))
)

# Check that they are equivalent to those produced using apollo
all(round(conditionals_lh, 10) == round(conditionals$r_lh, 10))
```

```
[1] TRUE
```

It is hard to overstate the importance and benefits of visualising the results of your analysis. Visualisation transforms abstract numbers and complex models into intuitive, easily interpretable insights. By visually exploring the data, you gain a deeper understanding of its underlying patterns, trends, and distributions, which might not be immediately apparent from raw statistics alone.

One particularly effective method for visualising findings from RP-MXL models is a kernel density plot. This tool provides a non-parametric way to estimate the probability density function of a random variable, offering a smooth and continuous representation of the data distribution.

Unlike histograms, which rely on predefined bins and can obscure finer details, kernel density plots allow you to observe the shape of the data more clearly, identifying important features like multiple modes, skewness, and the spread of the data. By leveraging such visual tools, you enhance your ability to interpret and communicate the results, leading to more informed decision-making and a better understanding of the underlying data. The following code chunk demonstrates how to create a kernel density plot of the individual-specific means of the conditional distributions we have just generated using the `ggplot2` package (See Fig. 10.8).

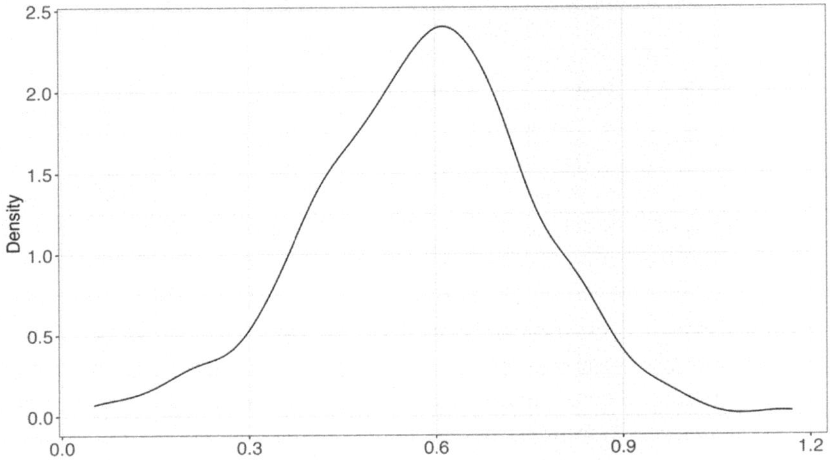


**Fig. 10.8** Marginal utility for low turbines (conditional means)

```
# Kernel density of the means of the conditional distribution
conditionals_lh |>
  ggplot(aes(x = post_mean)) +
  geom_density() +
  labs(
    x = "Marginal utility for low turbines (conditional means)",
    y = "Density"
  ) +
  theme_bw()
```

Reflecting back on the sub-sample of individuals who are 40 years old, male, and have the lowest level of education that we examined earlier when discussing the unconditional distribution, we find that there are three individuals in our sample who fit these criteria. To help illustrate the distinction between unconditional and conditional distributions, we now consider how their individual-specific means compare and whether we can identify their positions within the broader distribution.

It is important to remember that the individual-specific mean is merely a single point estimate on their conditional distribution. To demonstrate the nature of individual-specific distributions, we plot the midpoints of equally spaced bins against the total weights of the unconditional draws that fall within these bin boundaries for each of the three individuals. This line plot, resembling a frequency polygon, provides a clear visual representation of the distribution's shape, highlighting the central location and where the majority of the density is concentrated for each individual.

By overlaying the distributions for all three individuals (See Fig. 10.9), we can directly compare them, revealing any similarities or differences in their marginal utility estimates. Additionally, adding the distribution produced from the unconditional distribution (the red dashed line) allows us to contrast the individual-specific distributions with the broader, unconditional one.

This visualisation underscores the key concept that the individual-specific conditional estimates are not just single values but distributions in themselves. Typically,

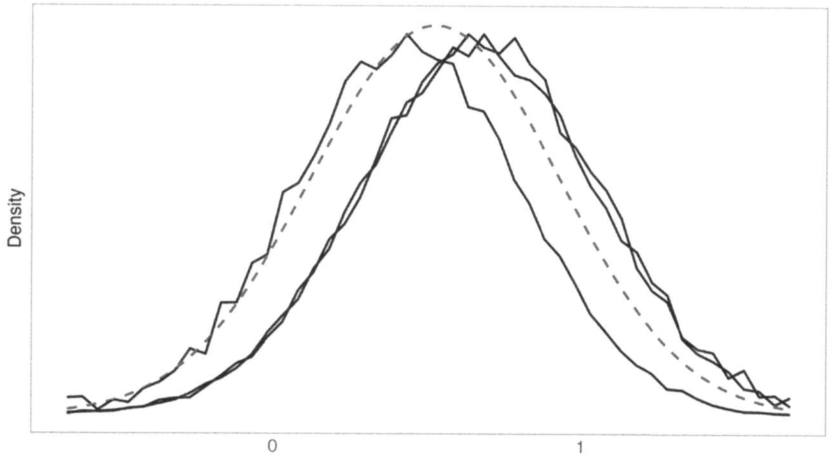


**Fig. 10.9** Marginal utility (individual-specific conditional distribution)

we focus on the mean of these distributions and occasionally consider the standard deviation, but this visualisation reminds us that these estimates are part of a larger probabilistic landscape. This deeper understanding is crucial when interpreting the results of models that account for heterogeneity in preferences across individuals.

Although the individual-specific means of the conditional distributions represent just a single point within the broader distribution, they remain highly valuable and informative. These means serve as the expected value or weighted average, providing the best estimate of where an individual is likely to fall on the distribution, all else being equal.

Essentially, given the model specification (e.g. type and number of draws, distributional assumptions), the resulting parameters, the data, and the choices made by the individual (hence why they are termed "conditional" estimates), these means offer our most reliable estimate of each individual's marginal utility. Consequently, one of the key advantages of conditional distributions is the ability to explore and examine differences across various subgroups. For example, we can compare conditional distributions by different socio-demographic variables. See the code chunk below, where the means of the conditional distributions are first separated in Fig. 10.10 by *gender* and then in Fig. 10.11 by *education*.

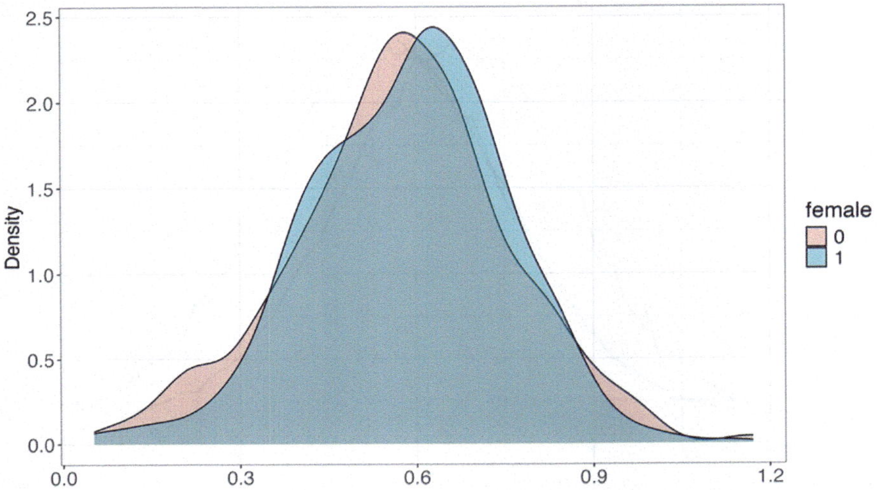


**Fig. 10.10** Marginal utility for low turbines (conditional means) by gender

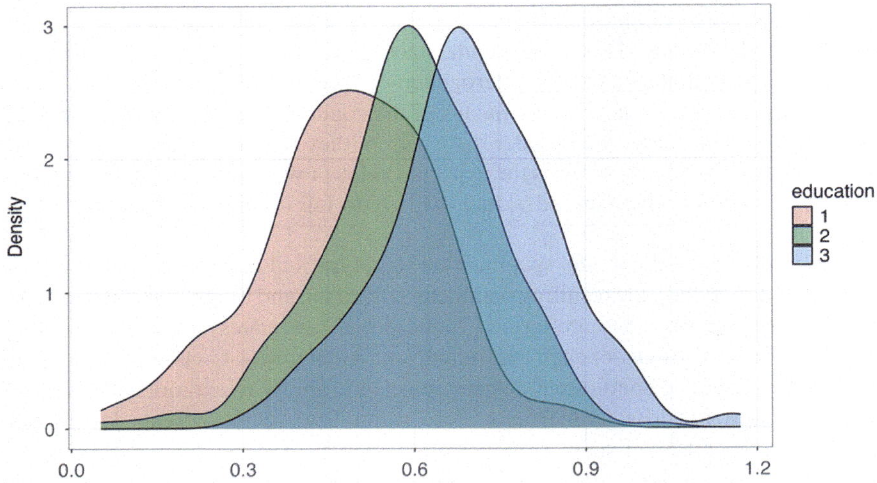


**Fig. 10.11** Marginal utility for low turbines (conditional means) by education

```
## Plotting the conditionals ----
conditionals_lh <- database |>
  select(id_individual, age, female, education) |>
  distinct() |>
  right_join(conditionals_lh, by = "id_individual")


conditionals_lh |>
  mutate(
    female = factor(female)
  ) |>
  ggplot(aes(x = post_mean, fill = female)) +
  geom_density(alpha = 0.4) +
  labs(
    x = "Marginal utility for low turbines (conditional means)",
    y = "Density"
  ) +
  theme_bw()


conditionals_lh |>
  mutate(
    education = factor(education)
  ) |>
  ggplot(aes(x = post_mean, fill = education)) +
  geom_density(alpha = 0.4) +
  labs(
    x = "Marginal utility for low turbines (conditional means)",
    y = "Density"
  ) +
  theme_bw()
```

As discussed in Sect. 3.1, knowing the distribution of marginal utilities alone provides limited insight because it is affected by scale issues, such that the distribution is not directly comparable across individuals or models. As we have seen earlier in this chapter, measures like mWTP and consumer surplus, which require the consideration of multiple random parameters, are far more useful. To compute mWTP here, you need the random distributions for both a non-cost attribute and the cost attribute. Since we already have the respective unconditional distributions (stored in `unconditionals`) and the corresponding weights for each draw (stored in `w`), we can easily derive the means of the conditional distributions.

The code for this is provided below. Note that if the RP-MXL model is estimated in WTP space (see Sect. 9.3.1.2.2), the mWTP distributions are directly obtained from the estimation process. However, in cases where the model is estimated in preference space, such as the model used in this chapter, the mWTP must be calculated as the ratio of the coefficients, which is precisely what we do in the code chunk below.

A key aspect of applied work in environmental economics and policy implementation is understanding how policies affect various segments of the population. Policymakers may want to know, for example, whether men or women are more significantly impacted by a given policy, or if individuals living closer to new wind farms experience greater effects than those further away.

Often, we tackle these questions by comparing mWTP values for different population segments. In the code chunk below, we present kernel density plots for the means of the individual-specific mWTP distributions, grouped by specific socio-demographic variables (gender and education) in the data, to illustrate how the impacts vary across different groups. Figure 10.12 illustrates these distributions by gender, while Fig. 10.13 focuses on education.

```
# Add the means of the conditional marginal WTP distributions to the tibble
conditionals_lh <- conditionals_lh |>
  mutate(
    post_mean_wtp = rowSums(w * (- unconditionals$r_lh / unconditionals$r_ct))
  )


# Plot the results
conditionals_lh |>
  mutate(
    female = factor(female)
  ) |>
  ggplot(aes(x = post_mean_wtp, fill = female)) +
  geom_density(alpha = 0.4) +
  labs(
    x = "Marginal WTP for low turbines (conditional means)",
    y = "Density"
  ) +
  theme_bw()
```

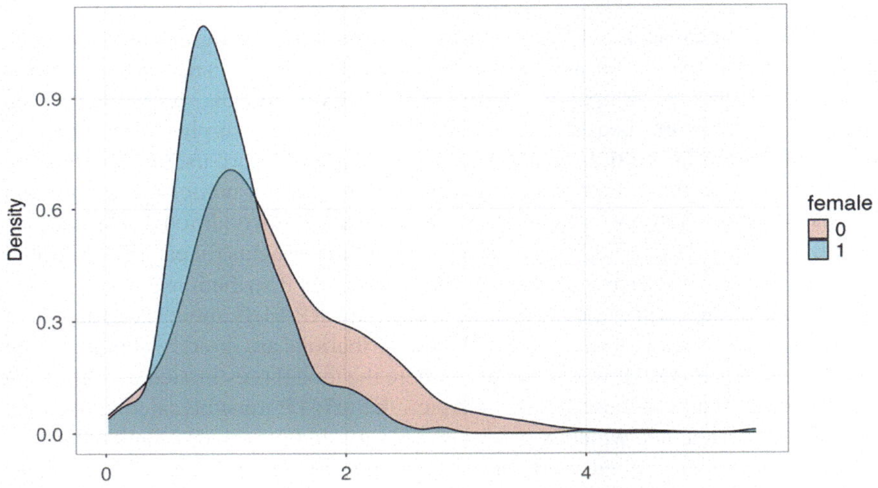


**Fig. 10.12** Marginal WTP for low turbines (conditional means) by gender

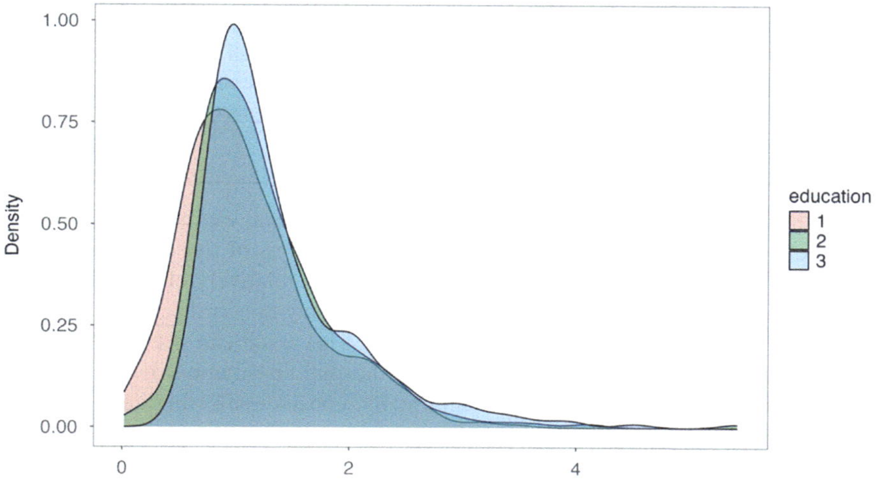


**Fig. 10.13** Marginal WTP for low turbines (conditional means) by education

```
conditionals_lh |>
  mutate(
    education = factor(education)
  ) |>
  ggplot(aes(x = post_mean_wtp, fill = education)) +
  geom_density(alpha = 0.4) +
  labs(
    x = "Marginal WTP for low turbines (conditional means)",
    y = "Density"
  ) +
  theme_bw()
```

**Ensuring well-defined moments in mWTP distributions**

As discussed in Chap. 9, certain popular distributions used for monetary coefficients in RP-MXL models can result in infinite moments for the distribution of mWTP. For example, when dividing by a random variable that follows a normal distribution, which ranges from minus to plus infinity, there is a non-zero probability that the divisor will be very close to zero. This can lead to outcomes that are not well-defined and cause the resulting distribution to exhibit extreme variability, often resulting in infinite variance.

Daly et al. (2012) offer comprehensive discussions on this issue and present a theorem that outlines the specific assumptions about the population-level distribution of the random parameter for the cost attribute necessary to ensure that the moments of the mWTP distribution are well-defined.

> Our focus here is specifically on zero values in the denominator of the continuous distributions assumed for the coefficients in an RP-MXL model, rather than zeroes that might occur due to sample variation in the maximum likelihood estimates. For a detailed discussion of the distinction between these two types of zeroes, we refer readers to Daly et al. (2023).

For these reasons, as part of the post-estimation analysis, we recommend examining both the unconditional and conditional distributions of the cost attribute. If these distributions contain a high proportion of values relatively close to zero, the resulting mWTP distributions are likely to exhibit heavy tails or become undefined in regions where the denominator is very small. This issue can occur even if the cost attribute is modelled using a negative log-normal distribution. If you observe this problem and the data supports it empirically, consider selecting an alternative distribution for the cost attribute that ensures it remains strictly negative.

#### 10.3.2.2 The Poe Test for Differences in Distributions

The kernel density plots generated above for different sub-groups provide valuable insights into the distribution of mWTP. At a glance, it is evident that the distributions overlap (see Fig. 10.12 and Fig. 10.13). If there were no overlap—or very minimal overlap—it would be straightforward to conclude that the means of the individual-specific conditional distributions are statistically different. However, in cases where there is clear overlap, a more rigorous approach is needed.

When analysing mWTP distributions for various subgroups, a key question arises: is one subgroup willing to pay more or less than another for the same change in the provision of an environmental good? For instance, the kernel density plot in Fig. 10.12 suggests that the distribution for males is shifted to the right compared to that for females, indicating a potentially higher mWTP among males for this attribute. However, without a formal statistical test, this observation remains speculative.

The Poe test (Poe et al. 2005) is a statistical test that can be used to compare two distributions of mWTP. The test is based on the idea that if two distributions are equal, then the probability that a random draw from one distribution is less than or equal to a random draw from the other distribution is 0.5. The test relies on a convolution process, which considers all possible pairwise combinations between the two distributions. The test statistic represents the proportion of times that a draw from one distribution is less than or equal to a draw from the other. This proportion is then compared against a critical value to determine if the two distributions are statistically different. As a non-parametric test, the Poe test does not make assumptions about the underlying distributions, offering a flexible and robust approach for comparing distributions, especially when the data may not satisfy the assumptions required for parametric tests.

We can easily perform the Poe test in R to compare two independent distributions. The code chunk below demonstrates this process. Here, we consider two distributions: `wtp_female` and `wtp_male`, which represent the means of the individual-specific mWTP distributions for female and male individuals in our sample, respectively.

```
# Extract the mean of individual-specific marginal WTP distributions for females
wtp_female <- conditionals_lh |>
  filter(female == 1) |>
  select(post_mean) |>
  pull()

# Extract the mean of individual-specific marginal WTP distributions for males
wtp_male <- conditionals_lh |>
  filter(female == 0) |>
  select(post_mean) |>
  pull()

# Compare each element of wtp_female with all elements of wtp_male
condition <- rowSums(outer(wtp_female, wtp_male, `<`))

# To obtain the test statistic gamma, sum over the condition vector and weight
# by the inverse of the product of the lengths of the vectors
n_female <- length(wtp_female)
n_male <- length(wtp_male)
statistic <- sum(condition) / (n_female * n_male)

# Print the resulting test statistic
print(statistic)
```

```
[1] 0.4748874
```

Specifically, this code tests the null hypothesis that the two distributions are equal against the alternative hypothesis that `wtp_female` < `wtp_male`. The reported statistic of 0.475 indicates that we fail to reject the null hypothesis at 5% significance level, leading us to conclude that `wtp_female` is not significantly lower than `wtp_male`. The code calculates the proportion of pairwise comparisons where `wtp_female`<`wtp_male`. Specifically, 118,492 out of 249,516 total comparisons support the alternative hypothesis. The *p*-value is computed as $118,492/249,516$, which equals 0.475. If we were testing the reverse hypothesis (`wtp_female` > `wtp_male`), the *p*-value would be 0.525 (i.e. $1 - 0.475$) and the conclusion would be the same. We fail to reject the null hypothesis at a 5% significance level.

The Poe test is a versatile tool that extends beyond comparing subgroups based on socio-demographics within a sample. It can be broadly applied to compare any two distributions, making it valuable in various research contexts. For instance, the test can compare the distributions (either unconditional or conditional) of two random parameters for different attributes within the same model. This is particularly useful if you want to determine whether the distribution of mWTP for one attribute significantly differs from that of another attribute.

The Poe test is especially beneficial when evaluating what effects different model specifications and distributional assumptions have on distributions of interest. It is also useful when examining differences in distributions derived from models that capture distinct behavioural decision-making heuristics, such as attribute non-attendance, elimination by aspects, or satisficing (Alemu et al. 2013; Daniel et al. 2018). Additionally, the test can be used to assess differences in distributions arising from different data treatments, such as variations in framing or the use of cheap talk scripts in stated choice experiments. In all these scenarios, the Poe test provides a robust method for determining whether the distributions are statistically different, making it a highly flexible tool in applied research, particularly in environmental economics and stated choice experiments.

We highlight the Poe test because it is frequently employed in environmental economics and is less commonly discussed in standard statistical or econometric textbooks compared to more widely used parametric and non-parametric tests. It is important to emphasise that relying solely on the Poe test when comparing two continuous distributions is not advisable. While the Poe test is a valuable non-parametric tool for comparing distributions, it is just one of many statistical tests available. Your choice of tests should be guided by the specific characteristics of your data and the nature of the comparisons you wish to make.

Parametric tests, such as the $t$-test and $F$-test, are widely used when the data meets certain assumptions, such as normality and the homogeneity of variances. The $t$-test is particularly useful for testing differences in means between two distributions, while the $F$-test assesses differences in variances. However, these tests may not be appropriate if the data violates the underlying assumptions, such as when the data is non-normally distributed or has outliers. In such cases, non-parametric tests provide robust alternatives.

The Mann–Whitney U test (also known as the Wilcoxon rank-sum test) is useful for comparing the central tendency of two distributions without assuming normality, as it focuses on the ranks of the data rather than the actual values. The Kolmogorov–Smirnov test is another powerful non-parametric test that compares the distributions, making it suitable for detecting differences in shape, location, and scale between two samples.

Given the diversity of available tests, you should assess which tests are most suitable for your analysis. We always recommend implementing multiple tests to ensure the robustness of your results—if different tests lead to the same conclusion, it strengthens the validity of your findings. Doing this not only provides greater confidence in your findings but also enhances the credibility of your policy recommendations.

#### 10.3.2.3 Moving Beyond the Mean

When conducting post-estimation analyses, and especially when reporting results, it is essential to go beyond reporting just the mean of the distribution. This, unfortunately, is common in the DCE literature, with researchers focusing solely on the mean in their analysis of mWTP and welfare changes. While the mean is an important point estimate, it is only one aspect of the distribution. The goal of implementing more complex models such as MXL models is to go beyond the mean, and not taking advantage of these results means throwing away much of the time and effort required for their estimation. Indeed, if all you want is a point estimate, you might as well stick with an MNL model.

The strength of the RP-MXL model lies in uncovering heterogeneity, so it is vital to describe the full distribution of key variables like the mWTP and welfare change, rather than just reporting the mean. The mean alone offers little insight into the distribution's shape and variability. Indeed, understanding not only the mean but also the distribution's shape, variability, and key percentiles (e.g. median, quartiles, and bottom and top deciles) is beneficial for policymakers. This information allows them to better assess how their decisions might impact different segments of the population. By considering the full distribution, policymakers can make more informed choices that account for the diverse effects of their policies across various groups.

Retrieving key percentiles of marginal utilities—such as the median, quartiles, and bottom and top deciles—is relatively straightforward for continuously defined random parameters in an RP-MXL model, as these are typically modelled using common parametric distributions like the normal, log-normal, or uniform distribution (with R functions `qnorm`, `qlnorm`, and `qunif`, respectively).

However, in practice, we are often interested in transformations involving multiple random parameters, such as calculating the mWTP (a ratio) or welfare changes (using the log-sum formula). The distribution of these transformed variables is usually not a standard one with a closed-form expression for its mean, variance, or percentiles. Computing these requires integrating over the joint distribution of all random parameters involved, which can be complex. To approximate the mean, variance, and percentiles of interest, a common approach is to use simulation, generating numerous samples from the distributions involved, calculating the variable of interest for each sample, and then averaging the results.

#### 10.3.2.4 Sampling Variation

As discussed earlier with respect to the MNL model results, we must account for the variability introduced by the sampling error. This represents an additional layer of variability beyond what we have discussed so far in the context of RP-MXL models, where the focus has primarily been on variability due to preference heterogeneity. It is important to distinguish between these two sources of variability. To deliver defensible and robust findings, whether for academic purposes or policy-making, it is important to acknowledge and clearly report both types of variability in your results and analysis.

The literature offers methods for translating sample variation into measures of uncertainty for continuously distributed coefficients (see Bliemer and Rose 2013; Scaccia et al. 2023). In the code chunk below, we focus on generating confidence intervals for the mWTP for *LowHeight*. We use the Krinsky-Robb method because the interaction of multiple socio-demographics in the numerator and denominator of the mWTP calculation is relatively complex when using the Delta method. Additionally, as emphasised earlier, it is crucial to move beyond focusing solely on the mean estimate. The Krinsky-Robb method simplifies the retrieval of confidence intervals for any summary statistic of interest.

The code chunk begins by extracting the draws used in the *Apollo* estimation process, along with the socio-demographic variables interacting with the random parameters. We then define a function called `randCoeff`, which mirrors the definition of random parameters in `apollo_randCoeff`. This function retrieves the unconditional distributions of the random parameters given the argument `params`. It essentially performs the same task as `apollo_unconditionals`, but is more efficient (since it is tailored to this setting) and optimised for repeated applications in a large number of Krinsky-Robb simulations.

Next, we generate unconditional draws based on the model estimates. Although this step could be skipped since the draws were already retrieved using `apollo_unconditionals`, it is included here for clarity. We then calculate the distribution of the mWTP of *LowHeight*. This distribution is unconditional, with a length equal to the number of draws used in the model estimation (which utilises the draws element in `apollo_inputs`) for each individual in the sample. Assuming no sample weights and that the sample is representative and random, obtaining a summary statistic that represents the sample level is straightforward—simply flatten the matrix into a single vector and calculate the summary statistic from that vector. This approach accounts for both preference heterogeneity within the sample and the observed sources of heterogeneity explained by socio-demographic variables.

We then compute the mean, standard deviation, deciles, quartiles, and median of the distribution. Following this, we use the previously defined `sim_dists` function to generate 10,000 draws from the empirical distribution. For each of these draws, we derive the associated distributions of mWTP and calculate the same summary statistics. Finally, we combine the statistics predicted using the model estimates with the 2.5th and 97.5th percentiles of the corresponding simulated values to provide 95 percent confidence intervals for each statistic. The results are printed in Table 10.9.

**Table 10.9** mWTP summary statistics for *LowHeight* from RP-MXL model accounting for sampling variation

| Statistic | Predict | Lower_ci | Upper_ci |
|---|---|---|---|
| Mean | −0.12 | −21.77 | 18.92 |
| SD | 0.07 | 0.42 | 31.29 |
| D1 | −0.21 | −49.08 | 5.33 |
| Q1 | −0.15 | −27.86 | 8.42 |
| Q2 (median) | −0.11 | −13.77 | 14.21 |
| Q3 | −0.08 | −6.78 | 24.06 |
| D9 | −0.06 | −3.54 | 37.91 |

```
# Extract the first row of untransformed draws(standard normals) for each individual
draws <- apollo_firstRow(apollo_inputs$draws, apollo_inputs)

# Extract socio-demographic variables for mean shifts
socio_demo <- apollo_firstRow(database, apollo_inputs)[, c("age", "female", "education")]

# Transform untransformed draws using model parameters (matches apollo_randCoeff, optimised   for Krin
sky-Robb simulations)
randCoeff <- function(params) {
  with(as.list(params), {
    list(
      r_mf = mu_mf + sd_mf * draws$draws_mf + delta_mf_age * socio_demo$age + delta_mf_female * socio_
demo$female + delta_mf_educ * socio_demo$education,
      r_sf = mu_sf + sd_sf * draws$draws_sf + delta_sf_age * socio_demo$age + delta_sf_female * socio_
demo$female + delta_sf_educ * socio_demo$education,
      r_mh = mu_mh + sd_mh * draws$draws_mh + delta_mh_age * socio_demo$age + delta_mh_female * socio_
demo$female + delta_mh_educ * socio_demo$education,
      r_lh = mu_lh + sd_lh * draws$draws_lh + delta_lh_age * socio_demo$age + delta_lh_female * socio_
demo$female + delta_lh_educ * socio_demo$education,
      r_rk = mu_rk + sd_rk * draws$draws_rk + delta_rk_age * socio_demo$age + delta_rk_female * socio_
demo$female + delta_rk_educ * socio_demo$education,
      r_md = mu_md + sd_md * draws$draws_md + delta_md_age * socio_demo$age + delta_md_female * socio_
demo$female + delta_md_educ * socio_demo$education,
      r_ct = -exp(mu_ct + sd_ct * draws$draws_ct + delta_ct_age * socio_demo$age + delta_ct_female * s
ocio_demo$female + delta_ct_educ * socio_demo$education)
    )
  })
}

# Generate draws based on model estimates
randCoeff_model <- randCoeff(model$estimate)

# Calculate marginal WTP for variable of interest
wtp_lh_model <- -randCoeff_model$r_rk / randCoeff_model$r_ct

# Summarise predicted WTP distribution
wtp_lh_summary <- c(
  mean = mean(wtp_lh_model),
  sd = sd(wtp_lh_model),
  quantile(wtp_lh_model, c(0.1, 0.25, 0.5, 0.75, 0.9))
)

# Set number of Krinsky-Robb simulations
nsims <- 10000

# Generate empirical distributions for simulations
sim_dists <- simulate_dist(model, nsims)

# Summarise WTP distributions across simulations
wtp_lh_summaries <- t(apply(sim_dists, 1, function(row) {
  randCoeff_s <- randCoeff(row)
  wtp_lh <- -randCoeff_s$r_lh / randCoeff_s$r_ct

  c(
    mean = mean(wtp_lh),
    sd = sd(wtp_lh),
    quantile(wtp_lh, c(0.1, 0.25, 0.5, 0.75, 0.9))
  )
}))

# Combine predictive distribution and confidence intervals
wtp_lh_dist <- tibble(
  statistic = c("Mean", "SD", "D1", "Q1", "Q2 (median)", "Q3", "D9"),
  predict = wtp_lh_summary,
  lower_ci = apply(wtp_lh_summaries, 2, quantile, probs = 0.025),
  upper_ci = apply(wtp_lh_summaries, 2, quantile, probs = 0.975)
)
```

**ⓘ Parallelising your computations**

In the context of an RP-MXL model, the Krinsky-Robb approach involves simulating unconditional distributions over a large number of draws from the empirical distribution, which can be computationally intensive and time-consuming. However, because these simulations involve independent computations, you can significantly improve the efficiency and reduce the processing time by using parallelisation.

This can be achieved by distributing tasks across multiple cores or processors. While this topic lies beyond the scope of the book, it is worth noting that R packages like `parallel` and `foreach` offer excellent tools for task-based parallelisation, allowing tasks to be easily divided into smaller units and executed concurrently across multiple cores or processors.

Table 10.9 provides the information needed to assess the statistical significance of various summary statistics of a continuous distribution derived from an RP-MXL model. Specifically, it focuses on a mWTP estimate, where the numerator follows a normal distribution and the denominator follows a negative log-normal distribution. Both the numerator and the denominator incorporate three mean shifters based on socio-demographic variables in the dataset. Consequently, calculating the empirical marginal distributions involves a total of 10 parameter estimates, each with its associated variance, along with 45 covariances that need to be accounted for.

Given this complexity, alongside the spread in the socio-demographic variables in the dataset, a high degree of variability is expected, which is evident in the results. This highlights the importance of not taking initial model results at face value and accounting for sampling variation. Additionally, considering a broader range of summary statistics beyond just the mean is crucial, as it provides policymakers with deeper insights into the distribution.

The uncertainty inherent in parameter estimates carries over to the derived conditional distributions. This implies that the means and standard deviations of these distributions are also subject to variation. While it is possible to derive standard errors and confidence intervals for these parameters, applying the Delta method can be complex and less stable due to the non-linear transformations involved. In such cases, the Krinsky-Robb method is generally more suitable.

To demonstrate how sampling variation affects the mean of an individual's *conditional* distribution, we focus on the marginal utility of *LowHeight* for the first individual in the sample. The estimated mean of this individual's conditional distribution, based on the model's parameter estimates, is 0.573. This value represents our best estimate of their marginal utility for this attribute, conditional on the model, data, and observed choices. However, because of sampling variation, a different sample (but still including this individual) could lead to a different set of parameter estimates, resulting in a different individual-specific conditional mean. To assess the uncertainty around this estimate, we simulate an empirical distribution using the same methodology as the Krinsky-Robb approach.

We generate 10,000 multivariate normal draws centred on the model parameters, using the robust variance–covariance matrix as the variance–covariance of the distribution. For each draw, we calculate the conditional mean of the individual's marginal utility of *LowHeight* and store these means. This process results in 10,000 different conditional means, reflecting the variability due to sampling. The histogram of these simulated means is shown in Fig. 10.14, providing a visual representation of the distribution. From this, we extract the 2.5th and 97.5th percentiles to construct a 95% confidence interval. We can now state that the individual's marginal utility is 0.573 (95% CI: [−5.238, 6.468]), accounting for the inherent sampling variation in the conditional distribution.

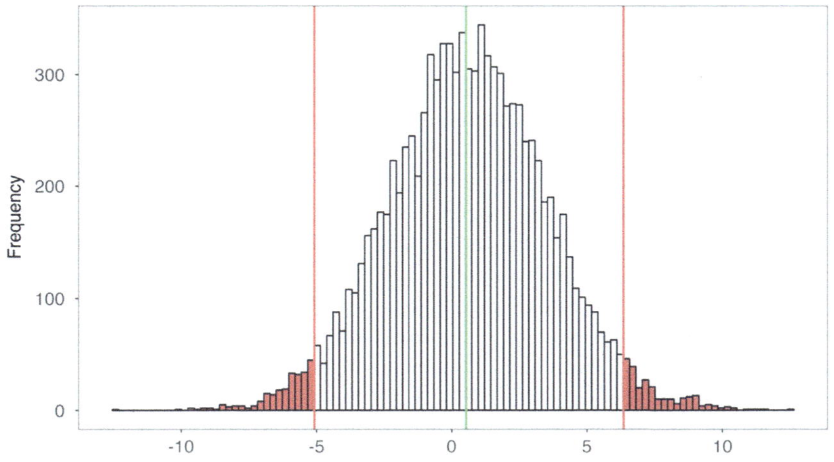


**Fig. 10.14** Marginal utility (mean of the conditional distribution for individual 1)

> **Important**
>
> The means of conditional distributions are often used for further analysis, such as regression modelling (see Campbell 2007) or exploring spatial variations in environmental economics (see Campbell et al. 2009). However, these analyses frequently overlook the sampling variation inherent in these means, treating them as definitive points on the distribution without accounting for their associated variance. As shown here, sampling variation also affects these estimates. This oversight is similar to ignoring the variance from the first stage in a two-stage modelling approach, leading to biased and inconsistent estimates in the second stage. When the uncertainty from the first stage is disregarded, standard errors are underestimated, resulting in overly narrow confidence intervals and overstated statistical significance. This increases the risk of Type I errors, falsely identifying significant relationships between variables.
>
> To ensure the validity of an analysis based on the means of the conditional distributions, it is crucial to properly account for the variance from the first stage. One effective approach is to incorporate sampling variation into this type of secondary analysis by repeatedly conducting the analysis with different draws from the empirical distribution, thereby capturing the uncertainty in the conditional distributions.

### *10.3.3 LC-MXL Model*

Moving on to the latent class model, we will now focus on the results of the two-class LC-MXL model presented in Eq. (9.12) in Sect. 9.3.2. The parameters estimated from this model are shown in Table 10.10. To interpret an LC-MXL model, it is important to recognise that it explains the data through a finite number of distinct parameter sets, each corresponding to a latent class. Within each class, preferences are assumed to be homogeneous, while heterogeneity exists between classes. The LC-MXL model is not a classification model, as respondents are not assigned to classes. Instead, the model estimates class-specific parameters and the unconditional probability of belonging to each class. What distinguishes an LC-MXL from an RP-MXL model is the fact that it assumes discrete distributions as opposed to continuous distributions.

Since preference homogeneity is assumed within each latent class, each class functions as its own MNL model. This means that you can apply the same post-estimation analytical techniques used for MNL models to analyse the results within each class. For instance, if you want to retrieve class-specific mWTPs and their associated standard errors using the Delta method, you can simply use the parameters estimated within that class.

**Table 10.10** LC-MXL model estimates

| | Estimate | Std_err | t_stat | p_value |
|---|---|---|---|---|
| cl1_asc_alt1 | 0.000 | NA | NA | NA |
| cl1_asc_alt2 | 0.594 | 0.017 | 35.399 | 0.000 |
| cl1_asc_alt3 | 0.589 | 0.024 | 24.634 | 0.000 |
| cl1_b_medium_farms | 0.240 | 0.027 | 8.790 | 0.000 |
| cl1_b_small_farms | 0.316 | 0.007 | 42.756 | 0.000 |
| cl1_b_medium_height | 0.443 | 0.037 | 11.979 | 0.000 |
| cl1_b_low_height | 0.928 | 0.020 | 45.797 | 0.000 |
| cl1_b_red_kite | −0.046 | 0.000 | −103.646 | 0.000 |
| cl1_b_min_distance | 0.493 | 0.019 | 26.016 | 0.000 |
| cl1_b_cost | −0.746 | 0.018 | −42.061 | 0.000 |
| cl2_asc_alt1 | 0.000 | NA | NA | NA |
| cl2_asc_alt2 | 1.224 | 0.014 | 90.029 | 0.000 |
| cl2_asc_alt3 | 1.227 | 0.010 | 122.913 | 0.000 |
| cl2_b_medium_farms | −0.534 | 0.012 | −45.930 | 0.000 |
| cl2_b_small_farms | 0.128 | 0.006 | 23.148 | 0.000 |
| cl2_b_medium_height | −0.769 | 0.021 | −35.931 | 0.000 |
| cl2_b_low_height | 0.411 | 0.006 | 63.398 | 0.000 |
| cl2_b_red_kite | −0.059 | 0.000 | −147.477 | 0.000 |
| cl2_b_min_distance | 0.193 | 0.002 | 100.601 | 0.000 |
| cl2_b_cost | −0.300 | 0.006 | −47.329 | 0.000 |
| cl1_cst_alloc_fun | 0.000 | NA | NA | NA |
| cl1_b_age | 0.000 | NA | NA | NA |
| cl1_b_female | 0.000 | NA | NA | NA |
| cl1_b_educ | 0.000 | NA | NA | NA |
| cl2_cst_alloc_fun | −0.154 | 0.354 | −0.436 | 0.663 |
| cl2_b_age | 0.020 | 0.006 | 3.318 | 0.001 |
| cl2_b_female | −0.851 | 0.166 | −5.129 | 0.000 |
| cl2_b_educ | −0.305 | 0.098 | −3.125 | 0.002 |

```
# Settings for the function apollo_deltaMethod
deltaMethod_settings <- list(
  expression = c(
    cl1_wtp_medium_farms = "-cl1_b_medium_farms / cl1_b_cost",
    cl1_wtp_small_farms = "-cl1_b_small_farms / cl1_b_cost",
    cl1_wtp_medium_height = "-cl1_b_medium_height / cl1_b_cost",
    cl1_wtp_low_height = "-cl1_b_low_height / cl1_b_cost",
    cl1_wtp_red_kite = "-cl1_b_red_kite / cl1_b_cost",
    cl1_wtp_min_distance = "-cl1_b_min_distance / cl1_b_cost",
    cl2_wtp_medium_farms = "-cl2_b_medium_farms / cl2_b_cost",
    cl2_wtp_small_farms = "-cl2_b_small_farms / cl2_b_cost",
    cl2_wtp_medium_height = "-cl2_b_medium_height / cl2_b_cost",
    cl2_wtp_low_height = "-cl2_b_low_height / cl2_b_cost",
    cl2_wtp_red_kite = "-cl2_b_red_kite / cl2_b_cost",
    cl2_wtp_min_distance = "-cl2_b_min_distance / cl2_b_cost"
  )
)

# Apply the Delta method to calculate the standard errors of marginal WTP
wtp_results_delta <- apollo_deltaMethod(model, deltaMethod_settings)
```

```
Running Delta method computation for user-defined function using robust standard errors

             Expression   Value   s.e. t-ratio (0)
   cl1_wtp_medium_farms  0.3219 0.0290       11.11
    cl1_wtp_small_farms  0.4239 0.0069       61.25
  cl1_wtp_medium_height  0.5936 0.0355       16.71
     cl1_wtp_low_height  1.2441 0.0042      296.14
       cl1_wtp_red_kite -0.0614 0.0016      -37.75
   cl1_wtp_min_distance  0.6605 0.0106       62.56
   cl2_wtp_medium_farms -1.7806 0.0762      -23.36
    cl2_wtp_small_farms  0.4268 0.0122       34.86
  cl2_wtp_medium_height -2.5618 0.1252      -20.47
     cl2_wtp_low_height  1.3683 0.0096      141.80
       cl2_wtp_red_kite -0.1979 0.0051      -38.70
   cl2_wtp_min_distance  0.6434 0.0166       38.86
INFORMATION: The results of the Delta method calculations are returned invisibly as
  an output from this function. Calling the function via
  result=apollo_deltaMethod(...) will save this output in an object
  called result (or otherwise named object).
```

While analysing within-class preferences is valuable, it is equally important to consider the size of each latent class. Remember that the LC-MXL model is not a classification model, so the size of each class does not represent the proportion of the sample (or population) that belongs to each class. Additionally, an individual's true preferences cannot be determined with certainty, meaning they remain latent. As a result, we cannot (and should not) assign individuals to any specific class. Based on observed choice behaviour, the existence of each class-specific set of parameters can only be inferred probabilistically, with the probability distributed across all classes for each individual.

The model parameters allow us to derive unconditional class membership probabilities, which represent the prior likelihoods that the different sets of marginal utilities correspond to an individual's actual marginal utilities. These unconditional class membership probabilities can be uniform across individuals or vary according to observable traits such as socio-demographic characteristics. In this analysis, we have chosen the latter approach, leading to unique class membership probabilities for each combination of socio-demographic variables. The code chunk below demonstrates how to retrieve these probabilities and their associated standard errors using the Delta method, specifically for a 70-year-old female with the lowest level of education.

```
# Settings for the function apollo_deltaMethod
deltaMethod_settings <- list(
  expression = c(
    cl1_prob = "1 / (1 +
exp(cl2_cst_alloc_fun + cl2_b_age * 70 + cl2_b_female * 1 + cl2_b_educ * 3))",
    cl2_prob = "exp(cl2_cst_alloc_fun + cl2_b_age * 70 + cl2_b_female * 1 + cl2_b_educ * 3)
/ (1 +
exp(cl2_cst_alloc_fun + cl2_b_age * 70 + cl2_b_female * 1 + cl2_b_educ * 3))",
    logit_cl1_prob = "log(
  (1 / (1 + exp(cl2_cst_alloc_fun + cl2_b_age * 70 + cl2_b_female * 1 + cl2_b_educ * 3)))
  /(1 - (1 / (1 + exp(cl2_cst_alloc_fun + cl2_b_age * 70 + cl2_b_female * 1 + cl2_b_educ *
3)))))",
    logit_cl2_prob = "log(
  (exp(cl2_cst_alloc_fun + cl2_b_age * 70 + cl2_b_female * 1 + cl2_b_educ * 3) / (1 + exp(c
l2_cst_alloc_fun + cl2_b_age * 70 + cl2_b_female * 1 + cl2_b_educ * 3)))
  /(1 - (exp(cl2_cst_alloc_fun + cl2_b_age * 70 + cl2_b_female * 1 + cl2_b_educ * 3) / (1 +
exp(cl2_cst_alloc_fun + cl2_b_age * 70 + cl2_b_female * 1 + cl2_b_educ * 3)))))"
  )
)

# Apply the Delta method to calculate the standard errors
lc_prob_results_delta <- apollo_deltaMethod(model, deltaMethod_settings)

Running Delta method computation for user-defined function using robust standard errors

     Expression    Value   s.e. t-ratio (0)
       cl1_prob   0.6199 0.0598       10.36
       cl2_prob   0.3801 0.0598        6.35
 logit_cl1_prob   0.4890 0.2539        1.93
 logit_cl2_prob  -0.4890 0.2539       -1.93
INFORMATION: The results of the Delta method calculations are returned invisibly as
  an output from this function. Calling the function via
  result=apollo_deltaMethod(...) will save this output in an object
  called result (or otherwise named object).
```

When dealing with estimates of class membership probabilities that must lie between 0 and 1, testing the null hypothesis against 0 does not make sense, because a true probability of exactly 0 is a boundary condition rather than a typical value within the distribution.

Moreover, the standard error should be interpreted with caution. The standard error is based on the assumption of normality, and while this can approximate the distribution of an estimate under certain conditions, the normal distribution itself extends infinitely in both directions. For probabilities, this means that a standard error-based confidence interval might suggest values less than 0 or greater than 1, which are not valid probabilities. These issues can be solved by using the transformation detailed below.

Despite these challenges, the normal distribution properties of the estimate can still be useful, particularly when the probability is not near the boundaries of 0 and 1. However, when the estimated probability is close to these boundaries, the normal approximation becomes less reliable.

In any case, it is usually more appropriate to use a transformation, such as the logit transformation ($\log(p/1-p)$), which maps the probability onto the entire real line. After calculating the confidence interval on the transformed scale, it can be back-transformed to the original probability scale, ensuring that the interval remains within the 0–1 range. This approach maintains the validity of the confidence interval while adhering to the properties of the normal distribution.

In the code chunk above, we apply the logit transformation to the unconditional class membership probabilities, resulting in estimates of 0.489 (95% CI: [−0.009, 0.987]) and -0.489 (95% CI: [−0.987, 0.009]) for Class 1 and Class 2, respectively. After back-transforming, we obtain the corresponding unconditional class membership probabilities of 0.620 (95% CI: [0.498, 0.728]) and 0.380 (95% CI: [0.272, 0.502]).

Observant readers will notice that in this two-class model, the standard errors are identical for the unconditional probabilities and their logit transformations. Additionally, the complement of the lower confidence interval for one probability is the upper confidence interval for the other, and vice versa. This occurs because the two probabilities sum to one. As a result, it is only necessary to calculate the probabilities, standard errors, and confidence intervals for one of the classes, since those for the other class can be inferred directly. This can be generalised to models with more than two classes: in such cases, you only need to compute these values for all classes except one; the remaining class's values can then be derived.

#### 10.3.3.1 Unconditional and Conditional Distributions

Moving beyond the unconditional class membership probabilities for a specific subgroup within the sample, we recommend exploring these probabilities across the entire sample. This can be done using the `apollo_unconditionals` function, which is also applicable to latent class models. In an LC-MXL model, this function returns a list with elements corresponding to each random coefficient, and an additional element containing the class allocation probabilities. Moreover, as with the RP-MXL model, examining the conditional distributions, specifically the class membership probabilities, is important. These are also known as individual-specific posterior class membership probabilities, representing the likelihood that an individual belongs to a particular latent class given their observed choices and characteristics.

According to Eq. (3.24) in Sect. 3.3.2, the conditional class membership probability for an individual belonging to a specific class can be computed using Bayes' theorem:

$$\widehat{\pi}_{c_q,n|\mathbf{i}_n^\star} = \frac{\widehat{P}_{n|c_q}\widehat{\pi}_{c_q,n}}{\sum_{s=1}^{Q}\widehat{P}_{n|c_s}\widehat{\pi}_{c_s,n}} \tag{10.6}$$

This results in a set of probabilities for each class and individual, indicating the likelihood that the individual belongs to each class based on their observed behaviour and characteristics. The `apollo_conditionals` function can also be used within an LC-MXL framework, where it returns a matrix with conditional class membership probabilities. Below, we retrieve both the unconditional and conditional distributions for the LC-MXL model and then compare their histograms (Fig. 10.15) side by side.

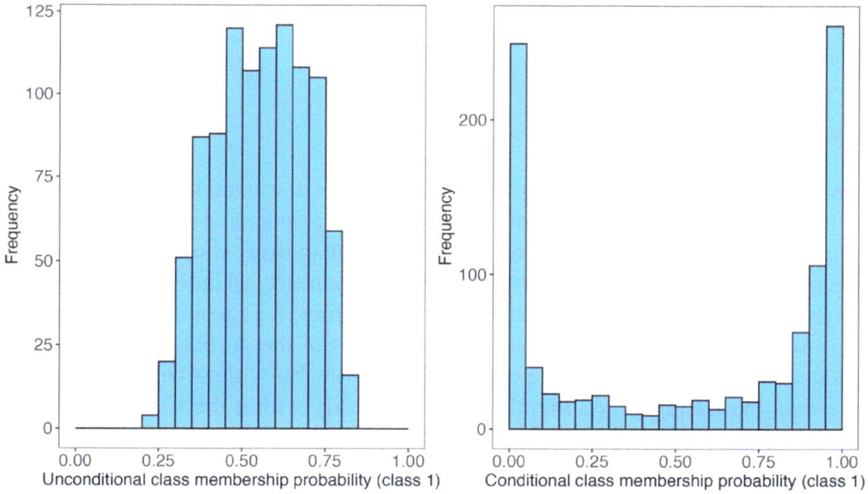


**Fig. 10.15** Class membership probabilities for LC-MXL model

```r
## Unconditional distributions ----
unconditionals <- apollo_unconditionals(
  model,
  apollo_probabilities,
  apollo_inputs
)

## Conditional distributions ----
conditionals <- apollo_conditionals(
  model,
  apollo_probabilities,
  apollo_inputs
)

# Plot results ----

tibble(
  probs = apollo_firstRow(unconditionals$pi_values$class_a, apollo_inputs)
) |>
  ggplot(aes(x = probs)) +
  geom_histogram(breaks = seq(0, 1, by = 0.05), color = 1, fill = "#87CEEB") +
  labs(
    x = "Unconditional class membership probability (class 1)",
    y = "Frequency"
  ) +
  theme_bw()
tibble(
  probs = conditionals$X1
) |>
  ggplot(aes(x = probs)) +
  geom_histogram(breaks = seq(0, 1, by = 0.05), color = 1, fill = "#87CEEB") +
  labs(
    x = "Conditional class membership probability (class 1)",
    y = "Frequency"
  ) +
  theme_bw()
```

We can see in Fig. 10.15 that the distribution of the unconditional probabilities is more entropic, with the probabilities more evenly spread across the classes. In contrast, the distribution of the conditional probabilities shows lower entropy, reflecting a much more skewed distribution where, for nearly all individuals, membership in one class is much more likely than in the other. As a result, the conditional probabilities are more concentrated at the extremes of the probability distribution. This outcome is expected, as the unconditional probability distribution effectively represents the average class membership probability within the sample (or, more precisely, within the subsample of individuals who share the same socio-demographic characteristics).

To maximise the insights gained from conditional class membership probabilities, it is useful to compare these distributions across different sub-samples of interest. The code chunk below demonstrates how to achieve this by comparing the distributions for males (left panel) and females (right panel), as depicted in Fig. 10.16.

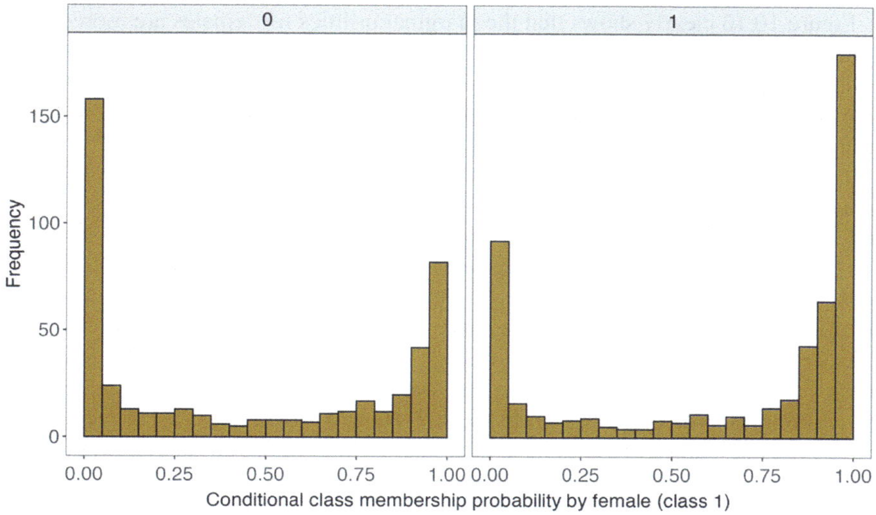


**Fig. 10.16** Class membership probabilities by gender

```r
# Merge the conditional probabilities with demographic data and plot
conditionals |>
  select(ID, X1) |>
  right_join(
    database |>
      group_by(id_individual) |>
      slice(1) |>
      ungroup() |>
      select(id_individual, age, female, education),
    by = c("ID" = "id_individual")) |>
  mutate(
    female = factor(female)
  ) |>
  ggplot(aes(x = X1)) +
  geom_histogram(breaks = seq(0, 1, by = 0.05), color = "black", fill = "#B8860B") +
  labs(
    x = "Conditional class membership probability by female (class 1)",
    y = "Frequency"
  ) +
  facet_wrap(vars(female)) +
  theme_bw()
```

Figure 10.16 clearly shows that the marginal utilities for females are more likely to be better explained by the parameters in Class 1, while for males, the marginal utilities are better described by the parameters in Class 2. However, it is important to note that there are still significant numbers of both males and females whose marginal utilities align with the other latent class.

This observation underscores that the latent class model, with its socio-demographic interactions in the class membership functions, captures both observed and unobserved sources of heterogeneity. The noticeable differences in the distributions between males and females are largely driven by observed preference heterogeneity. Nonetheless, the considerable variability within each distribution reflects the influence of unobserved heterogeneity.

Note that the term $\widehat{\pi}_{c_q,n}$ in Eq. (10.6) is essentially equivalent to the term $w_{nr}$ defined in Eq. (10.5), which denotes the weight assigned to a specific draw from the continuous distribution for individual $n$. Here, $\widehat{\pi}_{c_q,n}$ represents the weight (or probability mass function) associated with each specific value in a discrete probability distribution, where the discrete points along this distribution are determined by the class-specific values of the marginal utility estimates. Using the individual-specific class membership probabilities, we can derive conditional estimates of marginal utility for each individual.

However, the LC-MXL model does not impose constraints to ensure that marginal utilities across different classes are on the same scale. Each class's utilities are estimated independently, leading to potential variations in magnitude due to differing scales or variances. This makes a direct comparison of marginal utilities across different classes challenging. However, ratios of marginal utilities can be compared directly, as scale differences cancel out.

Below, we provide the code to retrieve the conditional mWTPs from this LC-MXL model. To demonstrate how the conditional class membership probabilities influence the resulting distributions, we have plotted the conditional mWTP distribution for the *RedKite* attribute in Fig. 10.17. As expected, the distributions are quite similar in shape, reflecting the underlying class membership probabilities.

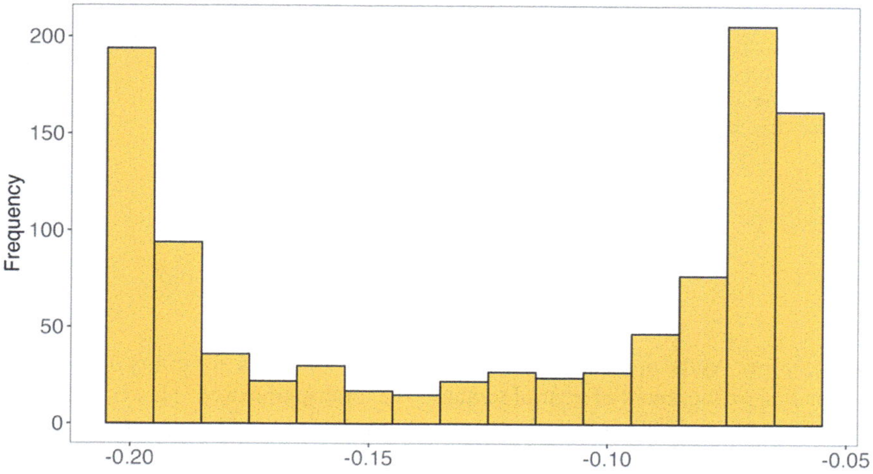


**Fig. 10.17** Marginal WTP for red kites (€ per month)

```
# Compute conditional marginal WTPs for all specified names ----
wtps_lc <- lapply(
  c("b_medium_farms", "b_small_farms", "b_medium_height",
    "b_low_height", "b_red_kite", "b_min_distance"), function(name) {
      wtps_name <- mapply(
        function(x, y) {-x / y},
        unconditionals[[name]],
        unconditionals[["b_cost"]]
      )

      # Calculate the conditional marginal WTPs
      wtps_name[1] * conditionals$X1 + wtps_name[2] * conditionals$X2
  }
)

# Plot the resulting distribution of marginal WTP
tibble(
  wtp = wtps_lc[[5]]
) |>
  ggplot(aes(x = wtp)) +
  geom_histogram(binwidth = 0.01, color = 1, fill = "#F1C40F") +
  labs(
    x = "Marginal WTP for red kites (€ per month)",
    y = "Frequency"
  ) +
  theme_bw()
```

Just as with the RP-MXL model, it is important to extract and report more than just a single mean estimate when analysing the distribution of conditional estimates from an LC-MXL model. In the context of a two-class model where the conditional class membership probabilities exhibit a U-shaped distribution, relying solely on the mean can be misleading. In such cases, the median can be a more informative measure of central tendency.

However, even the median might not fully capture the distribution's essence if the probability mass is concentrated in regions far from the median or mean. Both the mean and median could end up in regions where the density of the distribution is

**Table 10.11** mWTP summary statistics for *LowHeight* from LC-MXL model accounting for sampling variation

| Statistic | Predict | Lower_ci | Upper_ci |
|---|---|---|---|
| Mean | −0.12 | −0.22 | −0.04 |
| SD | 0.06 | 0.01 | 0.09 |
| D1 | −0.20 | −0.26 | −0.09 |
| Q1 | −0.19 | −0.26 | −0.04 |
| Q2 (median) | −0.10 | −0.24 | −0.02 |
| Q3 | −0.07 | −0.22 | −0.01 |
| D9 | −0.06 | −0.18 | −0.01 |

relatively low. As the number of classes in the model increases, the utility of the mean and median as measures of central tendency generally improves. This is because a larger number of classes can lead to more nuanced conditional distributions, which might be better represented by these measures.

However, this is not guaranteed, and each case should be assessed individually. Regardless of the number of classes, it is always useful to extract and report a range of percentiles from the distribution. Reporting a range of percentiles will offer a clearer picture of how conditional mWTPs are distributed across the entire range, giving a more complete and insightful appreciation of the distribution's characteristics.

In the following code chunk, we utilise the Krinsky-Robb method to generate confidence intervals for summary statistics of the mWTP associated with *RedKite*, mirroring our previous analysis of the RP-MXL model (presented in Table 10.9). The process begins by generating conditional mWTP draws based on the model estimates. We then calculate the mean, standard deviation, deciles, quartiles, and median of this distribution, and we create 10,000 draws from the empirical distribution and compute the corresponding mWTP distributions for each draw. We then calculate the same summary statistics as before, and finally, we combine the model-predicted statistics with the 95% confidence intervals for each statistic. The results are presented below (Table 10.11).

```
# Calculate marginal WTP for variable of interest
wtp_rk_model <- -unconditionals[["b_red_kite"]][[1]] / unconditionals[["b_cost"]][[1]] * co
nditionals$X1 +
  -unconditionals[["b_red_kite"]][[2]] / unconditionals[["b_cost"]][[2]] * conditionals$X2

# Summarise predicted WTP distribution
wtp_rk_summary <- c(
  mean = mean(wtp_rk_model),
  sd = sd(wtp_rk_model),
  quantile(wtp_rk_model, c(0.1, 0.25, 0.5, 0.75, 0.9))
)

# Set number of Krinsky-Robb simulations
nsims <- 10

# Generate empirical distributions for simulations
sim_dists <- simulate_dist(model, nsims)

# Define a function to compute the summary statistics for each simulation
compute_wtp_summary <- function(sim_row) {
  # Change coefficients to simulated draw
  model_s$estimate <- sim_row

  # Unconditional distributions for simulation draw
  unconditionals_s <- apollo_unconditionals(model_s, apollo_probabilities, apollo_inputs)

  # Conditional distributions for simulation draw
  conditionals_s <- apollo_conditionals(model_s, apollo_probabilities, apollo_inputs)

  # Compute class-specific marginal WTPs for simulation draw
  wtps_s <- mapply(
    function(x, y) {
      -x / y
    },
    unconditionals_s[["b_red_kite"]],
    unconditionals_s[["b_cost"]]
  )

  # Calculate the conditional marginal WTPs for simulation draw
  wtp_cond <- wtps_s[1] * conditionals_s$X1 + wtps_s[2] * conditionals_s$X2

  # Calculate summary statistics for simulation draw
  stats <- c(
    mean = mean(wtp_cond),
    sd = sd(wtp_cond),
    quantile(wtp_cond, c(0.1, 0.25, 0.5, 0.75, 0.9))
  )

  return(stats)
}

# Use apply to process simulations
wtp_rk_summaries <- t(apply(sim_dists, 1, compute_wtp_summary))

# Combine predictive distribution and confidence intervals
wtp_rk_dist <- tibble(
  statistic = c("Mean", "SD", "D1", "Q1", "Q2 (median)", "Q3", "D9"),
  predict = wtp_rk_summary,
  lower_ci = apply(wtp_rk_summaries, 2, quantile, probs = 0.025),
  upper_ci = apply(wtp_rk_summaries, 2, quantile, probs = 0.975)
)
```

Unlike RP-MXL models where random parameters follow continuous distributions, the LC-MXL model assumes discrete distributions. This means that each draw from the empirical distribution results in a conditional mWTP distribution that is bounded, with the lower and upper bounds defined by the minimum and maximum class-specific mWTP values. Since all conditional class membership probabilities are strictly between 0 and 1, the expected mWTP for each individual must fall within these bounds.

In contrast, the mWTP distributions in RP-MXL models reported in this book (and commonly used in environmental economics) are derived from unbounded distributions for the non-cost attributes. As a result, these distributions typically exhibit greater variability in both unconditional and conditional WTP estimates compared to those obtained from an LC-MXL model. Whether this increased variability is desirable depends on the specific empirical context. It is crucial to evaluate how well your model and its distributional assumptions produce plausible estimates that are appropriate for your research setting.

Just as in the RP-MXL model, the variability introduced by the sampling error also influences the conditional distributions in the LC-MXL model. This means that when conditional class membership probabilities, mWTPs, or welfare estimates derived from an LC-MXL model are used for further secondary analysis, it is necessary to account for this variability. Failing to do so can lead to misleading conclusions, as the inherent sampling error may cause significant fluctuations in the derived estimates. By thoroughly accounting for the variability in conditional distributions, you ensure that your analysis remains rigorous and that the conclusions drawn are both valid and reliable in the context of real-world decision-making.

## 10.4 Key Takeaways

- Interpreting models is just as important as building them. Constructing an econometric model is only the first step—its true value lies in interpreting and applying the results effectively, especially for discrete choice models, where each model demands a unique approach.
- In DCEs, the post-estimation analysis is key to deriving meaningful insights like marginal willingness to pay and changes in consumer surplus, which have practical, policy-relevant implications.
- Understanding the sampling error is vital for hypothesis testing and determining the statistical significance of model estimates. Recognising this variability ensures robust, reliable conclusions that guide better decision-making.
- Models that account for preference heterogeneity introduce additional variability distinct from the sampling error. It is essential to differentiate these sources of variability to avoid possible misinterpretations.
- When analysing models with unobserved preference heterogeneity, it is important to distinguish between unconditional and conditional preference distributions, while going beyond the mean for a more complete understanding of preferences and behaviours.

# References

Alemu MH, Mørkbak MR, Olsen SB, Jensen CL (2013) Attending to the reasons for attribute non-attendance in choice experiments. Environ Resour Econ 54(3):333–359. https://doi.org/10.1007/s10640-012-9597-8

Armstrong P, Garrido R, Ortúzar JD (2001) Confidence intervals to bound the value of time. Transp Res E: Logist Transp Rev 37(2–3):143–161. https://doi.org/10.1016/S1366-5545(00)00019-3

Bliemer MCJ, Rose JM (2013) Confidence intervals of willingness-to-pay for random coefficient logit models. Transp Res B Methodol 58:199–214. https://doi.org/10.1016/j.trb.2013.09.010

Campbell D (2007) Willingness to pay for rural landscape improvements: combining mixed logit and random-effects models. J Agric Econ 58(3):467–483. https://doi.org/10.1111/j.1477-9552.2007.00117.x

Campbell D, Hutchinson WG, Scarpa R (2009) Using choice experiments to explore the spatial distribution of willingness to pay for rural landscape improvements. Environ Plan A 41(1):97–111. https://doi.org/10.1068/a4038

Daly A, Hess S, Train K (2012) Assuring finite moments for willingness to pay in random coefficient models. Transportation 39(1):19–31. https://doi.org/10.1007/s11116-011-9331-3

Daly A, Hess S, Ortúzar JD (2023) Estimating willingness-to-pay from discrete choice models: setting the record straight. Transp Res a: Policy Pract 176:103828. https://doi.org/10.1016/j.tra.2023.103828

Daniel AM, Persson L, Sandorf ED (2018) Accounting for elimination-by-aspects strategies and demand management in electricity contract choice. Energy Econ 72:80–90. https://doi.org/10.1016/j.eneco.2018.05.009

Hess S (2010) Conditional parameter estimates from mixed logit models: distributional assumptions and a free software tool. J Choice Model 3(2):134–152. https://doi.org/10.1016/S1755-5345(13)70039-3

Hess S, Palma D (2019) Apollo: a flexible, powerful and customisable freeware package for choice model estimation and application. J Choice Model 32:100170. https://doi.org/10.1016/j.jocm.2019.100170

Krinsky I, Robb A (1986) On approximating the statistical properties of elasticities. Rev Econ Stat 68(4):715–719. https://doi.org/10.2307/1924536

Krinsky I, Robb A (1990) On approximating the statistical properties of elasticities: a correction. Rev Econ Stat 72(1):189–190. https://www.jstor.org/stable/1924536

Oehlert GW (1992) A note on the delta method. Am Stat 46(1):27–29. https://doi.org/10.2307/2684406

Poe GL, Giraud KL, Loomis JB (2005) Computational methods for measuring the difference of empirical distributions. Am J Agric Econ 87(2):353–365

Scaccia L, Marcucci E, Gatta V (2023) Prediction and confidence intervals of willingness-to-pay for mixed logit models. Transp Res B Methodol 167:54–78. https://doi.org/10.1016/j.trb.2022.11.007

# Chapter 11
# Final Thoughts

**Abstract** This book has provided a foundational overview of designing, collecting, and analysing discrete choice experiments (DCEs) in environmental economics using R. However, it is not intended to be a definitive guide on the subject: mastery of DCEs will require further reading and exploration beyond the content covered in this book. We carefully selected what we believe to be the essential elements of a DCE project to provide a solid foundation, while aiming to spark curiosity and encourage further inquiry. As we conclude this book, we offer some final thoughts and additional pointers to consider as you continue your journey of mastering DCEs.

## 11.1 Beyond Discrete Choices

This book focuses exclusively on discrete choices, in which individuals select a single alternative from a finite set of options. However, it is important to acknowledge that variations of this approach exist and are used in the environmental economics literature. For instance, one extension is a ranked choice experiment that involves ranking alternatives, in which individuals rank multiple options in order of preference. Such a model can be estimated using an exploded logit model, which assumes that each choice is made conditionally based on the remaining alternatives in each step of the ranking process (see Scarpa et al. 2011). Another extension is best–worst scaling, in which individuals select their most and least preferred options from a set. This is modelled using a MaxDiff model, which assumes that individuals choose the combination that maximises the difference in utility between the best and worst alternatives (Flynn and Marley 2014).

Both of these ranking approaches provide a deeper insight into preferences and, can enhance statistical efficiency by extracting more information from each choice task and can be especially useful in environmental economics for eliciting preferences and trade-offs. However, such methods might not always align with real-world decision-making processes. This can raise concerns about their ability to produce meaningful and welfare-consistent measures (which align measures or models with the preferences and utilities of individuals or society, ensuring that changes reflect



P. Mariel et al., *Environmental Valuation with Discrete Choice Experiments in R*,
The Economics of Non-Market Goods and Resources 17,
https://doi.org/10.1007/978-3-031-89338-4_11

actual improvements or reductions in overall well-being), such as marginal willingness to pay (mWTP) and expected changes in consumer surplus. Despite this, these methods still fundamentally rely on discrete choices.

However, choice modelling goes beyond discrete choices. Unlike discrete choices, in which respondents pick between distinct options, *continuous choices* involve a range of responses, such as amounts, levels, or quantities, and have a long history in environmental economics. While many examples exist in revealed preference methods, they also appear in stated preference methods. A basic example is the open-ended contingent valuation question, in which respondents provide a specific monetary amount they are willing to pay for a good or service. More closely related to the DCEs discussed in this book are volumetric choice experiments (see Carson et al. 2022), which capture quantities rather than just discrete choices, allowing individuals to choose how much of a good or service they wish to consume.

A more complex approach is the *multiple discrete–continuous choice experiment* (see the progression of these in Hanemann 1984; von Haefen and Phaneuf 2003; and Bhat 2005), in which individuals make both discrete choices (whether or not to choose an option) and continuous choices (how much to consume) across multiple goods or services. While *volumetric choice experiments* typically focus on a single good, multiple discrete–continuous choice experiments involve multiple goods, in which the respondent selects which options to consume and in what quantity. Both approaches go beyond the realm of traditional discrete choices and highlight the broad scope of choice modelling. This is why being precise when referring to choice modelling is important, as it is a broad term encompassing both discrete and continuous choices. When focusing specifically on discrete choices, as we do here, using the term discrete choice modelling is more accurate.

While there is limited use of volumetric choice experiments in the environmental economics literature, there are multiple applications that make use of discrete–continuous data (e.g. Kabaya and Kuriyama 2021; Calastri et al. 2023), and they can offer valuable insights beyond traditional DCEs. While the *Apollo* package includes functionalities for modelling multiple discrete–continuous choice experiments, other R packages may be better suited for modelling count data such as those collected in volumetric choice experiments. One example is the rmdcev package (Lloyd-Smith 2020), designed specifically for Kuhn-Tucker and multiple discrete–continuous extreme value model estimation and simulation in R. While we do not have space to elaborate on these further in this book, it is worth exploring these methods if they align with your research goals.

## 11.2 Alternative Decision Rules

All models presented in this book are based on the assumption that individuals adhere to fully rational utility maximisation principles. This theory states that individuals make *fully compensatory decisions*—that is, they consider all relevant factors associated with each choice, alternative, and attribute and make trade-offs between these aspects. In doing so, consciously or unconsciously, they calculate the overall utility for each alternative, considering every component, and then choose the alternative that offers the highest utility.

We model these decisions using a random utility maximisation (RUM) model. This approach assumes that the decision maker has complete knowledge of the utility of each alternative. However, from the analyst's viewpoint, observing or measuring every factor influencing the individual's decision is impossible (Manski 1977). To account for this uncertainty, a random component is introduced into the utility function, reflecting the analyst's inability to capture the individual's utility fully. It is crucial to emphasise that this randomness reflects the analyst's uncertainty, not the decision maker's: from the individual's perspective, their decision-making process remains deterministic and rational.

In a typical DCE, individuals are asked to choose between multiple alternatives, each described by different attributes, and fully compensatory utility maximisation is assumed. However, it has been argued—and demonstrated—that such a strict decision-making rule (requiring individuals to evaluate all attributes of every option and trade them off perfectly) may not hold in many DCEs. Given the complexity of the tasks in DCEs, it is often unrealistic to expect all individuals to consider every attribute in every alternative in a perfectly compensatory manner, calculating and summing up each part-worth to derive a total utility and then selecting the alternative with the highest utility.

There is substantial evidence of deviations from fully compensatory utility maximisation in revealed preference data, highlighting that individuals often do not evaluate all available alternatives and trade-offs in a manner assumed by classical economic theory. Therefore, as practitioners of stated preference methods, we should not be surprised to observe the adoption of heuristics (i.e. mental shortcuts or simplified rules), non-compensatory decision rules, or violations of strict utility maximisation in our data, as no real person can perform the instantaneous calculations that utility maximisation requires. Nonetheless, it is important to recognise that even with these deviations, utility maximisation models can still predict many aspects of behaviour with considerable accuracy. However, as these deviations become more pronounced, the model's predictive power will likely diminish, making it difficult to generalise its accuracy across contexts. Despite its limitations, the utility-maximisation framework remains valuable because it assumes individuals behave as if they made such calculations, providing a consistent and robust foundation for modelling choice behaviour (Hess et al. 2018).

The field of behavioural economics has increasingly acknowledged and attempted to model the complexities that arise from how people actually make decisions. Within environmental economics, several studies have relaxed the assumption of fully compensatory decision rules (see Veldwijk et al. 2023 for a recent review), exploring semi-compensatory rules, such as lexicographic decision-making, attribute non-attendance, and elimination by aspects instead. These rules suggest that people apply simplifying heuristics to reduce the complexity of the decision-making process. However, after these simplifications are applied, they revert to a utility-maximisation approach. For example, individuals may eliminate options that fail to meet a specific criterion before fully evaluating the remaining alternatives.

Hess et al. (2010) classify different types of behaviour that can lead individuals to not make trade-offs between all attributes across each of the alternatives (as assumed in standard DCEs) into the following behaviour patterns: non-trading behaviour (respondent always chooses the same alternative across choice sets), lexicographic behaviour (respondent applies a strict hierarchical ordering of attributes, for example by choosing the cheapest alternative), and inconsistent behaviour across choice situations (respondent's preferences vary in ways that appear irrational or non-systematic).

In addition to semi-compensatory rules, researchers in behavioural economics have explored non-utility maximisation decision rules. One prominent example within environmental economics is the random regret minimisation (RRM) model. Rather than selecting the alternative that maximises utility, the RRM model posits that individuals compare attribute level values across alternatives and choose the option that minimises regret—the feeling of dissatisfaction that may arise when a chosen alternative performs worse for certain attributes than a non-chosen one.

Chorus (2012) presents a comprehensive review of the RRM model and its applications. Other decision rules include satisficing (e.g. Sandorf and Campbell 2019; Sandorf et al. 2022) and prospect theory (e.g. Aravena et al. 2014; Heutel 2019). Each offers different perspectives on how individuals make choices in complex environments. These models, including non-utility-maximising rules, can be easily implemented in *Apollo* (Hess and Palma 2019).

In light of the examples above, it may be worth considering relaxing the strict assumption of fully compensatory utility maximisation when modelling choices in your data. In fact, you may even want to explore decision rules that do not rely on utility maximisation at all. Doing so could allow you to model and describe choices more accurately. Ideally, the model's assumptions should reflect the true decision-making process underlying the data. If the model is built on an incorrect decision rule, its ability to explain choices is significantly diminished, and its predictive power may be compromised. To address this, take proactive steps to ensure that the model reflects the true decision-making process by analysing the decision context, incorporating behavioural insights, testing assumptions against observed data, and iteratively refining the model to better capture true behaviour.

Nonetheless, the basic model of choice that economists use to explain individual behaviour remains grounded in utility maximisation. This assumption has long been a cornerstone of neoclassical economics and remains a foundational concept in decision theory. It is precisely this framework that allows us to infer welfare-consistent measures of mWTP and consumer surplus from the models discussed in this book (see Hess et al. 2018).

Crucially, any departure from fully compensatory utility maximisation can make the derivation of welfare- measures consistent with microeconomic theory extremely challenging, if not outright impossible. Therefore, if your primary objective is to derive marginal WTP or welfare measures, your best approach remains adhering to utility maximisation, as it provides a direct and robust link between individual choices and welfare economics. Any departure from this should be approached with caution, as you risk undermining your ability to obtain reliable welfare estimates.

As emphasised earlier, even when substantial deviations in behaviour from strict utility maximisation are evident in the data, random utility models often continue to predict many aspects of choice behaviour with reasonable accuracy. In these cases, you may still obtain useful results and be able to retrieve welfare-consistent measures, despite the presence of non-compensatory decision-making. However, if your focus shifts away from deriving welfare measures and towards improving choice prediction, exploring models that depart from the random utility maximisation framework—especially those that relax the strict assumption of utility maximisation—may prove advantageous.

In cases where you aim to retrieve both welfare-consistent measures of mWTP and consumer surplus, while accurately capturing the choices made by individuals who may not adhere to utility maximisation, one approach is to use probabilistic latent class models that accommodate different sets of behaviours, with each class reflecting a distinct decision rule. An appealing feature of these models is that the class probabilities offer insight into the proportion of individuals adopting each decision rule. Moreover, mWTP and welfare change estimates can still be obtained from the class that assumes utility maximisation. A substantial body of research has utilised this approach to account for deviations from fully compensatory decision-making rules (e.g. Campbell et al. 2011; Hess et al. 2011; Boeri and Longo 2017; Jourdain et al. 2022).

## 11.3 Alternatives to Maximum Likelihood Estimation

Maximum likelihood estimation is the most commonly used method for analysing choices in a DCE, and it is the primary focus of Chapter 8 in this book. All model outputs discussed in Chapter 9 are based on maximum likelihood estimation. However, you may benefit from exploring alternative methods beyond this book's scope.

Bayesian estimation is one such alternative. Unlike classical maximum likelihood estimation, Bayesian estimation incorporates prior information or beliefs about parameters into the analysis. This can be particularly advantageous when dealing with limited data or when strong prior knowledge exists, as it allows researchers to update prior information or beliefs with new evidence.

Another approach is machine learning, which includes techniques such as decision trees, random forests, and neural networks (e.g. Hillel et al. 2021; van Cranenburgh et al. 2022; Ali et al. 2023). These methods can be valuable when the relationships between variables are complex or non-linear, which maximum likelihood estimation may not capture effectively. Machine learning approaches are ideally suited for large datasets and can reveal patterns that traditional methods might miss, making them suitable for scenarios that require high predictive accuracy and complex data structures. Additionally, the expectation–maximisation algorithm (see Train 2009, Chapter 14), which iteratively updates the model parameters, can be a helpful method.

In R, Bayesian estimation, machine learning, and expectation–maximisation can be integrated into DCE analysis. The *Apollo* package supports Bayesian estimation as an alternative to classical methods. It also includes expectation–maximisation routines for RP-MXL models, in which all parameters are treated as random and a full covariance matrix is estimated, as well as for LC-MXL models, in which parameters vary across different classes. While the *Apollo* package does not support machine learning techniques, R provides numerous packages for applying machine learning methods.

As this is a rapidly developing area, we ask the reader to do their own research for the latest packages. Although these alternatives to traditional maximum likelihood estimation are beyond the scope of this book, being aware of these approaches can help you enhance your DCE analysis by providing alternative approaches to data analysis. Bayesian and expectation–maximization approaches are particularly useful for handling missing data, estimating latent variables, and accommodating complex model structures. Machine learning methods, on the other hand, excel at managing large datasets, capturing non-linear relationships, and improving predictive accuracy. By integrating these techniques, you can gain deeper insights into choice behaviour and develop more scalable, flexible, and robust models for analysing DCE data.

## 11.4 Balancing Complexity and Practicality in Model Selection

In this book, we aim to convey the complexities and potential pitfalls of analysing choices from DCEs. There are numerous modelling options, and while we have covered some key specifications, the range of possible models is virtually limitless. Each model has assumptions, some of which may be more robust than others. Unfortunately, we cannot evaluate the suitability of every possible model for every DCE.

So, what guides us in choosing the right model? How do we decide when to stop modelling? The saying "a good artist knows when to stop" applies equally to econometricians. A good econometrician knows when to stop refining their model, understanding that while no model is perfect, some are better than others. The goal is not perfection but rather to describe the data as accurately and simply as possible.

We recommend avoiding using overly complex models when simpler ones will suffice, considering the model's end users and what they need to extract from it. Sometimes, adding complexity is necessary to ensure the model's robustness and defensibility. However, complex models should be used judiciously and only when they genuinely enhance the understanding of the data.

It is important to avoid using model assumptions to obscure data inadequacies. Models should *never* be used to engineer results in a particular direction or to mask flaws in the data. Instead, the focus should be creating a transparent, defensible, and helpful model for the intended audience. Strive for clarity and simplicity wherever possible, and make sure your choices are guided by the data and the specific research questions you are trying to answer.

Choosing the right model is a challenging task. However, as you gain more experience, you will develop a deeper understanding of which models are suitable for specific datasets, often even before you begin estimating them. This intuitive grasp of model suitability is invaluable in guiding your modelling choices, but takes time to hone. Remember that the modelling process is inherently iterative and exploratory, and avoid rushing straight into what you believe will be the final model. Many less experienced researchers jump to complex mixed logit models without sufficient model exploration simply because many published papers only feature results from a single mixed logit model. However, these models are usually the culmination of extensive evaluation and testing of numerous other models, and you must do the same in your research.

During the modelling process, you will encounter many decision points along the way where your choices can significantly impact the outcome of the analysis. At these crossroads, following a logical process and documenting your decisions thoroughly is essential, providing as much justification as possible. To guide your model selection, consider using multi-model inference techniques (Burnham and Anderson 2002).

As detailed in Chapter 9, the output from models estimated using *Apollo* includes several goodness-of-fit statistics, such as the Akaike Information Criterion and the Bayesian Information Criterion, which you can compare across models to assess their suitability for your DCE. These and other information criteria (accessible from the stored model output) are helpful not only in selecting the best model but also in guiding model averaging (Hancock and Hess 2021; Hancock et al. 2020). Using an information criterion, you can compute model weights, allowing you to combine estimates from multiple models by averaging estimates according to these weights, and thereby incorporate the uncertainty and variability among models in your estimation. This method enhances the robustness and comprehensiveness of your data analysis, leading to more informed modelling decisions (e.g. Layton and Lee 2006; Campbell et al. 2018).

## 11.5 R Shiny for Data Visualisation and Decision Support

As discussed in Chapter 6, R Shiny is a powerful web application framework for R. In this book, we demonstrated how it can be adapted to facilitate the creation, distribution, and data collection for an online DCE survey. However, this is not its primary intended use. Shiny is fundamentally designed to enable users to build interactive, dynamic web applications directly from their R scripts, simplifying the process of creating web-based dashboards and visualisations, without requiring extensive web development expertise.

The real strength of Shiny lies in its ability to integrate data analysis workflows with user-friendly interfaces, allowing non-technical stakeholders to explore, manipulate, and visualise data interactively. This provides flexibility in creating applications ranging from basic data visualisations to sophisticated, real-time data processing platforms. For researchers conducting DCEs, particularly in applied fields like environmental economics, the greatest utility of Shiny apps may be in their role as a tool for communicating results to stakeholders rather than as a primary data collection platform.

In many funded research projects, delivering a decision-support tool has become a key project outcome. These tools are designed for policymakers and decision-makers, allowing them to explore various policy scenarios interactively. Shiny is particularly well-suited for developing such dashboards and decision-support tools tailored to diverse users and stakeholders. The functionality of these tools can vary greatly based on user needs. At its simplest, a Shiny app could serve as an interactive tool that lets users view outputs from different models, allowing them to compare outcomes across scenarios. A more advanced tool could provide visually rich results, such as data displayed on a map with multiple layers, offering a deeper level of engagement with the data.

An example of such a Shiny application is provided by Hess et al. (2022) and is available at https://stephanehess.shinyapps.io/COVID19_Shiny/. This tool allows users to simultaneously predict the uptake of different COVID-19 vaccines across 18 study areas. Users can create custom scenarios by configuring vaccine characteristics, including efficacy, protection duration, the risk of side effects, waiting time, and costs, and adjusting the levels of infectiousness and severity of circulating COVID-19 variants. Developing a fully customised R Shiny app for such cases requires substantial explanation and depends heavily on the intended functionality and user needs. Thus, we do not include a detailed walkthrough of how to create such an app in this book. For more information on R Shiny and detailed guidance on fully customising it to meet your specific research needs, we encourage you to review *Mastering Shiny* by Hadley Wickham (Wickham 2021). This book offers a thorough exploration of Shiny, covering everything from fundamental concepts to advanced features.

## 11.6 Stay Updated and Adapt

Data science is a fast-moving field: everything from storing, processing, and using data to the data itself constantly evolves. Three of us authors have been working with DCE data since long before internet panels and online surveys were an option, and our key takeaway is this: nothing stays static—so you have to stay flexible, open to learning, and adaptable to new advances in technology.

While R is a valuable platform for analysing DCEs right now, no one knows how long this will be the case. Several alternative software options already offer similar flexibility and ease in estimating discrete choice models, and there is no doubt that more will emerge in the future. Staying open to exploring different tools will ensure your research stays at the cutting edge. Software like Python, Stata, MATLAB, Julia, or specialised programs such as Ngene, NLOGIT, Biogeme, or Latent GOLD can offer unique algorithms, faster processing, and user-friendly interfaces tailored to specific modelling needs (or experimental designs, in the case of Ngene). Expanding your toolkit will give you access to these features and allow for greater flexibility in your analysis.

By diversifying your software use, you can enhance the robustness of your models and ensure that you are employing the best tools for your research. So, while this book covers R extensively for designing, conducting, and analysing DCE experiments, we encourage you to look beyond R and embrace all of the tools at your disposal—just like a carpenter, the more tools you have, the more tasks you can tackle.

At the same time, new types of data and sources are becoming available. Be open to incorporating these emerging datasets when they align with and enhance your research. We are already seeing how these datasets can complement, or even replace, traditional stated preference data, a trend that will surely only grow as more data becomes accessible. Embracing these changes will keep your research relevant and forward-thinking.

As we wrap up this book in the beginning of 2025, we are already seeing how AI is reshaping the research landscape. It is impossible to know how the changes it brings will affect how DCEs are conducted or analysed in the future—if they even will be. We are well aware that the content of this book may become obsolete sooner than we think, and we are all for it—that is just how science evolves. So, while this book might not stand the test of time, we hope it offers some practical guidance for now. And hey, if nothing else, maybe it will be a fun resource for future historians!

## Bibliography

Ali A, Kalatian A, Choudhury CF (2023) Comparing and contrasting choice model and machine learning techniques in the context of vehicle ownership decisions. Transp Res Part a: Policy Pract 173:103727. https://doi.org/10.1016/j.tra.2023.103727

Aravena C, Martinsson P, Scarpa R (2014) Does money talk?—the effect of a monetary attribute on the marginal values in a choice experiment. Energy Econ 44:483–491. https://doi.org/10.1016/j.eneco.2014.02.017

Boeri M, Longo A (2017) The importance of regret minimization in the choice for renewable energy programmes: Evidence from a discrete choice experiment. Energy Econ 63:253–260. https://doi.org/10.1016/j.eneco.2017.03.005

Bhat CR (2005) A multiple discrete–continuous extreme value model: formulation and application to discretionary time-use decisions. Transp Res B Methodol 39(8):679–707. https://doi.org/10.1016/j.trb.2004.08.003

Burnham KP, Anderson DR (eds) (2002) Model selection and multimodel inference. Springer, A practical information-theoretic approach. https://doi.org/10.1007/b97636

Calastri C, Giergiczny M, Zedrosser A, Hess S (2023) Modelling activity patterns of wild animals—an application of the multiple discrete-continuous extreme value (MDCEV) model. J Choice Model 47:100415. https://doi.org/10.1016/j.jocm.2023.100415

Campbell D, Hensher DA, Scarpa R (2011) Non-attendance to attributes in environmental choice analysis: a latent class specification. J Environ Planning Manage 54:1061–1076. https://doi.org/10.1080/09640568.2010.549367

Campbell D, Mørkbak MR, Olsen SB (2018) The link between response time and preference, variance and processing heterogeneity in stated choice experiments. J Environ Econ Manag 88:18–34. https://doi.org/10.1016/j.jeem.2017.10.003

Carson RT, Eagle TC, Islam T, Louviere JJ (2022) Volumetric choice experiments (VCEs). J Choice Model 42:100343. https://doi.org/10.1016/j.jocm.2022.100343

Chorus CG (2012) Random regret-based discrete choice modeling: a tutorial. https://doi.org/10.1007/978-3-642-29151-7

Flynn TN, Marley AAJ (2014) Best-worst scaling: theory and methods. In: Hess S, Daly A (eds) Handbook of choice modelling. Edward Elgar Publishing, pp 178–201

Hancock TO, Hess S (2021) What is really uncovered by mixing different model structures: contrasts between latent class and model averaging. Eur J Transp Infrastruct Res (EJTIR) 21:38–63. https://doi.org/10.18757/ejtir.2021.21.3.3949

Hancock TO, Hess S, Daly A, Fox J (2020) Using a sequential latent class approach for model averaging: benefits in forecasting and behavioural insights. Transp Res Part a: Policy Pract 139:429–454. https://doi.org/10.1016/j.tra.2020.07.005

Hanemann WM (1984) Discrete/continuous models of consumer demand. Econometrica 52(3):541–561. https://doi.org/10.2307/1913464

Hess S, Stathopoulos A, Daly A (2011) Allowing for heterogeneous decision rules in discrete choice models: an approach and four case studies. Transportation 39:565–591. https://doi.org/10.1007/s11116-011-9365-6

Hess S, Daly A, Batley R (2018) Revisiting consistency with random utility maximisation: theory and implications for practical work. Theor Decis 84:181–204. https://doi.org/10.1007/s11238-017-9651-7

Hess S, Lancsar E, Mariel P et al (2022) The path towards herd immunity: predicting COVID-19 vaccination uptake through results from a stated choice study across six continents. Soc Sci Med 298:114800. https://doi.org/10.1016/j.socscimed.2022.114800

Hess S, Palma D (2019) Apollo: a flexible, powerful and customisable freeware package for choice model estimation and application. J Choice Model 32:100170. https://doi.org/10.1016/j.jocm.2019.100170

Hess S, Rose JM, Polak J (2010) Non-trading, lexicographic and inconsistent behaviour in stated choice data. Transp Res d: Transp Environ 15(7):405–417. https://doi.org/10.1016/j.trd.2010.04.008

Heutel G (2019) Prospect theory and energy efficiency. J Environ Econ Manag 96:236–254. https://doi.org/10.1016/j.jeem.2019.06.005

Hillel T, Bierlaire M, Elshafie MZEB, Jin Y (2021) A systematic review of machine learning classification methodologies for modelling passenger mode choice. J Choice Model 38:100221. https://doi.org/10.1016/j.jocm.2020.100221

Jourdain D, Lairez J, Striffler B, Lundhede T (2022) A choice experiment approach to evaluate maize farmers' decision-making processes in Lao PDR. J Choice Model 44:100366. https://doi.org/10.1016/j.jocm.2022.100366

Kabaya K, Kuriyama K (2021) Discrete and continuous preference heterogeneity in a Kuhn-Tucker model: beach recreational demand. Land Econ 97(3):548–561. https://doi.org/10.3368/le.97.3.548

Layton DF, Lee ST (2006) Embracing model uncertainty: strategies for response pooling and model averaging. Environ Resour Econ 34:51–85. https://doi.org/10.1007/s10640-005-3784-9

Lloyd-Smith P (2020) Kuhn-Tucker and multiple discrete-continuous extreme value model estimation and simulation in R: the rmdcev package. R Journal 12(2). https://doi.org/10.32614/RJ-2021-015

Manski CF (1977) The structure of random utility models. Theor Decis 8(3):229–254

Sandorf ED, Campbell D (2019) Accommodating satisficing behaviour in stated choice experiments. Eur Rev Agric Econ 46(1):133–162. https://doi.org/10.1093/erae/jby021

Sandorf ED, Campbell D, Chorus C (2022) A simple satisficing model. PLoS ONE 17(10):e0275339. https://doi.org/10.1371/journal.pone.0275339

Scarpa R, Notaro S, Louviere J, Raffaelli R (2011) Exploring scale effects of best/worst rank ordered choice data to estimate benefits of tourism in alpine grazing commons. Amer J of Ag Econ 93:813–828. https://doi.org/10.1093/ajae/aaq174

Train K (2009) Discrete choice methods with simulation, 2nd edn. Cambridge University Press, New York. https://doi.org/10.1017/CBO9780511805271

van Cranenburgh S, Wang S, Vij A et al (2022) Choice modelling in the age of machine learning—discussion paper. J Choice Model 42:100340. https://doi.org/10.1016/j.jocm.2021.100340

von Haefen RH, Phaneuf DJ (2003) Estimating preferences for outdoor recreation: a comparison of continuous and count data demand system frameworks. J Environ Econ Manag 45(3):612–630. https://doi.org/10.1016/S0095-0696(02)00024-4

Veldwijk J, Marceta SM, Swait JD et al (2023) Taking the shortcut: simplifying heuristics in discrete choice experiments. Patient 16:301–315. https://doi.org/10.1007/s40271-023-00625-y

Wickham H (2021) Mastering Shiny. O'Reilly Media, Inc. https://mastering-shiny.org/

The manufacturer's authorised representative in the EU is Springer Nature Customer Service Centre GmbH, Europaplatz 3, 69115 Heidelberg, Germany. If you have any concerns regarding our products, please contact ProductSafety@springernature.com

Printed and bound by CPI Group (UK) Ltd, Croydon, CR0 4YY
30/09/2026
02225572-0016